Becoming Americans in Paris

BROOKE L. BLOWER

# Becoming Americans in Paris
## Transatlantic Politics and Culture between the World Wars

OXFORD
UNIVERSITY PRESS

# OXFORD
UNIVERSITY PRESS

Oxford University Press is a department of the University of Oxford.
It furthers the University's objective of excellence in research, scholarship,
and education by publishing worldwide.

Oxford   New York
Auckland   Cape Town   Dar es Salaam   Hong Kong   Karachi
Kuala Lumpur   Madrid   Melbourne   Mexico City   Nairobi
New Delhi   Shanghai   Taipei   Toronto

With offices in
Argentina   Austria   Brazil   Chile   Czech Republic   France   Greece
Guatemala   Hungary   Italy   Japan   Poland   Portugal   Singapore
South Korea   Switzerland   Thailand   Turkey   Ukraine   Vietnam

Oxford is a registered trade mark of Oxford University Press
in the UK and certain other countries.

Published in the United States of America by
Oxford University Press
198 Madison Avenue, New York, NY 10016

© Oxford University Press 2011

First issued as an Oxford University Press paperback, 2013.

Library of Congress Cataloging-in-Publication Data
Blower, Brooke Lindy, 1976–
Becoming Americans in Paris : transatlantic politics
and culture between the World Wars / Brooke L. Blower.
   p.   cm.
Includes bibliographical references and index.
ISBN 978-0-19-973781-9 (hardcover); 978-0-19-992758-6 (paperback)
1. Americans—France—Paris—History—20th century. 2. Paris (France)—Intellectual life—20th century.
3. Politics and culture—France—Paris—History—20th century. 4. Political culture—United States—
History—20th century. 5. United States—Relations—France. 6. France—Relations—United States.
7. United States—Civilization—French influences. 8. France—Civilization—American influences.
I. Title.
DC718.A44B66   2011
305.813'04436109042—dc22       2010018235

9 8 7 6 5 4 3 2 1

Printed in the United States of America
on acid-free paper

*For Jamie*

I DIDN'T KNOW IT AT THE time, but the defining moment for this book came in the middle of the index room of the Bibliothèque Historique de la Ville de Paris (BHVP). My purpose in coming to France was to reexamine the history of Americans in Paris after the Great War. When I was young, I loved the modernist work of expatriates, but tales of their carefree days abroad had come to seem flat and predictable. I wanted to look beyond the conventional stories, to breathe new life into the subject by seeking out French sources as well as American ones. I wanted to write something rich and messy, full of the period's weighty politics and the day-to-day problems of urban life. My motivations were largely methodological. Even before I had heard of "transnational" history, I was interested in resonances between European and American culture, and I expected this topic to allow me to pit two different historiographies against each other in creative, unexpected ways. My goal was to bring wider contexts and Parisian points of view to bear on American claims. Surely, I thought, evidence of all sorts of encounters was simply waiting to be plucked from the collections of the BHVP and the city's other archives.

So there I was, in the library's impressive index room with its wall-to-wall card files stuffed with potential. But those catalogues yielded nothing useful under headings like "Américain" or "Etats-Unis," and I found myself standing there, unable to think of other subjects to check. I didn't want to trace the movements of one particular class of people—writers, reformers, or businessmen. Others had done that well already, and besides, I was interested in connections and conflicts that cut across different groups. "Paris" wasn't a useful category either. The whole place was devoted to the city. Just what did

I think I was doing there anyway? I had imagined that whole new dimensions to American culture and politics could be revealed by breaking out of the usual frameworks that bound historical inquiry to its national compartments. But the only discernable trace of the United States in that index room was my own sheepish, obviously American self. All my plans seemed to fall away, rolling towards the corners of the room like so many groceries spilling out of the broken bottom of a paper bag. Archives were not designed for the kind of work I was trying to do. Yet without foreign research, I could not help to reconceptualize American history in international perspective. People switch topics mid-archive all the time. But I was in the wrong country.

To turn this crisis into an opportunity, I had to cast a very wide net and think in greater detail about the relationship between Americans and those sections of Paris most transformed since the war. I read every chronicle of the interwar capital I could find, and at the Archives de la Préfecture de Police I finally started turning up a productively dissonant set of sources to set against Americans' stories about the capital. Full of undercover reports, letters from concerned citizens, and other documents related to the governance of the capital's political and social affairs, the files of the police offered an entrée not into the private mentalities of artists but instead into the very public life of the Paris streets. Scratching away at the cultural opacities of a world peopled by rioters, reactionaries, and intrusive paraders, I realized that rather than cataloguing exchanges between individual Americans and Parisians, I needed to theorize a middle ground between them—that my story would be about the contested spaces of the city itself.

For encouraging me to take on the ambitious task of picking up those pieces and for helping me to put them together in a compelling way, I have many people to thank. At Princeton University, where this project began as a dissertation, I received crucial financial support from the History Department, the Davis Center for Historical Studies, and the Graduate School. Fellow graduate students provided much-needed humor, inspiration, and commiseration over the years. For their thoughtful comments on chapter drafts I am indebted to Katherine Holt, Jolie Dyl, Jane Murphy, Daniela Bleichmar, Matthew Wisnioski, Gretchen Boger, Drew Levy, Todd Stevens, Nicole Sackley, Molly Loberg, and Eric Yellin. I very much appreciate the advice and encouragement I received from Princeton faculty as I developed this project, including from Nell Painter, Kevin Kruse, Dirk Hartog, and William Jordan. I cannot thank enough the members of my dissertation committee, not only for their mentoring but for the examples they set in their own work. Anson Rabinbach offered valuable direction in the field of interwar Europe. Philip Nord's inquisitive approach to history and skillful analysis of urban transformations and French politics offered an inspiring model. I am deeply grateful to Christine Stansell for her insights into the subtle but all-important issues of tone and characterization. She has enriched my scholarship in profound ways that are difficult to delineate but evident everywhere, I believe, in the development of my work over the years. My advisor Daniel T. Rodgers nobly weathered my vague proposals, panicked e-mails from France, and muddled drafts. This project would not have been possible without his talent for conceptualizing the big picture and his nuanced understanding of the challenges of writing transnational history. As an outside reader, Thomas Bender generously lent his time, pushing me to think more carefully about class and cultural politics, the project's overall structure, and so much more.

As I set about transforming the dissertation into a book, I have been lucky to join an engaging community of scholars at Boston University. My thanks go to the entire History Department faculty for their warm welcome and intellectual camaraderie. For specific help with the manuscript, I thank Bruce Schulman, Julian Zelizer, Arianne Chernock, Charles Capper, James Schmidt, Jonathan Zatlin, Charles Dellheim, Jon Roberts, Eugenio Menegon, Simon Payaslian, Louis Ferleger, Marilyn Halter, and Nina Silber. Generous funding from Boston University's Humanities Foundation and the Peter T. Paul Career Development Professorship provided time and resources during the critical stage of revision. In Boston, I have also discovered with delight a wider circle of historians and friends, who have helped to shape this book in important ways. For their incisive reading of various chapters, I thank David Engerman, Christopher Capozzola, Meg Jacobs, Marilynn Johnson, and David Quigley. Many others, too numerous to name, offered exciting observations and pointed questions at various conferences, seminars, and talks in Princeton, Boston, London, and Washington, D.C. I also benefited greatly from the expertise of the French historians Stephen Schloesser, Clifford Rosenberg, and Jeffrey Jackson.

A host of archivists and others assisted with the research and book production. Staff at the BHVP and the Archives de la Préfecture de Police were resourceful and more than patient with a young American with dubious French skills. Librarians at Case Western Reserve Library kindly granted permission to cite from the Myron T. Herrick papers. Sean Casey at the Boston Public Library allowed me the wonderful opportunity to mine the stacks of the Felicani Collection's unprocessed materials. David Mislin, Kate Jewell, Jonathan Koefoed, Sara Georgini, and Amine Rahmouni El Idrissi provided sharp research and production assistance in the manuscript's final stages. Thank you also to Joyce Seltzer for the suggestion of the title. I would like to thank those at Oxford University Press who worked on this book as well for their skill and enthusiasm, beginning with my readers, whose feedback was a great help. It has been a pleasure to work with Susan Ferber, whose intelligent editing and commitment to this project has made all the difference.

Finally, family both in California and Northern Ireland deserve special gratitude for their unflagging support and understanding over the years. Closest to home, thank you to Ailish Webster for her impeccable timing and to Jamie Webster, for everything else.

Brooke L. Blower
Somerville, 2010

CONTENTS

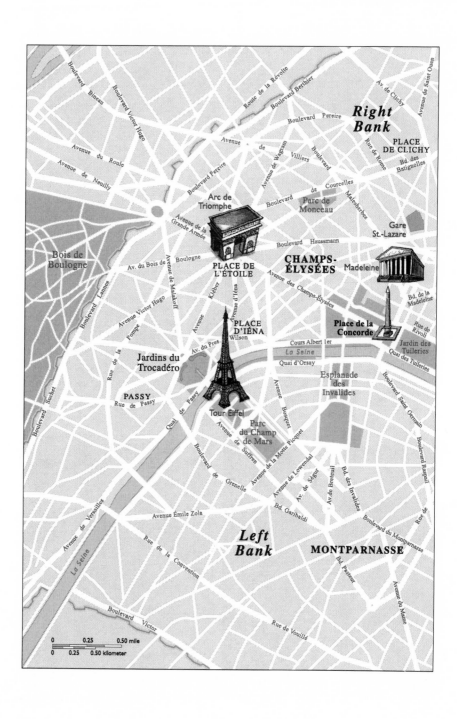

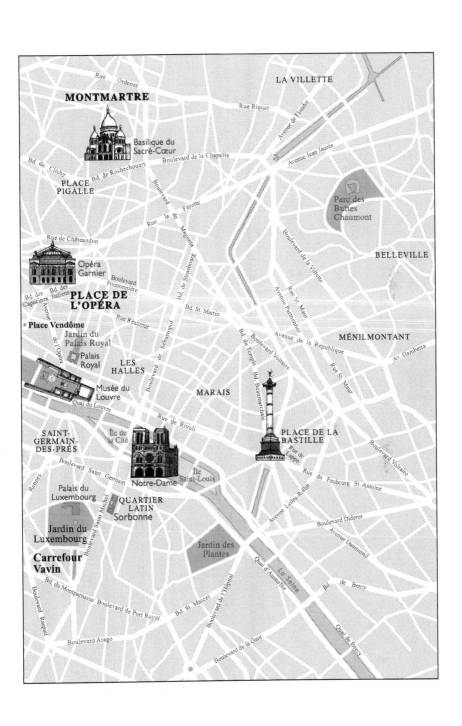

LA VILLETTE

MONTMARTRE

Rue Ordener

Rue Riquet

Avenue de Flandre

Basilique du
Sacré-Cœur

Bd. de Clichy

Bd. de Rochechouart

Boulevard de la Chapelle

Avenue Jean Jaurès

PLACE
PIGALLE

Parc des
Buttes
Chaumont

Boulevard

Rue la de Fayette

Bd. de Strasbourg

Rue de Châteaudun

Boulevard de la Villette

BELLEVILLE

Opéra
Garnier

Boulevard
Poissonnière

Rue St. Maur

Avenue Parmentier

Bd. des
Capucines

Bd. des
Italiens

PLACE DE
L'OPÉRA

Bd. St. Martin

Avenue de la République

MÉNILMONTANT

Av. Gambetta

Avenue de l'Opéra

Place Vendôme

Rue Réaumur

Jardin du
Palais Royal

Boulevard Voltaire

Rue St. Maur

Bd. du Temple

Palais
Royal

LES
HALLES

Boulevard de Sébastopol

Bd. Beaumarchais

Musée du
Louvre

Quai du Louvre

MARAIS

Rue de Rivoli

PLACE DE LA
BASTILLE

Boulevard Voltaire

SAINT-
GERMAIN-
DES-PRÉS

Île de
la Cité

Rue de Lappe

Rennes

Boulevard Saint Germain

Notre-Dame

Île
Saint-Louis

Rue du Faubourg St. Antoine

Palais du
Luxembourg

Boulevard Saint Michel

QUARTIER
LATIN
Sorbonne

Avenue Ledru-Rollin

Boulevard Diderot

Jardin du
Luxembourg

Avenue Daumesnil

Carrefour
Vavin

Jardin des
Plantes

La Seine

Bd. de Bercy

Bd. du Montparnasse

Boulevard de Port Royal

Bd. St. Marcel

Boulevard de l'Hôpital

Quai d'Austerlitz

Quai de Bercy

Boulevard Raspail

Boulevard Arago

Boulevard de la Gare

# Introduction

*The Age of World Wars*

PARIS AFTER WORLD WAR I has long been portrayed as a refuge for American talents. Seduced by visions of Gertrude Stein presiding over her disciples, Langston Hughes writing verse in a rundown attic room, or Ernest Hemingway hunched over his well-lit café table, many have celebrated the capital as "Gay Paree," a fabled land of nightclubs, sidewalk terraces, and a surfeit of personal freedom, where visitors lived artistic lives untroubled by their Parisian hosts. The outlines of this tale are familiar: fleeing the repressive climate of the postwar United States, all kinds of individuals made their pilgrimages to a city that seemed just as distant from American problems as it did from French politics. Jazz performers escaped American racism; literary women slipped past the watchful eyes of their families; nonconformists skirted the condemnation of puritans. As the story goes, Americans fled from political commitments during the 1920s by going to Paris, only to renew those ties as they renewed their connection to American soil in the 1930s. Paris after World War I has been remembered as a simpler time and place *before* politics happened to Americans—one that sometimes nurtured personal development but almost always preceded political awakening.[1]

It is hard to resist such romanticizing. Unquestionably, freer mingling in the French capital offered African Americans a welcome reprieve from the deep and violent inequalities of their hometowns. Without a doubt, the expansive distance Paris put between young women and their families eased the social expectations many daughters sought to escape. All kinds of newcomers found life in France to be exciting and, with the exchange rate, affordable.

Yet behind these patent truths lies a richer, darker, more consequential history of Americans in Paris. Drawn into the capital's conflicts, buffeted by the often harsh judgments of others, Americans in Paris became key participants in a new, more integrated age of transatlantic experiences. Paris would be more than a destination for temporary overseas adventures. Instead, it presented a concrete terrain on which to grapple with increasingly pressing questions about Americans' relationships to a wider world of political and cultural affairs. To overturn those enduring myths about "Gay Paree," in short, is to discover beneath them a largely forgotten story about the multisided, transnational quest to define modern America itself.

At the dawn of the twentieth century, Americans' place in the world had been far from certain. The United States had encompassed a patchwork of social worlds—a nation fractured along class lines, dominated by regional tensions, divided by languages, religions, and races. Americans may have sometimes imagined themselves to be leaders in industry and democratic politics, but culturally they continued to take many of their cues from Europe. There were few traditions deemed worthy enough to study as American art and literature in the universities. In manners and tastes, the middle and upper classes followed the dictates of British and continental mores. European elites, for their part, looked on the United States as dynamic and exotic, to be sure, but an inferior place.[2] The title of the English journalist W. T. Stead's exposé of Americans' impact abroad in 1901 sounded prescient— *The Americanization of the World*—but he was talking less about the consumer goods and mass entertainments that would come to define American culture in future decades than about raw foodstuffs, bulk wheat, and such.[3]

Yet by the 1920s and 1930s, observers inside and outside the United States began to discern the contours of a new and, many thought, utterly distinctive American society populated by distinctively American inhabitants. The years between the wars were critical ones for wide-ranging social consolidation in the United States, when a fractured and far-flung population, drawn into the orbit of emerging national markets and media, increasingly began to imagine themselves as a united people. Through radio entertainments and advertisements, through sporting events and Gallup polls, people in the United States were learning to see themselves as pioneers of a strikingly modern era and a compelling "American Way of Life," a slogan coined in the 1930s to capture these crystallizing definitions of national character.[4] Before, Americans had looked to Europe for cultural models. Now, celebrating their own arts and traditions—cultivating self-consciously American styles and postures—they were becoming a more self-aware and integrated population while simultaneously building up their economic and political clout around the world. By 1941 the publishing mogul Henry Luce could famously proclaim the ascendancy of the "American Century," an age defined not just by U.S. military might and skillful enterprise but also by intangible qualities—values and practices which Luce and others celebrated as "infinitely precious and especially American."[5]

The process by which most Americans learned to define themselves as Americans during the 1920s and 1930s is often portrayed as largely reflexive. Progressive reformers, businessmen with big plans, and Harlem Renaissance luminaries eagerly sought international exchanges. Yet other Americans are still popularly imagined as intensely inward-looking, even isolationist, during the interwar decades.[6] The 1920s seem dominated by political retrenchment and disengagement—a heyday for immigration quota making and economic conservatism, when radicals and labor unions floundered and most Americans were only daring at cocktail parties. Many Americans endeavored to be modern in the twenties, but in terms of their orientation toward the broader world, they have been remembered—largely based on the refusal of Congress to ratify the League of Nations charter—as loath to involve themselves in international affairs. The 1930s may be regarded as more politically engaging years, but the kind of activism Americans embraced during the Depression is also often thought of as profoundly insular. This, after all, was the decade of folksy murals celebrating "the people," of record high tariffs, and of neutrality acts. Nationalism, or Americanism as it was often branded, was such a strong force on the left as well as the right that it seemed to have overwhelmed other affinities and sensibilities.[7]

Depicting American society as introspective, however, obscures the importance of international terrains of maneuver for the development of such national affiliations. Americanness—that collection of sensibilities, values, and forms of social organization that "America" evoked during the first half of the twentieth century—did not derive from domestic preoccupations alone. It also emerged as an international concept at a time when Americans and Europeans became enmeshed in an interrelated web of controversies and causes. Ironically, the divergence of American culture from European models, as imagined by journalists, politicians, artists, and others, took shape amidst a powerful convergence of concerns that brought people on both sides of the Atlantic closer together in the age of world wars. What follows, then, is a story about how "America," in all kinds of competing incarnations, became a potent symbol in transatlantic political culture during the decades prior to World War II. How modern American culture would be defined, how Americans would be imagined as critical players in global affairs—these questions were worked out at the edges of American society as well as at its center. Nowhere was this process more clearly displayed than in Paris, the destination for hundreds of thousands of Americans between the wars and a key crossroads for international popular politics. Immersing oneself in the seductive atmosphere of this world city became a paradigmatic American experience during this era, and as sojourners from the United States settled into their hotel suites and rented rooms, as they combed the capital's side streets and corner cafés, they entered a complex local political scene, ultimately helping to reconfigure it in important ways.

In the early twentieth century, Paris stood as a renowned center of arts and commerce, an industrial powerhouse, a continental transportation hub, and the seat of French government. But what most often appealed to Americans were its small delights: the uneven silhouette of steep mansard rooftops, a medieval courtyard stumbled upon by chance. In 1927, as the capital's *Annuaire statistique* recalls, the city boasted 87,775 trees for lovers to embrace under and 7,774 benches for wizened old men to sit on. Café terraces—Paris's signature public grounds—covered 67,346 square meters of sidewalk. There were miniature boats to sail in the fountain of the Jardin des Tuileries and fish to catch off the quiet quays along the Seine. For shoppers, the metropolis's open-air markets promised a cornucopia of sweet-smelling fruits and exotic game, its riverside book stalls a smorgasbord of opinions, its flea markets and department stores a bonanza of bargains.[8]

Achieving this semblance of harmony proved no small feat in one of the world's largest and most densely populated cities. An impressive infrastructure made such crowded living possible for the nearly three million people residing within the capital's compact seventy-eight square kilometers and, by the late 1930s, two million more in its surrounding suburbs. Beyond the city's outer arrondissements a patchwork of fruit orchards and vegetable plots, along with imposing refineries of mustards, pâtés, and wines, helped feed its inhabitants. In the city center, fluid movements below ground signaled the capital's mastery of modern priorities. Millions of commuters filed onto the Métro each year, while state-of-the-art sewers formed other subterranean passages tangled with water mains, telephone lines, and suction tubes filled with compressed air, shooting millions of messages called *pneumatiques* speedily across town. The capital's growing *banlieue*, or suburbs, pulsed with the factory production of ceramics, glassware, cars, and perfumes. Cargo from the vast reaches of France's empire clogged its railroad stations and waterways: jade, ivory, rubber, and feathers from Asia and Africa. Central artisan neighborhoods buzzed with the making of luxury items from these raw materials—the jewelry, corsets, and *articles de Paris* for which the city had become famous—while the cramped workshops of nearby quarters churned out cheap furniture and clothing. Along the boulevards, offices rattled with the typing and chatter of white-collared men and neatly frocked women.[9]

The capital's impressiveness in the early twentieth century seemed to turn on this combination of charming detail and arresting magnitude, on the city's ability—despite its manifold activities and historic monumentality—to retain a sense of being a deeply human place. "I cannot think of anyone," one writer asserted, "for whom there is not in Paris some answering chord, some link with a great aggregate of humanity, which has lived and wrought and piled up history and romance and experience for two thousand years, all under the one banner of Paris." The young American poet E. E. Cummings remembered sheer ecstasy upon his first glimpse of the capital when he arrived as a volunteer ambulance driver during the Great War. He thought that whereas "New York had reduced mankind to a tribe of pygmies, Paris (in each shape and gesture and avenue and cranny of her being) was continuously expressing the humanness of humanity."[10] This notion of the capital's accessibility and universal relevance—the sense that its beauties and lessons belonged to anyone who proposed to look for them—elevated Paris to the status of a world city. Exploring and interpreting it was thus seen by many across the globe as a requisite life experience, essential for coming to terms with the dawning modern age.

No less than others, Americans looked to Paris as a source of wisdom and inspiration, and after World War I they came to the capital in droves. The city became for many of them a springboard into the wider world. Americans had long been involved in transnational movements—forced and voluntary migrations, relocations of the rich and poor, through a Native American hinterland, across North American borderlands, from European and Asian homelands to American cities and back. And in many ways, the conditions that propelled Americans beyond their own shores during the interwar years grew out of the big, transformative developments of the nineteenth century—the accelerated growth of industrial capitalism and its concomitant networks of transportation and communication.[11] What was new in the age of world wars, however, was the ascendant economic and political clout of the United States, which challenged even that of the leading nation-states of Europe, and the perception of Americans' increased presence and influence abroad. Indeed, after the Armistice in 1918, despite the isolationist proclamations and nativist politics of many, Americans launched an unprecedented array of movements eastward across the Atlantic, expanding their foreign correspondence activities, student exchanges, overseas commerce, and tourist travel. These outward forays proved to be critical, if sometimes underestimated, forces that helped to shape Americans' political culture and sense of themselves.

Also new was the way in which all these trajectories guiding Americans' movements abroad intersected in Paris. The French capital had of course been a destination for prominent Americans since the sojourns of Benjamin Franklin and Thomas Jefferson, and by the late nineteenth century, it nurtured a colony of American elites who led primarily quiet, cloistered lives dedicated to social proprieties or intellectual distinctions. The overseas mobilization of more than two million troops and support staff during World War I, however, utterly transformed the size and nature of the American community in Paris. As home now not only to survivors of the patrician prewar colony but also to forward-thinking cadres of businessmen, diplomats, and journalists, a small but vibrant African American crowd, bohemian cliques of illustrious lights and eccentric riffraff, and troupes of college students and fellows, the city took on new political, economic, and cultural roles for Americans, displacing even London as the headquarters for a diverse lot of sojourners and their overseas endeavors. Observers on the continent began to talk somewhat overdramatically about an invasion, or, as one British onlooker put it, an "American occupation of Paris," dating "from a year or two after the close of the Great War."[12] The number of permanent American residents in the city rose from 8,000 in 1920 to 32,000 in 1923 to an estimated 40,000 at a high point during the mid and late twenties. Adding to that, hundreds of thousands of American tourists descended on the capital each year.[13] Unlike previous Grand Tour travelers, who had come to absorb the refinements of the Old World, these postwar Americans, including many larger-than-life personalities and flashy big spenders, flaunted the habits and tastes of the New World instead. If going abroad challenged Americans' sense of themselves and their culture, their arrival would also have important implications for others.

This American subculture in Paris developed substantially by the mid and late 1920s, and, contrary to common belief, it encompassed far more than the well-known Montparnasse bohemia haunted by famous writers and the nightlife of Montmartre crowned by jazz virtuosos. In the French capital, Americans discovered to their delight practically all the amenities they enjoyed back home. They had access to a variety of places to worship, including a Friends' Center and an American Baptist Foreign Mission Society. At the Methodist Episcopal Church on the boulevard Haussmann, members made use of the modern gymnasium with two basketball leagues and classes in sewing and stenography as well as free aid for the poor. They could seek assistance from scores of American doctors, lawyers, and dentists; they could shop at American grocery stores stocked with Campbell's soup, Aunt Jemima's pancake flour, marshmallows, cornflakes, and peanut butter; they could slake their thirst at American saloons and fill up at American diners, like the Chicago-Texas Inn and the Little Brown Jug, which satisfied cravings for fried chicken and corned beef hash.

Like people at home, Americans enjoyed a well-rounded civic life in Paris, choosing from among a blossoming array of clubs and charity organizations. Members of the very first American Legion post and the Benjamin Franklin Chapter of the Daughters of the American Revolution commemorated patriotic holidays, while others filled two Masonic lodges every other Monday. Adolescents enrolled in two local Boy Scout troops as well as special boarding schools and summer camps. Teenagers attended the American High School of Paris, preparing for college entrance exams, playing sports, joining the glee club.[14] "It's no longer 'Paris'; it's just my address," one resident wrote at the peak of the colony's activities. The Americans here, he realized, "play golf and bridge, do church work, follow the market, go in for charity 'drives,' serve cocktails, and talk about children and servants and football exactly as at any dinner party in the States."[15] Through these activities, Americans in Paris manifested an offshore extension of their national life, projecting an image of the nation as something not rooted in fixed physical geography but made up of movable social institutions and cultural parts. Gertrude Stein's quip that America was her country and Paris was her hometown seems not so fanciful in light of all this community building.[16]

Especially since World War II, however, many aspects of this remarkable outpost have been forgotten, while the exploits of Stein and other celebrities have been amplified and mythologized. The actual city, in all of its textured complexity, usually appears as little more than a static backdrop for American escapades. All but forgotten are the thousands of businessmen, journalists, scholars, and others who poured into Paris alongside the more famous expatriates. And beyond the artistic impact of musicians, painters, and writers, little attention has been paid to Americans' influence in the city or the ways in which Parisians protested their presence, sometimes violently.[17] Instead, Americans have commonly portrayed the capital as a vast reserve of leisure and indulgence. It seemed to function, as one journalist put it, "like a big seaside resort: 'The Americans' Playground,'" with the French only there "as scene-shifters to keep the show running." Another magazine writer agreed in 1926: "Real life, we seem to think, goes on in the United States; the rest of the world is a funny show."[18] Since studies of Americans in Paris have relied almost exclusively on American accounts like these, they cannot help but absorb such mythmaking tendencies.

Even a brief review of interwar French history, however, dispels these notions about Paris as a carefree playground. France had suffered disproportionate damage and casualties during World War I, leaving eight million acres in ruin and permanently disrupting family and village life. The national government, mired in partisan squabbling and corruption, faced continuous opposition between the wars from extremists on both the left and the right eager to see the downfall of the Third Republic. The rationing of coal and other goods stretched far beyond the Armistice, and the economic uncertainties of the immediate postwar period carried over into disruptive fluctuations in the value of the franc, anxieties over astronomical war debts, and finally, after 1931, widespread depression.[19] France's capital stood out for its particularly volatile dynamics. All kinds of new groups taxed its infrastructure and stoked acute levels of xenophobia among French residents. World War I and its aftermath pulled newcomers into the capital's orbit who otherwise might not have come. Its position near the front brought displaced peasants from the north, supporters from allied countries, and troops from the colonies. Hosting the peace conference, too, ensured that the city would remain after the war a clearinghouse for international news and diplomacy. Labor shortages, a direct consequence of the conflict, encouraged the influx of workers from other European countries as well as from Africa and the Caribbean—an unprecedented wave of immigration that intensified even further as Americans restricted access to their borders. As France became the world's leading destination for immigrants, Paris and its suburbs housed a higher percentage of foreigners to total population than any other European city, reaching about 10 percent by the mid-1920s. Furthermore, its location a short train ride from the ocean liner ports of Cherbourg and Le Havre positioned the capital as a leading destination during the first era of mass tourism, bringing boisterous, wealthy travelers, especially from Latin America, the United States, and Great Britain, who helped transform the city into a far more cosmopolitan and, to some, far less French place.[20]

The city sat poised on the brink of an increasingly unstable and politicized world. The Bolshevik Revolution and subsequent civil war in Russia reconfigured international politics, splitting the radical left across the modern world into warring camps of communists, socialists, and anarchists and spawning in reaction a bevy of right-wing movements. Radical actions, from general strikes and insurrections to terrorist acts, were met with severe backlashes in the United States, Europe, and the colonies alike. New commitments to parliamentary democracy, celebrated in the Versailles

Treaty, slowly crumbled in Eastern and Southern Europe, and Paris absorbed an explosive mix of their refugees and activists. Taking advantage of the capital's easy reach by railroad as well as its relative tolerance of exiles, all sorts of unpredictable characters of clashing ideological persuasions slipped in as the situation deteriorated elsewhere: White Russian émigrés, Italian and Central European antifascists, nationalist militants from Indochina and North Africa, Soviet operatives, royalist plotters, Spanish Loyalists, and Nazi spies. Paris during these decades was, arguably, among the most polarized places in the world. One of the largest concentrations of communists and socialists anywhere built up their strength in the city's infamous suburban "Red Belt," while one of the world's most powerful police forces and a staunchly right-wing municipal government simultaneously ruled its center.[21] This was decidedly not Gay Paree as Americans have thought of it.

Even on a day-to-day basis the capital could disappoint romantics. Building façades and scaffolding were plastered with unwieldy, oversized billboards, loud flashing neon advertisements, and shrill political posters—signs of visual chaos. The metropolis, at times, could be a "clamorous hell," too, starting before dawn with the scavengers who clanked and banged their way through the contents of trash cans. In 1927 residents slopped a whopping 701,585 tons of garbage onto the streets. Muddy litter clogged the gutters and antiquated cesspool tanks. Bedraggled early birds were invariably showered with debris beaten from rugs slung out of windows overhead. Neighborhood policemen struggled to keep under control various other disturbers of the peace, making collars for lewd displays, belligerent drunkenness, and urinating *en plein air*—an especially gratuitous act in a city with over a thousand conspicuous public urinals. Factories polluted the air on the outskirts of town, producing their oils, fertilizers, and chemicals. Sometimes oozing gas meters exploded; electric lights flickered on and off. The resident American writer Elliot Paul remembered that functional telephones, iceboxes, and soundproof bathrooms "belonged to another world" far from places like his crooked street on the inner Left Bank.[22]

Residents increasingly worried about the future of their capital. Between the radicalizing immigrants and workers in the suburbs and the growing community of affluent foreigners who seemed to dominate social life in the center of the city, "the Paris of Parisians," as French nationalists often called it, was now imagined to be smothered between two menacing extremes. On the one side, visualized the French writer and future Vichy supporter Paul Morand, encroached the outer districts: "home of the proletariat and hot-bed of communists," jammed like ghettos with their "jumble of imported labour." On the other, he envisioned an even more unsettling development: "at the very heart of all, in a vortex of molten heat, the Paris of today, modern and American, like the crater of a volcano in ceaseless eruption."[23] For different people in different ways, these particular fault lines in the capital dramatized the central tension of interwar politics writ large: the clash between well-established traditions of liberalism—promoting individualism, laissez-faire capitalism, permissive cosmopolitanism, and democratic compromise—and the new, more strident movements of the left and right that challenged this center.

Thus, from the mundane dilemmas of modern city governance to the extraordinary challenges presented by urban mass politics, Paris captured the critical problems of the age. Experiences in the capital carried great symbolic value. Contrary to today's myths about their escapist potential, they were weighted with import and often highly politicized. People imagined that something beyond local control was at stake in the city's public affairs. During the Great War, the Allies' hopes and fears had fixated on whether Paris held or fell. Then, during the peace deliberations, across Europe and the Middle East, victors and vanquished alike awaited the fate of their borders, to be decided in Paris. From across oceans, colonial subjects trained their sights on the push for self-determination. Surely, they thought, what began in Paris would end in their own lands. Communists and fascists, who mounted the most formidable challenges to liberal democracy between the wars, also keenly followed the capital's affairs. Despite their divergent beliefs, both groups betrayed a view of human destiny as unfolding progressively through a series of revolutionary moments and an assumption about the centrality of Paris to that process. In both worldviews, that is, to command Paris—the capital of revolution, birthplace of bourgeois society and republican values—was to control the path of history.[24] Thus, in the battles of the day, the metropolis became both a staging ground and the coveted prize. A sense for this would guide members of the far left and right, as well as so many others wedged in between, who shaped the city's history between the long months when the Allies had victoriously defended the capital during World War I and those disturbingly short weeks it took for the Nazis to conquer it in 1940.

With these broader developments in mind, the pages that follow move past the truthful notion that many Americans found Paris an enjoyable diversion from unfavorable realities at home. They draw out instead the political implications behind all the pleasure seeking and socializing in the capital that have so far been left to stand as innocuous and entertaining side notes to the more serious history of the period. Analyzing both American and European perspectives, this book does not ask *why* Americans went to Paris—the primary question driving much of the literature on the subject—but what happened once they became conspicuous participants in the capital's public life. What impact did they have on the city? How did Parisians and other Europeans interpret their presence? And what difference did this overseas movement make to Americans' sense of themselves and their culture? Changing the motivating questions—and, to answer those questions effectively, opening up the analysis to Parisian archival research and European historiography— these methodological shifts reveal this topic to be not simply an amusing interlude but a crucial chapter in modern American history.

In the wake of the Great War, Americans' place in Paris, and by extension their role in the world, became the subject of intense discussion. Part I establishes the parameters of these debates, first through the eyes of arriving Americans and then from the point of view of other Paris residents. As chapter 1 shows, the creation of a prominent colony in Paris provided an occasion for Americans to celebrate their prosperity and imagine their own national ingenuity, even as that colony privileged certain visions of American culture over others. Telling stories about their triumphs abroad offered Americans a way to think about themselves as pioneers of an emerging way of life. Europeans also wrestled with the significance of this incursion. While some looked to arriving Americans as exemplars of exciting new possibilities, others began to associate them with a host of unwelcome changes that had arisen in Paris since the war. Chapter 2 details how many Parisians discovered that vocally protesting against perceived American encroachments—signs of which proliferated, from neon advertising campaigns to more liberal mixing in the nightspots—became one way to make sense of these jarring developments and to disassociate them, no matter what their complicated origins, from their own image and agendas. Together, the chapters of part I demonstrate how, for visitors from the United States as well as for their hosts, arguing about newcomers' impact on the capital provided an opportunity to sharpen distinctions between American and European culture. Such definitions were not predetermined. What stood out as American was not simply created within the borders of the United States and then exported in the form of complete products. Americanness was not simply American-made. It also took shape through a myriad of interactions abroad.

This transatlantic history encompassed more than cultural discourse. By the mid and late twenties, arguments over the place of Americans in Paris also began to overflow into tense, physical confrontations on the city's streets. Part II explores these backlashes, first on the left and then on the right, uncovering the ways in which efforts to combat American influence in the capital figured prominently in new forms of Parisian cultural politics. As chapter 3 documents, the far left's use of "anti-American" tactics reached a peak during the Sacco-Vanzetti affair. Rioting against the Massachusetts executions of the two Italian anarchists in August 1927, protesters singled out institutions and symbols in Paris they associated with American privilege and exploitation. Within days of the riots, the Paris police began their own rigorous crackdown on the pleasure grounds so popular with visitors from across the Atlantic—an aggressive antivice campaign to address growing uncertainties about the capital's international reputation. As chapter 4 uncovers, right-wing Parisians who supported this police "purging" saw Americans as agents who hastened the invasion of foreign immoralities and portended French national decay. These intriguing incidents, which have yet to receive sustained analysis by historians, reveal not only the richness of the pre–World War II history of anti-American politics but also the extent to which others helped to determine what Americanness would come to stand for in the new century.

Not simply targets, Americans were also players in the capital's popular conflicts, and they drew on their experiences abroad to hone their own convictions. Part III, therefore, also pairs chapters on the right and left, this time to analyze the development of American political culture in international contexts. Chapter 5 delves into the significance of the American Legion's much-publicized Paris convention in September 1927, when some twenty thousand veterans commandeered the city for a massive parade. Taking place only weeks after the Sacco-Vanzetti riots, this controversial march highlighted the Legion's affinities with those right-wing groups on the rise in Europe, and it gave such "pilgrims" the means to infuse their movement with greater strength and legitimacy, drawn from a sense of international relevance. The capital also nurtured American politics on the left. A hotbed of radicalism as well as avant-garde art, a place bubbling with talk of foreign affairs, the metropolis became a gateway for artists and writers who would wade even farther out into the world of mass politics by the late twenties and thirties. Chapter 6, therefore, reconsiders those most famous Paris expatriates, revealing how their time in the capital represented not a flight from responsibility, as commonly believed, but a key turning point for developing a particular brand of internationalism that enriched the emerging culture of the Popular Front. Together, these final chapters illustrate how, in Paris, Americans on both sides of the spectrum began to fashion new models of engagement overseas that sharpened their political stances. Just below the formal business, policy, and diplomacy networks studied most often by historians were layers of more casual interaction that proved to be defining ones for Americans working to understand their role in the world and to give shape to their own modern political culture.

Taken together, visions of rioters smashing the windows of famous cafés and ruffling American pedestrians, scenes of police rounding up nightclub clientele and placing bars popular with Americans under surveillance—these images undermine the myth of a postwar Gay Paree that has endured in popular American memory. Moving from broad comparative and transnational relationships to the ways in which specific encounters played out on the capital's streets reveals the extent to which, amidst mounting crisis, Americans in Paris, along with their hosts, enlisted themselves in a shared culture of political engagements. Here, at the intersection of European and American history, where the fluid sweep of international networks meets the rooted context of an urban landscape, a new story emerges about how Americans helped to shape the cultural politics of interwar Paris, and, at the same time, how Paris helped to shape American political culture.

The methods used to unearth this new narrative depart somewhat from the approach most often taken by those studying the history of American culture in transnational perspective. Scholars in this field most readily conceptualize their charge as one of tracing connections and exchanges. They highlight, above all, the intellectual cross-fertilizations and literary translations, the personal correspondence and art publications, trailing along the complex social circuits forged by migrants and sojourners. The cultural history of Americans' engagements abroad has been written largely as a history of productive dialogues, though not without their setbacks. For Americans eager for new experiences, all kinds of foreign locations, like Paris, have been important spaces to rethink their sense of self, to forage for new insights, and to sharpen critiques that had seemed harder to articulate back home. As such, the world beyond the borders of the United States, even with its disappointments, looms large as a terrain of opportunity for Americans.[25]

And this it has surely been. Yet cross-cultural encounters in the early twentieth century were not always as transcendent as scholars, or the people they study, often imply. They were not always foremost about reciprocities, traded in art anthologies or gathered up by reformers, poets, and other receptive intermediaries. In many ways, modern transatlantic culture has been built out of a series of jolting, messy, not-so-productive exchanges. Interactions across national lines have been uncomfortable as well as exciting, and they have been suffused with power struggles as difficult as those that could be found at home. They have been as much about confrontation as about collaboration, as much the product of disconnects as of connections. Inspiring poets and other wanderers to great heights, the international circulation of people, goods, and ideas has also stirred disenchantment, inflamed prejudices, and provoked new angers. It has spread reactionary as well as progressive agendas. It has led, frankly, to all kinds of bad behavior. Outside the famous salons, down on the streets, this was the situation Americans frequently discovered in the French capital between the wars.

This could not but have been the case from the start of the First World War to the end of the Second, an era aptly christened by Eric Hobsbawm as the "thirty-one years' world war," a "general age of catastrophe and crisis in the affairs of the world." Americans, as well as those responding to them, had to work their way through a challenging set of global crosscurrents during these years—forces at once nationalist and international. On one hand, the Great War redoubled the movement of manpower and materiel. Newsreels and mass publications scattered information over ever vaster distances. Congresses and conventions promoted the spirit of internationalism. Two-way traffic spiked between metropoles and colonies. Airplanes surveyed foreign lands. But at the same time, nationalist movements boomed, and patriotic imperatives cut across and mixed with cross-national allegiances at all points along the political spectrum. The nationalisms that took shape on both the left and the right during the interwar years were not the uneven and incomplete state-building projects of the nineteenth century but new, culturally thick varieties, which envisioned the state as the inspiration for an entire way of life. These new nationalisms were the stuff of uniformed crowds in the streets, of overblown symbols and modal figures, of national cinemas, official art styles, and imposing, iconic leaders. Americans' searches for a distinctive, modern political culture were part of this worldwide move toward more strident forms of nationalism. Yet as avid participants in Hobsbawm's thirty-one years' world war, they, like others, would do their searching on an international field of action.[26]

Ultimately, this age of world wars and political polarization was experienced as both a widely interconnected and a deeply particularized conflict. Local controversies, such as the Sacco-Vanzetti affair and plans for a Legion parade in Paris, were propelled into international scandals, and then, as transnationalized events, they were in turn refiltered through local conditions and national concerns. These are the dynamics explored in this book, because it is this interplay between broad, international developments and increasingly important national affiliations that made up a vibrant transatlantic culture in the early twentieth century, shaping the popular politics of many nations, not least of the United States. These are the dynamics that became one of the defining features of an era of accelerated global interaction and foundering world markets, of communisms and fascisms—of a time, as we shall see, when a local court case in a small New England town snowballed into worldwide uproar, and droves of supposedly provincial veterans thought it natural to caravan thousands of miles across the Atlantic for a victory march.

PART I | # The Specter of Americanization

*Many voices, native and foreign, clashed in intermittent debate over the country's destiny.*

—Matthew Josephson, *Life among the Surrealists*

CHAPTER ONE | Triumphant Arrivals

T HE TYPICAL AMERICAN ENTRÉE INTO the French capital began with a
taxi ride—a harrowing crash course in the streets of the city by the
Seine. Paris taxi drivers were advised to be nice to these guests. *"Donnez
confiance au client,"* counseled a contemporary manual, "by not crossing streets
without slowing down," and don't forget, it prodded, that a red light means
stop. For newcomers, the ride was a shock nonetheless. Americans emerged
from their boat trains onto the grimy platforms of the Gare Saint-Lazare,
scrambling to collect their trunks and make their way past somewhat
welcoming, somewhat disconcerting signs posted in English: directions to
special trains, departures to New York via Le Havre, and warnings to "Beware
of Pickpockets."[1] Amidst the din of horns outside, they surrendered themselves to daredevils in caps and moustaches who whisked them away toward
the hotels near the place de l'Opéra.

At peak hours, the place de l'Opéra looked less like the cynosure of an
imperial city plan than the bumper car arena at an amusement park. Newcomers' taxis along with top-heavy delivery vans and hasty Citroëns mixed
with rickety pushcarts and brazen jaywalkers in what one visitor described as
a "raging, disputing clash of cross-currents." In a typical year during the
1920s, more than 150,000 people would crash their cars and more than
11,000 people would crash their bicycles in traffic-jammed thoroughfares like
this one—accidents that unfolded on poorly paved avenues and in cobblestone
alleys, accidents due to excessive speeding, drunken drivers, drivers ignorant
of road regulations, vehicles without brake lights, surfaces slick with snow or
frost. Americans recounted this first taxi journey as a death-defying adventure,

giving rise to a "legend," as one *Scribner's* columnist related, that drivers sped "wildly through the swirl of traffic, grazing pedestrians on the place Vendôme, taking the Rivoli corner on one wheel, and careening toward the river, always coming within a hair's breadth of disaster, but always miraculously escaping."[2] The taxi ride became a stock scene in Americans' accounts about the capital, reappearing again and again in personal writings, magazine articles, and novels.

On one level, this virgin taxi ride story was about risk in a foreign land. It referred to the need Americans had long felt for guidance to get around the intimidating capitals of Europe. From the back windows of a taxi, the French metropolis that zoomed past appeared wild and perilous. For Sinclair Lewis' autobiographical protagonist Sam Dodsworth, "it was a motion picture produced by an insane asylum . . . a telephone bell ringing just after he'd gone to sleep; it was lightning flashes and steam whistles and newspaper extras and war." Few Americans bothered with the city's slow and crowded public transportation between the wars. And, with the favorable exchange rate, taxis were cheap. Thus, even though cabmen seemed gruff and impetuous, they became essential pilots just as commissioned guides had been for travelers in the nineteenth century. Privy to the capital's quirks and short-cuts, such chauffeurs ensured that although the passage was frightening, under their charge, as one survivor testified, "Somehow—with luck—one escape[d] death."[3]

And yet, if on the surface this familiar setup spoke of narrow escapes, if it recalled Americans' long-standing fears that they might be out of their depth in the grand capitals of Europe, tested by the centuries, it also hinted at a departure from such old insecurities. For more and more Americans after the war, the trip from the train station stood out not as the first in a series of foreign dislocations, but more likely as the last moment of uncertainty before confidence took over. Surviving the taxi ride was thrilling. It seemed to mark for them a rite of passage not only into the Paris experience but also onto the world scene. This was a success story, alluding to the manner by which unlikely visitors from across the Atlantic would take Paris by storm and make it their own. It was at heart a tale about American derring-do.

The Paris that Americans saw between the wars tended to be one they created in their own image. Once they had conquered that taxi ride, the city seemed to open up for them a bounty of evidence attesting to their own growing impact abroad. Sojourners quickly discovered in the western half of the Right Bank the epicenter of a rapidly expanding American world, a community made up of tens of thousands of permanent residents and hundreds of thousands of visitors. This was no modest overseas outpost, nor was it merely an extension of the exclusive, high-society American colony of the prewar years. Newcomers marveled at the wealth of novel American institutions clustered along the avenues near the Opera, from banks and beauty parlors to soda fountains, and they admired the conspicuous, lively presence of their compatriots—new kinds of arrivals who had not been there before but now packed the area's restaurants, bars, and hotel lobbies. Circulating in this buzzing social scene, Americans approached the capital as a glorious stage set, an exciting backdrop against which they could model a newfound self-assurance.

Through American eyes, Paris glimmered, shimmied; it was not a part of war-spent Europe or demoralized France so much as an independent, modern mecca, the site where George Gershwin scored his brassy, triumphant symphony, where Cole Porter perfected his playful rhymes. During the twenties and early thirties, gushed one *Saturday Evening Post* commentator, Paris "seems to have been what Broadway tried to be, what Greenwich Village yearned to be, what Fifth Avenue was determined to be—all at once and all in American terms."[4] Statements like this one are often taken at face value as evidence of Americans' carefree, inconsequential time in the City of Lights. Yet Americans' descriptions of Paris did not simply reflect the city's realities. More precisely, these were claims—stories Americans told themselves about how they had come into their own as members of a leading nation. The notion that Paris could be possessed "all in American terms" pointed to the capital's role as a pivotal place for Americans to refashion themselves in this age of world wars.

Americans' commanding presence in interwar Paris appears especially remarkable in light of recent assumptions about their cultural inferiority. During the nineteenth century, critics on both sides of the Atlantic regarded Americans as but pale imitators of Europe's high standards, a people who had selected false teeth and the Colt revolver to represent themselves at the Crystal Palace exhibition—remarkable inventions perhaps, but hardly the stuff of greatness for the ages. Occasionally, onlookers shared Charles Baudelaire's worries about becoming *"américanisé,"* but by and large Americanization still referred to the acculturation of immigrants in the United States. European celebrities, from Charles Dickens to Sigmund Freud, seized on their travels to the New World as occasions to pose as better-knowing outsiders, mortified by the violence and vulgarity of American life. After his two trips west at midcentury, Matthew Arnold famously blasted that "in culture and totality, America, instead of surpassing us all, falls short," an assessment elites in the United States resented but feared was too often true. The nation's money-grubbing hustle and bustle similarly assaulted the sensibilities of Rudyard

Kipling during his visit in 1891. Enslaved to a crude notion of progress, building cities of "grotesque ferocity," Americans were more barbarian than the barbarians he had encountered in the colonies, Kipling declared. Not all Americans were unmannered philistines and not all Europeans superior intellects, of course, but these clichés had staying power, coloring the expectations of travelers who traversed the Atlantic in both directions.[5]

By the early twentieth century, however, the tides of cultural influence seemed to be turning. Manufacturing in the United States soared, and the principles of industrial organization piloted by Frederick Winslow Taylor's scientific management and Henry Ford's factory work system became famous the world over. The emergence of a vibrant, distinctively American culture during the first half of the century, however, entailed not just these new modes of production but other, more subtle or diffuse changes—innovations smuggled into everyday life by the bold graphics of Madison Avenue, the blinking neon lights of the Great White Way, the fast talk and streamlined fashions of Hollywood films, the blowout sounds of big band jazz. A modern American ethos would evoke a whole constellation of styles and practices, new designs for living that promised to shatter the stiff old Victorian rules and sweep away the stuffy traditions of Europe. It exuded a confidence, a novelty that seemed full of excitement and democratic potential. For all its problems and failures, "America" stood for a seductive way of life not only for those living in the United States but also for millions beyond it, and the rise of an "American" Paris was part and parcel of this development.

The growth of an elaborate American world in Paris showcased many of the behaviors and trends gaining popularity back in the United States, but it also made modern American culture seem more coherent and distinctive than it actually was. During these decades, Americans had been searching to define their national traditions, but this process was marked by intense conflict. Would the nation be driven by small-town rhythms or big-city energy? Would rigid moral values hold over from the nineteenth century or would new, more cosmopolitan and egalitarian sensibilities prevail? In Paris, the latter strains of American culture came to the fore where they did not have to compete with alternative visions of the nation on display back in the United States. The local American community—dominated by investors and other go-getters, jazz performers, freelance journalists, adventurous students on new junior year abroad programs, and young bohemians experimenting with life and art—offered a particularly liberal and urbane image of the United States, set starkly against alternative ways of life abroad. Envisioning their role in postwar Paris offered Americans an occasion to come to terms with their new cultural standing and forward-looking orientation. Those arriving by taxi would play a crucial role in helping to define what would come to be regarded as quintessentially "American" in the twentieth century—even though their Paris colony highlighted only certain aspects of American life.

Surveys of Americans in Paris between the wars almost always focus on two famed locales—Montmartre and Montparnasse—and the illustrious "expatriates" who populated their renowned jazz joints and rowdy cafés. These storied quarters, however, actually appeared on the periphery of most Americans' mental map of the capital. The heart of the city, as visitors saw it, could be found instead on the inner Right Bank between the Jardin des Tuileries and the grand boulevards in the vicinity of the Paris Opera. This is where, for arrivals, the uneasiness of the taxi ride began to abate as the quarter's much-anticipated sights came into view. Here were the sidewalk canopies, the cluttered kiosks, the arches leading to the Métro, the aproned waiters, the steady traffic policeman, the sauntering *Parisienne*. On streets like the rue de la Paix, luxury boutiques dazzled American women with their world-renowned names: Cartier, Worth, Paquin. Visiting men appreciated instead the friendly look of American saloons lurking on side streets where institutions like Harry's New York Bar—with pendants of Harvard and Yale hanging in its latticed windows—promised spirited camaraderie. Newcomers dutifully noted the area's monuments, but the place de l'Opéra became their prime reference point. This imposing square emerged during the 1920s as the main hub for the rapidly growing American colony—a nexus around which grand hotels did a brisk transatlantic business, where tour buses lingered and scores of American companies set up shop. With the terraces of the popular Café de la Paix at its side, the place de l'Opéra became the crossroads where husbands and wives rendezvoused after spending their mornings apart and where, a young American gratefully discovered, "one is certain to encounter friends from home." Revealingly, it was the place disoriented tourists looked for when they got lost.[6]

Unprecedented numbers of Americans set sail for Paris and the place de l'Opéra between the wars. The dawn of such mass tourism could be glimpsed as far back as the Paris Exposition in 1867, when Thomas Cook escorted his first group of Americans around the city, and, at the same time, Mark Twain gathered fodder for his humorous travelogue, *The Innocents Abroad*. Possibilities for middle-class touring increased further during the late nineteenth century thanks to improved transportation and the rising popularity of commercialized leisure. Between 1880 and 1900, the annual number of American steamship passengers en route to Europe shot up from 50,000 to 125,000.

That amount doubled again by 1913. World War I interrupted this impressive movement, and even into the early twenties visits would be blighted by passport and visa difficulties, steep prices, and shortages of fuel, food, even coin currency.[7] But by the mid-twenties, skyrocketing numbers of Americans ventured abroad. Between 1924 and 1930, tourist travel to Europe rose again by more than 100 percent. Visitors headed especially for France. Only a reported 15,000 Americans visited the country on the eve of the war and only 30,000 in 1919, but 100,000 made the trip in 1921 and an impressive 400,000 in 1925.[8]

Such democratized travel had been spurred on by the postwar economic boom in the United States, by the strength of the dollar, and, indirectly, by the new quota restrictions on immigration. As transatlantic working-class migration slowed to a trickle, once congested, now underbooked steerage compartments on steam liners were reincarnated as budget-friendly berths sold under the label "Tourist Third." Upon its debut in 1925, fewer than 20,000 people traveled Tourist Third, but only three years later that number reached almost 80,000. The young were especially amenable to these modest accommodations. Below deck in a no-frills atmosphere, one *New York Times Magazine* writer explained, flourished a "kind of intensified college life—instruction, sport and romance in the kaleidoscope of shipboard days." Sandwiched between this flaming youth and the wealthy who made the passage in spacious first class, retired businessmen and their wives, eager schoolteachers, the grown-up children of immigrants, and others embarked on much-anticipated trips of a lifetime across the Atlantic. American church groups orchestrated packaged-tour pilgrimages. Professional organizations arranged overseas conventions, such as the American Bar Association, which held its meeting in Paris in 1924, and the Rotary Club, which descended on Belgium in 1927. Dutifully investigating Europe's industries as well as its entertainments and historic treasures, wandering police commissioners, union leaders, and social reformers combined business with pleasure.[9] Paris, one correspondent pointed out, now sat at the "center of the American tourist's universe." The city's central location made it a depot for all kinds of comings and goings on the continent. One California couple passing through on their way to a physiology congress in Zurich were delighted when they ran into friends from home: "They were going to Geneva to the League conference on hormone standardization. We laughed over liqueurs till morning."[10]

Catering to the coming hordes, American establishments peppered the busy inner Right Bank. By 1928, from the vantage point of the place de l'Opéra, American banks and bureaus stood "at nearly every corner," one *New*

*York Times* correspondent reported.[11] Between them sprouted pharmacies like Scott's Drug Store, afternoon rest stops like the Rivoli Anglo-American Tea Room, bookstores like Brentano's, and American-style beauty parlors like the one run by the Ogilvie sisters in the Equitable Trust Building. On the boulevard des Italiens, Sam's, with its soda fountain, beckoned the homesick across from the Guaranty Trust Company. While shops and tearooms attracted American women in droves, the area's newspaper reading rooms achieved the status of informal clubs for men. Dozens of plush offices, stocked with oriental rugs and leather armchairs, dotted the neighborhood, including those of the *Chicago Daily News* opposite the Café de la Paix, the *Chicago Tribune* just around the corner, and from New York, the *World* and the *Herald Tribune* on the avenue de l'Opéra.[12] Havens from the bustle of the street, these rest stops offered places to seek out current issues of home papers and sign social registers, appealing especially to businessmen as great places to check the price of stocks or peruse the sports page while talking conservative politics over a cigar.[13]

Hotels in the western half of the Right Bank, too, became important social centers for Americans, where patrons often rented suites for weeks or even months at a time. In 1928, between mid-July and mid-August alone, a quarter of a million Americans would register at Paris lodging houses.[14] Americans revered the luxury establishments especially, swarming the Ritz, the Majestic, and the flamboyant new Claridge, popular with Hollywood movie stars. With elevators and revolving doors, special cable privileges to New York, English-speaking concierges, and English-sounding names, such grand establishments scorned the charming quirkiness of smaller pensions in favor of a crisper, more impersonal tone that delivered the feel and comforts of big-city American hotels. They were, by one account, "pure, unadulterated New York." After the war, the Astoria near the Arc de Triomphe had been "brought up to the highest standard of hotel perfection," according to its English-language advertising, and transformed into a place to "Meet Your American Friends."[15] What concierges at these imposing places failed to arrange could be had from travel agencies nearby. The Auto-Confort Touring agency rented luxury cars with English-speaking drivers from the place Vendôme, and Helen Scott's American Service Bureau just behind the Madeleine procured theater tickets, personal shoppers, and information about local schools and housing. Most popular of all, American Express lured clients to its premises just a stone's throw from the Opera itself. By 1927, during the high summer season some 13,300 people filed through its doors every day. Even iconoclasts like Emma Goldman and Henry Miller relied on it as their Paris mailing address.[16]

After World War I, Americans gravitated to the bustling, traffic-snarled Opera district. The busy American Express, topped by a gigantic electric sign, appears on the far right. Mario von Bucovich, *Paris*. New York: Random House, 1930.

This rising postwar world of Americans in Paris contrasted sharply with the smaller, insular American colony that had existed in the nineteenth century. Based in the tony residential neighborhoods of the far west, by the 1870s this community had leveled off at about five thousand members—diplomatic and commercial representatives, Confederates fleeing the aftermath of the Civil War, members of the leisure classes of New York or Boston—along with some eight thousand temporary visitors, mainly upper-class participants in the continental grand tour. The capital also attracted a smattering of students and artists, worldly and often affluent Americans such as John Singer Sargent, born and raised in Europe, who made his living painting portraits for society notables. To confirm their wealth and status, American elites once clamored for admission to Napoleon III's court and promenaded on the grounds of the Bois de Boulogne. They kept in touch with national affairs through the nearby American legation, the offices of the newspaper *American Register*, the Washington Club for men, and two esteemed American Protestant churches. Most members of the colony, however, made little use of other public spaces. Retreating into their parlors, established families followed the seasonal exigencies of the aristocratic society that still held sway over the area, making careful contacts with their

compatriots through elaborate systems of social calling that scarcely registered in the street life around the Champs-Elysées. Their enclaves remained
highly exclusive before World War I, as suggested by the daily customs of
the novelist Edith Wharton, who permanently settled in Paris in 1907. Like
other colonists, she delighted in the civility of her small circle of literary and
old society friends—"people who shared my tastes," she explained.[17]

After the war, followers of respectable society continued to keep house in
the timeworn mansions of Passy and other select quarters, but they were
clinging to a vanishing order in the face of a changing Paris, its streets, Edith
Wharton regretted, now marred by "hideous advertisements," its buildings
and fountains "torn from their mystery by the vulgar intrusion of flood
lighting," the Champs-Elysées clearly in its "last expiring elegance."[18] Long-
standing residents like Wharton would also be overwhelmed and outpaced
by all kinds of new Americans on the scene—ambitious State Department
employees, perky department store buyers and copyeditors, recent graduates
off on a lark. Eclipsing the cloistered, high-society worlds of the prewar colonists, the capital's proliferating landscape of American shops and haunts,
where one could eat layer cake or make friends over a newfangled cocktail,
would make Paris appear open and accessible in ways it had not seemed
before. Claiming a greater share of the public spotlight, these new arrivals
would not remain cooped up in museums like dutiful travelers of old. Nor
would they choose to be cultural chameleons, taking on European demeanors
like the status-conscious characters of a Henry James novel. Instead, they
fancied themselves brave and original participants in a city begging for their
business and awed by their enthusiasms.

Americans' invasion of the Opera area and its surrounding districts signaled
a turning point in their international relations. Before the twentieth century,
investors tapped the markets of Latin America and the Caribbean, leisure
travelers set sail for Europe, and globetrotters and missionaries plied the
ports of the Far East, but on the whole more people poured into the United
States than left it for foreign shores. By the turn of the century, however,
American networks abroad began to thicken as politicians, businessmen, and
others became increasingly intent on building up the nation's commercial
and military empires. Such international movements accelerated further in
the wake of World War I. Opportunities and imperatives born of the
conflict—in exports, banking, journalism, diplomacy, and humanitarian
aid—helped inaugurate a new phase of overseas activities for Americans, particularly in Europe, helping to quash those old chuckles about philistines and
false teeth. The emerging web of social, economic, and political connections

abroad, all intersecting through the French capital, was made by a range of ambitious Americans—each, in their own way, at the forefront of national innovation in the early twentieth century. Fittingly, when John Dos Passos sketched out a geography for his great American novel, *Nineteen Nineteen* (1932), he simply drew a circle labeled Paris surrounded by other cities in its orbit.[19]

World War I decisively rerouted Americans' energies through the French capital. Trailing some two million combat troops, Red Cross nurses, YMCA chaplains, Salvation Army hut workers, and military support staff poured into France, many making their way to Paris. Situated so close to the front, the city served as a headquarters for intelligence and humanitarian work. American volunteers staffed a host of relief groups for war orphans, wounded men, and the rebuilding of the devastated regions, several of which would carry on their efforts after the cease-fire. Many war-related ventures would become fixtures in the postwar city. The American University Union first opened in 1917 as a base for enlisted collegians, and the Paris edition of the *Chicago Tribune* and the well-patronized American Library had both been founded initially as resources for American soldiers. With the peace, some Americans never returned home. Others—African Americans enamored of the prospect of life without segregation, white middle-class youths wooed by their adventures as ambulance drivers and burning with literary pretensions—quickly drifted back to Paris. Just after the Armistice, decommissioned officers, MPs, and an especially troublesome underworld of army deserters boosted the city's resident American colony to some six to eight thousand people. During the peace conference, masses of United States delegates and journalists, too, cluttered up the city's central quarters, signaling the greater role Americans would play in the capital in the wake of war. That spring, Dos Passos remembered, "it looked as if every man or woman in the United States who could read or write had wrangled an overseas job. Relief was the great racket," he thought, but "those who couldn't disguise themselves as relievers came as journalists or got attached to government commissions."[20]

After Versailles, the wave of unruly doughboys and conspicuous convention-goers would ebb, but the journalists were there to stay, and they helped to set the tone of the postwar American colony. The growth of syndicated news networks and the war itself had stoked interest back in the United States for overseas news of all kinds. Once considered career suicide, appointments to posts in continental Europe became some of the most coveted positions in journalism. Before the war, when London dominated the transatlantic cable system, fewer than a dozen American reporters had languished in the backwater of Paris's news offices. But by 1926, London's monopoly had been broken, and more than eighty official American correspondents, in addition to scores of unofficial ones, made the French capital a clearinghouse for current events just as it had been a depot for wartime personnel. Young journalists, fresh out of college or the army or straight from the rosters of regional papers, became familiar sights trolling for society column fodder on the platforms of arriving boat trains and scooping leads in the lobbies of opulent hotels. Many of those who would become pioneers in the emerging field of foreign correspondence, such as Dorothy Thompson, William Shirer, and Martha Gellhorn, began their careers in Paris, freelancing for American newspapers and magazines eager for stories about the French capital, or taking positions as beat reporters for the capital's growing English-language press. Trading stories in the cluttered workrooms of the local *Paris Herald* or bantering over banquet meals at the Anglo-American Press Club before dashing off to cover turmoil in some other part of the continent, American journalists in Paris fashioned themselves into gutsy breaking-news reporters. A job at the *Herald* furnished a "passport," the paper's managing editor argued, offering aspiring writers entrée into a burgeoning profession and a world of new experiences.[21]

Like the daring foreign correspondent, the businessman represented another new breed of American in postwar Paris. In the nineteenth century, when raw materials dominated exports from the United States, American wholesalers typically had arranged the bulk sale of unfinished products like cotton, wheat, and tobacco on the basis of samples, dealing with few overseas purchasers and having little concern for the fate of shipments past their ports of delivery. In the French capital, American commerce had been brokered primarily by a small cluster of shipping agents and luxury goods traders. Yet American manufactured exports, increasing steadily since the 1880s, surged during and after World War I, riding on the new status of the United States as a creditor nation and filling the vacuum left by the beleaguered industries of Germany, France, and Great Britain. Dealing increasingly with finished merchandise, many American merchants no longer concluded their transactions at the docks of Liverpool or Le Havre. Growing ranks of advertisers, maintenance men, consultants, and other experts ensured that American enterprise in postwar Europe would involve not only transporting industrial wares but also transferring designs, capital, and distribution methods.[22]

Despite language considerations, Paris began to rival London as the preferred headquarters for Americans doing such business on the continent. When it was founded in 1894, the Paris American Chamber of Commerce counted only eleven members, and just after the Armistice, it still claimed only about six hundred. By 1927, however, thousands of firms and representatives from every region of the United States were listed in its directory, supporting that group's depiction of Paris as the "business center of Continental Europe." Local American agents specialized above all in machines—pressing and dying machines; adding, copying, and automatic numbering machines; wrapping, washing, and waxing machines. Laying the foundation for Americans' dramatic inroads into the markets of twentieth-century Europe, such businesses often gained their foothold by first attracting the patronage of their compatriots. Local branches for American advertisers, insurance agents, and corporations hawking all kinds of enticing wares cropped up across the capital. Firms such as Frigidaire, the radio supplier Atwater Kent, and the Crane Company, featuring the latest plumbing fixtures, established showrooms on the Right Bank's side streets and advertised aggressively in local English-language publications, suggesting that Americans looking to modernize their French apartments comprised a sizable portion of their clientele. The financial capital of Americans in France was far from negligible. Even the year of the stock market crash, Americans spent more than $137 million there, roughly triple what they dispensed in England or Germany. Targeting these customers, salesmen peddled an array of specialty goods and services from American-style dry cleaning and dairy home delivery to permanent hair waves and Spalding sporting goods. Practically everything Americans desired, writers routinely claimed by the mid-twenties, could be purchased in Paris, thanks to the local entrepreneurship of American risk takers.[23]

American bankers also played a more prominent role in the capital following a series of federal reforms in the United States legalizing foreign branches and export combinations. The war, too, proved a watershed. At the outset of the conflict, few American banks had been located in the French capital, but soon several firms arrived to handle the accounts of the military and other war-related groups. The growth of the Guaranty Trust Company of New York was typical. One of the first American banks to establish a Paris office, it opened in 1916 in a third-floor apartment with only four employees. Less than a decade later, with 265 employees occupying the corporation's largest overseas office on the rue des Italiens, its branch was by then only one of the many American financial institutions with a strong ranking on the Paris clearinghouse. Others stood at even more prestigious addresses, including J. P. Morgan's bank and the Bankers Trust Company on the place Vendôme and the National City Bank of New York on the boulevard Haussmann.[24]

Not unlike relief workers aspiring to reconstruct whole villages or journalists taking on the continent's complex political tensions, American bankers and businessmen exuded self-assurance in Paris, proudly manning their companies' local branches, yukking it up at Chamber of Commerce luncheons, and milling around the bar at the Ritz. As a former banker and a veteran of Ohio Republican politics, the ambassador to France, Myron T. Herrick, typified their worldview. Herrick championed an expansive role for American enterprise abroad, espousing what he called "manifest responsibility," a blend of expansionist expectations and level-headed investment. A favorite of American traders and investors in Paris, Herrick peppered his speeches with history lessons and "darky" jokes, rallying his compatriots with calls for them to be "something else than mere business men" by taking on a grander mission as emissaries for the "great power and wealth" of the postwar United States.[25]

Students, too, took advantage of easier access to the French capital after the war. During the nineteenth century, Paris had drawn American art and architecture students and handfuls of other serious scholars, but beyond the École des Beaux Arts and the Académie Julien, French universities—with their rigid qualifications and dearth of social facilities—attracted few American registrants, who often preferred coursework in England or Germany. Desperate for revenue, however, French officials began courting students from across the Atlantic after World War I, beginning with plans to provide instruction to almost six thousand demobilized American soldiers. At the same time, the Sorbonne expanded its summer school programs and initiated special French civilization classes for visitors anxious for the prestige of a Paris education without the rigor necessary for regular coursework. In addition, more funding from institutions such as the Guggenheim Foundation, increasingly diverse and affordable tour options, and the sharp rise in American college attendance in general ensured that study overseas would no longer be reserved for serious preprofessionals and the leisured wealthy. Touting student exchange as a force for world peace as well as fitting preparation for the nation's future business leaders, university faculty shuffled collegians from one historically significant corner of Europe to the next, lecturing on everything from art appreciation to banking practices. France and especially Paris, where the University of Delaware initiated the very first junior year abroad program in 1923, became a perennial favorite. Full-time American enrollment at French universities shot up from a few hundred in the early twenties to substantially more than five thousand by the end of the decade. For middle-class youths, spending a summer in the footsteps of Michelangelo and Shakespeare or earning a certificate of attendance from the Sorbonne had become as much a rite of passage as college itself. "To the true college girl the European venture . . . is well-nigh indispensable," a writer for *Scribner's* announced in 1928, and, "first and last," her desire was "to see Paris."[26]

To regulate and structure all these young travelers' experiences in the capital, a plethora of student clubs sprang up, especially in the Latin Quarter. At various alumni associations and church-sponsored community centers, American students enjoyed art exhibitions, "smokers," and Thanksgiving dinners. The American University Union on the boulevard Saint-Germain handled mail and maintained an information bureau and workroom with typewriters for its guests. Local American student life had become so well established by 1923 that the Barnard graduate Marguerite Loud found it hard to juggle her Sorbonne studies and busy social schedule. "There are so many girls we know in Paris that it has been a whirl of teas & lunches," she reported to her mother. American students could find in and around the Latin Quarter brand-new libraries, poolrooms, baths, and other facilities established just for them. Loud's quarters at the American University Women's Paris Club, later known as Reid Hall, featured such amenities as steam heat and electricity and housed an average of 154 young women per month by 1927, only six years after its opening. Boasting similar accommodations, the British-American YWCA's Foyer International des Etudiantes reopened in 1928 on the boulevard Saint-Michel with celebrated American conveniences, including a quick-service cafeteria. For visitors like Loud, studying abroad not only offered a landmark year intellectually, it opened out onto new social horizons. "I'm simply blooming in health," Loud exclaimed, sending home to her parents frank but reassuring descriptions of the "darn good time" she was having with the man she would later marry. "We spent a conventional 'Young America' evening & played around in taxis & cafes & danced," she wrote in one letter; "I was perfectly thrilled & felt as though I owned Paris!" she exclaimed another day.[27]

Sharing space with such keen students on the Left Bank were those legendary expatriates. Fleeing the reactionary climate in the postwar United States, these self-styled refugee artists were a much more heterogeneous lot than the privileged East Coast figures who had filled the pantheon of expatriates past. Across the gangplanks to Europe came droves of independent women, Midwesterners and natives of the West Coast, Jews and Catholics, sons of immigrants, daughters of the ghetto. The capital's sojourning novelists, philosophers, painters, and poets, white and black, became simultaneously the dispossessed of American modernity and the vanguard creators of American modernisms. Their ranks included Harlem Renaissance writers such as Langston Hughes and members of musical entourages like the clarinetist Sidney Bechet and the dancer Josephine Baker, who joined the troupe assembled in 1925 for the milestone La Revue Nègre. They included pathbreaking publishers like Sylvia Beach, who took on James Joyce's *Ulysses;* experimental composers like George Antheil and Virgil Thomson; writers such as Gertrude Stein, Ernest Hemingway, and Henry Miller, who revolutionized the tenor of American literature; and artists like Alexander Calder and Man Ray, who catapulted American art onto the world stage. The city captivated, at least for a time, those who would produce some of the most defining American cultural achievements of the twentieth century: William Faulkner, Aaron Copland, Alain Locke, Walker Evans, and Grant Wood, among many others.

Gravitating to the salons of the up-and-coming quarter of Montparnasse, these artists and intellectuals eagerly contributed to the area's avant-garde presses and little magazines, and they crossed paths at Sylvia Beach's bookstore and lending library Shakespeare and Company or at the Dôme, the Rotonde, and other famous cafés. Left Bank bohemians cast themselves as the social opposites of the Right Bank's American entrepreneurs, but their tight-knit cliques were not so different. In Montparnasse, one writer discovered, friends gathered in modest studios to "eat hot waffles cooked in an electric waffle-iron by the Vassar-bred wife of a Princeton sculptor," to dance to jazz records, to "say 'gee whiz' and 'gosh,' and argue about Picasso . . . and the Ku Klux Klan and next year's American League prospects."[28] Often posing as aloof and intellectually superior to the vast majority of other newcomers from the United States, expatriates nevertheless could be as rowdy as common tourists. Promoting themselves as creative geniuses who would reveal to the world the wonders of modern American art, they could be as self-aggrandizing and boosterist as the most confident businessman or banker. Far from renouncing their nationality, they remained very much a part of the broader, rapidly expanding American community in Paris. From Montparnasse they traveled to the Right Bank for work, to draw funds and mail from the big American banks or the American Express, to borrow books from the American Library, or to stock up on goods from American specialty stores. Many financed their stays with scholarships and grants from American institutions, while even more supported themselves by writing for local American newspapers, syndicated news networks, or periodicals with circulations back home. Oftentimes the line separating famous expatriates from ordinary students and journalists merely came down to the success or failure of a first novel. As hundreds of thousands of Americans streamed through each year, expatriates could not avoid the crowds shuffling along the boulevards, gawking at the café terraces from their tour buses, filling up the nightclub tables each night. By the mid-twenties, exiling oneself to Paris had become about as effective as banishing oneself to Coney Island or Atlantic City.

A few African Americans, such as the writers Gwendolyn Bennett and Countee Cullen, both on fellowships, also lived and worked on the Left Bank, but others gravitated to the nightlife district at the foot of Montmartre. At hangouts like one café dubbed the "Flea Pit," saxophone players, pianists, bouncers, and dishwashers trickled in for afternoon breakfast before setting off for all-night work at clubs such as Zelli's and the Palermo. Like other self-proclaimed exiles from American life, black expatriates glorified Paris as an escape from the problems of home, a place, in the words of one resident, where there were "no more bars to beat against." African American artists and writers discovered numerous opportunities in the capital to branch out and forge connections with other people of color, collaborations which have been celebrated and thoroughly explored by scholars. Nevertheless, they, too, continued to feel the pull of the broader American community. Most importantly, they depended on the patronage of their compatriots. Some African Americans found only menial work in the city, shining customers' shoes in the basement of the American Express or working as doormen for other establishments. Performers in turn depended on the business of white audiences, who often expected entertainers to model stereotypical versions of blackness ranging from French fantasies about natives in the African jungle to white Americans' romances about mammies and field hands in the old plantation South. Some struggled with a profound ambivalence about their enduring affinity for American life, feelings which often grew even more acute in Paris, where nationalist and internationalist impulses rubbed up against each other in interesting if uneasy ways. Gwendolyn Bennett, for one, was startled by an unexpected onset of homesickness during her Paris residence in 1925. She marveled at the "strange new patriotism" she felt about the United States, but reassured herself that this appreciation for her nation remained distinct from the negative "'home' feeling" she got watching white Americans "jostle each other about the American Express."[29]

Like their white compatriots, Bennett and other African American intellectuals and entertainers discovered in Paris new ways to envision themselves. Not just an escape from racism and a route into the world of black internationalism, the capital also paradoxically made it possible for them to participate more fully in American life. It presented, for many African Americans, a place to pursue a set of rags-to-riches American dreams. Josephine Baker, for example, had been a child of East St. Louis at the time of the gruesome race riot in 1917, and an impressionable nineteen-year-old chorus girl who could hardly read or write when she arrived in Paris. Marveling at the capital's lack of formal segregation, its opportunities to date white men, and her ability to negotiate her own terms of employment, Baker treated her own rapid rise to stardom as a Cinderella story. Sleeping past noon, tossing her designer gowns in a heap on the floor of her lavish quarters, receiving interviewers in a disheveled bathrobe, Baker mimicked the starlets of Hollywood film and luxuriated in being "manicured, pedicured, pampered, perfumed." Many others, too, sought out fame and fortune, so highly valued yet elusive for people of color back in the United States. African Americans operated some of Montmartre's most profitable clubs, such as Chez Florence, owned by Palmer and Florence Embry Jones, and Le Grand Duc, managed by the enterprising veteran Eugene Bullard, who gave Langston Hughes a job washing dishes. The Grand Duc's red-haired headliner, known as Bricktop, eventually opened her own club near Josephine Baker's late-night spot, Chez Joséphine, taking pride in hosting rising talents like Louis Armstrong as well as famous customers like F. Scott Fitzgerald and Cole Porter. Hobnobbing with dignitaries and celebrities, African Americans like Bricktop, no less than their white counterparts, cast themselves in the role of trendsetters and cultural innovators, delighting in how their blues music and jazz dance had helped to transform Montmartre into a "jumpin' hot town." Their contributions to the quarter offered a vision of what urban American life might have been like if success had been based on talent and merit rather than race. In Montmartre, Sidney Bechet raved, "Everybody had a kind of excitement about him. Everyone, they was crazy to be *doing*."[30]

The enormous impact of the war, the expansion of foreign correspondence and overseas commerce, the explosion of tourist travel, and other factors helped to draw Americans abroad during the interwar years and created channels that led them specifically to Paris. In their eyes, the capital had become the "hub of the European wheel."[31] It was no accident that all these different groups descended on Paris at the same time, a moment when American prosperity and energy welled up as never before. Businessmen and bohemians may have been social opposites, but they, like other Americans, shared an optimism about their expanding roles in world affairs, especially as those roles were being fashioned in the French capital. Americans in Paris exuded a sense of national mission, from investors propping up the continent's flailing economies and investigative journalists opening their readers' eyes to the era's greatest challenges to musicians seeking to capture all this enthusiasm in new sounds and rhythms and students playing the role of ambassadors of goodwill. Paris provided a space for more inclusive participation by those who had previously found themselves at the edges of American culture but who were central to its twentieth-century remaking. American women enthusiastically adopted more public roles in the capital, foregoing the chaperones and rigid gender roles of old. Paris offered African Americans a new sense of empowerment, too, as a place where club owners could eject racist patrons without fears of reprisal and where casual outings through the city were not blighted by a minefield of racist laws and etiquette. In a city that had plenty of room for extremist politics, most American sojourners gravitated toward liberal orientations instead—either the economic "liberal-developmentalism" of its business and diplomatic leaders like Herrick or the cultural liberalism of its artists.[32] Even in a metropolis dedicated to commerce and secular republicanism, Americans stood out as proponents of laissez-faire social and business relations. They eagerly marketed and bought new products and entertainments. They embraced avant-garde experimentalism or cosmopolitan tastes for jazz and Latin American dance. They joined the vanguard crowds that welcomed more informal mingling in the city's cafés, and they tried out for themselves an anything-goes attitude that before the war had been the purview of marginalized radicals. For Americans, imagining "Gay Paree" often doubled as an exercise in discovering their own liberal values.

After World War I, Americans reinvented their national life in Paris, transforming what had been a modest colony or outpost into a colony in the more grandiose sense of the term—a foray into foreign space that threatened to dominate and redirect local life. American accounts of this process, however, did not simply document their actual impact on the city. They overflowed with hyperbole, attesting most of all to Americans' growing sense of self-importance. With characteristic flair, a writer for the *Independent* compared the impressive movements of Yankee travelers to the "shifting of whole populations in the Middle Ages." Next to Americans' hectic convergence upon Europe's historic cities, he argued, the "pace of the Klondike gold rush seems lethargic." Americans reconceived Europe, and Paris especially, as a new frontier after the war, an exciting territory to be conquered by peppy, resourceful pioneers from across the Atlantic coming to strut their stuff. "I have begun to see that my fellow-citizens are far more important than they imagine even in their most eagle-screaming moments," the popular novelist Louis Bromfield wrote at the beginning of his fourteen-year residence just outside Paris. The American abroad, he argued, was "unmistakably a man just born," a commanding player with the "power of an immense and wealthy nation at his elbow," a successor, Bromfield suggested, drawing on a common analogy, to the ancient Roman citizen. "God damn the continent of Europe. It is of merely antiquarian interest," F. Scott Fitzgerald proclaimed even more forcefully during his first trip across the Atlantic, "We will be the Romans in the next generations."[33]

Such unabashed stories about American conquests abroad were not at all a given in the early twentieth century. The idea of the United States as a pioneer civilization or a unified nation was only just gaining ground as

Americans filed off of their boat trains in postwar Paris. In fact, back in the United States residents had long found themselves "living in pieces of a nation rather than a consolidated whole," as the historian Thomas Bender writes. The dramatic upheavals between the Civil War and the Great War made this seem especially so. Sectional tensions persisted even after federal troops withdrew from the South in 1877. Out west, settlers and town boosters in newly incorporated territories resented Northern industrialists as much as white Southerners did. Beneath these tectonic rifts rested even more finely cut differences. Across the states, immigrants clung to their own languages, habits, and values, and the sheer number of newcomers arriving to American shores during this period was staggering. By 1910, one-third of Americans had been born abroad or had at least one foreign-born parent. Except for those spectacular, short-lived occasions when laborers banded together to stage wildcat strikes, more often they found themselves pitted against each other over jobs and housing. Native workers snubbed the foreign-born; whites scorned Asians and African Americans. Manning segregated work crews, huddling in their own neighborhoods policed at the edges by gang rivalries, patronizing their own churches and corner stores, migrants immersed themselves in mutually suspicious subcultures, often gearing their emotional lives back toward the overseas homelands to which one-quarter to one-third of them would eventually return. Millions of people residing in the United States felt themselves apart. "My people do not live in America," one Slavic immigrant recognized, "they live underneath America."[34]

Even for the middle and upper classes, those 10 percent of Americans who came out on top, class imperatives often trumped national affinities. Deeply ambivalent about or even hostile toward the booming working classes in their midst, elites cultivated distinctions that set them off from the multitudes. If, from their ghettos, immigrants lived with their gazes fixed back on their homelands, affluent Americans, too, looked abroad for their tastes and values from their privileged social circles. For them, the highbrow traditions of the Old World were synonymous with civilization, essential antidotes to the leveling and anarchic character of their own increasingly complex and fragmented society. Educated in Swiss boarding schools or refined by grand tours and seasons spent in London or Rome, the wealthy professed to be more at home in the capitals and resorts of Europe than in the Little Italys, Chinatowns, or Jewish quarters of their own cities. Even less affluent Americans infused their lives with European fashions, stocking their homes with faux aristocratic furniture and imported collectibles to dramatize their belonging to a white, international elite. Like the mansion builders of Newport, Rhode Island, installing their class legitimacy stone by stone from overseas palaces, other turn-of-the-century Americans excelled as cultural borrowers, believing that their status derived more from their mastery of European models than from their ability to fashion new, distinctively American customs.[35]

For all the nation's economic might and democratic promises in the decades before World War I, Americans still feared that trends across the Atlantic fueled its intellectual energies. Trying to think their way past such cultural dependency, leaders in arts and academia made tremendous efforts to establish libraries, museums, and other institutions that would enable them, as the liberal intellectual George William Curtis suggested, "to dispense with Europe." Nevertheless, the great accomplishments of the era—the gondola-plied lagoons of Chicago's White City, the well-proportioned facade of New York's Metropolitan Opera House, the lavish period rooms of Isabella Stewart Gardner's Boston museum—only reinforced how Americans' desire to compete with Europe locked them into the practice of appropriation. Literary critics, too, labored under enduring assumptions about the paucity of their own canon. Echoing the *Edinburgh Review*'s famous 1820 query—"In the four quarters of the globe, who reads an American book?"—Van Wyck Brooks concluded sadly in 1915 that it was "of no use to go off into a corner with American literature." It was a common refrain to profess that the United States was still a young nation in need of a coming of age.[36] Even in the early twenties, this familiar lament continued to carry weight. Jaded writers such as Harold Stearns and Malcolm Cowley decried the barrenness of American culture and the alienation intellectuals felt now more than ever amid a thriving business civilization monopolized by men with little patience for lofty ideas or poetic experimentation. Artists and writers, Cowley elegized, had explored all possible outlets in the United States, but "one after another they had opened doors that led only into the cupboards and linen closets of the mind." Embracing self-banishment to Europe as the only way out, Harold Stearns edited his farewell manifesto, *Civilization in the United States* (1922), a series of essays by prominent American critics. In light of its contents, the collection's title proved mildly sarcastic: in the modern United States, the book argued, civilization, in any commendable form, simply did not yet exist.[37]

Soon, however, fresh points of view would begin to open outward from the old dilemmas about national distinction and civilized worldliness, laying the groundwork for exciting innovations in American arts, entertainment, and design. Some of the basis for these new, more confident traditions stemmed from the fact that, as divided and diverse as Americans were in the early twentieth century, they were also being pulled together by strengthening centripetal forces. The economic and territorial incorporation of outlying regions, knitting the continental United States together with railroads and denser communication links during the late nineteenth century, provided a foundation for greater cultural unification in the twentieth century. Brought together by shared experiences—world fairs and popular amusements, public rituals and schooling, as well as budding national markets and media—Americans saw themselves more and more as members of a modern nation-state. During World War I, swelling popular patriotism combined with an expansion of government power accelerated these nationalizing tendencies. The war had revealed "a new type of American" and a "new and more virile Americanism," binding citizens together with common purpose, Myron Herrick rejoiced shortly before reassuming his post as ambassador in Paris. Taking up Theodore Roosevelt's famous condemnation of the nation's social fragmentation, Herrick looked forward to the conflict's end, when, he predicted, "this nation is going to exert a power and influence in the world greater even than it wields now because it will be a nation of thorough-going Americans and not merely an international boarding-house."[38]

During the coming decades, through the shared agonies of war and depression, Americans further embraced values of national belonging, and the idea of a distinctive American culture reached its fullest potential through national advertising, mass magazines, radio, and film. The apogee of American Civilization, as it was called in the 1920s, or the American Way of Life, its formulation thereafter, showcased a powerful if ultimately temporary synthesis of artistic and commercial energies—an audacious challenge to the past that seemed best conveyed by calling up a collage of modern people and elements, a tapestry of gangsters and molls, admen and newspaper reporters, cigarettes and fedora hats, trolley bells, Tin Pan Alley accents, and red-lipped blondes. Overseas, observers watched this invention of American traditions—this reconceptualization of American people, American sass, American style—with both interest and trepidation. Americans, many claimed, were pioneering the future, an alternative path that was both a promise and a threat, overstocked with washing detergent, cheerful slogans, and canned food.[39]

And yet this synthesis was never quite as complete as it looked from the outside, and it was only just dawning in the 1920s. Indeed, during the years surrounding the Great War, what American culture would come to stand for seemed more up for grabs than ever as the old genteel proprieties of the nineteenth century came under siege by intellectual and political radicals. As longtime authorities lost their ability to dictate the values of the nation, popular challenges bubbled up from below. New cultural forms buzzed with what Matthew Josephson from Paris labeled the nation's "urbanized folkways": the slang of immigrants, the syncopations of jazz, the daring tastes of city youth. By the 1920s and 1930s, as the United States was transformed from a rural society into an urban, industrial one, Americans of all classes increasingly embraced the excitements of commercial culture with its critical if often veiled contributions by Jewish, Italian, African American, and other previously marginalized talents, who had found common ground in the era's media and urban entertainments. This new productivity and vitality, however, met with formidable opposition. Religious leaders opposed the nation's seemingly more secular orientation, while others campaigned against "hyphenated Americans," who threatened to dilute a purportedly purer Anglo-Saxon national past. The early twentieth century bristled with reactionary movements—the nationwide revival of the Ku Klux Klan after 1915, the persistence of antisemitism, backlashes against feminism and radicalism. Even as the population of the United States became more urban, old agrarian myths, claiming that the true heart of the nation rested in its farms and small towns, gained new resonance. Just what constituted "Americanness," just who could speak for the nation, grew even more hotly contested as Americans moved out into the world in new roles after World War I.[40]

The version of America showcased abroad seemed to flatten out all this debate and complexity. In Paris, the urban, commercial, liberal side to American culture traveled most readily and shone brightest against a foreign backdrop. Understanding how this part of American life came for a time to eclipse other versions of Americanness requires seeing its ascendance not just as something developed by marketers, entertainers, and scholars inside the United States but as something worked out in international contexts. Americans did not simply retain their national identification when they went abroad. More precisely, they often discovered overseas just how they wanted to be American.

Writers and artists in Paris most famously contributed to this process. Rather than retreating into their own private worlds of exile, expatriates consumed themselves with the task of defining and even promoting a modern national culture. Encouraged in their endeavors by small but select sets of European intellectuals enamored of the machine-age artifacts of American life—from the architect Le Corbusier and the painter Fernand Léger to surrealists and *négritude* writers—Americans in Paris began to see how they might capture vibrant national idioms, how they could construct new aesthetics and attitudes by rubbing them up against other subjects, traditions, and techniques. In Paris, composers such as Aaron Copland transcended their classical training and seized the sounds of the streets and the rhythms of popular music to meld them into American symphonies. For Copland, jazz had seemed pedestrian back in his hometown of Brooklyn, but rediscovering it in Europe, haunting the Paris cafés where it played, was "like hearing it for the first time." For Langston Hughes, too, distinctively American music came alive in new ways in the after-hours jam sessions of Montmartre: "Blues in the Rue Pigalle. Black and laughing, heartbreaking blues in the Paris dawn, pounding like a pulse-beat, moving like the Mississippi!" Paris provided a key vantage point for the critic Gilbert Seldes, who penned *The Seven Lively Arts* (1924), his groundbreaking treatise celebrating American popular entertainments from the Keystone Cops to Krazy Kat, while holed up in a borrowed Paris apartment, writing briskly from memory with nothing but a few clippings and comic strips on hand. The "home products" of the United States, the writer Matthew Josephson, like others, argued, could be seen from across the Atlantic with newfound appreciation, their "authentic beauty" and "outlandish departures from the past or from previous European traditions" at last deserved intellectuals' attention.[41]

Rather than abandoning the battle over American values, then, expatriates transported the debates to new grounds, growing increasingly confident that usable national traditions could be made right there from Paris—that as expatriates, they would be the ones to create a modern American culture worthy of international recognition. Expatriates never stopped thinking about the United States while outside of it; indeed, they tended to think about it even more and, they thought, more perceptively with the distance. This notion was behind Gertrude Stein's famous formulation that "writers have to have two countries, the one where they belong and the one in which they live really," and it gave confidence to numerous others who wrote inspiringly from afar about early-twentieth-century American experience, not least Sinclair Lewis, who wrote *Babbitt* (1922), and F. Scott Fitzgerald, who completed *The Great Gatsby* (1925) while abroad. "Transplanting yourself," Hemingway discovered, had great imaginative payoffs. "In Paris I could write about Michigan," he recalled of his days composing his first successful short stories. From painters to poets, others also viewed Paris as a nursery for developing new visual and literary languages that could capture the magnificence and grotesqueness of America's urban life, the peculiarities of its small towns, the greatness and pettiness of its people—often in ways that appeared so quintessentially American that they would come in time to seem wholly removed from international influences. William Carlos Williams's essayistic ruminations on national character for *In the American Grain* (1925), the siren wails of George Antheil's *Ballet Mécanique* (1927), Walker

Evans' documentary-style photographs of the New York subway, and Grant Wood's iconic painting *American Gothic* (1930)—all had tucked within them lessons from Paris apprenticeships.[42]

Not just writers and artists, but all kinds of Americans, time and again related how they felt a sense of Americanness most sharply overseas. In an article about going abroad and "Discovering One's Own Country There," one *Century* columnist captured a conventional set of realizations Americans reported during their trips. "It has become a commonplace that one of the best spots in which to study America in our time is Europe," he noted. Amidst another culture, elements "characteristically American" stood out "in almost brazen relief." Subtle cues betrayed by traveling Americans spoke volumes. The "tilt of a hat" or the "touch of bright brassy humor"—the smallest detail "spells America." Watching for such clues among their countrymen, he asserted, Americans abroad began "to frame an impression of a civilization": their own. These insights amounted to more than discrete personal revelations. Rather, they formed the basis for shared understandings about the emerging power of the United States and the perceived distinctiveness of American culture. The United States had "already taken from Europe all that it has to offer in culture," contended one patriot, who announced that years of living abroad had made him American. "America, you feel and you know, is in movement," he rhapsodized. By contrast, he pronounced, "Europe is standing still." Accumulating common wisdom like this had unmistakably triumphalist overtones. "In these days an American abroad tends only toward becoming more American," Louis Bromfield concluded. "America as a nation has come of age," he declared, "and the American abroad knows it well enough."[43]

New quests for the pleasures of the street, new emphasis on play, modern technologies, personal expressiveness—these sensibilities traveled to Paris more readily than the agrarian values of the United States, partly because of the kinds of Americans going there after the war and partly because these sensibilities resonated best with the tradition of urban spectacle already long established in the French capital. Americans' styling of themselves as trend-setters in Paris, however, would also depend on the dynamics that governed how they moved through the city and interacted with others. Americans often gave the impression that they commanded Paris at large, but more often visitors and residents pursued only a limited range of experiences there. Such selective movements fundamentally shaped how they would perceive their role in the capital.

To take Americans' accounts of Paris as simple fact is to imagine them as overrunning the city, dictating its trends, monopolizing its nightlife. The "number of Americans in the region of the Opera" struck one aspiring writer as among the "most amazing phenomena in Paris." African Americans' styling of Montmartre as akin to Harlem similarly exaggerated their dominance over the area, since no more than a few dozen of them resided there by the mid-twenties. Nevertheless, in these districts Americans constantly marveled at their compatriots' presence. "One can't walk a block without bumping into someone from home," averred an American diplomat. There was, he thought, "something almost epic" about these "vast hordes" descending annually on the place Vendôme, which "blossomed out suddenly in straw hats," and the rue de Rivoli arcades, reverberating "with American voices."[44] For every visitor or resident reassured by the sight of compatriots, another complained that these invading masses ruined their own authentic experience of the capital. One young Tourist Third traveler had been disappointed with the vaunted night-life of Montmartre, its clubs "overflowing with Americans," the place Pigalle "cluttered with American college boys" and looking like Sixth Avenue. She resented, too, her travel mates' insistence on sitting and watching the "pageant of Savannah and South Bend and Birmingham" in front of the Café de la Paix. "I'd been devoting my energies to insisting how foolish it was to come clear to France just to hang around the American quarter," she regretted. Whether visitors welcomed or abhorred this kind of insular socializing, it encouraged Americans to approach the city as a place where they were both ubiquitous and quite at home. Familiarity bred a certain sense of ownership or control. "These teeming noisy boulevards are crowded with Americans; where there were formerly tens there are nowadays hundreds of them," one typical traveler recorded, "Really the Americans have had a greater effect upon Paris than any other people."[45]

Despite these assertions, Americans sometimes oversold the idea that they were right at home in Paris. The city may have seemed from certain angles like colonized territory, but in many ways it remained an inscrutable and challenging place, hints of which occasionally peeked through the upbeat tone of American reports. "It was a bit terrifying at first," one arrival wrote home, "plunking down in a strange city, with strange money to handle, and a strange language in my ears. God, it is foreign. I had no idea Europe could be so European." As they made their way through the streets, many discovered, in the straightforward terms of one guidebook, that they "must be prepared to see some things done that neither he nor his friends in America do." Americans abhorred sanitation conditions in the capital and pined for familiar conveniences. They fretted about unapologetic public displays of affection—about couples kissing and black men holding white women's hands. They were made nervous by solicitations from prostitutes and street guides. They worried about drinking the water and were terrified that they would be served horsemeat without their knowledge. Amid growing resentments over the war debts, Americans flooded the embassy with queries about the capital's safety each time the press reported attacks on tourists. Indeed, taxi drivers presented only the first of a host of sullen, vaguely hostile characters visitors had to contend with, even if they never strayed from the inner Right Bank. The only other option would be hiding out in their hotel rooms. One newspaperman, outraged over "the indignities suffered by American residents of Paris," relayed to Ambassador Herrick that he had been sneered at in shops, had tips thrown in his face, and been served tainted food and "gouged by a thieving and insolent cook." "It has reached a point where members of my family," he admitted, "prefer to remaine [sic] in the seclusion of our home than facing the annoyances of going out."[46]

Most Americans, of course, did venture forth, but they moved through the capital in predictable ways, limiting their exposure to such unpleasantness and ensuring that, for the most part, they encountered only the Paris they had been conditioned to expect from movies, Broadway hits, and bestsellers back home. By the mid-1920s, Paris appeared everywhere in the mass entertainments and magazines fast becoming central to American life.[47] More and more, American audiences were expected to have detailed familiarity with not only the city's famous monuments but also other, more obscure places and people. To be culturally literate required understanding references to the Arc de Triomphe and the Louvre, but also to the *bouquinistes*, the races at Longchamps, the Ritz, and Zelli's. Even before they alighted from their boat trains, therefore, Americans would have been prepared for the temperament of the city's taxi drivers. They would have known why postcard sellers were notorious and why café drinks came with saucers; they would have gotten sly asides about the lobby of the Folies Bergère. What commentators felt compelled to explain to their followers in the immediate postwar period—the centrality of the Opera, the excitements of the Pigalle area—they would take for granted as common knowledge only a few years later, invoking well-known locales without any undue orientation. In the early twenties, for example, magazine articles patiently instructed readers about the artist colony in Montparnasse and the importance of the "Café Rotonda" as "the headquarters of American 'Bohemians' of Paris." Such lecturing (and misspelling of the Rotonde) rapidly became unnecessary and uncommon. "It was inevitable we go to Montparnasse," one young visitor reported home only a few years later, "Telling about the Café du Dôme and its sister the Café de la Rotonde is like reciting 'to be, or not to be.' There's so much precedent."[48]

Thus, once Americans arrived to Paris, they knew exactly where to go. Privileging certain areas while neglecting others, their routine activities mapped the city in highly selective ways. Standardized guidebook tips steered Americans over and over to similar itineraries—seeking out lunch, shopping, and tea or cocktails near the Opera; dinner and a show on the Champs-Elysées or in the Bois de Boulogne; Montmartre or Montparnasse for late-night carousing; followed finally by early-morning onion soup at the central markets of Les Halles. Travelers' lore secured the notoriety of certain establishments that became well-known referents—Montmartre nightclubs like Florence's, Montparnasse cafés like the Jockey and the Dôme, as well as Fouquet's, an essential watering hole on the Champs-Elysées. Readers of Anita Loos' bestselling *Gentlemen Prefer Blondes* (1925) would have been well versed in the hunting grounds stalked by the seemingly innocent yet shrewdly manipulative Lorelei Lee during her stay in Paris. Hitting all the must-see stops in search of rich men—Ciro's, the Ritz, Château Madrid, the Café de la Paix, and "The Foley Bergere"—she bumps into the same Americans again and again. "You really would think you were in New York and it was devine," she exclaimed.[49] All this accumulated popular wisdom ensured that Americans swarmed the most commercialized and spectacular neighborhoods of the capital while consistently passing over others.

Large sections of the capital therefore remained inaccessible to or ignored by Americans during the 1920s and 1930s. Few penetrated the faubourg Saint-Germain to participate in aristocratic salons. The sanctuaries of bourgeois foyers and inner courtyards remained for the most part secret. Few paused to consider the world of the homeless and itinerant tradespeople under the Seine's bridges—crannies where indigents and ragpickers crouched around tents and pots and pitchers and built fires between concrete blocks, where women repaired mattresses and men collected cigarette butts. On the outskirts of town, from the windows of trains, newcomers might have glimpsed the unreal encampments of wooden shacks hammered with plaster-board and corrugated metal along dirt roads beyond the pale of municipal utilities. If some Americans did comprehend the poverty of "the zone"—packed in the shadows of the city's fortifications where some 42,000 *zoniers* eked out existences in converted wagons, broken-down railroad cars, and other makeshift structures—it was only because they were redolent of the shantytowns of the old American West, the dilapidated quarters of black Southern sharecroppers, and the worst tenement districts of northern cities, or, later, their Hoovervilles. Americans' itineraries did not for the most part take them through any of these alternative universes in Paris, nor, except when escorted by policemen or other guides promising glimpses of the city's underworld, did they take them into the working-class neighborhoods to the east, stretching up from the place de la République to Ménilmontant and La Villette. The city teemed with immigrants after the war, too, but the Jewish quarter in the Marais, as well as enclaves to the north that absorbed waves of Chinese laborers, Algerians, Poles, and others, would have seemed doubly foreign to an unsuspecting American wanderer.[50]

Other sections of the capital they experienced only selectively. By the mid-twenties, trips to Montmartre and Montparnasse had become especially popular, but American forays into these regions tended to be superficial. Some traveled by day to the Butte—the top of Montmartre, by Sacré-Coeur and the charming place du Tertre. For most Americans, however, "Montmartre" was a nighttime destination centered on a cluster of clubs at the base of the hill. Visiting crowds tended not to look beyond the glare of neon lights, disregarding the quotidian life of the neighborhood. Montmartre housed a mishmash of immigrants and laborers all struggling to survive and coexist. It harbored a tough, rundown, crime-ridden world, which touched the lives of resident African Americans but which white Americans conveniently overlooked in their pursuit of the latest thrill. Most Americans' exposure to "Montparnasse" proved equally cursory. For those who were not scholars or artistic types, the entire Left Bank represented an outlying region. Whereas guidebook writers imparted knowledge to their readers about a Right Bank replete with social and geographical complexities, the city on the other side of the Seine loomed as a vague mass, often referred to in toto as the Latin Quarter or Montparnasse. Yet once the cafés at the intersection of the boulevards du Montparnasse and Raspail gained a lively reputation, going there became an obligatory outing to "see all the Nuts and all the Freaks." Whizzing off in their taxis to "hit it up" in Montparnasse, past the stone walls of the bourgeois sixth arrondissement or the bleaker, broken-down parts to the east—or racing north to the hotspots of Montmartre—many Americans treated these destinations as nightlife islands surrounded by unknowable (and perhaps even uninteresting) French life. After a certain hour, one joke had it, if Americans hailed a taxi, no matter where they were or asked the driver to go, he would invariably take them to Montmartre.[51] Similar truisms surrounded rides to the Left Bank. As one American visitor marveled, "'Montparnasse' is enough for the American visitor to say to the chauffeur, and he will deposit his fare in front of the Café Rotonde, the Dôme, or the Coupole."[52]

This kind of selective movement through the capital magnified impressions of Americans' influence in those areas they did frequent, making these quarters seem even more "American." Surely, one writer suspected, French visitors came in from the provinces, "but where they stop in Paris is a mystery. Certainly it is in no quarter of the city that Americans frequent." Visitors often reveled in the way some Paris neighborhoods seemed to be emulating the tempo and styles of American places, particularly New York City. The Opera area recalled Broadway, observers frequently noted, and the avenue des Champs-Elysées loomed as a counterpart to Fifth Avenue. Montparnasse, many argued, was Greenwich Village transported, and Montmartre, with its tacky tourist traps, a version of Chinatown. Americans routinely imagined that the capital reflected back to them their own national genius. The "way to see America," in one observer's estimation, was "to get a chair at the Café de la Paix." The place Vendôme, quipped another, was the "most beautiful square in America." Congregating in the same corners of the city, patronizing the same cafés and hotels, Americans looked around and saw an urban landscape replete with signs of themselves. American newspapers announced as a fait accompli that the French capital was "getting Americanized at a rate which reminds one of the growth of a Middle West city twenty or thirty years ago."[53] In Paris, visitors and residents could see in action the ways in which "Americanization" no longer applied only to reforming immigrants back home or supposedly uncivilized races in the colonies. The Paris of Americans offered a model of cultural and economic expansion even into European centers of world power.

Americans did not simply arrive at conclusions about their relative importance in Paris among themselves. In many respects, they were also responding to cues by shopkeepers who welcomed their presence. After the war, diplomatic ties between France and the United States grew increasingly strained, and by 1926 Americans had to sink into a state of denial in order to ignore the surge of "anti-American feeling" in Paris, which some, like Cornelius Vanderbilt Jr., doubted privately could "ever be straightened out again." But next to these tensions, opportunistic forms of pro-Americanism flourished among those hoping to profit by sojourners' patronage. In districts frequented by Americans, proprietors embraced the use of English to attract visitors' business. Such a practice departed from past expectations that foreigners should conduct themselves in French or suffer the consequences of confusion or intimidation. During the nineteenth century, American arrivals often felt "practically deaf and dumb," thanks to the grinding difficulties of even simple tasks like ordering food and securing a hotel room in French.[54] These language difficulties, however, became less common as a theme in visitors' writings during the twenties as English proliferated in Americans' favorite quarters of the city. Proprietors hired waiters who spoke "fluent salesman-English" and offered translations for menus and entertainment programs. Department stores employed interpreters as a courtesy service (except at La Samaritaine, one writer noted, where the whole staff spoke English). Policemen near the Opera and along the Champs-Elysées wore blue armbands to indicate that they had participated in special English-language training programs, and by the thirties, taxis contained translations explaining their rates. Especially near the Opera, billboards advertising American bars, grill rooms, and *dancings* punctuated the horizon, while hotels and shops commonly promised in their windows, "English Spoken Here." Signs beckoned visitors to "Quick Service" or "Five o'clock tea at all hours" and dutifully warned of "Wet Paint."[55] More ominously, for a time a Montmartre club cautioned that it restricted admission to "Whites Only." "Be glad you aren't here!" one American exclaimed to those back home, "you would hear as much American-English spik-ed on the streets as French. One of the once-French, once-famous restaurants advertises Vermont sassidge and maple syrup." English seemed so prevalent that the student Marguerite Loud resorted to writing letters to her parents in French for practice: "Il y a tant d'Américains et d'Anglais en France qu'on a de la difficulté d'apprendre à parler le français ici!"[56]

The spread of English facilitated Americans' integration into the commercial life of the city. At the same time, it intensified their belief that they commanded special attention from their hosts. Because visitors were "confronted everywhere by signs in the two languages," one writer pointed out, they had the "uncanny impression that it is the foreigners who are in the middle of things and the Parisians who are the outsiders." Reflecting such newfound linguistic arrogance, American guidebooks and magazines actually began suggesting that a complete lack of French language skills would serve their readers better than imperfect ones. In 1930, one *Saturday Evening Post* article went so far as to argue that "the only really safe way to do France" was to learn only two words, *oui* and *non*, and cultivate a "great deal of explosive impatience." There was always someone nearby, the magazine assured, "who can speak a form of understandable English, and if enough fuss is made he can be had." Harking back to doughboys' crude, wartime attempts to "parlez-vous" French women, sentiments like these suggested that where English flourished, French, the language of cultural excellence, had ebbed to a few insensitive uses for Americans—namely to make sexual advances or to put French men "in their place."[57]

Perhaps even more than speaking English, carrying U.S. dollars eased Americans' passage through the city and solidified their association with its most modern and commercial quarters. Money matters governed the vast majority of Americans' daily encounters in the capital, and Americans' status

Cartoons may not offer accurate representations of the city, but they reveal a lot about popular perceptions. This one alludes to how, from the vantage point of the Café de la Paix, Americans fancied themselves as right at home in Paris, casually dominating its public life. *Life Magazine*, August 18, 1927. Courtesy of Harvard College Library, Widener Library, P267.2.

as customers became a central organizing principle for their stay. At times, the whole city of Paris seemed to visitors to run on the pettiest of financial transactions. Pittances were required for even the smallest of pleasures— sitting on a chair along the Champs-Elysées or requesting extra condiments over lunch. In pensions, meters calculated how much electricity guests burned up in their private rooms. At cafés, waiters tabulated bills based on carefully written notations on each drink's saucer. At the markets, perishables were sold in the most trifling of quantities; it did not pay to buy in bulk. "The French could support the nation on the waste of America," remarked one traveler, frustrated by the "incredible and exasperating" fact that Parisians were overly economical in everything but their use of time. "The French are the most franc-loving, sou-cluching, hard-faced, hard-worked, cold and half-starved set of people I've ever seen in my life," Langston Hughes similarly complained to Countee Cullen; "You even pay for a smile here."[58]

Worse still, Americans faced a slew of special taxes levied on foreigners as well as unofficial discriminatory practices. Staff at hotels and restaurants padded visitors' bills or employed two sets of prices, offering more expensive menus to unwitting guests. The fleecing of Americans in Paris became legendary back in the United States thanks to magazine articles that painted pictures of the city's "free-booting" taxi drivers and other villains who treated tourists as "suckers" and victims "to be scalped."[59] Conspicuous, big-spending Americans found themselves vulnerable not only to the exorbitant prices charged in tourist traps but also to theft and blackmail by bottom-feeders who trolled the nightlife spots looking for prey. In the summer of 1927, such hapless marks included a man from Wyoming whose papers and return ticket to the United States went missing in a rue Fontaine brasserie, a sailor whose wallet was swiped by a woman he picked up in Zelli's and took to a nearby hotel, and a New York journalist who had been stripped of all his belongings during a mugging but was too inebriated to remember the details. Sporting telltale American shoes, haircuts, eyeglasses, or overly formal evening wear, Americans faced relentless harassment by street peddlers and panhandlers, too. "An opera hat causes an eruption of rug merchants," warned one guidebook.[60]

Yet prosperous Americans, made even richer by favorable exchange rates, proved well positioned to take advantage of an urban environment governed above all by commerce. In spite of the hassles of being singled out, Americans nevertheless relished their status as some of the city's prime customers, believing that the power of the dollar afforded them preferential treatment. "When in doubt, tip everyone in sight and be liberal," one American touring with her family advised, "whatever difficulties you are in at the moment will miraculously smooth themselves out." Another guidebook put it even more bluntly: "With a certain class of people, the American dollar speaks French." An even more effective universal language than English, the dollar gained Americans special access to exclusive restaurants and nightclubs, and it helped defuse run-ins with the natives. Travel exposés constantly stressed the dollar as a local form of carte blanche; it was, a young Ernest Hemingway reported to the *Toronto Star*, "the key to Paris."[61] Francs, by contrast, seemed to many like "so much confetti," as one writer opined, or "stage money," as another ventured. Pinning five- or ten-franc notes to their hats or pasting them to their luggage like hotel labels, some patrons of tourist charabancs even threw change to children, like beggars, in the street below.[62]

During the interwar years, Americans did not simply work out definitions of themselves and their culture at home and then go abroad already sure of themselves. For many, traveling overseas offered a prime opportunity for self-discovery and self-assertion. Especially against the popular backdrop of postwar Paris—picturesquely foreign and yet astonishingly familiar and accessible—Americans gained a sharper sense of themselves as Americans. Impressed by the confident movements of so many compatriots, flattered by local proprietors who responded to their whims, Americans often imagined that they were transforming the city, almost single-handedly, into a booming success—into a snappier, snazzier capital for the new century. "The foreigner comes to Paris as an invader, wresting from the French themselves the fairest quarters and most delectable resorts of their city," claimed one popular writer. Remove them, he insisted, "and you take away two-thirds of her characteristic flavor. Gay Paree, indeed, can scarcely be regarded as a French institution at all." By touting their impact on Paris, Americans were able to think about their own distinctiveness and begin to imagine for themselves a larger role in world affairs—even if in largely unofficial capacities. American travelers, one reporter summed up this sentiment, had become a "dominant factor in the modern world," standing as frontline propagators of American commerce and democratic expression. Tourists "make history," he wrote, "and as a factor in international relations, both economic and cultural, they constitute nothing less than a major element in the growth of modern civilization."[63]

If there was one American entrée into the capital more celebrated than the taxi ride, it was Charles Lindbergh's arrival in the *Spirit of St. Louis* on May 21, 1927. Touching down amid swarms of welcomers at Le Bourget airport, the lone pilot became an instant sensation, drawing rapturous acclaim from people of all national and political affiliations. No one offered a more idealistic model of the new American abroad than this most heralded visitor to Paris in the twenties, with his display of technological know-how and faith in progress, matched by plucky independence and plain good looks. Melding the ambitions and enterprise of modern industry with the grounding of small-town values, Lindbergh seemed to his fans back home to reconcile the growing tensions in American culture between urban and agrarian ways of life. He is "our dream," one *American Magazine* writer exclaimed, "of what *we* really and truly want to be." The aviator embodied the "American spirit," many gushed with newfound national pride. "In this age," a Florida Methodist minister decided upon hearing of the pilot's safe landing, "It is better to be an American than to be a king."[64]

Following Charles Lindbergh's historic flight in May 1927, the aviator and Ambassador Myron T. Herrick greet joyous crowds in the Paris streets from a balcony of the Aero Club. ©Bettmann/CORBIS

In Paris, Lindbergh was held up as a figure who stood above politics. He was "unspoiled, unspoilable," Ambassador Herrick put it simply.[65] Josephine Baker—that other most famous American in Paris associated with St. Louis—remembered her own reaction that evening in May. She excitedly broke the show-stopping news to the audience of the Folies Bergère, half full with Americans. "I forgot that Lindbergh was a white man and that he came from St. Louis and might not have liked Negroes," she explained, "I only remembered that he was an American and that he had done something great for the progress of the world." Parisians forgot for a moment, too, their angers over the war debts and fears about Americans' expansionist objectives on the continent. French officials trumpeted enduring affinities between the two republics and gloried, as the Police Prefect Jean Chiappe put it, in the "incomparable beauty" of Lindbergh's accomplishment. "You are one of these men," the president of the Paris Municipal Council told the aviator, "in whom a great nation recognizes the image of its ideals." French onlookers, wanting to be a part of Lindbergh's adventure, sent him scores of gifts—commemorative coins, radiator ornaments, paintings, and a blue leather collar for the flyer's cat. "Lindbergh's sheer, unassuming simplicity," one reporter claimed, "has given the people of France a new and very much needed glimpse of the real America."[66] To many, he exemplified the positive, liberating force Americans might be, and often thought they were, in the French capital.

Like Lindbergh, Americans in interwar Paris thought they embodied an idealized image of the United States, one that would inspire others around the world. Their influence, as they saw it, extended beyond the promotion of a form of political economy summed up by references to Fordism or Taylorism. They offered more generally enticing, liberal glimpses of American life in the new century. The liberalism Americans often embraced in Paris—as forward-thinking as it often seemed—nevertheless had important limits. After the war, visitors from across the Atlantic championed the sensational thrills and novelties afforded by the capital's avant-garde cafés and nightclubs, but going to Chinese restaurants or ogling Latin American tango dancers remained, as it did at home, a particular form of cosmopolitanism perfectly compatible with enduring strains of nationalism and racism. Fights between white and black Americans, for example, routinely broke out in restaurants and bars, as tourists protested the lack of Jim Crow facilities. For both French and American proprietors, profitability often determined whether informal segregation would be tolerated. Even the most successful African Americans in Paris recounted instances where they were asked to leave hotels, theaters, and other establishments because the management dared not offend white American patrons. The very night of Lindbergh's arrival, Josephine Baker was nearly thrown out of one fashionable restaurant when a neighboring couple insisted to the headwaiter that serving a black woman simply was "not done."[67] White Americans soaked up jazz in the city's exotic nightspots to show how worldly they were, not to fashion a new, better era of American race relations.

The American community in Paris may have been liberal in the classic sense of the term, but this did not, on the whole, equate to the kind of political liberalism that would become such a cornerstone of mid-twentieth-century American politics. Geared toward the excitements of the marketplace rather than the promises of reform or the pursuit of social justice, politically the colony appeared on the whole more conservative than progressive. True, some residents stood out for their leftist convictions. During the Sacco-Vanzetti affair, some Americans joined Parisians in petitioning for a new trial and battling their reactionary compatriots in stormy café arguments that often drew the attention of police. The dancer Isadora Duncan famously held protest meetings in her Left Bank studio, where she kept a photograph of Governor Fuller on her mantle, scribbled with the slogan, "Down with Philistines!" In her final public act, only weeks before her death, Duncan stood wrapped in a red shawl in silent candlelight vigil for the two prisoners outside the American embassy.[68]

Most Americans in Paris, however, professed instead what they called "responsible opinion." "I am a liberal-minded man," one told a British journalist when asked about the Sacco-Vanzetti case. Worried that anarchy would sweep the United States if the two prisoners were not executed, he said that "if they are really innocent I would give them only life imprisonment." Residents of the Right Bank, Democrats or Republicans, most often shunned causes like the Sacco-Vanzetti affair, which put pure politics over business. Leaders in banking and diplomacy—prime movers in the Chamber of Commerce and the local American church organizations—tended to be internationalists of a kind, but devoted themselves to foreign policies that protected American interests abroad and opposed left-wing radicalism at all costs, even if it meant colluding outwardly with the far right. The colony's leading newspapers, headed by the *Herald*, with a daily circulation of 35,000 by 1929, espoused views farther to the right than their home editions. The *Herald* "did not bother much" with reporting on rising hostilities against Americans in the capital, its editor admitted. Promoting the agendas of Europe's right-wing states, which seemed to offer bulwarks against "reds" on the continent and at home, the paper, one critic charged, offered "the frankest advocacy of Fascism." The immensely popular Ambassador Herrick, who so skillfully took Lindbergh under his wing, similarly exemplified the political affinities of much of the colony he represented. As ambassador, he willingly socialized with and relied on intelligence from the militant royalist group Action Française. He honored the late Mexican dictator Porfirio Díaz, whom he had befriended in Paris before the war, and praised Marshal Lyautey, the far-right French governor of Morocco, for his occupation of that "backward" territory. The members of the center-left coalition, the *Cartel des gauches*, who gained temporary control of the French government in 1924, he regarded as "extremists." At the mere mention of the Sacco-Vanzetti case, the ambassador became apoplectic—understandably, since he had been the target of an anarchist supporter's bomb.[69]

Americans in Paris also tended to be highly class-conscious even as more open socializing overshadowed the old society atmosphere that had prevailed before the war. Graced by the frequent presence of Vanderbilts, Morgans, and Hearsts, along with a parade of flashier celebrities—from the movie stars Douglas Fairbanks and Mary Pickford to New York mayor and high-life connoisseur Jimmy Walker—Americans invested enormous time in Paris trying to see and be seen. Their adulation for royalty of all kinds, even those with dubious claims to their titles, was hardly exaggerated by the period's popular jokes. As a child, Josephine Baker had dreamed of lands with kings and queens; as a star, she cashed in on the similar fantasies of her compatriots, adding an accent to her name for her club Chez Joséphine to recall the Empress Bonaparte, and staging a fake marriage to the Count Giuseppe Abatino—in reality a plasterer by trade and gigolo by practice. Like her fellow Americans, Baker loved pomp and circumstance. Developing a taste for designer gowns, folding French expressions into her colloquial American speech, she began to distance herself from other African Americans in Paris, those whose presence might belie the fairytale.[70] She was not alone in admiring Mussolini and other rulers who styled themselves as benevolent leaders of their people. The economic and cultural liberalism Americans subscribed to in Paris, therefore, included many paradoxes—it denoted a cosmopolitanism with room for racial hierarchies and nationalist pride, and it pointed to a democratic ethos with strong class pretensions and a soft spot for nobles and dictators.

Like the symbol for innocence abroad Charles Lindbergh had become, Americans in Paris liked to envision themselves as politically neutral figures, the envoys of beneficial laissez-faire policies, the architects of new designs for living in the twentieth century. In the myths made by novelists, memoirists, and magazine writers, Americans' activities overseas were emptied of complicated or contentious motives, like the image of Gay Paree itself. But buried beneath these supposedly harmless tales lay ideas about expanding American power. Parisians would prove sensitive to such undertones, drawing far less optimistic conclusions from all this American cavorting in their city. However much they liked to see themselves as removed from the factional struggles of interwar Europe, Americans would nevertheless find themselves at the center of controversy in the French capital. The contours of the Paris of Americans—and the shape and significance of modern American culture more generally—would soon be brought into even sharper relief by conversations, arguments, and protests staged all around its edges.

CHAPTER TWO | Reluctant Hosts

A MERICANS RENDERED THE FRENCH CAPITAL as dashing, exciting—a panorama that reflected back to them their own dawning greatness. Next to the stories Americans told themselves about their triumphs abroad, however, divergent narratives began to emerge. Struggling to make sense of Americans' excursions in the capital, other Paris residents linked these newcomers from across the Atlantic to numerous postwar changes. Their assessments provide an important counterweight to Americans' self-congratulatory claims, even if they are no less inclined towards hyperbole. "The foreigners who have colonized Paris since the war have transformed its physiognomy," one author complained in a popular French middle-class magazine. "Just as they raised whole cities on virgin prairie soil," he wrote, "they have here built up places of diversion to their taste." The unnamed "they" in diatribes like this one clearly alluded to those arrivistes fresh from the land of bustling St. Louis, Chicago, and New York.[1] Such worries about the transformation of the capital into an American urban frontier, echoing Americans' own celebration of the city as a place to be conquered, proliferated especially from the mid-twenties to the early thirties. By then, as one American correspondent relayed, fears of "Americanization" in Paris had reached the level of "an obsession."[2] But how did onlookers differentiate between so-called American encroachments and the capital's other traditions? What exactly would be counted as "American" in interwar Paris?

Analyzing how this obsession took shape in the specific context of the French capital adds new dimensions to the study of "Americanization" and "anti-Americanism" in Europe, searching deeper into the period before

World War II when definitions of modern American culture were still in formation. Conventional wisdom suggests that during this era French animosity toward Americans centered primarily on formal diplomatic disagreements. Goodwill between the former allies dissipated rapidly after the Armistice as it became clear that the United States would not join the League of Nations but would push for disarmament and debt repayments. To most French people, who had made such sacrifices during the conflict, it seemed that Americans had profited by the war and then forfeited on unspoken promises to ensure peace and prosperity in the aftermath. In the early twenties, some French industrialists and state officials admired American production techniques, but their enthusiasm for adopting business models from across the Atlantic lagged far behind that found in Weimar Germany. At the same time, frustrations mounted over policies drafted back in the United States. The Washington Naval Conference (1921–1922), relegating France to secondary-power status, deeply unsettled French observers. Worse still, in 1924 American policymakers instituted the Dawes Plan, helping to revitalize the German economy with loans while withholding capital from allies to force them into a payment schedule for their war debts. Especially after the Dawes Plan, anger directed at American creditors and politicians grew fierce all along the political spectrum in France.[3] Caricaturists personified the United States as "Uncle Shylock" and imagined it as a land of rapacious, insensitive "Yankee millionaires." Shocked and disappointed, French citizens routinely muttered, "They fought the war *with* us; they make the peace *against* us."[4]

Beyond these clear conflicts of interest, antagonism towards Americans between the wars, it is commonly believed, found its appeal through popular French travelogues exploring social conditions in the United States. During these decades, critics such as Georges Duhamel and André Siegfried combed Chicago's stockyards and Manhattan's speakeasies, looking uneasily for the meaning of American industry, materialism, and conformity. Such writers helped to shift Europeans' view of the United States as a raw, unfinished backwoods full of unmannered roughnecks, as many had portrayed it in the nineteenth century, to a sense of it as an overprocessed, ultraurbanized land, albeit one still teeming with vulgarity and violence.[5] These exposés deeply impressed educated French readers, giving sharper shape to their vague emerging prejudices. Focusing on these texts alone, however, leaves the impression that French opposition to Americanism during this period amounted to an elite response to an American culture still confined within the borders of the United States. No wonder notions that Americans enjoyed a kind of benevolent neutrality in early-twentieth-century Paris persist.

Instead, World War II has been widely regarded as the watershed for American influence in Europe. Following the midcentury ascendance of the United States as a military and economic superpower, the growing presence of Americans, their products, and methods abroad indeed elicited passionate reactions, especially in France. Those on the receiving end of American culture, as many have shown, took up complicated processes of appropriation, manipulation, and resistance. When scholars do look to the roots of these dynamics before World War II, they often interpret them as the prehistory of what was essentially a postwar encounter between seductive American consumer goods and the war-torn societies and antiquated business practices of Europe.[6] "It was the Second World War that brought America and Americans into the French landscape," Richard Kuisel concludes in his now classic *Seducing the French*, "Up to then, the New World had been of marginal interest except to the writers who sketched its negative stereotype."[7]

To the contrary, on the streets of interwar Paris Americans represented more than an abstract menace across the ocean, more than a stingy nation of creditors promoting a frightening but still distant version of modernity. Siegfried, Duhamel, and others did not have to go all the way across the Atlantic to think about what modern American culture stood for or what it would mean for them. In the 1920s, Parisians of various political leanings developed an acute sense that Americans had formed a vibrant and troubling subculture right at the heart of their city. Aware of Americans' growing confidence and changing relationship to the capital, Parisians deplored how visitors paraded brashly though the city center as if Paris existed solely for their own enjoyment. Urban chroniclers, preservationists, and others worked to link this American presence to a host of alarming developments, evidence of which extended beyond the obvious impact of American banks and other institutions in the capital. In time, Americans became associated with a broad range of social practices, cultural aesthetics, and other subtle details—a perceived influence far greater than that delivered by motion pictures or safety razor imports alone. Responses to this apparent threat fed into a compelling ideological position that many French writers and others would take up—an "anti-American" posture cast against a cluster of values and symbols believed to be characteristic of a uniquely modern and urban civilization modeled by the United States. Such flexible anti-American thinking helped Parisians to assess their own hopes for the capital and to better understand themselves.

The history of "Americanizing" forces in Europe is often written as a contest between two fixed, opposing cultures already preformed. What would "Europe" do when "America" came knocking? Then, as now, many assumed that modern American culture stood for a coherent way of life already running full throttle back in the United States and ready for transfer abroad, where it would precipitate, according to Victoria de Grazia's masterful account, a "transatlantic clash of civilizations."[8] But in the early twentieth century, the age of skyscrapers, admen, and chain stores was only just dawning. Urban nightlife, Hollywood movies, and modern manners were just beginning to gather cross-class appeal, and they faced plenty of skepticism and resistance. Debates about American influence in the French capital, therefore, proved to be more than simply reactions to an invading force, a reception of something already made in the United States and then exported whole. Rather, all this talk in the city helped to constitute what would be understood as "American" to begin with. Ironically, many of the foremost signs of urban modernity that would be attributed to "Americanism"—automobiles, cinema marquees, neon advertising, commercial spectacle in general—had actually been pioneered in Paris. But many French critics began to disassociate these innovations from their own national heritage, just as more and more Americans embraced the components of cultural and economic liberalism as quintessentially their own. Labeling them American, despite their more complicated origins, became one important strategy for defining an idealized French way of life and preserving it from foreign corruption. Ideas about modern Frenchness and modern Americanness would develop in tandem in interwar Paris. Understanding how requires situating the experiences of Americans in the capital's broader social contexts. It requires mining the points of view of others and digging down into the vivid perspective of the day-to-day street scene.

Before the gaslights had been extinguished, before the pigeons left their roosts, men began rinsing the streets with water, a ritual that made each Paris morning feel like a fresh, promising start. With daylight, concierges—the sentries of private residences—swept out entryways and placed cushions on windowsills for their cats and dogs. At bus stops, commuters in hats and overcoats tore off numbered slips and waited patiently to board the charabancs that lumbered past. Especially in the early morning, Paris seemed a city of sensible order and comforting routine.[9]

Urban historians now often remember the interwar capital, bookended by two catastrophic wars, as a place of such relative calm, but for Parisians in the 1920s and 1930s these pleasant impressions did not always last long past the dawn. Behind the city's picturesque façade, many knew, lurked all kinds of dark truths. Newspapers wove the city's *faits divers* into a tapestry of jewelry heists, traffic accidents, and other urban calamities. Police announcements bristled with political extremism and criminal acts. Anxieties about urban chaos infused municipal records, which officials kept with obsessive exactness. Definitions for the city's troubling parts, catalogued in its weighty *Annuaire statistique*, multiplied after the war, as though the vulnerability of Paris to disaster could be contained with bureaucratic categories. Each year, clerks meticulously disaggregated the mounds of tainted foods confiscated from the city's markets—the millions of rotten eggs, decomposing vegetables, or rancid meats. They tabulated the hundreds of uncontrollable fires, the thousands of ambulance rides that swept through the city's streets, and the steady number of people who suddenly dropped dead on its sidewalks.[10] Paris certainly had its macabre side. The city's subterranean recesses, after all, contained not only the infrastructures of modern plumbing and transportation, but also ancient catacombs stacked with millions of bones. If Americans' tributes time and again began with an invigorating taxi ride that foreshadowed their ultimate mastery of the capital, Parisians' commemorations often ended with forebodings of their own demise.

Daily life in Paris right after the Great War was much more interesting and more fraught than is suggested by references to the stereotypical *"années folles,"* the French equivalent to Americans' "roaring twenties." Joy and frivolity became newly possible with the Armistice, of course, but for Parisians problems endured. How to mourn the almost two million who died during the war, they wondered, and to mend broken families? How to deal with the sight of more than a million amputees and other shattered veterans?[11] Postwar Parisians never knew the severe unemployment levels suffered by Berliners or Londoners, but working-class residents nevertheless strained to make ends meet. Those with more resources, too, sensed their position becoming more precarious. France's international standing seemed to be slipping, and many Parisians imagined they lived in an unfriendly world. The Germans, they insisted, still posed a grave threat. The Americans and British may have remained important allies, but Parisians distrusted their motives and doubted their resolve to guarantee France's security. New powers loomed on the horizon—the Soviet Union, Japan—and murmurs of discontent rumbled across the Empire. At home, middle and upper-class urbanites felt besieged as well. Labor militants, many of them veterans of war or exiles fresh from conflicts abroad, boldly demanded a greater share of political influence. Rising prices, blamed on affluent tourists, and the devaluation of the franc, linked to unfair debt arrangements, ate into family savings and fixed incomes. Parisians believed themselves to be suffering at the hands of others. Indeed, one of the darkest truths in postwar Paris was the multifaceted and growing xenophobia of its residents.

Americans were far from the only foreign colony in the city and far from the only group of newcomers Parisians found suspicious. The number of foreigners in the capital doubled during the 1920s, reaching more than 10 percent of the city's population. Almost three times as many foreigners landed in Paris than in Germany as a whole. Disproportionate numbers of unskilled, single men filed into the city, eclipsing the largely skilled migrants who had made the trek before. By the mid-twenties, 20 percent of the manual workers in Paris were foreign-born. Outnumbering all others, more than one hundred thousand Italians, in search of employment or fleeing Mussolini's regime, settled into the eastern neighborhoods and northern suburbs of Paris, forming a steady supply of hands for the city's building trades. Traditionally, the bulk of the capital's migrants had come from France's own provinces and from neighboring countries—Belgium and Switzerland as well as Italy. Now, they were joined by arrivals from further afield. In the wake of the Bolshevik Revolution, Paris became the headquarters for Russian émigrés. Refugees, running from famine and civil war, and "Whites," who had opposed the Red Army, doubled the city's Russian population by 1926, amassing in its outer southwestern arrondissements as well as Montmartre, where they picked up the pieces of their lives as taxi drivers, automobile workers, and railroad porters. Czechs, Armenians, Greeks, and others, too, built dense, insular communities richly evocative of some faraway village life. The Marais district blossomed into a similarly exotic Jewish enclave a short walk from the Seine. Since the 1880s, a steady stream of Eastern European Jews had made their way to the dilapidated quarter, seeking educations and escaping persecution. By the 1920s, the streets around the rue des Rosiers offered a hodgepodge of specialty shops, peddlers' carts, and Yiddish signs for the area's hatmakers, garment workers, and furriers. Though fewer in number, subjects from France's colonies also added to the capital's social diversity. Men from the Caribbean, Indochina, and North Africa—many of those who had soldiered or labored for France during the Great War—drifted back to the capital after the peace in search of freedoms denied in the colonies. Driven by drought and famine at home, young Algerian men formed the largest chain of migration from the French colonies, moving to the metropole to take up work in chemical factories and metal works. With only some six hundred resident Algerians before the war but sixty thousand or more by the late twenties, Paris supplanted Marseilles as the capital for colonial subjects in France.[12]

Native-born residents looked on apprehensively as these crowds inundated the city's poorest neighborhoods, exacerbating the postwar housing crunch, filling the streets with the sound of their languages and the smell of their foods. Parisians' reactions to foreigners ranged widely from tolerance, or more likely avoidance and indifference, to outright hostility. Immigrants filled deficits in the postwar labor force, but their living quarters, researchers averred, were a blight. Health workers and others wrung their hands over high rates of disease that thrived especially in areas deemed *îlots insalubres*, pockets of congestion and squalor that had somehow eluded Haussmann's demolition crews. Tuberculosis, typhoid fever, whooping cough, dysentery: all regularly claimed lives in interwar Paris, and foreigners often comprised a disproportionate number of the sick. Crowds of young men, cut loose from communities back home but unintegrated into French society, seemed to onlookers to be marred by irregular status, poor hygiene, and poor judgment. Ghettoized housing estates crammed with immigrants, France's pioneer scholar of immigration contended, constituted "true hotbeds of moral and physical contagion," their inhabitants mired in a form of "promiscuity" and "repulsive filth." Playing on such prejudices, right-wing politicians regularly fulminated against newcomers as parasites who stole jobs, sapped the city's services, and overran its hospitals and jails. Newspaper writers mocked immigrants' strange habits and accents. They used the word *étrangers*, "foreigners," as a pejorative and even resorted to nastier epithets like *métèques* or *indésirables*.[13] The capital undoubtedly appeared as one of the world's most important beacons for the desperate and the displaced. For outsiders, however, it did not always live up to its universalist promises.

Established residents had long resented newcomers, of course, and Parisians were far from unique for expressing this kind of nativism in an era of intense international migration. The proliferation of foreign colonies in Paris after the war, however, elevated such concerns to a whole new level, because they gave graphic, local dimensions to big, geopolitical worries. Like other great migrant destinations in the early twentieth century, Paris served as a cauldron for nationalist politics, perhaps ironically given its status as a meeting ground for so many different people. While Americans felt more sharply their Americanness in Paris, other immigrants, too, discovered patriotic allegiances that back home had paled behind regional and village loyalties. Rising ethnic convictions, uniting Poles, Czechs, and others, made the assimilation of such groups even more elusive, while violent struggles among their different factions threatened to ensnare France in diplomatic imbroglios. Paris, for example, served as a base for Mussolini's spies and hit men, just as it offered refuge to those who defied the Blackshirts and plotted their downfall. Political intrigue, spilling over the Italian border, led to no less than twelve assassinations in Paris between 1923 and 1929. For most Parisians, however, Bolshevism, cloaked amid all the arriving crowds, posed the most serious peril. Authorities had crushed the militant strikes during

France's own red scare in 1919–1920. Many, however, continued to view leftist agitation of any kind as an extraterritorial force capable of instigating an uprising in the capital, a notion seemingly confirmed in 1921 when Paris authorities caught communists smuggling funds from Soviet agents through American Express.[14]

If arriving European exiles accentuated fears about political extremism, the growing presence of colonial subjects compounded a range of racial anxieties. Parisians liked to pride themselves on being more enlightened about such matters than Americans, who perpetuated such a violent culture of segregation, but they remained the beneficiaries of a vast empire with its own inequalities. Increasingly, the uncertain fate of French imperialism seemed tied to the activities of the capital's own colonial populations. Parisians digested news about the Moroccan fighter Abd el-Krim's victories in the Rif War of the early twenties alongside sensational stories about crimes committed in Paris by North Africans. They got word of independence movements in Tunisia, Egypt, and India while learning about the militancy of their local Southeast Asian and Antillean populations. The city indeed nurtured the empire's rebels—the future Ho Chi Minh is only the most famous to have lived in Paris during this period—and calls for self-determination, issued in the metropole's small but committed anticolonial circles and publications, threatened to seep out to the territories overseas. Talented people of color may have enjoyed celebrity in Paris during its *tumulte noir*, but this vogue for Africana, jazz, and other so-called exotic phenomena did not undermine many Parisians' deep ambivalence about what some referred to as a rising tide of color.[15] Racialized clichés, perpetuated by advertising posters beaming forth comic black faces to sell bananas and department store displays and anthropological exhibits showcasing natives in their "primitive" habitats, persisted alongside affirmations that all potentially could be equal in *la plus grande France*. While communists and surrealists rooted for the end of empire from the margins, most Parisians listened to more mainstream pundits somberly predicting "the twilight of the white nations."[16] French authors were swimming in the same current of arguments about racial threats posed by foreign populations as Oswald Spengler in Germany and Madison Grant and Lothrop Stoddard in the United States, reactionary ideas that streamed across borders as readily as their subjects or the politics of anti-imperialism did.

Historians have documented Parisians' worries about working-class immigrants amassing on the city's outskirts—all those single laborers, radicals plotting revolutions, and strange others who flouted French ways of doing things. Less attention, however, has been paid to objections about growing numbers of tourists and wealthy residents, not least Americans, making an impact at the city's very center. While some had been drawn to Paris by labor opportunities and others attracted by a sense of the metropolis as a dramatic stage for mass politics, affluent visitors came as a result of new possibilities that had opened up in urban life during the past several decades. In the nineteenth century, leisure travelers often bypassed cities for spas, resorts, and natural beauties. When they came to great capitals like London, Paris, and Rome, they did so mostly to enjoy private society, view famous monuments and museums, or shop at exclusive retailers. Wandering the streets and rubbing shoulders with the crowds remained the purview of a few middle- and upper-class figures such as charity and social workers, male slummers, and journalists. Victorian cities were chaotic, potentially dangerous places, and often rigidly compartmentalized. By the end of the century, however, better transportation and the spread of upscale shopping districts and luxury hotels made them more hospitable destinations. As the range of people who visited and settled in urban areas widened, new activities and attitudes exploded the old limitations on mixing and movement. Bohemian enclaves offered unconventional spaces where individuals could flout the old proprieties and embrace the transformative possibilities of metropolitan life. Revolutionary ways of seeing and thinking about city life emanated not only from high cultural forms—avant-garde art, music, and literature—but also from the everyday sights and sensations, the chance encounters, the inspiring contrasts offered by the metropolis itself. Urban tourism became increasingly popular after the 1890s, and by the twentieth century, visitors longed not just to see the museums and monuments but also to soak up the atmosphere and sample the streets.[17]

Paris had been a forerunner for such urban exploration, drawing spectators earlier than most cities to its arcades, department stores, and international expositions, and by the early twenties all kinds of affluent newcomers descended on the capital in search of excitements. Spanish nobles, for example, became prominent seasonal visitors, migrating to Paris each year to buy the latest fashions, to enjoy the pleasure grounds, to be seen. Latin Americans, reportedly even more wealthy, took up residence for much longer. Like others, they descended on the most expensive restaurants and hotels in the city's western half. Better-off Russian émigrés joined the mix, too—successful professionals and those living off squirreled-away family fortunes. English expatriates, among the most numerous of this cohort, settled in the capital by the tens of thousands. Many supported themselves by working for the Paris branches of British banks and trading firms. Others made up a sizeable leisure class. It was cheaper to keep up appearances in Paris than in London.

Retired civil servants and dowagers stretched their fixed incomes there further than they could have at home.[18] All together, these crowds made up a worldly jet set of which Americans were only one part, infusing the fashionable districts of Paris with a cosmopolitan flair, serving as patrons for Argentine tango clubs, Caucasian cabarets, African American jazz joints, and other novel additions to the urban scene.

Such big-spending sojourners contributed appreciably to the local economy, a fact acknowledged by shopkeepers who tailored their menus to the tastes of their new guests. Parisians nevertheless complained frequently about these arrivals. To many, they posed even more trouble than working-class migrants, since they grouped not on the city's outskirts but right in its center, leaving their mark on the most cherished quarters of the capital. Structural renovations to the city center between the wars may have been nothing compared to its dramatic Haussmannization during the last century, but residents nevertheless became acutely aware of shifts in public life. "Especially since the World War," a member of the French Academy voiced a widespread opinion, Paris had been "completely transformed in its outward aspect," particularly "in its centres of pleasure and luxury."[19] Parisians attributed these changes in no small part to the influx of energetic, well-heeled foreigners who gravitated to those centers. Sensing that others dictated social trends, that local cultural control was shifting away from native residents, they feared the capital was modernizing according to foreign rather than French models. And no one would be singled out as primary agents of this new brand of urbanity more than the arriving Americans.

"Open revolt breaks out in Paris," reported the *Christian Science Monitor* in May 1920, only the second spring since the ceasefire. Discontent had been brewing in the hilly neighborhood of Montmartre, north of the city center where revolution had erupted a half century before. Declaring their independence as another Free Commune, locals invoked Wilsonian self-determination and pledged to "live henceforth far removed from the tumults of the barbaric Plain." The barbaric Plain of which they spoke with such contempt was Paris, the urban sprawl below, whose faster ways, flashier lights, and commercial enterprises had been slowly encroaching on the lofty eighteenth arrondissement since its incorporation into the city limits in 1860. "Proprietors without scruples, without spirit and without heart have dishonored the Butte," railed a circular by the Anti-Skyscraperist Party, which would carry the much-advertised mock election for this Free Commune thanks to its ambitious calls for an autonomous Montmartre, free of modern construction, but also, in proper French revolutionary fashion, because of its agenda of more expansive reforms. The party's platform evoked a fiefdom of utopian whimsy—Montmartre's streets and squares would be protected from outside aggressors and equipped with mechanical escalators and public fountains that spouted wine instead of water. Over the years, the successor to the Free Commune, the Republic of Montmartre, inspired outlandish demonstrations to promote neighborhood camaraderie and the "most wholesome of *gaîtés*." Avowing to keep French spirit alive and prevent the quarter's "invasion by vandals and *métèques*," by sundry night-owl intruders and hoity-toity tourists, the organizers of these movements faced off defensively against a changing cityscape.[20] Their aspirations may have been particularly colorful, but their discontents were widely shared.

Looking down across the Paris landscape from the heights of Montmartre, four districts in particular loomed as beachheads for changes that threatened to make French Parisians strangers in their own city. The closest, the Pigalle district of Montmartre, sat at the foot of the Free Commune's precious hilly regions; beyond that, towards the Seine, appeared the Opera area; jutting off to the right was the Champs-Elysées; and farther in the distance south of the Seine rose the neighborhood of Montparnasse. Each of these areas had its own distinct history, its own specialized atmosphere, but more and more they shared key characteristics that made them stand out from the rest of the cityscape. Together, these four districts emerged as the capital's most vibrant commercial quarters between the wars, with bars, nightclubs, and other pleasure grounds that attracted an affluent clientele. They were like pockets of the Jazz Age in a more earnest, even somber, urban context. Although many Parisians enjoyed these regions for their novelties, others loathed them as commandeered sections of the city, where rich foreigners promoted a deleterious form of cosmopolitanism. The lights and noise of these quarters drowned out the authentic cultures of the capital, many charged. "The true face of Paris," the French novelist Pierre Mac Orlan put it, had been hidden behind "the international mask of its multiple, nocturnal attractions."[21] Tourists and other privileged foreigners were not solely responsible for the evolution of these areas, but in commentary on neighborhood change, they appeared everywhere, and before long, debates about of these quarters became bound up with ideas about an American or Americanizing Paris.

Arguments about foreign influence reverberated through public discussions of the transformation of interwar Paris, not least through the city's popular urban chronicles. Part guidebook and part cultural essay, these numerous volumes simulated the musings and ramblings of the flâneur or the leisurely man-about-town, seeking to capture the capital's peculiarities in extraordinary detail. Leading writers in this genre were often well-regarded intellectuals, sometimes members of the French Academy, who chose the urban exposé as a medium for thinking through theories about neighborhood development and their attendant cultural politics. Among the more prolific chroniclers, writers such as Charles Fegdal, André Warnod, and Jules Bertaut betrayed conservative political leanings and a nostalgia for the order and hierarchy of Second Empire and Belle Epoque Paris. They evinced, by contrast, an outright disdain often mixed with morbid fascination for the postwar capital, its relaxed rules governing social and sexual relations, and, most especially, its foreign elements. "Since the last war, we are less sure of our Paris," André Warnod admitted in one of his many tracts: "Our guests, welcomed too eagerly, have spoken like masters and we have listened to them." Regretting the "negroes who have invaded with their jazz and their dances," the "Jews of Central Europe and their spirit of destruction," and the "Americans with their banks," Warnod asked futilely: "Paris, my dear Paris, will you know how to remain Paris for long?"[22] Although the majority of urban chroniclers stood right of center politically, their suspicions of outsiders resonated with others. Similar conceptions of Paris and its neighborhoods appeared in memoirs and newspaper editorials by those of all sorts of political persuasions.

Montmartre offered a ready target for critiques about urban change. Once the domain of grain mills, vineyards, modest art studios, and the bistros of anarchists and disgruntled Boulangists, Montmartre began to attract curious day-trippers and night revelers around the turn of the century, visitors who even then started to drive the folksy, politically edgy ways of the Butte into retreat. This process intensified further during World War I, when each evening American doughboys crowded the smoke-filled rooms of once charming venues like the Lapin Agile, which, Warnod regretted, now "took on the airs of bars *du Far-West*."[23] After the Armistice, more outsiders streamed in like carpetbaggers. At night, tuxedoed and evening-gowned visitors arrived in chauffeured automobiles to hot spots at the base of the hill. Along the streets splintering off from places Clichy and Pigalle, there had been only a handful of night resorts at the turn of the century. Now there were scores of them. Seemingly interminable trails of taxis and fancy cars snaked along narrow roads not made for them, and all around the Pigalle region arose a glaring nightscape—a collage of illuminated signs for *soupers* and American bars, the façades of spectacular resorts like the Moulin Rouge and the Gaumont movie palace ablaze with electric bulbs.[24] Like the animated members of the Free Commune, other traditionalists depicted a quaint quarter of old threatened by a nightmare, nighttime Montmartre of jazz and tacky imported revelry, a "huge cosmopolitan pleasure-fair," by one account, advertising itself "by every kind of illuminated device likely to attract the

The place Pigalle exemplified the city's most commercialized districts after the war, courting tourists and other revelers with its "new" nightclubs and "American Bars." For critics, however, this electrified streetscape signaled the invasion of a brash cosmopolitanism, threatening to overrun the capital's quieter, supposedly more authentic quarters. Mario von Bucovich, *Paris.* New York: Random House, 1930.

foreign visitor's eye." The electrification of the streets of the Pigalle area, its crush of taxis and cars, and its tawdry theme bars became causes for constant criticism.[25]

Onlookers decried the apparent foreignness of this startling new night-scape on display at the foot of the hill. Montmartre was indeed the most diverse quarter of Paris. By official count, it housed one foreigner for every three French residents, and that did not even include the waves of tourists and others who swamped the faubourg at night and then retreated to their hotels and apartments in the city below. To urban critics, these wealthy temporary visitors seemed more offensive than the Russian taxi drivers, West Indian bouncers, and other foreigners who made up the area's workforce, because they were the rapacious customers who drove local businesses to adopt all the same jazz tunes and tangos, the same gleaming décor and over-priced champagne. Practically all the area's resorts, one bystander declared, "exist entirely for the benefit of foreigners, who generally soon begin to complain loudly that they meet nothing but other foreigners in them. They are becoming more and more Americanised and are thereby steadily losing their individual character." Unsympathetic authors who combed the night places of Montmartre declared them flashy but seedy and empty of substance. "Montmartre commercializes itself under the flood of foreigners, Anglo-Americans especially," one sneered. This was not the old Montmartre *"qui pense* [that thinks]," but the new Montmartre *"qui dépense* [that spends]." Here, he regretted, after midnight people spoke anything but French in restaurants "more or less *anglo-américains*, full of light and noise but empty of ideas."[26]

Detractors asserted that Montmartre nightlife offered nothing but prefabricated entertainments no matter how spontaneous they appeared—signs of that same standardization travelers like Siegfried and Duhamel had found in such profusion in the United States. Famed music halls such as the Folies Bergère and the Casino de Paris illustrated this most graphically, with their identical chorus girls who kicked and shimmied in unison on stage to please equally conformist viewers. These places, critics scowled, teemed with the automatons of a decadent metropolitan culture—denationalized citizens of the world, who all danced the same dances, wore the same clothes, hummed the same inane tunes. The music hall promoted precisely those new urban values traditionalists wanted to resist. With names like "Paris qui jazz," "Paris-Vertige!," or even "Boum! V'ian! Pif-Paf!," their revues capitalized on the jarring sights and sounds of the modern city itself. Cynics contended that because their emphasis lay not with verbal repartee or clever lyrics but with elaborate visual feasts of lights and sequins, they pandered to visitors who did not speak French and wanted only to be "dazzled into a stupor." Many feared that the importation of "Anglo-American morals, tastes and pleasures," as one music-hall reviewer put it, would lead the average Paris dweller to sacrifice substance and intellect for the same superficial diversions that seduced non-French-speakers.[27]

For some, the incorporation of African American music and dance into the music-hall repertoire after the success of La Revue Nègre in 1925 posed the gravest danger. That sensation, headlined by Josephine Baker, unleashed the "most direct assault ever perpetrated on French taste," asserted one intellectual, claiming that this "lamentable transatlantic exhibitionism makes us revert to the ape in less time than it took us to evolve from it."[28] Such amusements, many prophesied, would bring upon Paris a racial contamination commensurate with the "mongrelization" from which American culture already purportedly suffered. In the nightspots of Montmartre, even a fan of the music hall elegized, *la tumulte* had replaced harmony, frenzy had replaced spirit, and the classic features of Parisian entertainment had retreated "before the invasion of negro music and barbaric dances." Jazz performers from the United States earned the appreciation of self-styled urban sophisticates and modern music connoisseurs, but to others they posed a double threat. They were seen paradoxically as carriers of both an overworked, mechanized American spirit and an uninhibited African primitivism. Beating to the rhythms of the jungle, many envisioned, jazz at the same time furnished the soundtrack for "mass-produced men."[29]

Both the African Americans on stage and the white Americans filling audiences each night clearly added to the cosmopolitan feel of Montmartre and similar night destinations. But why would Parisians blame Americans in particular for postwar changes in the city? They were not the only foreigners to put their stamp on Montmartre and the capital's other commercial quarters. British visitors and residents, for example, swarmed the same places and sought the same thrills, not to mention the fact that Parisians had long reserved special ire for English tourists. Nevertheless, sojourners from the United States increasingly bore the brunt of local resentments. The British presence in the capital now seemed less consequential than that of Americans, whose economic and cultural influence had soared in the wake of the war. More and more, when French pundits talked about "Anglo-Saxon" or "Anglo-American" threats to "Latin" values, their arguments often devolved into more specific grievances about Americans.[30] Americans seemed to be the most aggressive and threatening trendsetters. They were the ones who most profited by the exchange rate. Moreover, British writers in Paris worked assiduously to distance themselves from Americans. Their hostility towards visitors from across the Atlantic was often as visceral as that of French residents.

On the streets of Paris, fears about the shifting international balance of power dovetailed with concerns about the local impact of that paramount symbol of Americans' unfair advantages, the dollar. With the devaluation of many European currencies during the 1920s, Americans had crisscrossed the continent conspicuously in search of good deals. Inflation in Eastern Europe may have been steepest, but France actually drew the most American buyers. In 1927, Americans spent $190 million there, more than four and a half times the sum dispensed in Great Britain, more than six times that spent in Italy, and approximately nine and a half times that spent in Germany. That September, American Legionnaires and their wives alone dropped an estimated $4.5 million in Paris during their convention week. To French witnesses, this cavalier spending smacked of exploitation. "The Yankees, enriched by the war, spread the cult of the almighty Dollar across the world and disembarked, in joyful caravans, on the old Continent still poorly recovered from its wounds," one French novelist wrote. "Armed not with pistols but with dollars," he deplored, they ransacked Parisian boutiques, bought princely manors "for a mouthful of bread," and snatched up luxury items and artwork "for a derisory price."[31] Accusations that profiteering Americans treated Paris as a giant bargain basement reverberated across the political spectrum, appearing in everything from the Catholic newspaper *Le Croix* to the labor-oriented *Le Peuple*. In the moderate *L'Œuvre*, one editorialist characteristically complained that the "American invasion" had only caused an increased cost of living. "France is becoming an Anglo-Saxon colony," he wrote: "There are too many of these parasites here, eating our food, drinking our wine, going untaxed, and paying ridiculously little for everything they consume, thanks to the exchange."[32] When the exchange rate reached an all-time high of some fifty francs to the dollar in July 1926, such sentiments even exploded in a wave of street attacks on American tourists. Right-wing protesters had massed in front of the Chamber of Deputies to vent their irritations about the record plummet of the franc and the inability of the government to cushion the fall, but they soon turned their sights on Americans, singling them out for abuse on the boulevards and in Montmartre. Tensions peaked in late July when several thousand people gathered to boo the patrons of "Paris by Night" charabanc tours, which departed from the Opera area. Mobs stormed the buses, smashing their windows and forcibly removing their passengers.[33]

The gratuitous display of American purchasing power struck at the pride of many observers in Paris. A writer for the Catholic *L'Echo de Paris* discovered that railroad porters gravitated to foreigners who promised better tips. "It is no recommendation to be a Frenchman," he concluded sadly; "Paris is now suffering from an invasion." Others lamented time and again that the capital's best establishments had become too expensive for Frenchmen but a steal for others. One Parisian, struggling with her vastly depleted postwar income, told Ambassador Herrick that she could not help but feel "irritated and impatient," to feel, in fact, "vanquished," when, she saw "everywhere you Americans filling the restaurants and the hotels and taking away our art treasures, and invading all France, you who are so rich and prosperous and smiling." Such residents felt estranged in districts like Montmartre, where, one British guidebook writer reminded readers, visitors may have paid in francs, but it was the "weight of dollars that sets the wheels a-going and the tinsel flags a-flying." The inner Right Bank, too, another writer regretted, had become "practically prohibited" to "the natives" who did not "produce or sell something." The city seemed to be dividing into two distinct regions with their own economies, one where Americans bought and the other where they did not. "What business have we natives with our paper francs in Paris, that fair ground for Americans?" queried Paul Morand. Beyond American banks and American Express, a host of more subtle clues pointed to how Americans were helping to reshape local commercial life. "Read the nationalities of these red or sallow faces; listen to the babel of talk; and, if you are still skeptical, look at the bill," a writer for the middle-class *L'Illustration* urged. "What can this new Paris be called," he wondered, "if not 'the Paris of the dollar'?"[34]

Next to Montmartre, the Opera district captured the attention of the city's doomsayers—not surprisingly, since the quarter had become such a beacon for visiting businessmen, shoppers, and others. Since the war, many insisted, the area had been overrun by American crowds and institutions. Here, one German writer noted, amidst the international branches and banks, every other person who passed was a foreigner or an individual who made his living by them. For him, the area revealed one potent indication that even "*la belle France*" risked being transformed into "a sort of *colonie américaine*" or, even worse, "a copy of America." In another characteristically derisive account, a Danish woman sputtered: "If you go to Paris in August, you go to America." Echoing Americans' own conclusions, Paul Morand declared that the "Place de l'Opéra might well be Times Square." The whole area was now "a blaze of merchandise" and "superficial luxury," with electric signs, loudspeakers, and tour busses crammed with sightseers. One French periodical put it even more bluntly in 1930: "When a Yankee lands in Paris, he sees a conquered land."[35]

In truth, the place de l'Opéra and its surrounding streets had been a blaze of merchandise for decades. In the early nineteenth century, arcades cut ethereal passages through the solidness of stone city blocks, carving out spaces not only for vending mass-produced wares but also for practicing new modes of spectatorship. Here, in gaslit pavilions of glass and iron, the wandering poet Baudelaire discovered that Parisian modernity began. Even more dramatically, during the second half of the nineteenth century Haussmann's wider thoroughfares, updated middle-class housing, and more expansive retail premises pushed out poorer residents and transformed the area into the capital's most fashionable and accessible shopping district. Full of multistory emporiums with new plate glass windows, as well as big restaurants and cafés, this depopulated and commercialized section stood in contrast to the Right Bank's more residential working-class east as well as its older business districts—like the arcades and the Palais Royal—now past their heyday. The knot of Métro lines in the region, the densest in the entire city, hastened these trends. By the 1880s, the Opera quarter exemplified the *embourgeoisement* of the city center and symbolized France's economic grandeur.[36] It was to participate in the commerce and street life of these famed thoroughfares that legions of Americans streamed off those boat trains after the war.

A renovated Opera district had at first heralded the ascendancy of the capital's traders and their bourgeois customers, but the coming of Americans and other leisured foreigners signaled to many a shifting balance of power away from the middle-class beneficiaries of Haussmannization and early Third Republic politics. It became commonplace to imagine the district as a foreign concession or international quarter where the natives were not welcome except in service roles. Like the vogue for overseas music and arts in the clubs of Montmartre, the prominence of wealthy foreigners in the Opera area threatened to invert narratives about the superiority of French culture. As one popular refrain had it, the colonizers, once destined to bring *civilisation* to the world, were becoming the colonized. Americans, many began to theorize, practiced a new form of overseas domination, not a "military imperialism, booted and helmeted," but rather an insidious form of economic and cultural control. Commentators used bitter humor to make this point. The right-wing newspaper *Le Figaro*, for example, ran a series of letters written by a fictionalized American in Paris. "What has happened to the Parisians is just what happened to the Indians at home," the imaginary correspondent related nonchalantly to readers back in the United States, "the people here used to have their own odd ideas of what was proper and fitting and agreeable,—sort of a Chinese code of etiquette, you know . . . Now, thank God, that's over."[37]

This sense of colonization boomeranging back on the capital only grew stronger as the use of English proliferated on the inner Right Bank. By the mid-twenties, Europeans' plaints about its prevalence had overshadowed Americans' remarks about incomprehensible French speakers. Near the Opera, "French has long since ceased to be the popular language," one Frenchman characteristically lamented. Reporting for the *Frankfurter Zeitung* in the summer of 1925, Joseph Roth similarly recoiled from all the visitors in the city talking in a discernibly American twang. "Everywhere," he exclaimed, "you encounter lanky figures in flat shoes, with big horn-rimmed glasses," bunches of conspicuous tourists clutching their Baedekers and converging on the city's sights, where "they sing out their 'wow!'"[38] English-language signage, adopted to please the city's "most profitable patron, the Yankees" and demarcating the "Paris of the tourist," became cause for special outrage. Municipal councilors and others repeatedly proposed to tax signs not written in French, or even those that used the language incorrectly. In a typical rant against such "gibberish," *L'Œuvre* denounced the slogans "made from scraps of French, fragments of English and also expressions imported from who knows where" that stood out in sparkly, metallic letters on the façades of luxury boutiques—"barbarisms" that affronted the integrity of the language that was central, just like the franc, to Parisians' sense of self.[39] To those uncertain about the capital's growing internationalism—its transformation into a troubling "Babel"—signs of the Anglophone invasion seemed to jump out of the general landscape, leading to skewed impressions of its scale. French, of course, remained predominant in central Paris, but many nevertheless depicted the cityscape as monopolized completely by the plaques, products, and colloquialisms of transatlantic guests. The spread of English made the city much more legible to visitors from across the Atlantic, but at the same time it became disturbingly less so for native residents.

Billboards, electric lights—all sorts of objects punctuating the horizon—were often interpreted as omens of a debasing cosmopolitanism or an invading Americanism ready to overtake the capital's charms. After the war, public postings in general washed over the city's surfaces. Political campaign material and entertainment schedules vied for space on columns and kiosks. Towering billboards jutted up above the roofs of apartment buildings or draped down covering several stories of windows. Advertisements for soap and liqueurs, for the Moulin Rouge, coated multistory scaffolding and the sides of neighborhood stores, shouting their brand names at passersby. Relaxed limitations on the press in 1881 had opened up the possibility for this greater public posting, but it was not until the 1920s that city officials and others determined that advertisements had collectively grown all out of proportion to their surroundings. The Commission Municipale du Vieux Paris, the capital's premier preservation society, had addressed complaints about individually offensive signs before the war. Members' prewar efforts to combat such inappropriate *affichage*, however, proceeded case by case, with no overbearing sense of urgency to take on what they considered at the time a "very delicate question."[40] By the mid-twenties, however, *affichage* loomed as one of the Commission's most pressing concerns. Speakers filled their meeting minutes with disclosures about a city under siege by the abuses of advertising made "regardless of the most elementary rules of taste, of measure and good sense." The group spearheaded a crusade against the "uglification of Paris," working to reform tax laws regulating signage and to protect more sites from defacement.[41]

Preservationists, like others, linked Americans to this troublesome explosion of imagery on the streets, partly because of their contributions to recent advertising innovations. American corporations, such as the J. Walter Thompson Company, which opened its Paris branch in 1928, had forged ahead into international markets, helping to popularize hard-sell, advice-filled

Around the corner from the place de l'Opéra in 1925, a billboard for Ford automobiles almost completely covers the building that housed, from left to right, the "General Ticket Office" of the Wagons-Lits tour company, the *Chicago Tribune* reading room, and the Hôtel Scribe. Such publicity, even when it did not so obviously promote imports from the United States, evoked an "American" city experience that many Parisians found troubling. A poster from the notorious Cadum baby campaign appears in the bottom center. ©Albert Harlingue/Roger-Viollet/The Image Works

campaigns underscored by subtle, psychological strategies to pique desires. Even if products advertised with these methods on the streets of Paris were not American in origin, they were often thought of as such. Joseph Roth, like others, deplored the famous spokesbaby for Savon Cadum, whose oversized visage began to pop up around the city in the mid-twenties. "The baby may be the brainchild of a French soap manufacturer, but it's more than just an ad," he insisted, it was "a symbol of America: America over Paris." Pierre Mac Orlan similarly believed that historians in the future would find these curious, flat monuments the "vestiges of a fleeting religion dedicated to the cigarette, to alcoholic spirits, to the automobile and to Mary Pickford."[42]

Americans, however, became implicated in the spread of advertising not simply because of the style and content of signs, but also because such signs demarcated those urban corners most sought out by individuals from across the Atlantic. According to the records of the Commission Municipale du Vieux Paris, the Opera area and the Champs-Elysées stood out as those quarters most thoroughly conquered since the war by "colossal posters of the worst taste, for the large part foreign." And nothing evoked "*l'américanisme*" to Vieux Paris commissioners like the proliferation of electrified advertisements, no matter what their actual origins. In a typical conflation of American and English objects, preservationists' singled out both the American Express office's enormous rooftop sign and Selfridge's nearby "*Gazette lumineuse*" as their bêtes noires. By the Commission's estimation, these forces for Americanization represented an "apotheosis of advertising" and an affront to Parisians' "good sense." The British department store's ticker tape sign seemed particularly offensive, delivering "right at the heart of Paris" the news of the day in both French and English. The Commission did constant battle against such blinding eyesores, but they were outmatched by defiant proprietors who knew that such signs would lead more customers to their doors. Spotlighted posters, neon letters, and electric bulb arrangements sprouted up overnight like pesky mushrooms. No sooner had the Commission compelled the removal of one sign than another would surreptitiously take its place.[43]

Like the propagation of English and the American dollar, electric signs helped to develop the capital's modern side, while also undermining some of its previous characteristics. "The ability to saunter and idle" past twilight, regretted one Frenchman, had been damaged by the "winking and blinking gleam of fantastic and many-colored lights from electric signs." "Dazzling from roof to basement," he recorded, advertisements inscribed "their splendors in letters of fire on the eyes and on the minds of the passerby" and seemed "to bar the streets off as with massive blocks of radiant light." Artificial lights, some believed, endowed the establishments they advertised with an extraordinary, almost tyrannical authority over the rest of the evening cityscape. In the city's new cultural hierarchy, institutions of commerce and the popular haunts of foreigners literally outshone other establishments. After much maneuvering, the Commission finally did secure a government order for the removal of the cursed *Gazette lumineuse* on the final day of 1927.[44] It was a symbolic yet small victory in the battle over the surfaces of the Paris streets.

The Opera district had long been a center for trade and business, a fact that was only emphasized by the arrival of greater numbers of assertive Americans and other wealthy foreigners, just as Montmartre's nightlife had intensified amid the wave of wartime and postwar revelers. To the west, however, the area around the avenue des Champs-Elysées commercialized in sync with the growing tourist traffic, making it a particularly revealing location to document urban changes suspected of being driven by outsiders. Here, too, along the avenue's tree-lined flanks, observers located symptoms of "American" incursions most readily in the evolving cityscape itself.

Before World War I, the Champs-Elysées had been prized more for its pastoral charms than its glitzy nightlife. During the nineteenth century, the revered district had featured stately horse-drawn carriages making their way past chestnut trees and private mansions known as *hôtels particuliers*. As late as the 1880s, the area remained predominantly the domain of riding schools, stables, and select cafés. Even when, in the early years of the new century, the open-air *café-concerts* Alcazar and Ambassadeurs began to attract middle-class visitors—including American patrons of Karl Baedeker's guidebooks and Thomas Cook's tours—commercial life along the Champs-Elysées still paled next to that of the grand boulevards. The commercialization of the city center, however, soon encroached on this exclusive residential enclave. The number of private mansions along the avenue declined sharply after 1900, and on the eve of war the thoroughfare already housed more than 130 businesses, making it a principal nexus of bourgeois activities. Fashion *couturiers* began relocating their showrooms there from the vicinity of the place Vendôme during the war, and after the Armistice the westward migration of upscale shops continued apace, with banks and theaters following the trail of car dealers and luxury traders. "At the birth of this century there was but one shop in the Champs-Élysées," remarked a British observer in the late twenties, "now this scintillating avenue is lined with motor shops, dressmakers, jewelers, hatters, who jostle the few remaining *hôtels particuliers*."[45]

During the interwar years, change beset the expansive avenue. Encrusted from top to bottom with temporary fences and workers covered in plaster, the strip had become a "vast demolition and reconstruction site," observed one writer for *L'Œuvre*. The entire neighborhood, he testified, "peaceful, aristocratic, closed off" before, had been transformed abruptly into "an artery largely open, lively, pleasant, illuminated, sparkling" and *irrésistible* to the crowds. Motorcars especially symbolized the avenue's growing popularity and energy, dominating it not only from its paved middle but also from behind the plate-glass windows of the automobile showrooms that lined its sides. Although cars plied the Paris roads by the turn of the century, their full weight was not felt on the Champs-Elysées until the 1920s, when their greater numbers began to draw the avenue more firmly into the orbit of the city's center by making it more accessible to shoppers and pleasure seekers. Whereas before the war, the capital's densest traffic had accrued at the junction of the rue de Rivoli and the boulevard Sébastopol east of Les Halles, after the war its worst snarls tied up the large intersections farther to the west.[46] Now, at peak hours police on the Champs-Elysées could hardly contend with the congestion. By the early thirties, between three and seven o'clock, an estimated 20,000 automobiles emerged onto the avenue from its northwest entrance alone. That old byway of horses and fiacres had been transformed into a vast field of asphalt, clogged with idling, honking cars. The resulting commotion pierced though the quarter's former stately grace. The exhaust fumes took their toll on the chestnut trees.[47]

The avenue's hotels and other establishments owed their booming success in part to the patronage of foreigners. Here, luxury shops and commercial entertainments catered openly to Americans and other affluent visitors who had become prominent members of the capital's rich social set, often referred to as *Tout-Paris* (many joked that it might as well have been called *Tout-Etranger*). This cosmopolitan clientele poured into cafés like Fouquet's and the Select, with their proudly advertised American bars, and new, opulent pleasure grounds like the Lido, where police once detained F. Scott Fitzgerald for jumping into its sparkling pool. Detractors such as Robert de Beauplan, writing for *L'Illustration*, portrayed Frenchmen as a dying breed in these chic and expensive venues, overtaken by crowds of irrepressible *étrangers*. "The noisy throng has penetrated the Champs Élysées as far as the Étoile," he reported, "and the serenity of the Arc de Triomphe is likely to be

Le Select draws an international clientele on the Champs-Elysées in 1927. Along with other "American Bars" on the avenue, it would be attacked by Sacco-Vanzetti rioters. ©Albert Harlingue/Roger-Viollet/The Image Works

disturbed by a jazz-band restaurant that has recently opened only a hundred yards away." Even that idyllic garden *café-concert* Ambassadeurs, de Beauplan pronounced, was "now Americanized, too." Remade as a "monumental palace" for dancing and dining, it sported towering colonnades and a stage "where an amazing orchestra with big, shiny instruments sits."[48] The new Champs-Elysées shared the daytime hustle and bustle of the Opera district, and it also sported, to many residents' chagrin, some of the brash nighttime qualities of Montmartre.

The transformation of the Champs-Elysées, like that of the Opera area and Montmartre, offers insight into how Parisians and other Europeans first grappled with the possibility of Americanization. Yet historians have largely overlooked concerns about neighborhood change and the ways in which they helped critics to articulate antipathies towards a perceived invading American culture. Instead, scholars have focused most often on questions of production and consumption, zeroing in on business methods and consumer goods as prime categories for assessing Americans' impact abroad between the wars. The "fugitive pleasures" of Hollywood, as Duhamel called them, have been identified most readily as a vanguard force, winning audiences across Europe, not to mention in its colonies, while also eliciting early defenses against such foreign encroachments. As many have noted, European critics regarded American movies as potentially dangerous vehicles of cultural imperialism, tempting foreign viewers to emulate American behaviors and covet American goods. Comprising between 50 and 80 percent of the pictures shown in France in the mid and late twenties, the content of such pictures deeply troubled commentators such as André Bellessort, who deplored their ridiculous plots and "*clowneries absurdes.*" "These are the American foodstuffs on which we feed the popular imagination," he sighed.[49] Most famously, to curb these effects, officials in France, as in other European countries, inaugurated quota restrictions in 1928 to reduce the proportion of American feature films shown in French theaters.

The content of films indeed became an important source of apprehension about Americanization in Europe after the war, but only taking note of these imports without considering their social context misses the way in which such fears also stemmed from the changing dynamics of specific public spaces. Even before urban dwellers took in the plots and scenery of films, they were overwhelmed by the startling appearance of cinema façades and movie posters on the street. Designed to draw viewers into the theater, flashy marquees and advertisements met pedestrians with startling images—the threatening visage of a Wild West villain or the chilling sight of a damsel in distress. Cinemas lent the city's boulevards and avenues "an exotic note," one

Frenchman determined, and, like other novel "American" additions to Parisian life, they were hard to miss. At night, one French intellectual noted, these "innumerable" new structures opened up "great canyons of light amidst the masses of dark buildings on either side." Even the classic paean to American film by the surrealist Philippe Soupault began not with the motion picture itself but with the dissonance movie posters made with their urban surroundings. Before the cinema became a glaring presence on the Paris streets, Soupault recalled the "boredom of evenings that drew out like cigarette smoke." But then, he related, "one day we saw hanging on the walls great posters as long as serpents. . . . We imagined that we heard galloping hoofs, the roar of motors, explosions and cries of death. We rushed into the cinemas and realized immediately that everything had changed."[50]

Americans' role in promoting the cinema in the capital was far from imagined. After the war, they owned or controlled a reported three-fourths of the best class of movie houses in France. By 1927, in Paris alone these included several high-profile establishments, among them the Gaumont theaters (acquired by Metro-Goldwyn-Mayer) and the Marivaux Theater on the boulevard des Italiens (bought by United Artists). Grumblings against both French cinemas that displayed the trappings of American movie theaters and actual American-owned venues peaked in 1927, when Paramount Pictures converted the Théâtre Vaudeville at the top of the boulevard des Capucines into one of the grandest and best-equipped movie palaces in Europe. This huge monument at the heart of the city—the "insolent and luxurious Paramount," as Bellessort called it—did away with the petty financial transactions that had annoyed Americans about French *salles*, offering free telephone booths and toilets as well as bilingual ushers who did not require tipping. It also featured a mobile orchestra pit, state-of-the-art ventilation, and almost two thousand plush pink seats.[51] Better-off residents poured into such venues, and surrealists like Soupault sang the praises of American movie culture for its shock value, so creative, they thought, yet tantalizingly destructive to stale traditions. Yet for the same reason, others regarded movie palaces "as nothing short of sacrilege." Like department stores in the last decades of the nineteenth century, such mammoth institutions seemed to threaten the autonomous, authentic character of single neighborhoods. On the Champs-Elysées in particular, their influence would become overwhelming as the avenue emerged as cinema's main hub in Paris. By the end of World War II, no less than sixteen cinemas, signs ablaze, would be established on the prestigious avenue.[52]

Automobiles and car culture offered a similarly layered story about American influences in the capital that went deeper than concerns about the private enjoyment of prepackaged imports. Although motorcars had been invented decades before, the advent of the automobile in Paris dated from the 1920s, when their swelling numbers intensified residents' sense of rapid urban change. Parisians had registered only 3,800 automobiles in 1901 and 25,000 in 1914, but by 1925 this figure skyrocketed to 150,000. France remained the leading producer of automobiles in Europe throughout the decade, but American luxury vehicles—along with six-cylinder engines, lavish seat upholstery, four-speed transmissions, and new and improved shock absorbers—also began to infiltrate French markets. American production methods and advertising strategies, too, helped to revamp the industries of French automakers.[53] As proponents of Taylorism and Fordism, of new technologies and Fords, Americans were commonly blamed for the emerging car culture, even though many French Parisians also embraced it after the war. These associations, however, stemmed not simply from business methods and quantifiable consumer purchases; they also related to qualitative shifts in public life. To many, the growing ranks of motors of all kinds on the city streets signaled the invasion of an abrasive, rough-and-tumble sensibility more commonly identified with the American metropolis. Automobiles now assaulted the senses of the avenue stroller, critics charged, and undermined beloved traditions of promenading and *flânerie*. On the streets of postwar Paris, wrote one writer for the London *Observer*, the pedestrian ventured forth "in mortal terror" against the "nerve-racking noise and rush"—against "sirens that wail like a lost soul" and "horns that scream, groan, or hoot" in every "note of savagery."[54] On the Champs-Elysées, another remarked, people were "promenading for dear life." The car, many feared, would undermine local sociability. Whereas French Parisians had once strolled to after-theater suppers and other evening enjoyments, one *L'Œuvre* columnist argued, wealthy foreigners now dominated the capital's nightlife. Thus, "When he leaves the theatre or the movie the Parisian has only one idea—to find a taxi and to get home as soon as possible," he wrote.[55]

Like the automobiles with which they were associated, Americans were commonly blamed for a spreading quest for speed and increased productivity. Americans, André Bellessort noted, had injected into social relations a "*brutalité*" or "disdain for conventions" that, he contended, was not natural to French temperaments. Especially in areas like the Champs-Elysées, American customers threatened cherished routines—by demanding faster service, by promoting the abbreviated cocktail hour instead of the lingering aperitif, and, rather than adopting the protracted midday meal, by spreading the much-dreaded habit of the "quick lunch." "We want to go faster," the chronicler Charles Fegdal diagnosed as early as 1922, "we eat, we drink, we sleep . . . *en vitesse!*" Soon, in the service of convenience, Fegdal worried, nothing would be left of the city's former colorful and unexpected variety. Soon, for the sake of convenience, "like the barbarians of America," he warned, "we will number our streets and our boulevards." The present times, another writer argued in *L'Illustration*, had become so *bousculé*—"rushed" or "shaken up"—that Parisians had lost the principles that previously guided their lives. Propelled by cars, ocean liners, electricity, and other modern inventions, this undue *vitesse* instigated all sorts of pathologies and nervous disorders from insomnia to neurasthenia. Avant-garde artists such as Fernand Léger and Marcel Duchamp may have been experimenting with the sounds and artifacts of the Machine Age, but elsewhere anxieties like these multiplied. "From the time he gets out of bed the town dweller is caught up like a fly on the wheel, and when he returns at night, weary and exhausted, it is to listen to the clanging of the telephone and the babble of the radio," complained Jules Bertaut. Gone, critics like Bertaut lamented, was a prewar Paris of understated charm, a city that promoted appreciation for the finer details and simple pleasures of life, for intelligence and wit; gone, too, the ability to linger and loiter in the streets. It had all been trampled by the "infinite complications of modern life," by new urban rhythms and the general "orgy of tumult and speed" that powered thoroughfares like the Champs-Elysées. "Europe has decided to conduct her life to the tempo of the American symphony," Bertaut scowled, "and we of France have only fallen into step with all the rest."[56]

The metamorphosis of Montparnasse, that outlying destination to which Americans and other visitors began to travel in large numbers during the 1920s, was perhaps even more startling than the evolution of the Champs-Elysées. The quarter's new fame centered on the carrefour Vavin, a double intersection where the rue Vavin and the boulevard Raspail crossed the boulevard du Montparnasse. Anchored by its landmark cafés, the Rotonde, Dôme, Select, and eventually the Coupole, this quadrangle sat at the heart of the city's newest, most exciting bohemian enclave. This, however, would not be bohemia like that of the old Latin Quarter, but a flashier, commercialized version, a nexus not only for serious artists but also spectators and tourists. Here, the *Daily Herald* reporter George Slocombe recalled, a "modern mushroom colony" of nightclubs and American bars had remade the area after the war into something "as garish as Piccadilly or Broadway, hung with neon lights like a fair." Chroniclers routinely catalogued the sudden appearance of those same markers of modernity that had been the main preserve of the Right Bank: dense traffic, incandescent movie theaters, shining storefronts and restaurants, and multistoried luxury hotels. Taking stock of such evidence, many, like one British author, mourned "the coming of the hectic sophistication of the post-war Paris" to the Left Bank.[57]

As on the Right Bank, detractors often faulted Americans for these changes—for populating the quarter with poseurs and exhibitionists as well as those who came to ogle them and reducing the quarter to a tourist destination, just as bohemian Greenwich Village had become back in New York. American bars with their jazz bands, many claimed, had replaced more authentic literary cafés, and all kinds of American characters had supplanted the genuine French artists and students of prewar days. Eager to distance themselves from their fellow English-speakers, British commentators especially helped to popularize opposition to Americans' presence in the quarter. Though many visitors came to Montparnasse, they argued, the Americans seemed most intrusive, most self-aggrandizing. They were loud talkers. In the late morning, "you shall see them publicly eating grapefruit and grape-nuts on the café terraces. You shall hear them publicly talking," Sisley Huddleston complained; "In the afternoons they bring up their reinforcements, and in the evenings they are surely as numerous as the army of General Pershing." Of course, many Americans in Paris were discreet travelers and others hardworking, upstanding residents, but critics focused instead on their drunkest, most brazen compatriots, those who shouted and smoked and danced in the middle of the street, obnoxious American people, as one onlooker said, constantly "whirling round in taxicabs or private cars, whooping and waving."[58]

The carrefour Vavin, where Americans and others came to whoop and wave, had first gained its status as a prominent junction in 1911 with the completion of the boulevard Raspail, setting the stage for the remarkable development of this once remote and peaceful neighborhood south of the city center. At the beginning of the century Montparnasse did not yet constitute a destination of note. Its bottom half—with grazing prairies, fields of wheat, and stables—remained surprisingly agrarian. Its top half—distinguished by religious establishments with walled gardens, private schools, and a cluster of taverns on the rue de la Gaîté—was the territory of artisans, bourgeois families, and a sprinkling of artists and Sorbonne professors. Even into the early twenties, visitors to the region delighted in its village atmosphere. In those days, the Dôme was only an unassuming workmen's corner bistro with no outside seating, the Rotonde only a modest *zinc*. On the corner of the rue Vavin sat a furniture shop and across the street a coal-and-wood yard—the Select and the Coupole did not yet exist. But in 1923 the proprietor of the Dôme quadrupled the size of his property, signaling the commercialization that would rapidly overtake the area in the mid-twenties. The following year, his competitor at the Rotonde, too, "succumbed to the lure of the plush seat and the clean fingernail," as one patron put it, beginning renovations that would transform the old Bolshevik hideout into a sprawling café with a dance hall, upstairs banquet room, and ample gallery wall space.[59]

In the wake of these developments, elegies not just for a bygone carrefour Vavin but for an entire studious Left Bank multiplied.[60] The terraces of the new Montparnasse cafés showcased what seemed to many an almost absurdly cosmopolitan milieu, a "higgledy-piggledy confusion," in Huddleston's words.[61] The arrangement of long-haired or pointy-bearded Scandinavian poets, self-styled flappers from Iowa or the French countryside, and Asian artists in berets offered a parody of the international clientele that peopled the more esteemed "Tout-Paris" establishments on the Right Bank. The parade of aggressive women, the "motley assortment of races," and the "perpetual cosmopolitan carnival" that was postwar Montparnasse horrified conservatives like Jules Bertaut.[62] Reactionaries decried the so-called degeneracy spawned by the area's experimental art, and they scorned the endless patter at the cafés—the *"Babel montparnassienne."* Especially after the late twenties, when Camille Mauclair wrote a series of articles about the role of Jews and other foreigners in French art for *Le Figaro* and *L'Ami du Peuple*, theories about the Americanization of Montparnasse began to dovetail with increasingly vocal kinds of racism and antisemitism. Montparnasse harbored "the filth of Paris," Mauclair blustered, and he urged the police to raid it.[63] A few years later, a writer for another conservative newspaper found nothing more awful to contemplate on a Montparnasse terrace, as at a café on the boulevards, than the "horrible mélange of people with strange faces," with their "hooked noses" or "hair too black," their skin too copper or too pasty. Such hostility to the Left Bank's bohemia underscored the degree to which, in popular French parlance, the concept of cosmopolitanism had taken on a distinctly negative, debasing cast deriving from its decades-old association with Jewishness as well as from newer, pejorative connotations similar to mongrelization in the United States. Conspicuous visitors who inundated a district like Montparnasse, one writer warned, threatened to transform it into *"un banal quartier cosmopolite* where it does not do well to be French." If the situation spread, *Le Petit Parisien* similarly predicted, all of France risked becoming "a nation *banalisé, internationalisé."*[64]

Before long, the "France that was France" and "Paris the Gay City" will have "faded into a mere memory," cautioned the British journalist George Slocombe, replaced by "a new chemical landscape of jazz bars and jazz cars and by a terrifying fresco of sky-signs and moving electric fingers pointing to

When they die, good Americans, it was often said, go to Paris. The tabloid illustrator Pem pictures such an afterlife in "American-Style Piety." Helping to draw a distinction between American and French ways of life, Pem depicted Americans not as they were at home but as they appeared to be in the French capital—overdressed in evening finery, stirred up by jazz and alcohol despite their pious pretenses, and averting troubles abroad, thanks to "beware of pickpockets" and "lavatory" signs posted at the bottom left. *Fantasio*, September 1, 1925.

the end of an epoch."[65] Replete with new signs and new people, such an electrified landscape, less and less dependent on the French language, had made the city appear more accessible and hospitable to Americans and other visitors. Yet for Parisians and others skeptical of the new manners and morals, modern quarters like Montparnasse promoted an unsettling juxtaposition of people, which threatened to overturn the social order. Focusing on those four quarters of Paris most transformed since the war, urban writers reconceived the postwar city in concrete and provocative ways for their Parisian readers. Americanness proved one particularly effective concept for framing discussions about changes besetting the metropolis, changes denounced by those who wished Paris could return to prewar tempos, by those suspicious of newcomers and resentful of the liberties some were taking in the most celebrated corners of the capital.

Helping to mobilize an informal campaign against the perceived American invasion, journalists, chroniclers, and preservationists argued that American tastes and habits imperiled French tradition in ways both subtle and profound. To protect French values, therefore, Parisians repeatedly contrasted their own urban practices with those of their transatlantic guests. The very ways in which individuals moved through and perceived the modern city, they suggested, were determined by nationality. Americans, many claimed, had journeyed all the way across the ocean to "see Paris," and yet, for all their reliance on visual cues to get them around town, they remained practically blind when it came to discerning the capital's deeper complexities. Travel to the city, one Frenchman proposed, had "sealed [Americans'] eyes with impenetrable spectacles."[66] Visitors saw "nothing but a vibrant façade, a painted mask," agreed another; they discovered nothing of the subtle rhythms of the capital. Newcomers, weighed down by guidebooks and overly ambitious itineraries, slighted the treasures of Paris by visiting them *"en étranger,"* echoed Charles Fegdal. Instead, Fegdal advocated more discerning forays through the city's spaces—visiting them, in other words, *"en Parisien."* Ways of seeing, like ways of moving through the streets, separated the natives from the interlopers, André Warnod similarly imagined. Sneering at the "optical gluttons" who had invaded postwar Paris—indiscriminate creatures sated by any and all public scenes—Warnod declared, "We prefer the gourmet." With "only his imagination for a guide," this inveterate city-goer moved selectively and patiently through the streets. To Warnod, these antithetical approaches to urban life clearly corresponded to opposing national cultures. The gourmet, of course, was the quintessential French *flâneur.* To move about the city like an optical glutton, Warnod explained, was to *"flâner à l'américaine."*[67]

Like its inhabitants and visitors, the city itself seemed to promote two competing ways of life after the war. Grappling with the growing dissimilarity between those quarters deemed most modern and cosmopolitan and the capital's other, more modest and traditional enclaves, commentators frequently remarked that Paris was in fact two separate cities: one *étrangère,* guided by mindlessness, hedonism, materialism, and *américanisme,* and the other healthy, quiet, sensible, French. "There are two distinct Parises," one sojourner put it plainly, "the Paris of the Parisian and the Paris of the strangers." With mounting emotion, residents romanticized a prewar capital of grace, charm, good humor, and good taste that had supposedly existed before the onslaught of tourists, before conversation and clever repartee, as one said, had been consigned to the status of lost arts, and before eloquent talk had been trampled over by inelegant dancing.[68]

To combat these offensive intrusions and to shore up the values they deemed most French or Parisian, many of the capital's residents began to trumpet wit and conversation, exactly those things off-limits to non-French-speakers, as counterweights to the foreign and nonverbal languages that had eased outsiders into the social life of the city. French itself signified for some a defiant, local authenticity—a form of linguistic subversion acted out most obviously by patriotic shopkeepers who took to hanging sarcastic *"Ici on parle français"* notices in their store windows. The *café-concert*, surviving on the fringes of Paris's new nightlife, served as another particularly strong bastion of French resistance. Laden with slang, puns, and fast-paced humor, *caf'conc'* performances were an antidote to the superficial splendors of the music halls, and they would have been incomprehensible to many of those who filled the audiences of the Folies Bergère or the Casino de Paris. Here, jokes spun on current events and came at the expense of politicians, celebrities, and, most of all, foreigners.[69]

Neighborhood groups, too, inspired by the Free Commune of Montmartre, launched their rebellions. Reacting to the arrival of American expatriate writers and artists, who also wanted to escape the crowds in Montparnasse, residents of the quaint Ile Saint-Louis proclaimed their independence in 1924, threatening to appeal to the League of Nations to restrict American immigration to their tranquil island in the Seine. "Treacherous Paris" had sold their quarter to Americans, they charged, who corrupted the local cost of living with their dollars and monopolized the best restaurants and cafés, where "American" had become the de facto language.[70] For such renegades, theorizing a real Paris that stood in opposition to an American one helped to build a textured portrait of what Frenchness in the new century might look like. Juxtaposed against the behavior of visitors from across the Atlantic, what it meant to be a true Parisian became all the clearer. Americans might have been wooed by the glaring, wailing Paris of Montmartre, Montparnasse, the Opera district, and the Champs-Elysées, but to the Frenchman who moved about in his "real Paris," one writer ventured, the "only lights that matter are those that shine on the pavement outside his own favorite brasserie."[71]

Pinpointing the "real Paris" may have seemed straightforward to those who championed "French" ways of living in it, but ironies in fact riddled this kind of national thinking. As much as writers liked to think so, what it meant to be "French" was no more static or fully formed as a concept than what it meant to be American. Not unlike the United States, France encompassed a patchwork of different social worlds in the early twentieth century. Continuing to guard their own dialects, customs, and histories, the residents of outlying provinces were only just beginning to be pulled into the national fold through republican education, war, and other unifying forces. Even in the heart of Paris, defining what was French remained an ongoing project, labored over by intellectuals, advertised incessantly by international expositions, and indoctrinated through popular literature. Like early-twentieth-century Americans, French people wrestled over "modern" and "traditional" visions for the nation and its capital.[72] Oftentimes, the practices of Paris's residents contradicted the pronouncements of its traditionalist critics. For all the harangues against the crass urbanism of Americans, many French Parisians, too, avidly patronized those stores with their neon lights, the cinemas, and the grand resorts. Indeed, despite claims that Frenchmen appreciated the city's modest pleasures most, Parisians had been world leaders in urban sophistication. It was Americans who had often been the followers. Back in American cities, department stores, cabarets, and other venues had adopted Parisian names, menus, and revues, using the gloss of French commercial culture to make their institutions seem more upscale and appealing to those middle classes only beginning to embrace urban nightlife.[73] In the United States, French culture helped to legitimate those styles and activities that would come to seem classically American.

In France, however, those who wanted to envision their cultural heritage as something more properly grounded in rural, time-tested values had to obscure France's leading role in all these technological and commercial innovations, repackaging them in effect as American imports. This involved considerable selective remembrance. After all, going back to the establishment of those arcades that captivated Baudelaire, it had been Paris that gave birth to the art of everyday urban spectacle. Automobiles, department stores, advertising posters, and more had all in fact been pioneered in Paris. The Lumière brothers staged the first public viewing of moving pictures in Paris in 1895, and until World War I, French filmmakers produced more movies than anyone else in the world, inundating markets across the United States. The movies had to be domesticated by Hollywood studio executives and reformers in the United States before they could be imagined as indomitable agents of American civilization.[74] Neon tube lighting—identified so definitively with the American cityscape after the war—had actually been invented by a Frenchman, too. He exhibited his first neon sign in Paris in 1910 before exporting replicas to the United States in the early twenties.

Even Josephine Baker's Revue Nègre was not simply an American invention. The cast had come from the United States, but their routines were judged too tame and precise. A French producer reworked the entire show during rehearsals, enlarging the role that would make Baker a star.[75] Identifying the components of an ascendant American culture, therefore, did not simply involve a process of locating signs of an invasion. More precisely, it required a process of disavowing traditions that might otherwise be seen as quintessentially French. Making Frenchness and making Americanness were to be in the early twentieth century by-products of each other, and thinking in terms of exports and imports does not do justice to the processes by which such national definitions and identifications were made.

The 1920s marked a turning point in Franco-American relations. In 1919, many would still have agreed with the Frenchman who spoke of "a spiritual bond" between two sister republics "both motivated by the same divine rage for liberty." But only a few years later, the French official André Tardieu captured public sentiments better when he concluded that between these nations, "there is no common measure and no common political language." Differences between Americans and the French seemed increasingly irreconcilable—and increasingly liable to spill over into small but ugly incidents. When American rugby players scored an upset win over France during the 1924 Paris Olympics, for example, crowds stormed the field and chased the winning team out of the stadium.[76]

Such popular disillusionments—what might be called "anti-Americanism"—did not arise solely out of economic and diplomatic disagreements, although surely these were never far from mind. They also grew out of debates about the intersection of local and international affairs as they played out in the daily life of the capital. Anger directed towards Americans should not be dismissed, as it often is, as simply a rhetorical strategy for domestic squabbles between different French factions or as wild searching for convenient scapegoats. Americans clearly played a prominent role in the capital's postwar transformation. But at the same time, developments identified as forms of Americanization should not be thought of simply as the work of unilateral American actions. In interwar Paris, they derived from a complicated interplay of motives and activities by both residents and visitors. From the vantage point of a boulevard café terrace, or from the window of a taxicab approaching Montparnasse or Montmartre, the specter of Americanization did not appear as the work of abstract forces, sweeping indiscriminately across the entire metropolis. The presence of American people had an uneven, cumulative effect, inflecting some neighborhoods more than others. On this urban terrain, where the smallest details might be invested with enormous import, the way a toilet flushed or a drink was poured became emblematic of the difference of civilizations. And as visitors and residents leapfrogged from place to place in search of the capital's cosmopolitan side, some of what it meant to be American or what it meant to be French was created in the process.

No distant phenomenon, then, "America" was something encountered on the ground in the French capital after World War I. Important not merely for prefiguring later, more famous campaigns against Americanization, these early protests helped to shape definitions of American culture at that time—not least because so much of the discussion would be translated and excerpted for American readers back in the United States. Parisians helped to highlight the urban, commercial, and cosmopolitan aspects of postwar American culture as those elements which would most define the United States in the new century. Since critics employed a flexible, expansive sense of national character, many things in interwar Paris would be attributed to American influence even if their origins proved more complicated. Importantly, what would be construed as American was not only decided by products and policies created in the United States and then sent abroad. It was also determined by what came to be seen as distinctively American through processes of exchange and conflict with others at the edges of national life. As demonstrated by the ways in which different urban cues, no matter what their origin, became associated with foreigners from across the Atlantic, postwar Paris showcased not only the importation of Americanness, but also the creation of Americanness on-site.

Neighborhood groups had been galvanized and the ticker tape sign came down, but by the late twenties, preservationist efforts and publicity stunts still seemed outmatched by changes coded as American. All this talk, pitting Americans and Europeans against each other between the wars, pointed to the development of a growing nexus of political engagements, however strained. Americans would continue to be targets. Along with writers, humorists, and policymakers, others soon reacted just as symbolically, but not always as peacefully, to the liberal, capitalist, and cosmopolitan "American" world imagined at the city's core. From the outer leftist suburbs and from the ranks of authoritarian officials on the inside, many would soon challenge Americans' place in the capital in order to boost a variety of political aspirations. There would be action in the streets of Paris as well as words.

PART II │ Parisian Cultural
Politics

*Sous son sacrifice à la révolution grouillait un monde de profondeurs . . .*
—André Malraux, *La condition humaine*

| The Sacco-Vanzetti Riots

B Y THE MID AND LATE 1920s, the particular neighborhoods and businesses Americans frequented in Paris had become common knowledge. That Americans put their stamp on certain quarters of the city was taken for granted. Theories about this perceived Americanization would do more than supply fodder for urban chroniclers. They also provided loose ideological underpinnings for aggressive political actions forged in the city's streets. As revealed in the debates of preservationists, journalists, and others, this budding form of anti-Americanism did not correspond to a blanket, pathological hate for all things American but served instead as a flexible framework used to evoke a cluster of grievances. Its strength was its malleability. At the same time, however, so-called anti-Americanism would not be endlessly adaptable in Paris. It proved particularly amenable to campaigns pitched against the cosmopolitanism, capitalism, and liberalism embodied by the city center. Thus, those who would make the most of it between the wars—propelling such sentiments beyond the newspaper columns and municipal meetings out into the city's boulevards and squares—did so from the extreme ends of the political spectrum. For leftists, the cause that most opened up possibilities for using anti-American tactics was the Sacco-Vanzetti affair, a drama that consumed the attention of Paris activists for much of the 1920s and culminated on August 23, 1927, in widespread rioting.

That night, just after 10 P.M., one of the capital's commissioners telegrammed to police headquarters that people were building barricades at the intersection of the rue Réaumur and the boulevard Sébastopol. Less than an hour before, thousands of angry demonstrators had swarmed the area, erecting a blockade to stave off a phalanx of mounted policemen. Onto uprooted trees and an overturned cart, rioters piled materials pilfered from local businesses, iron grilles ripped up from sidewalk planters, and sacks of plaster stolen from a nearby construction site. From the shelter of this makeshift fortification, rebels let fly various projectiles in the direction of arriving authorities. The forces of order charged the barricades as stragglers holed up in sidewalk cafés pelted men in uniforms with a hailstorm of saucers and glasses. "What happened at the Réaumur-Sébastopol intersection," as one police report described it, constituted "a genuine pitched battle."[1]

That night disturbances like this one flared up across central Paris in what an officer charged with the retrospective inquest classified as "an evening tumultuous and eventful to the point of excess." Protesters ran through the streets across the Right Bank, smashing kiosks and slinging lampposts through glass storefronts, destroying display cases in confectioners, haberdasheries, and stationers. They raided Potin's grocery emporium and carried off shoes and clothing from looted shops. In particular, rioters set out to taunt Americans. By the Opera, despite careful police countermeasures, about one hundred people managed to congregate in front of the Café de la Paix, a spot always popular with Americans, screaming threats and insults. Not far north of there, a crowd staged a similar demonstration upon the debarkation of a boat train at the Gare Saint-Lazare, principal depot for Americans coming from Atlantic ocean liners.[2]

This turmoil broke following the announcement that at Charlestown Prison in Massachusetts, Bartolomeo Vanzetti and Nicola Sacco had been put to death in the electric chair. More than seven years before, police had charged Sacco and Vanzetti with the murder of a guard and paymaster during an April 1920 shoe factory robbery in South Braintree. Found guilty in July 1921, the two languished in jail for years, suffering numerous failed appeals before receiving death sentences. A shoemaker and a fish peddler, both men had immigrated to the United States from Italy in 1908. Faced with the strains of working-class life in the immigrant ghettos of New England's factory towns, each seized upon the offensive strategies of anarchist activism. As foreigners, extreme radicals, and reputed draft dodgers who spent the war in Mexico, they stood as prime examples of those who became targets of government and public backlash in the reactionary postwar period.[3]

People around the world, however, had been riveted by their plight. Many who followed the case questioned their guilt; even more doubted the fairness of the court proceedings, steeped as they were in an atmosphere of popular hysteria and steered by a prosecutor and judge openly prejudiced against the defendants' anarchist politics and Italian background. As the executions neared, a chorus of disapproval spread across borders and oceans, gripping cities and towns from Moscow to Milwaukee. There had been parades in Sydney and Mexico City, rallies in Pittsburgh and Paris. General strikes brought factories and mines, presses and public transportation, to temporary standstills from New York City to Montevideo, Uruguay. Crowds thickened around speakers in Hyde Park in London and orators who preached in a half dozen languages from their soapboxes in Chicago and Philadelphia. There were meetings in Stockholm and boycotts in Amsterdam. In Buenos Aires, prisoners staged a hunger strike from their jail cells—a gesture of solidarity with the two men. Brawls erupted over the case in the labor-oriented port cities of Le Havre and Marseilles. Demonstrators burned American flags in the colonial entrepôts Casablanca and Johannesburg. In Italian villages, underground networks smuggled pamphlets and letters about the affair past Mussolini's officials. Leaflets picturing Sacco and Vanzetti and calling for the downfall of American institutions littered the international quarter of Shanghai. Hours before the scheduled executions, one protester was killed in a clash with the police in Geneva, headquarters for the League of Nations. That same day, workmen scrolled a last-ditch plea in yard-high letters across the front of a building in central Berlin: "America's Christian murderous dollar justice is tonight murdering Sacco and Vanzetti. We raise our voice before God and mankind. Men, pause and think in this last hour."[4]

Nevertheless, after several delays—and all the false hopes that came with them—Sacco and Vanzetti were electrocuted just after midnight on August 23, 1927. When the two men died, the most logical place to expect unrest would have been Boston or New York, so close to the crime and subsequent courtroom dramas. Yet it was Paris where the most serious incidents of rioting took place. When news of the executions reached the French capital, leftist newspapers announced plans for demonstrations along the boulevards and near the American embassy. That night, peaceful gatherings degenerated into chaos and fighting when police forcibly dispersed the crowds. As participants scattered, smaller bands of agitators fanned out from the original points of demonstration. For more than three hours, rioters did battle with the authorities and bystanders from the avenue des Champs-Elysées to squares at the foot of Montmartre. Under the direction of the Police Prefect Jean Chiappe, an army of *gardiens de la paix* and mounted republican guards set out to restore order. Police arrested more than two hundred people and assaulted countless others. More than two hundred policemen were bludgeoned or stabbed in the melees. Morning light revealed a landscape strewn with broken glass and marble debris. All told, the turbulence that night posed one of the most serious threats to political stability in the capital since the Commune in 1871.

Its gravity would not be surpassed until the street violence that brought the city uncomfortably close to revolution in February 1934.[5]

An American named Edward Newton visiting Paris during the Sacco-Vanzetti affair marveled at how "a few agitators got the French so stirred up over the execution of two Italian murderers that one might have supposed that a group of French angels were being done to death by a mob of devils." What did the rifling of Paris shops and cafés, Newton wondered, have to do with the execution of two Italians in the United States?[6] One might argue, very little. Those caught up in the scenes on the boulevards included not only political militants but also unsuspecting locals, imprudent curiosity seekers, thieves, and teenage vandals. Even Paul Faure, Secretary of the Socialist Party, whose members had participated in the demonstrations, criticized the night's events as bereft of substantive meaning. He denounced the incidents as "impulsive gestures of a crowd without direction, left to its own devices, unthinking, capable of savage and cruel acts." Revolution was not made, Faure insisted, by stealing shoes or bursting car tires.[7]

The riots were indeed impulsive, as riots by definition are. Most likely, protesters did not steal shoes as a clever reference to how the scandal began with the robbery of a shoe factory but because they needed or wanted shoes. Still, scenes of unrest did not lack interpretable logic. Conflict over control of the city streets that night illustrated the interplay between the general spirit of the Sacco-Vanzetti campaign—the idea that it was an occasion for international working-class solidarity—and the more specific issues for which it became a vehicle in Paris. Leftists had wanted to dramatize their participation in the worldwide event presented by the case, but police barred them from demonstrating within the city's walls. As they defied those bans to protest the fate of Sacco and Vanzetti, rioters drew on local popular prejudices and cultural associations to stake their claims to the city center. In particular, Sacco-Vanzetti protesters tapped into widespread resentments against the conspicuous role of Americans in the postwar capital. To them, police hindrance combined with Americans' growing presence underscored the ways in which large, abstract questions about international power played out in local terms.

Such "anti-American" dimensions to the Sacco-Vanzetti affair illuminated how, for the far left, culturally nationalist sensibilities began to overlay traditional, economic orientations. In Paris, the Sacco-Vanzetti campaign not only grew out of and represented a last gasp of older forms of class politics, it also served as a turning point for activists who used the campaign to experiment with new types of cultural politics attuned to the particular challenges of the interwar period. A foundational moment for the anti-American passions that would become a staple of leftist protest, the Sacco-Vanzetti affair emerged as a key lens though which Americans' place in the early-twentieth-century world would be understood and defined.

Although American visitors often neglected searching inquiries into the political climate of the French capital in favor of lighter forays into its worlds of pleasure, the state of Parisian politics merited their attention. Turmoil in France may not have been as acute during the twenties as it had become in other former belligerent countries, but that did not lessen the sense of shock and fear wrought by the war and its aftermath. Like Americans, Parisians yearned for a return to an imagined normalcy. A widespread call for a resurrected prewar order—the *rappel à l'ordre*—bolstered all kinds of draconian impulses. Pushing against these urges, leftist radicals warred with their enemies and each other, growing more brazen in their claims and tactics. By 1924 they were winning impressive results in the local elections of greater Paris, forging Socialist and Communist strongholds in the Red Belt suburbs. At the same time, the forces of law and order built up their strength in the city center. The capital's Municipal Council, stocked with reactionaries, set the tone of politics at the heart of Paris.

Between the wars, French national governments rose and fell with alarming rapidity, proving incapable of mediating between class interests, lighting on an effective monetary policy, or winning concessions from crucial allies abroad. Such inefficacy badly eroded popular support for republican institutions. Mudslinging Communists and other militants spared no love for the compromises necessary to build coalitions in the Chamber of Deputies. Large segments of the French right, for their part, remained ambivalent at best about the reigning political system. Royalists, right-wing Catholics, self-styled fascists, and others radicalized by the war and leftist advances loudly assailed the Third Republic's secular, democratic aims. Moreover, members of the centrist Radical Party, incensed by the effrontery of communists and politicized foreigners, routinely traded their commitment to democratic rights for collaboration with the city's powerful police force and the far-right members of the Municipal Council. The capital's extensive collection of political daily newspapers, buzzing with confrontational language, reinforced these animosities. The threat of violence between the police and left-wing demonstrators seemed ever present.[8]

Beginning in 1921, the Sacco-Vanzetti affair emerged as a key conduit for the capital's radical politics. Even before most Americans had heard of Sacco and Vanzetti, residents of Paris and its suburbs joined the vanguard of those opposing the convictions. The editors of *Le Libertaire*, the main anarchist newspaper in Paris, were among the first to break news of the case in Europe in August 1921. French communists, too, rallied early to the cause. From Moscow that October, the Comintern's Executive Committee (ECCI) recognized the two men's incarceration as a chance to consolidate its power over a loose network of national parties, broadcasting appeals for followers to organize massive strikes—to fight the death sentences, which showed "that in 'civilized America' proletarian revolutionaries share the benefits of only one technical innovation, the electric chair." After the ECCI's directive, communists in Paris cofounded with anarchists a Comité d'Action to arouse workers' contempt for the "odious class justice of American capitalism," promoting local demonstrations through a barrage of posters and handbills. Meetings in and around the capital grew intense. During a gathering at the Salle Wagram, a grenade exploded, injuring a policeman. That same month, a bomb disguised as a gift box of perfume went off in the Paris home of American Ambassador Myron T. Herrick, catapulting the case to international headlines for the first time. The device, sent by an anarchist Sacco-Vanzetti supporter, inaugurated a series of explosions that autumn, damaging U.S. embassies in Lisbon and Rio de Janeiro and consulates in Zurich and Marseilles—the first of the waves of direct action protest that would arrive on the doorsteps of American diplomats in coming years.[9] The bomb targeting Herrick and its aftermath elevated the case back in the United States to a first-rate scandal and foreshadowed the importance the affair would have in Paris over the coming years.

The Sacco-Vanzetti campaign originated with the elaborate working-class, radical networks that had flourished across the Atlantic world since the second half of the nineteenth century. Connections forged by anarchists, socialists, syndicalists, and Italian migrants, joined by members of newly established Communist parties, drew activists in the United States, Latin America, and Europe early into the cause.[10] In locations where these different networks intersected, the case became particularly resonant—in places like New York, Chicago, and Boston, with their large immigrant working classes and established socialist traditions; in Latin American cities such as Buenos Aires and Rio de Janeiro, with their prominent Italian populations and active anarchist circles; and in European centers from London to Leipzig, where communists and other leftists worked doggedly to gain more ground. Individuals across the continents saw in the drama something of their own predicaments. Anarchists, hated and feared in so many communities, regarded Sacco and Vanzetti as comrades in arms, fellow victims of political intolerance whose ideals had been misconstrued. Italians across Europe and the Americas—of widely divergent political affinities—identified with the two men as *paisani*. Devotees of the fledgling Communist parties viewed the prisoners as casualties of a brewing class war, proletarian martyrs whose suffering would rally other oppressed peoples to the cause of revolution. Laborers and humanitarians of varying beliefs and nationalities saw the situation as simple and yet profound. They bemoaned the plight of two men who had been torn away from their families and subjected to the mental torture of years spent in jail awaiting death, men they imagined as subject to a "frame-up" by officials of unbending minds with more resources than they themselves might ever possess.

Paris was rich with all of these radical and working-class subcultures, making it a particularly fertile ground for the Sacco-Vanzetti campaign. Since the 1880s, the capital had been headquarters for French *libertaires* and anarchist exiles from elsewhere. In Montmartre's out-of-the-way bistros and other hideouts, members of a growing anarchist movement easily tapped into international currents and controversies. The city also hosted influential labor associations, most notably the Confédération Générale du Travail (CGT), a broad-based syndicalist union established in 1895, and the Section Française de l'Internationale Ouvrière (SFIO), which in 1905 brought socialist factions together into one increasingly successful constitutional party. Although membership for such organizations fluctuated wildly after World War I, the proliferation of factory work in the Paris region increased the capital's status as a magnet for industrial laborers and activists. At the same time, Italians emerged as the most numerous group of foreigners pouring into the capital and also one of the most politically outspoken—a further boost to the local Sacco-Vanzetti campaign. Forming their own community cooperatives, Italians in Paris also joined French political organizations, notably communist-aligned labor unions and the Italian-language wing of the French Communist Party (PCF). Parisian communists in general would exploit the case more effectively than many of their counterparts elsewhere, not least because the capital and its suburbs had been the undisputed center of French communism since the founding of the PCF in December 1920. The Paris region housed a substantial portion of the nation's party members, as well as those belonging to affiliated groups such as the Secours Rouge, the Jeunesses Communistes, the Association Républicaine des Anciens Combattants (ARAC), and the unions of the Confédération Générale du Travail Unitaire (CGTU).[11]

Tellingly, such workers and radicals—French and foreign-born—filled the ranks of Sacco-Vanzetti protests, and, eventually, the rosters of riot arrests. Those detained by the police would be predominantly male and young, between the ages of eighteen and twenty-eight. Police identified more than twenty of those arrested during the riots as active syndicalists, and even those whose political affiliations remained unclear earned their livings overwhelmingly by working-class jobs, among them many skilled manual craftsmen, including masons, builders, and mechanics. There were wage earners, too, from the semiskilled positions along the assembly lines of factories like Renault and Citroën: molders and turners and fitters of sheet metal and glass. Several practitioners of traditional *petits métiers*, including a mattress maker, a ragpicker, and a newspaper hawker along with a few homeless and unemployed individuals, also faced charges. Perhaps significantly in light of the rioters' hostility towards sites associated with American visitors, many of those arrested worked in the bottom rungs of those burgeoning industries of leisure and tourism, including several cooks, waiters, taxi drivers, and chauffeurs. Of 113 detainees whose nationality could be established, twenty-one hailed from foreign countries: one each from Romania, Portugal, Switzerland, the Netherlands, and Hungary; two each from Spain, Poland, and the United States; and ten—or almost half—from Italy. More than three-fourths of the forty-two people arrested during the riots whose political affiliations could be established were believed by police to have communist connections.[12]

Back in Boston, the Sacco-Vanzetti Defense Committee, tasked with spearheading the two men's legal defense, aspired to tap all this interest in the prisoners' fate mounting in Paris and other places overseas. Below posters in German, Italian, and Spanish, multilingual volunteers in the Committee's offices fielded telephone calls and written inquiries about the case from Latin America, Europe, and beyond. The Boston Committee had originated with the efforts of local anarchist immigrants, many of them acquaintances of Sacco and Vanzetti, including the Spanish cabinetmaker Frank Lopez and the Italian printer Aldino Felicani, and it would be through their personal correspondence and contacts abroad, along with those of lawyer Fred Moore and friend Carlo Tresca, that the defense would find some of its earliest and staunchest supporters.[13]

All of this overseas action, not least in Paris, would be vital to sustaining the campaign at the start, especially since forging a radical movement proved so incredibly difficult in the early 1920s. Internal divisions—differences of language, occupation, religion, ethnicity, and race as well as competing philosophies—constantly pushed against ideals of international solidarity and the efficacy of trade unions and other groups trying to mobilize their members. Beyond these persistent centrifugal forces, World War I dealt a particular blow to the radical left and transformed the conditions under which Sacco-Vanzetti supporters would eventually have to work. Leading Socialist parties, most notably those of France and Germany, along with the Labour Party in Britain, sacrificed long-held internationalist principles for nationalist alliances in hopes that they would translate into postwar rewards. American socialists' decision to oppose the war proved even more disastrous once the United States entered the conflict in 1917 and such a stance began to draw ire from a mobilized public. The war temporarily severed all kinds of vital communication networks, reducing transatlantic traffic to a crawl and blocking dialogue between those who found themselves on opposite sides of the trenches. The Bolshevik Revolution in October 1917 compounded such wartime disruptions. On one hand, the success of the Bolsheviks signaled new revolutionary possibilities, appearing to supporters across Europe and beyond as the overdue chance to make socialism a living reality. The Bolsheviks' victory in Russia, however, also forced a painful cleavage on the socialist left. In coming years, communist cells would eat into the organizations and campaigns of the noncommunist left. At the same time, the Bolshevik Revolution elicited an enormous reaction from moderates and conservatives, and activists of all kinds would share the brunt of this backlash. In the years immediately after the war, leftists faced unprecedented levels of censorship, incarceration, deportation, and vigilante attacks even in places with long-standing democratic traditions—not least in France and the United States.[14] As much as Sacco-Vanzetti protesters depended on well-established international networks, they also found themselves in the postwar period traversing a new landscape of radical politics.

These new realities sharply constrained the Sacco-Vanzetti campaign. From their shabby Boston headquarters, Defense Committee members struggled in the early twenties to drum up interest beyond their own immigrant, working-class circles in New England and New York. Boston liberals did contribute early to the campaign, and *The Nation* and *The New Republic* mentioned it in the initial months, but this alone could not elevate one particular cause above the many other contemporaneous arrests, deportations, and civil liberties violations that competed for public attention. During the January 1920 Palmer Raids, just months before Sacco and Vanzetti were detained, authorities arrested eight hundred people in New England alone for charges related to their radical activities. Those who knew about the case in its earliest stages therefore imagined it as little more than a typical Red Scare injustice. Broad support from liberals—so often foregrounded in histories of the campaign—would really only appear much later, and the Boston Committee knew all too well that sustaining their fight depended on the generosity of rank-and-file laborers. Donations to the defense reflected the modest means of early allies, averaging between ten cents and twenty-five dollars. Beset by their own struggles in the antilabor climate after 1919, however, common workers could only do so much. Hard-pressed striking miners and others wrote to the Committee, apologizing that they could not scrape together more funds.[15]

Facing Red Scare opposition themselves, and preoccupied with their own institution building and internal squabbling, communists, too, at first equivocated when asked to join the cause. Historians often credit the Comintern as the prime mover for worldwide agitation on behalf of Sacco and Vanzetti and imagine communist networks as the main international link for American leftists in the interwar period. Yet communists did not dominate this affair as they would the Scottsboro campaign. In the United States, their involvement proved belated and sporadic. Even though the case was "as old as the Party itself," Comintern informants admitted, during its early years "contact of the Party with it was very meagre."[16] In other parts of the world, communist prominence in the campaign also varied. In Latin America, syndicalists and anarchists more effectively mobilized followers. In Europe, the Comintern's main propaganda expert, Willi Münzenberg, failed to wage a centralized campaign, focusing instead on other now-forgotten controversies. Thus, with few funds arriving from prominent Americans or through the Comintern, the case at first seemed destined to unfold as the Haymarket tragedy had—a powerful moment for anarchists and their closest allies but with limited response from others. Already by the summer of 1922, the Boston Committee was bouncing checks.[17]

As evidenced by early successes abroad and difficulties at home, the campaign to save Sacco and Vanzetti did not simply spread outward from the United States to unsuspecting cities overseas, as U.S. State Department officials would be inclined to see it. The movement actually tacked back and forth between organizers in Boston and others overseas. Indeed, the Boston Committee recognized the task of looking for supporters abroad, where agitation often outpaced that in the United States, not as a supplementary endeavor but as a vital lifeline. While organizers in Boston struggled to expand their North American support networks, making inroads first into the Midwest and southern Canada, protesters in Latin America and Europe staged significant demonstrations for the two men. Substantial activities like those in Paris were under way in many parts of Europe by autumn 1921, despite the failure of the mainstream American press to highlight any actions other than the horrific bombings.[18] News of protests abroad, however, did galvanize workers in the United States. From the garment trades in New York to the West Coast divisions of the IWW, in their last burst of fire, union locals sponsored grassroots meetings and fundraisers, preempting or even contradicting the official positions of union leaders who generally limited their support to periodic formal resolutions. Scattered crowds around the country expressed their desire to be a part of the international movement: "We, citizens in mass meeting assembled in the city hall of

Minneapolis," one characteristic declaration began, "join in the world wide protest." Communist operatives reported back to Moscow: "For the first time the American working class has been part of an international working-class protest movement"; they had been "internationalised by the struggles of their fellow-workers in other lands."[19]

In communities across the Atlantic world, anarchists and other radicals started defense committees like the one in Boston, translating the stream of dispatches from New England into local actions that raised wider awareness about the case. In Paris, after joint actions with communists fell apart, anarchists formed the Comité Sacco-Vanzetti, a crucial mediator between the Defense Committee of Boston and the liberal and working-class public of the French capital in coming years. Under the leadership of Louis Lecoin, no stranger to political imprisonment himself, the Comité launched a determined petition campaign in 1926. "We stopped passers-by," Lecoin remembered, "we went to residences, we deposited lists to sign in union headquarters, newspaper offices, at shopkeeper's places." Paris anarchists even arranged for automobiles strapped with giant placards bearing inscriptions in favor of Sacco and Vanzetti to circle the city.[20] Overseas Sacco-Vanzetti committees, such as the one in Paris, helped make the controversy something more than Haymarket had been.

American historians most often take note of the Sacco-Vanzetti case because it stood out as a milestone in the political awakening of famous left-leaning writers such as Edmund Wilson, Malcolm Cowley, and Josephine Herbst. Viewing the affair in international perspective, by contrast, reveals how much the case at its heart should be regarded not as a tale about broad-minded intellectuals, who would claim so much credit for the campaign, but rather as a story about working-class radicals struggling to reconstitute their movements in the aftermath of the Great War. Especially in those early years, real energy for the cause bubbled up from below and from abroad. By 1926 and 1927, liberals would certainly become high-profile supporters, but during the first crucial years, working-class crowds and donors sustained it. It was the rank and file of labor unions, far-flung chains of Italian migrants, the members of socialist and communist organizations, and the adherents of the small but influential anarchist movement who filled petition sheets, packed rallies, and made the campaign a mass movement. Work for Sacco and Vanzetti, the Boston Committee periodically reiterated, had been "made possible all these years entirely by the workers of this and other countries," and without them, they surmised, the prisoners would not have lived as long as they did. "The classless or bourgeois intelligentsia followed belatedly," agreed the activist Eugene Lyons.[21] To internationalize the history of the Sacco-Vanzetti campaign, then, is to see the case as a window onto the development of the radical left after World War I, illuminating the synergy between such popular politics on both sides of the Atlantic.

Although the Sacco-Vanzetti affair began as a working-class movement, by 1926 and 1927 it had evolved into something much more. Entertaining new objectives and strategies, campaign organizers on both sides of the Atlantic ultimately transcended traditional class politics, drawing in a far wider array of supporters who altered the shape and tenor of interwar leftist politics. Early on, to elevate their cause above the general din of the Red Scare, orga-nizers began to liken Sacco's and Vanzetti's situation to Tom Mooney's sensa-tional conviction in San Francisco, since that labor activist's death sentence had been commuted to life imprisonment in 1918 after it became clear he had been framed for the bombing of a Preparedness Day parade. This precedent offered hope that at least modest success might still be had in the darkest days of Palmerism. Focused on the specific goal of securing a new trial for the prisoners, the Boston Committee encouraged allies to downplay the role of revolutionary violence in the movement and to operate above factional differ-ences. Aspiring to bring as many groups into their fold as possible, organizers sponsored theater events and spaghetti picnics. Volunteers also learned the importance of modern publicity techniques, amassing hundreds of newspaper contacts around the world and becoming more and more skilled at tailoring their pleas so that they would resonate effectively with different constituencies. For example, in a desperate push as the executions neared, the Committee launched a "Drive on Coolidge" to persuade the president to pressure state officials to stop the executions, as Wilson had done in the Mooney case. In preparation, Committee members dashed off a vast contact list, which conveyed the massive social networks they had put together over the years, connecting radicals around the world to prominent business and social leaders. Even William Randolph Hearst, a most unlikely ally, would be approached with an appeal to his own interests: "Levine to write special wire," the plan's scribbled notes directed; "We believe it will promote your ideal of international under-standing, particularly among English speaking people of the world. Point out Wells and Shaw interested."[22]

In Paris, Lecoin's Comité took these ideals to heart. Ignoring the criti-cisms of some anarchists who wanted to embrace more radical tactics, Lecoin, like his counterparts in Boston, courted moderates' involvement. The liberal League of the Rights of Man, the SFIO, and the CGT would join rallies in the Paris region, including the impressive July 23, 1927, demonstration at which some ten thousand people crowded the Cirque d'Hiver on the city's outskirts while ten thousand more amassed outside, chanting the names of the two condemned men.[23] Widening interest in the case also sent skyward the circulation of the capital's newspapers, those argumentative sheets that filled the arms of street criers, blaring the latest headlines. The Radical Party's *L'Œuvre* and the Socialist *Le Populaire* regularly dished out dramatic news about the affair in morning installments and special editions. The circulation of *Le Libertaire*, typically between 6,000 and 10,000 copies, soared to as many as 30,000 during the height of the campaign. The edition announcing the executions and calling for demonstrations sold out at 50,000 copies.[24] Such attention from the capital's diverse leftist press was instrumental in getting people out on the streets and headed for the American embassy, where anarchists, socialists, and liberals gathered the night after the executions.

Despite these successes, cooperation among different factions of the left— striving for a "united front"—proved elusive. Not surprisingly, attempts to reach out to liberals helped erode communists' already lukewarm participation in the coalition. By the mid-1920s, relations between the communist and noncommunist left had deteriorated on both sides of the Atlantic, due to local personality conflicts as well as changing Comintern directives.[25] Following the establishment of the International Labor Defense (ILD) in 1925, communists in the United States withdrew their delegate to the Boston Committee meetings and formed competing defense groups. Staging their own demonstrations in places like Chicago and Los Angeles, they collected money on behalf of the cause but siphoned off most of the proceeds for other priorities.[26] Nevertheless, communists in the United States never completely wrestled control away from the Boston Committee and its allies, as they would have liked. Distinguishing themselves from other activists by their unflinching view of the case through the lens of class analysis, they scoffed at the idea of cultivating liberal support. Reformers, communists charged, sought to shore up a system corrupt and broken beyond repair. To them, debating details about the trial and appealing for justice only helped "maintain in the minds of the workers the fictions of bourgeois legalism."[27] They remained mired in their own aggressively partisan, doctrinaire approach to waging political campaigns.

Just as they had in the United States, unified leftist actions in Paris, which seemed possible just after the war, quickly soured. French socialists had at first viewed the PCF as an upstart party, destined to disappear, and until 1924 they thought reunification a distinct possibility despite obvious ideological divides. Socialists, however, soon grew impatient with what they perceived as the flamboyant extremism of the PCF, painting communists as nothing but *"des anarchistes insurrectionnels cosmopolites."* News of repression in

Russia also widened the rift with anarchists who had at first supported the Soviet experiment. After the Kronstadt massacre in 1921, advocating for radicals imprisoned or executed by Bolsheviks moved to the center of French anarchists' preoccupations.[28] Like their American counterparts, Paris communists grew increasingly disruptive to united front efforts and proved unwilling to follow the directives of other leftists. During the Sacco-Vanzetti affair, they began staging their own, competing demonstrations, most impressively their August 7, 1927, rally in the Bois de Vincennes, attended by approximately 25,000. The evening after the executions, Paris communists and their followers would eschew the anarchist- and socialist-led rendezvous by the embassy, calling for an alternative protest on the grand boulevards.

Here, however, the parallels between communist politics on each side of the Atlantic diverged. Paris militants departed more readily from the party line and moved beyond arguments framed purely in class terms, tapping into a much broader range of their supporters' emotions. To craft such messages, like their socialist and anarchist competitors, they depended on the sensational qualities of the city's radical press. Party spokesmen wrote passionately about the case in their official organ, *L'Humanité*, which enjoyed a circulation of roughly 200,000, indicating that its readership vastly exceeded the party membership of some 50,000. This incendiary daily enjoyed record popularity during the culmination of the Sacco-Vanzetti affair, drawing in all kinds of casual readers and fellow travelers.[29] Like other leftist newspapers, *L'Humanité* not only communicated information about the case but also created interest and suspense on the streets of the city. In doorways and on café terraces, Parisians read translations of Vanzetti's touching letters along with incensed editorials. Huddled around some of those same kiosks that would be destroyed during the rioting, crowds scanned the most recent editions for their blaring declarations, photographs of the two prisoners, and news of the latest execution delays transmitted over one of the eighteen telegraph lines that had been specially installed in Charlestown prison itself.[30] By 1927, with headlines growing to the size of poster typeface and rhetoric rousing "interest into passion" and "pity into anger," as the unsympathetic *Le Figaro* asserted, the affair had evolved into a "serial novel of the front page."[31] The Sacco-Vanzetti case had successfully overcome its rocky beginnings to become a modern, media-fueled cause célèbre.

During the final months of the two prisoners' lives, the campaign had escalated into a riveting drama played out in large metropolitan centers like Paris, winning support not only from working-class radicals but also from middle-class liberals and others. By then, cables pleading for a retrial or sentence commutation poured into American diplomatic posts. Opinionated missives flooded Judge Webster Thayer's chambers, Massachusetts Governor Alvan T. Fuller's offices, and Calvin Coolidge's White House and South Dakota summer home. Appeals had been raised by an impressive number of public figures from Albert Einstein to Thomas Mann. Anatole France's early plea for clemency would be one of the last political stands the inveterate intellectual would take; Marie Curie's telegram to Governor Fuller would be one of her only such acts. Adding her signature to a student initiative in Paris would provide a formative moment in the political education of a young Simone de Beauvoir. Petitions were circulated in many countries, and they were impressive. One conveyed the sentiments of more than a dozen British MPs; another contained some 153,000 names gathered by the Swiss Union of Workers. In June 1927, a giant scroll calling for a public investigation of the affair arrived at the State House in Boston. On it appeared almost a half million signatures from around the world.[32]

By the summer of 1927, moderates, and even some on the right, became less inclined to ignore the continuous delays and the growing doubts surrounding the death sentences. Conservatives and reactionaries worried about how the case might tarnish the reputation of the United States and energize radical movements in multiple hemispheres. They, too, suggested that the incarcerated men had already suffered enough. Calls for pity and compassion crossed not only national borders but also partisan divides, forming a broad discussion about universal standards of justice. But widespread moral outrage proved complex. Oftentimes it fused with redirected angst and realpolitik. "The Sacco-Vanzetti case was exploited everywhere," contended the American journalist George Seldes; "radical mobs and the conservative press of fifty countries made of the two convicted Italians a means for demonstrating their own anger and fear." For Seldes, the executions of Vanzetti and Sacco brought the rising tide of postwar anti-American sentiment to a high-water mark, serving "to unite huge masses in Europe and South America and elsewhere against a common object of disdain and hate"—the United States.[33]

The case indeed seemed to accentuate common gripes against Americans and their government. Liberals in various countries, for instance, recalled the disappointments of Wilsonian democracy. Eastern and Southern Europeans, in turn, had not forgotten that they had been declared officially undesirable by U.S. immigration laws. Latin Americans linked the case to their northern neighbors' "Dollar Diplomacy" and imperialist ventures—to the Marines' return invasion of Nicaragua only months before, for example. For citizens of former allied nations who followed the affair, Americans' insistence that war debts be repaid often sprang to mind. Moreover, the trial seemed to confirm the lessons many had already drawn from American domestic events, such as the enactment of Prohibition, the Scopes Trial, and the persistence of lynching and racial violence. It offered "a register" of the intolerant, uncivilized character of American mentality, Austria's premier newspaper charged. It exposed, echoed a French critic, "a grave crisis of the social body." The Sacco-Vanzetti case, like the Dreyfus Affair to which it was often compared, became, as the English writer and socialist H. G. Wells articulated, a trial "by which the soul of a people is tested and displayed."[34]

Americans' interest in the case waxed and waned over the seven long years of legal battles, but by 1927 it had become divisive. Oftentimes, news of growing criticism abroad compelled Americans to take sides. No friends to anarchism, some found themselves nonetheless moved enough by the international demonstrations to protest to involved parties. Reciting their patriotic bona fides, letter writers described themselves as conservatives, Mayflower descendants, or simply "responsible American citizens," pleading for authorities to recognize, as one woman from Charlestown, Massachusetts, believed, that Americans should be too proud of their "State and Nation to blacken them with judicial injustice." The urgency, as another group reminded from Seattle, came from the responsibilities of facing a "watching World." Concerned citizens' potentially most effective if ultimately unsuccessful argument for mercy, offered in dispatches to Fuller and Coolidge, hinged on how the case marred the reputation of American justice abroad. Jane Addams's impassioned plea stood as only the most famous of such statements: clemency afforded a chance "for a real reconciliation between Anglo-Saxon and Latin peoples," she insisted to unmoved authorities. No state could "ignore the world's opinion," echoed a Mississippi resident. "France tried it in the Dreyfus case, but couldn't do it," he recalled. "Germany did it in the Edith Cavell case. . . . Will it help Massachusetts or America to lose the good opinion of the world?" he demanded.[35]

For other Americans, however, international agitation only hardened opinion against the two men. As the executions approached, George Seldes noticed, "men in the street began to say, 'We won't let damned foreigners interfere with us,' and 'They're Reds, anyway, so let them burn.'" American Legionnaires—patriots and nativists extraordinaire—applauded Governor Fuller for not caving to outside pressures. "Give 'em the juice," the evangelist Billy Sunday preached from similar convictions: "Burn them, if they're guilty. . . . I'm tired of hearing these foreigners, these radicals, coming over here and telling us what we should do." In an oft-repeated rebuke to Jane Addams's request that he address the international consequences of the executions, the chairman of the Senate Foreign Relations Committee, William Borah, scoffed at "foreign interference," claiming that it would be "a shameless cowardly compromise of national courage, to pay the slightest attention to foreign protests or mob protests at home." Mounting adumbrations of anti-Americanism, it seemed, would be met with redoubled resolve. The executions, Seldes concluded, were "considered by millions of Americans a fine answer to Europe."[36]

Nevertheless, the so-called impudence and interference of foreigners could not be simply willed away, and the trial of Sacco and Vanzetti could not so easily be separated off from its international ramifications—a predicament symbolized by the vulnerability of American embassies and consular posts during the affair. Back in the eighteenth century, Paris received the first United States legation in the world, but since the 1890s, American envoys in the French capital had belonged to an expanded, bureaucratizing Foreign Service designed to foster American commercial and diplomatic interests abroad. Foreign installations formed a chain of official structures that signaled the growing political and economic connections between Americans and other parts of the world.[37] They had, however, another unintended use, increasingly offering handy targets where people might register their anger about U.S. policies and scandals. During the Sacco-Vanzetti affair, beginning with the attempt to bomb Ambassador Herrick in Paris, the gates of American embassies and consulates formed frequent backdrops for violent scenes between police and civilians. Exasperated State Department officials prepared memos explaining to groups overseas that American federal employees had no direct bearing on the outcome of the case. Protesters around the world did not care about such constitutional nuances; appeals, threats, and bomb scares poured into diplomatic posts from Tokyo to London.[38]

The speed and intensity with which the Sacco-Vanzetti affair unfolded around the globe—the near simultaneity of protests on far-off continents in favor of the same two men—pointed to the unprecedented potential for transnational political mobilization during this new era of world integration. There was something about the aesthetics of the Sacco-Vanzetti demonstrations that anticipated what would become an increasingly familiar type of international reaction to miscarriages of American justice and other controversies over the course of the twentieth century. Scenes of people picketing American embassies, carrying signs, burning American flags would become a staple of the visual repertoire used by protesters in communities around the world. How Americans would be viewed, how "America" would be defined in the new century, derived in part from this emerging form of popular politics.

For leftists, the Sacco-Vanzetti campaign dramatized the problems and possibilities of waging grassroots campaigns between the world wars. More than a revival of old, working-class political action and much more than a

Moscow-led agenda, it helped to teach activists how to navigate new political terrain. Just what would a radical movement look like in a postwar age? Should demonstrations take place in lecture halls or out in the streets? Would a united front be possible, and would liberals play a part? Would it be pitched as a class struggle or a fight to rehabilitate American justice, or something else entirely? For almost a decade, the Sacco-Vanzetti case because a prime means for leftists to try to work out these dilemmas. And as the movement attested to the partial rebuilding of old class networks that had faltered during the war, it also revealed how new sensibilities could be grafted onto these tried-and-true channels. Radicals became increasingly attuned to the power and usefulness of broad-based campaigns built by modern mobilization tactics. This was to be a politics still motivated by class imperatives but also flexible, a politics not only tethered to the shop floor but in tune to the neighborhood and the daily press, to cultural appeals and popular prejudices— a politics centered especially on critiques of Americans and their culture. Supporters of Sacco and Vanzetti in Paris led the way in recognizing and exploiting such potential. Like many others, they felt inspired to be a part of this historic, worldwide incident. But they would also take the campaign in their own direction, responding to the dynamics of their immediate surroundings and transforming the affair into a deeply localized event, reaching its crescendo in the hours after the executions.

In an age when breaking news was something learned in the dense huddle of street crowds, people in cities around the world gathered in front of newspaper bulletin boards in the hours before the executions. As midnight neared in New York City's Union Square, thousands congregated in front of the offices of the Communist *Daily Worker*, waiting tensely for staff to post updates in the windows. As the hour of death approached, more and more newsflashes appeared:

> Bulletin: Paris crowds staying up all night. . . .
> Bulletin: Protesters in Geneva stoning the League of Nations headquarters. Stores carrying American products being sacked and destroyed. . . .
> Bulletin: Charlestown an armed camp. 500 police and state troopers with machine guns surround prison and block off nearby streets.

The window-front headlines portrayed the event as one unfolding on a global scale in real time.[39]

Thousands of miles south in Buenos Aires, an American journalist surveyed from her bedroom window the animated Avenida de Mayo below, where clusters of men stood reading the news flashes in the office windows of a leading newspaper. "They read," she explained, "then joined the procession moving slowly, angrily, resentfully, up the avenue." Across the Atlantic— where it was already early Tuesday morning—word of the executions broke just as many were rising for work. In Rome, crowds reportedly stood in stunned silence before the newspaper offices. In Paris, people had remained out late the night before, lingering around bulletin boards, awaiting the latest dispatches from the United States. "The city was tense as though it were something that was happening within the borders of France," remembered the visiting American labor activist Mary Heaton Vorse. "We sat around in groups feeling the hour of doom approaching," she said, feeling the "horrible anguish," the same grief "causing the massing of emotion in Union Square and the assembly of great crowds in Boston."[40]

After the executions, tensions only escalated in the French capital. *L'Humanité* hawkers trudged through the city's popular quarters with a special issue, intoning "*Sacco et Vanzetti électrocutés!*" On top of that edition—of which vendors reportedly sold 192,000 copies—the day's first subsequent run reached 290,000.[41] In anger and disbelief, activists filled other left-wing newspapers with plans for demonstrations that night. The Comité Sacco-Vanzetti and the Socialist Party issued a joint statement to the people of Paris. "*Lève-toi!*" they urged, "Demonstrate with dignity, peacefully, as befits free men." For days, in anticipation of this hour, heavily armed police had blockaded the area around the American embassy, giving the neighborhood, the *New York Times* reported, "the appearance of being in a state of siege." Nearby bus lines had been rerouted and the Métro closed, transforming the place d'Iéna into what one French newspaper described as a "vast zone of emptiness and silence."[42] By nine P.M., thousands would descend on the embassy area anyway, determined to gather in the vicinity of that highly symbolic building. Others packed the sidewalks of the grand boulevards. Particularly dense crowds accumulated in front of the newspaper offices of *Le Matin* on the boulevard Poissonnière, where bystanders recited slogans like "*Vivent Sacco et Vanzetti,*" "*Mort aux vaches,*" and "*À mort Fuller.*"[43] When it was all over a few hours later, hundreds would be detained—for carrying weapons (brass knuckles, guns, knives), for refusing to disperse, for looting and destruction of property.

The far-flung networks of migrants and radicals propelled the Sacco-Vanzetti case from a local miscarriage of justice into an international cause célèbre, and the position of Paris at the crux of these channels suggests how it came to be such a hotbed for dissent. But what led the protests to such a bloody conclusion on the boulevards? In preceding weeks, giant outdoor events in the Paris area had been staged with similarly heightened emotions and under equally intense police pressure—but without serious incident. On August 7, for example, some fifteen thousand paraded behind Vanzetti's sister, Luigia, through the Bois de Vincennes on the city's outskirts, confronted by a massive police presence. Unionized workers and suburban community collectives, ARAC veterans, revolutionary students, and members of various communist front groups—all fell into careful formation, chanting "Save Sacco and Vanzetti." Overhead, surveillance blimps monitored the human sea with its bobbing placards and billowing red flags, while officers on the ground discharged telegrams to police headquarters every five to ten minutes reporting on the scene. Despite the nervousness of the authorities and the resolve of the crowd, the day passed with remarkable calm.[44] So what, then, was the flashpoint that transformed this tense but peaceful face-off into the free-for-all bedlam that it became just sixteen days later?

The answer lay in the particular social geography of the Paris region and its accompanying spatial politics. During the 1920s, police prohibited all processions within city limits, excepting festival celebrations, national ceremonies, and other commemorations that received government authorization. In surrounding suburbs, gatherings such as the one on August 7 were *"tolérées"* if their purpose was not deemed "contrary to public order" or a "danger to the peacefulness of the population." Although in theory this policy made no distinctions regarding political affiliation, in practice it served to systematically exclude leftist demonstrations from the city's public spaces or *la voie publique*. Whereas right-wing groups—anchored through veterans' organizations and patriotic leagues—could couch their gatherings in the terms of national commemoration necessary to receive formal blessings, leftists were consistently denied access to the streets. According to one internal report, police classified fifty-one *manifestations* for the years 1920–1927 but approved only three gatherings in the city—marches by war veterans and victims, protesting insufficient pensions and the Washington debt accords. All leftist plans to demonstrate *au centre-ville* included on the list were, by contrast, formally banned. Tellingly, almost all injuries and arrests recorded had occurred when activists ignored police orders and headed for the gates to the city anyway.[45]

Arguably, the Sacco-Vanzetti affair represented a high point for this classic form of urban politics. Protecting public space from unruly crowds and protesters' escalating claims had become a major preoccupation of municipal authorities in Paris just as it had in other early-twentieth-century metropolitan centers. As in London's glamorous West End, the modernizing downtowns of Latin American cities, or the international concessions of East

Asia, workers were imagined as out of place in the center of Paris. In order to weather these limits on access, leftists immersed themselves in constant bargaining with the police. During the Sacco-Vanzetti affair, the elaborate choreography of moves and countermoves between the two became almost reflexive. Sacco-Vanzetti activists announced plans for tremendous gatherings; the police proclaimed them illegal. Organizers published Métro directions, rendezvous locations, and lists of sections and subgroups for marches to take place near the American embassy; police officials drafted color-coded maps and intricate memos, detailing special services and roadblocks to choke off access to the embassy area. Protesters entertained ways to subvert the restrictions in brainstorming sessions; police retooled their preparations based on undercover intelligence updates. Leftist leaders rescheduled demonstrations for the suburbs, promising the events would be orderly and devoid of seditious speech and signs; government authorities poured almost all of their manpower into patrolling them anyway—and blockaded the embassy area, too, just to be sure.[46]

When Vanzetti and Sacco died, this delicate pas de deux ended abruptly. Days before the executions, Prefect Chiappe reiterated the ban on protests in the

Communists take to the Paris streets to protest the fate of Sacco and Vanzetti. A worker in the foreground wears an armband to show his identification with the two martyrs. ©Roger-Viollet/The Image Works

city center and issued a particularly strident warning that any challenges to police authority would be met with force. Sacco-Vanzetti supporters interpreted these statements as a deliberate provocation—and responded with an unambiguous one of their own. They insisted on holding parallel demonstrations in front of the American embassy and on the central boulevards the evening of August 23, plans which police in turn regarded as willful affronts to their policy. One retrospective memo summarized the mindset of the police in the face of protesters' defiance that night: "When groups insist on demonstrating on the *voie publique* despite the prohibition of the Government, they are rebelling against authority and committing a seditious act that the police have the urgent duty to suppress." Just what triggered the rioting on the boulevards remains unclear. Whether it had been sparked by a gunshot from the crowd, a gunshot from a provocateur, or a premeditated, uninstigated charge by the police—all working theories at the time—mattered less than the simple but pivotal act of workers appearing collectively in the city center. As the abstract international battle for justice took on local, physical dimensions, protesters used the occasion to challenge their marginalization from the city's grounds. And although Sacco and Vanzetti had not been saved, some would consider the temporary occupation of the city in their honor a resounding victory nonetheless. Headlines for *L'Humanité* the following morning would celebrate in broad, bold type:

# Working-class Paris *maître du pavé!*
## Montmartre and the Center in State of Siege

Standing as the *maître du pavé*—"master of the streets"—was critical in the endgame of interwar Parisian politics.[47] Just who could claim such status was literally duked out on the city's boulevards and wrestled over in the debates that surrounded the affair.

Protesters' momentary ability to command the pavement would prove bittersweet and incomplete. They faced formidable opposition that night. Almost three thousand policemen had been stationed to greet them in eight battalions from the place de l'Etoile to the place de la République. On the grand boulevards, where the Communists called for demonstrators to mass, Prefect Chiappe stood poised to direct his human arsenal in person. At the appointed hour of protest, the boulevards bristled with the activity of strollers, diners, and curiosity seekers brushing shoulders with arriving demonstrators. Only moments later—as the throngs thickened—agents, with somber resolution and batons in hand, propelled themselves against the multitude with what the moderate *L'Œuvre* called *"violence extraordinaire."*

Mounted on horses, police parted the crowds with truncheons and drove individuals down narrow side streets. The charges came, one after another, rapid and intense. One Frenchman, passing by the offices of *Le Matin* on his way to catch a tram home, watched as "policemen drunk with rage" trounced pedestrians in successive charges. The flustered man narrowly escaped the battle he had wandered into inadvertently, his glasses smashed and his kidneys aching. Agents also "recovered" the area's abundant sidewalk establishments, which served as ready garrisons for agitators. On one terrace, reported *Le Petit Journal*, peaceful customers "rolled *pêle-mêle*" along with protesters across tabletops. The right-wing *Paris Herald* described the scene with glee: "Waves of sullen though battle-bent 'Reds' were rolled back time and again by the police."

In the aftermath, people would turn up at local pharmacies and hospitals with concussions and head wounds, chipped teeth, black eyes, and gashes in need of stitches. The ruthless affrays left the boulevards strewn with hats, torn clothing, and blood. "The disturbers of the social order have had the proof that they must give up the hope of descending into the street with impunity," Chiappe announced after it was all over. "The *manifestants* master of the streets? It is false!" he said, "We found ourselves before the 'pures,' before the professionals of the riot. We know how to act the next time."[48]

At a retrospective Chamber debate, the Communist Deputy Alexandre Piquemal noted how critics had been shocked that workers "had the gall" to appear en masse—as they so seldom did—in the center of Paris. The bourgeoisie tolerated protesters in the working-class suburbs where they did not have to see them, he realized, but, for laborers "collectively," the grand boulevards were "*interdits*." Piquemal himself had witnessed the riots from the boulevard Poissonnière, and the memory of police brutality fired his speech in front of the Chamber months later. "The right of *manifestation*," he railed, "you will not take it away from the working class any more than the imprescriptible right to revolution!"[49] In his long, impassioned defense of the historically guaranteed right to demonstrate, Piquemal intimated that Sacco-Vanzetti activists had hoped to regain access not only to the capital's physical center but also to its long-standing traditions of popular uprising. Standing triumphantly as masters of the city's streets, in other words, required that demonstrators also pose as inheritors of the city's past.

To many, the buildings and neighborhoods of Paris conjured up a living history, one shot through with the violent conflicts of previous centuries. The cobblestoned streets of the Marais recalled the barricades of 1830 and 1848, and the square before the Hôtel de Ville could seem haunted by past riots and gruesome public executions. Père Lachaise cemetery housed not only famous deceased residents in its garden plots but also the ghosts of the last Communards, gunned down against its outer wall. As the American expatriate Harold Stearns discovered, the city's streets were "soaked in blood." Traversing the capital, he explained, "You get a vivid feeling every now and then that the tolerance and the liberty you enjoy have all been fought for, have all cost a high price in human life. You get a feeling of heritage, much sharper than even I have in my own historical town of Boston." The urban landscape, charged with such historical associations, reinforced the idea of Paris as the capital of modern revolution. Strengthened over the course of the nineteenth century, this myth encompassed a malleable set of symbols that could be called upon to lend legitimacy to those who claimed the city's revolutionary heritage for their own.[50]

For this reason, contests over space in Paris often became simultaneously battles over the commemoration of time. Reshaping the city's revolutionary geography had been a preoccupation of artists, authorities, and insurgents since the French Revolution itself. Gestures to mute the capital's radical past were met with counteroffensives to raise it anew. In the 1830s, conservatives unveiled the Obelisk of Luxor on the newly renamed place de la Concorde, hoping the pillar's lack of congruence with its surroundings would blot out the square's past incarnation as the place de la Révolution, gory site of the guillotine. In 1871, Communards felled Napoleon's Column on the place Vendôme and posed triumphantly for photographs next to his broken statue. Their opponents later retorted by building Sacré-Cœur, which cast its long, clericalist shadow over Montmartre where the Commune began. For decades, the political right and left had fought back and forth to topple old monuments and erect new ones, to rename squares and streets, as though locked in a giant game of chess. The urban landscape, overlaid with markers of the city's checkered past, offered a fitting terrain for such a match.

In the game of symbolic urban politics after World War I, the Parisian right dominated. Once a staple holiday of the left, Bastille Day—and accompanying references to 1789—were refitted with nationalistic overtones by the center and the right, beginning with the Armistice parade on July 14, 1919. For their public displays, reactionary veterans' groups and those motley gangs of extremists known as the *ligues* flew the *tricolore* and imbued the Marseillaise with martial grace. Challenging this appropriation of the revolutionary spirit—taking back the *tricolore*, the Marseillaise, and Marianne—would be one of the left's most effective cultural messages, which began in earnest when organizers chose Bastille Day for the first Popular Front parade in 1935. As demonstrated by the actions of Sacco-Vanzetti protesters, however, disputing the right's monopoly on both the streets and their historical meanings began in more haphazard ways even before that impressive cortege through the eastern neighborhoods of Paris.[51]

On the night of the riots, the sight of angry protesters descending the boulevards in workmen's clothes and caps offered a visual reminder of previous popular occupations of the city center. Especially by attempting barricades—those ultimate architectural expressions of Parisian revolution—protesters identified their actions implicitly with past insurrections and joined in the ritual contest over the capital's symbolic dimensions. But amid the chaos of a riot situation, it proved difficult to stay focused on the poetics of history. Police determination to disperse large, static crowds led rioters to break up into smaller, highly mobile bands of people, who raced through the streets to unanticipated destinations before police could reposition their reinforcements. This tactic did not allow protesters to take over any one particular quarter of the city, but it did allow them to infiltrate many different areas, undertaking a string of destructive acts that stretched across ten arrondissements. In the heat of the moment, *manifestants* found it more expedient to attack sites charged with negative political connotations than to build positive associations with previous fights for liberty. For this reason, Sacco-Vanzetti supporters did not gravitate, as they might have, to the place de la République and the plebeian neighborhoods of the east where barricades had been raised many times before. Instead, they pressed into the western quarters of the city—the cherished domain of their political rivals.[52]

During the Sacco-Vanzetti affair, the battle between the rioters and others determined to maintain their stronghold on the commemoration of the city's past was best revealed in the scandal over the reported desecration of the Tomb of the Unknown Soldier. Interred under the Arc de Triomphe in 1920, the anonymous poilu had reinvigorated the status of Napoleon's Arch as a premier rendezvous point for the right. This sheltered spot and the adjacent Champs-Elysées, with its vista all the way to the Obelisk of Luxor, became a principal stomping ground for reactionaries throughout the interwar years. Leftists impulsively but mindfully invaded this territory the night of the riots. When police dispersed Sacco-Vanzetti supporters from the American embassy area, hundreds regrouped around the Arc de Triomphe, where they sang the Internationale and overturned chains that demarcated the sacred space. Some even allegedly threw rocks and spit on the Tomb. By raiding the monument at the center of the Etoile (a brash act later disavowed by many leftists), protesters did not intend so much to defame the enlisted victims of Verdun. They desired, rather, to despoil the territory of the *ligues* and veterans' organizations, the right-wing deputies and councilors, who used the site to exploit Parisians' patriotism and mourning for their own political gain.[53]

The American writer Elliot Paul speculated that, during the interwar years, "the only things the Parisians were not willing to laugh about were the price of bread and the Tomb of the Unknown Soldier." Indeed, the outburst at the Arch drew an intensely emotional backlash from Parisians. "The act of a few exalted criminals wanting to sully the tomb of modest and unknown heroes who personify the mourning of the whole country," the rightist *Le Figaro* explained, "had aroused a unanimous movement of disgust and anger." In the days after the riots, thousands joined ceremonies at the Etoile. Government officials and anonymous citizens alike placed flowers and wreaths on the Tomb to expiate the "odious profanation" by the rioters. Veterans of the Great War and the Franco-Prussian War stopped traffic on the Champs-Elysées. Sons of the dead, survivors of the Somme, the blind, the *mutilés*, and the *gueules cassées*—all came out to march without police interference to the spot that encapsulated their heroism and suffering. Through moments of silence and ritualistic relightings of the eternal flame, patriotic Parisians reconsecrated the monument and took it back from the "miserable agitators" whose spontaneous, symbolic deed had gone too far. In the coming weeks, rectifying the insult to the Tomb would not be limited to the participation of French citizens. Visiting foreign leaders, including King Boris of Bulgaria, paid their respects to the shrine, and the American Legion—in town for their annual convention—would offer a tribute to the Unknown Soldier at the start of their controversial parade down the Champs-Elysées.[54]

For the police, the city's conservative bourgeoisie, and its right-wingers, the clamor of protesters did not speak to a conscientious and collective mourning of injustice. For detractors, it was not about the freedom to demonstrate or the practice of historically guaranteed rights (which royalists and other extremists did not support anyhow). It portended, quite simply, an invasion. It was the onslaught of a ragtag army of tramps, Soviet minions, and foreign *indésirables*, trudging in from the putrid working-class districts that had grown up in recent years around the city. The "vermin of the world" had ravaged Paris, insisted one critic of the riots. The offensive that night betrayed a "clearly revolutionary character," argued another, with its communist columns and "low thieves from la Chapelle, Belleville, and la Villette." For Marcel Lucain of *Paris-Midi*, the events represented a waking urban nightmare. Like others, he concluded that meetings out in the Bois de Vincennes or Pré Saint-Gervais had been justified by desires to impress upon the United States the "powerful movements of crowds." But "direct action in the street" smacked of other motives. "It was Bolshevism agitating, destroying, taking possession of the *pavé parisien*," Lucain contended, fueled by "a majority of foreign subjects, refugees, undesirables, *métèques* of all colors . . . benefiting from our hospitality, our liberty, and our employment . . . howling in twenty languages their age-old hate of France."[55]

Lucain's conjuring of a thieving, conniving underclass recalled those infamous *classes dangereuses* that had long preoccupied the thoughts of the city's more privileged inhabitants. In part because of such fears, many of the cramped and dilapidated neighborhoods of the working poor—those breeding grounds for squalor, crime, and radicalism—had faced the wrecking balls of Baron Haussmann's urban renewal projects during the middle of the nineteenth century. The capital's luckless evicted had streamed to nearby industrializing faubourgs, which, growing steadily in the years before World War I, offered a new setting for worries about revolutionary masses.[56] After the Armistice, working-class suburban populations rose even further. Fleeing the city center's postwar housing shortage, Parisian laborers joined waves of arriving immigrants in the soot-clogged shadows of Clichy's gas works and the noxious miasma around the chemical refineries of Aubervilliers. Together with the patchwork of depressed farm communities and the marginalized world of squatters just beyond the city's fortifications, the industrial suburbs of Paris formed the fabled *"ceinture rouge,"* or Red Belt, that leaped into Parisians' imaginations following the impressive showing by the Communists and Socialists in the legislative elections of May 1924.[57]

For conservatives, the transfer of Jean Jaurès's ashes to the Pantheon that November 1 brought to life apocalyptic visions of a siege from the suburbs. In an exceptional event—made possible only by the temporary control of the government by the *Cartel des gauches*—Communists and Socialists staged massive parades through the city center. For moderates and rightists, the scene was terrifying. The sight of suburban workers bearing their banners and incendiary signs through the capital did not, for them, honor the father of French Socialism so much as it heralded, as one critic put it, "the funeral of the bourgeoisie." The paranoia stirred up by the *panthéonisation* of Jaurès helped to promote the right-wing *ligues* from a place on the extremist fringe to a position of influence and power. It gave rise overnight to paramilitary "defense" groups—including the Jeunesses Patriotes and the Faisceau—and replenished the ranks of reactionary veterans' organizations and the royalist Action Française.[58]

Sociological exposés of the Red Belt only reinforced Parisians' anxieties and set the stage for the kind of violence that erupted in 1927. In one bestselling foray into the "spiritual desert" that encircled Paris, published the same year as the Sacco-Vanzetti riots, the Jesuit Pierre Lhande searched desperately for traces of God and faith in a world where crosses and pious icons had been supplanted by inane magazine cutouts—or worse, portraits of Lenin and Trotsky. Among vagabonds and strangers, Lhande documented an "embittered and miserable population" encircling Paris with "formidable danger." For the "turbulent masses" of this forgotten place, there was only the "heavy atmosphere" of gritty bistros, where political talk in the murky light of oil lamps and pipe smoke stoked popular resentments. Here, Lhande feared, "visions of luxurious Paris that one brushes up against every day" made envy nag at the hearts of men for whom the daily commute stood as a "forced return journey from the comfort of the city to the misery of the slum." Worst of all, he cited "evocations of the '*grand soir*,' cleverly presented by the foreigners," which of course included Americans. These brash nightlife displays put on by affluent revelers, he suggested, were like beacons for the angers of the masses, rumbling "in expectation of the favorable hour for the great assault." Appearing at the same time, Édouard Blanc's influential survey similarly mused on a suburban wasteland where "the foundations of a civilized society: *religion, patrie, famille*" lay in ruin. While the bourgeoisie was busy knocking down the city's fortifications, communists were busy constructing "all along the abandoned barrier, a series of municipal fortresses," which stood, he contended, not as "defensive installations, but positions of attack." Blanc reminded his readers that armed rioters could easily sever the capital's communications, blockade its principal railroad lines, even transform its metallurgical foundries into factories for making "deadly machines."[59]

As paranoid as such prophesies sounded, these were not unwarranted concerns, especially after the revolutionary moment in 1919–1920, and as the far left, in France as in other places, moved toward new levels of extremism. Blanc's claim that insurgents could choke off communication and transportation to the city or co-opt suburban factories came straight from threats made by the famous Communist editorialist for *L'Humanité*, Paul Vaillant-Couturier, who had celebrated exactly those possibilities in a widely circulated article three years earlier. Flowing sometimes from heroic principles, the politics of communists, anarchists, and other militants just as often devolved into menacing terrorism. Even as they hit on important injustices, leftists trafficked in inflated rhetoric and provocation, even if it meant muddling issues or confusing causal relationships. These years saw a surge of bombings on both sides of the Atlantic—murderous plots that targeted public gatherings and private residences alike. These were not simply the secret acts of lone individuals. Oftentimes they were tacitly condoned or even egged on by blustering editorialists and soapbox firebrands. Even years later, that early bomb attempt against Ambassador Herrick still struck most

Parisians as proof of the unconscionable extremism of the left. Parisians adored Herrick for his support in the early years of the war. To attack him was to attack a great wartime ally who had selflessly defended the capital.[60]

In the weeks leading up to the Sacco-Vanzetti riots, ominous events in this vein only compounded Parisians' suspicions of radicalism. Right-wing newspapers gave prominent coverage to a string of explosions—bombs that gutted the platforms of downtown subway stations in New York City and London, shattered the stained glass of churches in Chicago and Philadelphia, ripped through Ford agency offices in Rosario and Córdoba, Argentina, and damaged the façade of the American consulate in Sofia, Bulgaria. One explosion in Oklahoma injured at least eight people and completely razed three houses. Another device detonated in a telephone booth at a tramway station in Basel, Switzerland, killed a mother of five, and severely wounded several others.[61] Leftist networks may have been on the defensive in many parts of the world, but terrorist tactics convinced others that, with the Communist Party as their perceived new vital center, radical movements still presented a serious danger.

This unsettling news, together with notions about the Paris suburbs as hotbeds for extremism, made it possible for opponents of the left to claim the city as their protectorate and to demonize protesters as troublemakers who did not belong. Le Temps, like many other papers, depicted the Sacco-Vanzetti affair as simply a "pretext seized with enthusiasm by the party of Moscow." "We have in Paris a party of the riot, of armed violence, of pillage," the conservative organ warned, but quickly added that "thanks to the energy of the prefect of police . . . at no moment were the revolutionaries masters of the streets." Prison terms as long as eighteen months for those caught rioting reflected the capital's tender political climate and widespread sentiment that the Massachusetts executions had been merely an excuse for "revolutionary maneuvers" by unsavory foreigners and the deeds of career criminals. Speedy tribunals handed down sentences averaging more than three months, and foreigners were deported. Ultimately, the rioters had been foiled, many rejoiced, in their plan to give "the appearance of the 'zone rouge'" to what Le Temps called the "liberated regions" of the city center—regions that had been freed from the machinations of the extreme left and from an all-too-usable revolutionary past, regions that were not to be open and accessible to all but reserved for the non-left and their paying guests. The Minister of the Interior Albert Sarraut—the Radical Party leader who had appointed Chiappe—drove the point home: "The evening was hot, but the police held and will continue to hold . . . the revolutionaries must know that the street does not belong to them and shall never belong to them."[62]

Moderate and right-wing newspapers did not let on, but foreigners and suburban interlopers by no means exclusively or even primarily perpetrated the Sacco-Vanzetti riots. The vast majority of those arrested during the unrest were Frenchmen who lived within the city's twenty arrondissements, particularly in the run-down neighborhoods around the central markets of Les Halles.[63] Nevertheless myths about the Red Belt prevailed. *Ceinture rouge*, land of the noble militant worker poised to reclaim his status as master of the Paris streets, and *ceinture rouge*, pestilent hideout for those who harkened for France's demise—these clashing images rendered the capital's geography in highly contentious terms, fostering the frustrations of the left, the fears of the right, and the mutual hatreds of both sides. But another mapping of the city was just as important to the dynamics of the Sacco-Vanzetti affair: the American one. The capital's American subculture, obsessed over by French preservationists, urban chroniclers, and Americans themselves, had just reached its peak of influence on the eve of the executions. On August 23, Sacco-Vanzetti demonstrators put their knowledge about Americans' presence in Paris to overt political use. Leftists' aims to support international worker solidarity, challenge police authority, and stake claims to the city center—this cluster of desires came together, albeit imperfectly and even paradoxically, as they trained their sights on places and things they associated with transatlantic visitors.

French officials tried quickly to divest the demonstrations of any meaningful gestures or political import, especially of any glint of criticism leveled at the United States, an interpretation readily taken up by the American press. "The mob felt no particular animosity toward Americans," the *Paris Herald* reported cheerfully; "It seemed, in fact, that the two Italian anarchists were entirely forgotten in the course of the evening." The *New York Times* similarly suggested that the majority of those who clashed with police "had but a hazy knowledge of the Sacco-Vanzetti case." The executions, rather, had been "seized upon by the radical leaders to stage one of their periodical displays of strength in the face of 'capitalistic' Paris. Proof of this," the *Times* claimed, came from "the fact that the majority of the places attacked were French conducted and had little or no connection with Americans or America."[64] The protests indeed targeted "capitalistic" Paris, but the *Times* editors and many other commentators overlooked the central role Americans and their institutions played in that modern, commercial part of the capital. Rioters did not aim solely for American people or things that night—there was plenty of classic anti-bourgeois action—but outbursts of an "anti-American" bent formed a significant thread in the unfolding unrest.

Americans in Paris faced considerable hostility as a result of the affair. The expatriate Matthew Josephson believed that he had narrowly escaped a "good beating" in a suburban café when a group of factory workers angry about the Sacco-Vanzetti case guessed his nationality. The literary critic Samuel Putnam remembered a parallel experience the night of the riots, when he and his wife found their regular café filled with workingmen who shot them menacing looks and gestures. The café proprietor asked the Putnams to leave: "'It is dangerous,' he said, 'You see, you are Americans, and—well, they do not like Americans—tonight.'" In his damage report to police, one brasserie owner on the boulevard Batignolles suggested that protesters had actually set out searching for Americans to confront that Tuesday evening. Men carrying axes and hammers smashed the windows of his business, he avowed, and one of them demanded if there were "any Americans" inside. Even the *New York Times* admitted that the initial clash on the grand boulevards had been sparked when a crowd gathered to hoot at a young American. The fact that the *Times* was headquartered in the *Le Matin* building on the boulevard Poissonnière—and brazenly advertised by oversized signs—may also explain why people gathered so densely in front of those particular offices.[65]

Still, Americans and their property would have faced more direct reprisals for the executions if not for careful police preparations. Stationing an army of officers around the U.S. embassy, authorities also issued formal instructions "concerning cinemas, banks and other American establishments." They told district commanders to take special measures to protect American newspaper offices and "the circulation of the cars of American tourists." An explicit directive also ordered police to make sure that crowd dispersal was "done in the direction of the place de la République and that we never chase the *manifestants* towards the Opéra"—a district replete with prominent American banks, ritzy hotels, and companies like American Express. Such meticulous precautions to insulate Americans and their businesses from the protests reveal that Paris authorities had known on the eve of the unrest what they would later downplay: that the demonstrations would include important anti-American dimensions.[66] Because of these police safeguards, demonstrators targeted those places with abstract associations rather than direct connections to Americans. In lieu of attacking explicitly American institutions, that is, rioters displayed a more subtle and diffuse understanding of the American presence in their city than the police had anticipated. Racing through the center of Paris and the streets of its western half—heart of the city's cosmopolitan spirit, kingdom of the rich, lair of its insidious *ligues*— rioters singled out with special intensity those aspects they imagined as evocative of American influence. When police dispersed the large crowds near the embassy and the grand boulevards, it was no accident that substantial minorities headed for the Champs-Elysées and Montmartre, districts well known for their American clientele.

Hostile bands—including those from the scene at the Tomb of the Unknown Soldier—descended the Champs-Elysées in small, destructive waves between nine and eleven o'clock. One raucous bunch of about five hundred marched down the avenue, accosting evening strollers. "They crossed the avenue des Champs Élysées *en file*," said one police brief, "interrupting traffic, insulting automobilists, looking to damage their cars, throwing projectiles." Several businesses on the luxurious street fell prey to the protesters' umbrage. Here, exclusive cafés were known as popular rest stops for Americans, and many also displayed English-language announcements and advertised American bars to woo customers. At upscale establishments like the Select, prominently advertised as an American bar, rioters threw objects through windows, broke up wicker chairs, and browbeat patrons. One Anglophone sign likely catalyzed an especially noisy *manifestation* in front of Fouquet's.[67] Above the restaurant's elegant awning hung the offending notice:

**HIGH CLASS
GRILL ROOM**

· · · · · · ·

**AMERICAN BAR
Dinners Suppers
Coffee Tea
Chocolate**

Markers like this one furnished some of the most important visual cues for American visitors. They made the city navigable for English-speaking monoglots and had become increasingly essential props for shopkeepers hoping to attract such patronage. At the same time, however, they also provided beacons for those offended by the rich and cosmopolitan practices on display in the capital's flashiest quarters. Parisian crowds had a history of displaying sensitivity to these kinds of symbols in the streets. The casual, destructive nationalism of Sacco-Vanzetti rioters recalled the actions of mobs in 1914, which had sacked shops and hotels with German-sounding names after the declaration of war.[68] Now, amid all those debates about the differences between American and French culture, rioters armed themselves anew with a set of notions about Americans' place in the capital.

Not far from Fouquet's, the Café Tortoni hosted one of the riot's most fiery skirmishes. By the café proprietor's account, several hundred individuals of a decidedly "sinister look" stationed themselves in front of the café's terrace around 10:30. When protesters began insulting patrons and throwing rocks, bedlam ensued. Shattered windows showered the café's clientele, which included, by the *Paris Herald's* count, "a score of Americans." As the windows came crashing down, they seemed to take with them some of those common American illusions about Gay Paree as a playground secluded from the mucky everyday hassles of politics. Bottles, saucers, and plates furnished ammunition for both sides. At least two gunshots were fired; one bullet blew through the back of a chair inside the establishment. The café's manager was injured by a siphon thrown by an agitator he later identified as a tall, blond, clean-shaven youth with no vest—clearly an agent of the revolution. One customer, the movie director Henri Diamant-Berger, claimed that the gunfire had come from a small mustached man wearing a cap—a picture-perfect image of the militant Parisian worker—but others insisted that a café guest actually fired off the shot.[69] To escape the pandemonium, Diamant-Berger and his injured wife took hasty refuge in the restaurant's basement bathrooms along with more than a dozen others. For half an hour, they huddled listening to the racket of overturned furniture overhead. Diamant-Berger tried to phone the police, but the line had been cut. Their leisurely evening abruptly ended, the rattled customers eventually succeeded in fleeing through the cellar.[70]

That night, events such as these played like enactments of the dire warnings that had punctuated the city's leftist press during past months. Only weeks before, for instance, one poster pasted up on public walls had assured the *"PEUPLE DE PARIS"* that if the United States electrocuted Sacco and Vanzetti, "their racketeers, their American Legion, their millionaires" would no longer enjoy "peacefulness," that they would no longer have "the right to the city." On the morning of the executions, the anarchist *Le Libertaire* echoed these sentiments. "The American executioners will not parade peacefully around the aristocratic streets of the capital," its front page insisted; *"Non,* the virtuous puritans of the New World will no longer get drunk on champagne in Parisian brothels after having intoxicated themselves on the blood of their victims."[71] The rioting later that evening, in light of such heated language, could be read as the momentary realization of a shared fantasy of dismantling the American subculture in Paris, a presence demonstrators saw as the most egregious local form of exploitative privilege. Of all the potential bourgeois or capitalist targets in the city, protesters went for those that were also evocative of and heavily frequented by Americans.

With its extravagant setting and reliably American clientele, the Champs-Elysées provided a ready target for demonstrators unable to approach the nearby American embassy. For the same reason, some of the most dramatic dismantling would take place in Montmartre. When police repelled crowds from the Communist-led demonstration on the grand boulevards, several thousand inspired individuals veered off north towards the city's premier nightlife destination, calling the names of Sacco and Vanzetti, calling for the death of Fuller. Heated exchanges between those who had traveled to Montmartre for pleasure and those who had come for politics degenerated into a flurry of destruction between the places Clichy and Pigalle. At the Brasserie Wepler it would cost approximately 20,000 francs to replace the eleven smashed windows, four broken marble tables, and mountain of cracked dishware left in the aftermath of one scuffle. Roving through some of the capital's best pleasure grounds, protesters damaged more than a dozen automobiles—those luxury possessions that conveyed the rich to their nighttime destinations. One rental car belonging to the American Auto-Confort Touring agency, known for its fully equipped luxury vehicles and English-speaking drivers, rioters singled out for special abuse. They not only smashed its windows and destroyed its paint but also removed its engine.[72]

Protesters' premeditated desires to reach those quarters known to cater to Americans and other wealthy visitors were compounded by spontaneous stimuli that set them off unexpectedly. The severe damage at the Brasserie Wepler, for example, might have been sparked by an English-language announcement in its window, as reported by the *Paris Herald*. Such a trigger definitely explained the fate of the Brasserie Mikado up the street from the Wepler. Around 10 P.M., a column of some 1,500 demonstrators heading towards the place Clichy passed in front of the Mikado, its proprietor Louis Soulanges later testified. "The head of the cortege had already passed before the Brasserie," he explained, "when, abruptly, the *manifestants* stopped, shouting 'Charleston, Charleston!'" The rioters had spied the Hôtel Charleston, located—to Monsieur Soulanges' misfortune—in the same building as the Mikado. For some of the angry pass-ersby, the name must have triggered an association with Charlestown prison where Sacco and Vanzetti had gone to the electric chair. But it also recalled the famous American dance, zealously practiced in nightclubs that catered to Americans. In either case, the word Charleston alone was enough to enrage the mob marching past. Seizing handfuls of stones piled for nearby road repairs and hurling them through the windows, rioters unleashed a *"grande panique"* among customers on the terrace, who stampeded inside.[73]

Events here at the edge of the eighteenth arrondissement had clearly been informed by the incendiary editorials of the Communist Deputy Paul Vaillant-Couturier, which dominated the front pages of *L'Humanité* that month. The dynamic Vaillant-Couturier had railed against the United States as a center of class exploitation and bigoted violence, and for him the Sacco-Vanzetti case laid bare a growing international struggle between colluding capitalist powers—led by the duplicitous "Republic of the dollar"—and a united working-class front. "The battle has now begun between the police at the orders of the American plutocracy and the proletarian conscience of the entire world," he asserted: "To the interdependent *capitalismes* engaging in the same repression against the defenders of the proletariat, the proletariat must respond by an act of *solidarité internationale!*" Vaillant-Couturier's sense of the Sacco-Vanzetti case as a profoundly international event was matched by his conviction that Paris stood as both the immediate terrain of contest and what was ultimately at stake in the affair. "Working-class Paris, although it can be believed on Wall Street, is not a colony of the dollar. . . . Rise up!" he exhorted Parisians. Vaillant-Couturier fixated on the approaching American Legion convention, branding the arriving veterans as representatives of those who condoned the executions of Sacco and Vanzetti and those who encroached on the sovereignty of the French capital. The day before the riots he wrote that "the fascists of the American Legion have been cheered by Paris, Friday night, at the Moulin Rouge." The next morning he blasted again: "Montmartre takes in the first wave of American Legionnaires patriotically drunk on memories of war, of champagne . . . of jazz and of Charleston."[74] Evoking the Moulin Rouge, Montmartre, and the Charleston in his exposés of the Sacco-Vanzetti case, the words of Vaillant-Couturier unfolded like a road map for some of the most serious incidents later that night.

So perhaps by no coincidence, the evening's most spectacular installment of rioting occurred when an imposing mob gathered on the boulevard Clichy with the intention of sacking the Moulin Rouge. During the ensuing fray, approximately fifteen gunshots were fired as a troupe of traffic cops made a desperate attempt to hold off an invasion of the theater before reinforcements arrived. Unable to keep the crowd at bay, police and business owners watched as *"perturbateurs,"* calling for vengeance in the name of Sacco and Vanzetti, set about demolishing the façade. In a frenzy of which Paris preservationists had only dreamed, rioters defaced posters advertising American performers and wrecked the music hall's overabundance of electric bulbs and neon signs. Demonstrators likewise destroyed the stained-glass marquee and illuminated decorations of the Bal du Moulin Rouge that abutted the music hall proper. During the assault, the "band of rowdies," proprietors grumbled, had also broken the Brasserie Graff's sign, a billboard six meters long made up of tiny lightbulbs that advertised garden terrace dining under the windmill blades of its more famous neighbor. The Moulin Rouge alone—that icon of Parisian spectacle, that premier destination for American visitors—would cost more than 50,000 francs to repair.[75]

Leftist editorialists, seeking to make meaning out of the night's incidents for a sympathetic readership, depicted the Sacco-Vanzetti affair on one level as a contest between those clashing economic coalitions that had long figured in Marxist imaginations. On one side, they envisioned the working classes; on the other, they pictured what Vaillant-Couturier called *"l'internationale de la noce"*—an alliance of cosmopolitan revelers with its troops of partygoers and consumers, a modern incarnation of the bourgeoisie whose brand of nighttime indulgence represented a "permanent insult to the misery of workers." For Vaillant-Couturier and others, these opposing blocs were locked in contest over Paris itself. In front of the famous Moulin Rouge, "while the anger of the people unfurled," Vaillant-Couturier rejoiced the morning after the riots, *"l'internationale de la noce* made the acquaintance of the real Paris, the Paris of the sons of the Commune, on the same soil where the last barricades were raised."[76] Against this new cosmopolitan and Americanized Paris threatening to sever those admired links to the city's tumultuous past, Vaillant-Couturier contrasted the one made up of those who had braved wet weather to participate in the protest in Pré Saint-Gervais only days before, those who represented what he called the "revolutionary heart of Paris." Their clothes soaked through with mud, their faces streaked with rain, crying *"Amnistie! Amnistie!,"* these urbanites had cheered, he related with a maudlin tone, for "the soldiers, the sailors, the imprisoned militants, those of France and those of the colonies, the victims of the executioners of Bulgaria, Poland, Romania, Yugoslavia, Italy, Hungary, Lithuania, and China." At their center, Vaillant-Couturier pictured the visages of "two innocents struck by the *capitalisme-exemple*, the *capitalisme yankee"*—Vanzetti and Sacco.[77]

Branding "Yankee capitalism" as exemplary and singling out Americans and their haunts for abuse, rioters and their defenders revealed that more had been at work in this controversy than pure class politics. The affair also signaled experimentation with new kinds of cultural politics. By juxtaposing images of an authentic, historic Paris against an imposing American one, Sacco-Vanzetti activists hoped to exploit popular desires to defend French culture. Radical Parisians' appeals to such nationalist sensibilities cut against their internationalist ideals and reversed previous notions, advanced most forcefully by Communist writers, that anti-American outbursts belonged to the French right. The incidents in Montmartre in particular contained an ironic element in light of events the previous summer. When, in July 1926, roving bands of right-wing Parisians targeted American tourists in Montmartre and near the Opera, *L'Humanité* had condemned the actions as "an explosion of chauvinist stupidity." Protests, the paper's editors argued, should not devolve into "manhandling an American drunk who, just like his bourgeois French counterpart, wants to make merry in Montmartre." Yet the versatile uses of anti-American invective proved too good to resist in the interwar capital, even if it contradicted leftists' promises to put class interests and solidarities above other allegiances. Indeed, French Communists' resort to such nationalist language and symbolism in their Sacco-Vanzetti campaign appeared so striking that, despite the PCF's ability, perhaps more than any other national party, to make something of the case, it drew a formal reprimand from the ECCI. Comintern officials took issue with the French Party's decision to frame their campaign in "sentimental" rather than class terms.[78] This kind of rustic nationalism of the left—just as opposed to modern, urbane visions of French culture as the pastoral dreams of the right—anticipated the aesthetics of the Popular Front, even as disapproval from Moscow held up its development.

Both in Paris and beyond, the Sacco-Vanzetti campaign served as a seven-year-long education in international grassroots organizing and propaganda techniques. The affair by no means united partisans of the left, but it provided the apparatus to regroup in the hostile climate of the 1920s. For anarchists and socialists, juggling between different factions and regions around the world presented a heady but stimulating challenge. Steeping themselves in knowledge about worldwide radical politics and the ways of modern publicity, such activists may not have saved the two men from the electric chair, but they emerged from the campaign with a better sense of how to appeal to different audiences and make the most of support from liberals and famous figures. For communists, the learning curve had been even steeper. French party members may have been reprimanded by the Comintern for their use of sentimentalism, but clearly, like their socialist and anarchist counterparts who used the same kinds of tactics, they were able to take advantage of the case in ways other communists who stuck to the framework of traditional class politics could not. Struggling to develop their movement in the 1920s and as yet still unsure what their strategies and traditions would be, communists found that the Sacco-Vanzetti affair made clear just how much single-issue campaigns, stirred up through advanced communications networks, could generate anger and mass action. The "propaganda schools in Moscow,"

John Dos Passos surmised in retrospect, learned from the case that "griefs and discontents, properly stimulated and directed, were more effective than armies in the world struggle for power." By the end of the twenties, as their fixed protocols began to emerge, communists therefore yearned to capitalize on incidents like it. The Sacco-Vanzetti drive may have failed in its immediate objective, but it would become a model for more successful campaigns waged during the Popular Front years of the 1930s on both sides of the Atlantic. Comintern operatives had been specifically searching for a case that "could be Sacco and Vanzettized to the ends of the earth" when they lighted on their most successful cause célèbre, the Scottsboro controversy.[79]

Others drew different lessons from the affair. Americans in Paris had followed the case with as much interest as anyone else, and they remained as bitterly divided on the subject as those back home. Some could not have cared less about the two radicals' deaths, sharing the sentiments of Billy Sunday or the Legionnaires, only days from setting up camp in the capital themselves. Others, like the writer Elliot Paul felt "utterly ashamed" simply for belonging to the nation that allowed this to happen. Grieving for the two martyred men, Paul also saw in the Paris riots a disturbing premonition of things to come. "That night started the preliminary rumblings of a series of quakes that jarred France's inimical classes apart and ended in the death of a nation," he later wrote of the Third Republic's fall.[80]

Indeed, the affair set in motion a chain of polarizing events that would continue the battle over control of the Paris streets. Right-wing responses to the night's events seethed with rage. The leader of the Jeunesses Patriotes, Pierre Taittinger, called demonstrators antipatriots, Moscow's executioners, a horde of murder apologists, and "the nebulous jokers of the League of the Rights of Man." The cranky royalist and antisemitic Léon Daudet thought the riots a natural outcome of the "democratic error." A writer for Le Figaro thundered, "If we want peace, we must strike hard and just and strike at the head" of those "criminal enterprises" filled with "international rabble," the enemies of civilization, society, and la Patrie.[81] Sentiments such as these prepared many Parisians to support with extra vigor the arriving American Legionnaires, whose takeover of the city would be even more urgent and satisfying after rioters had failed in their attempts at occupation. At the same time, the lessons of the Sacco-Vanzetti affair lent new legitimacy to right-wing desires to crack down not only on radicals but also on that provocative nightlife world that did not anger leftists alone.

| Prefect Chiappe's Purging of Paris

A S THE DESTRUCTIVE END TO the Sacco-Vanzetti affair suggested, between the world wars "Americanness," in its various guises, began to figure prominently in a transatlantic culture of political engagements. Targeting sites and symbols associated with Americans in Paris, however, would not be a left-wing preserve alone. Right-wing Parisians, too, marshaled popular support by opposing the liberalism linked with Americans and the districts that catered to them, a tactic employed most effectively in September 1927 by the reactionary Prefect of Police Jean Chiappe, who launched an *épuration*—a purging or cleansing—of those same districts just attacked by Sacco-Vanzetti rioters. Grappling with Americans' presence and the kinds of values they were believed to embody formed an important undertone in Chiappe's notorious reform effort, which has yet to be studied in detail.[1] Like the Sacco-Vanzetti affair, Chiappe's purge fused localized concerns to broader, international objectives. Drawing on connections between political and cultural subversion and the place of foreigners in the city, the prefect's initiatives aimed most of all to shore up the capital's reputation abroad.

Short and charismatic, balding but with a Corsican flair, Jean Chiappe was a man both easily admired and easily spoofed, a figure often likened, either with affection or disdain, to Napoleon and Mussolini. Popular with many Parisians and anathema to others, Chiappe had strong opinions about how the city of Paris should be. Capital of the arts, entrepôt of luxury trade and the pursuits of pleasure, "Paris must have a politics of prestige," he decreed. In the interest of the capital's international acclaim, the prefect prevailed upon Parisians and their guests to pursue their favorite urban pastimes with "decency and dignity." A career civil servant who rose through the ranks of the Ministry of the Interior, the prefect had a penchant for aphorisms. He always said: "Capital of good humor, Paris must be a capital of good manners."[2] Yet developments since the late war threatened to prove otherwise. From the dives of Montparnasse to the promenading galleries of Montmartre's theaters, the spaces that had become so familiar to American residents and visitors had been transformed, in the words of one worried observer, into a "tumultuous battleground of pleasures."[3]

During his seven years in charge of one of the world's largest and most modern police forces, Chiappe waged an ambitious campaign to counter these trends and transform the French capital into the orderly and robust metropole that he knew it could be. Beneath his punchy rhetoric lay Chiappe's deep discontent with the way things were going in the city and a growing predilection for the arguments and tactics of the far right. One American reporter would dub him the "best bet for French fascism." An admirer of Louis-Aldolphe Thiers, who had violently rid the capital of its insurgent Communards decades before, the prefect believed in a healthy dose of coercion to purge Paris of its objectionable moral and political elements and to mold its people into the upright inhabitants and industrious workers he envisioned. "Fear of the police," he instructed, "is the beginning of wisdom."[4] There would be no room in Chiappe's idealized Paris for outspoken radicals, colonial rebels, purveyors of vice, practitioners of alternative sexualities, or communists of any kind. For Chiappe, the rights recognized during the French Revolution represented a finite legacy, not an ongoing promise. In a city besieged by enemies internal and external, political and sexual, Chiappe discovered that the only sound way to save liberty would be to suppress it.

Chiappe's *épuration* officially began on September 1, 1927, one week after the Sacco-Vanzetti riots and little more than two weeks before the scheduled American Legion convention. As the nights grew longer, the prefect's agents descended on boarding houses and hotels, scrutinizing identity papers and guest logs. Plainclothesmen cased the backrooms of bars, cataloguing delinquencies that merited later raids, when whistle-blowing brigades would abruptly end after-hours drinking and dancing, cocaine use, and illegal acts of cross-dressing in public. They burst, too, into the dens of eccentric sex shows and bathhouses known as homosexual rendezvous. Organized into special *rondes de nuit*, patrolmen stacked in the backs of trucks or arranged into bicycle flocks scoured the streets, stopping passersby for questioning and detaining prostitutes, pimps, suspicious taxi drivers, and other self-appointed guides to the city's underworld of sex and danger. With particular zeal, Chiappe's men seized thousands of publications deemed pornographic from kiosk display racks and the bouquinistes' booths that lined the Seine, suspending sellers' permits, fining editors, and taking repeat offenders to court. Between September 1927 and March 1928 alone, Chiappe's dragnets resulted in more than 11,400 prosecutions for a variety of vice law infractions. More than 3,550 foreigners incurred fines for irregular identity papers; 849 others faced expulsion and other administrative verdicts stripping them of their right to remain in France. Police investigated more than 760 hotels and other establishments renting rooms in the city. They refused or rescinded music and after-hours permits for dozens of venues denounced for their "suspect" clientele, forcing many out of business. During those eventful six months, Chiappe's men interrogated more than 225,000 people.[5] That was only the beginning. The purge would continue for six more years.

Taking action against those who instigated the Sacco-Vanzetti affair, Chiappe's measures included new levels of surveillance in the city's working-class neighborhoods and suburbs. This campaign therefore took a crucial step toward greater police governance of immigrants, colonial subjects, and political dissidents, helping to provide the foundation for subsequent programs of internment and deportation under Vichy.[6] On Chiappe's watch, however, control of laborers and radicals often became most intense where their activities intersected with the cosmopolitan world of urban entertainments and nightlife. Chiappe and his supporters had discovered that the terrain of affluent foreigners and other night revelers needed policing as much as the turf of working-class migrants did.

Police prefects had purged Paris before, but Americans' heightened presence in the capital—and Parisians' reactions to them—allowed Chiappe new justifications for his épuration, which went beyond tested arguments about radical suppression and population control. If the explosive outcome of the Sacco-Vanzetti affair provided the initial catalyst for his measures, Chiappe also used the impending arrival of the Legionnaires—"our American friends," he called them—as a motivating factor. Both a crackdown on the irascible protesters who threatened more trouble during the Legionnaires' convention and a cleanup of those areas American veterans were destined to frequent would ensure the respectable presentation of the capital during that high-profile event. Furthermore, the general importance of American tourist dollars for the Paris economy and visitors' escalating concerns about the capital's unruliness provided Chiappe with a long-term justification for his campaign. Shortly before the riots, the prefect had learned that families abroad were hesitating to send their children to study in Paris, "fearing for them the dangers of the Capital." He learned at the same time, Chiappe later told the Municipal Council, that tourist agencies were reducing their itineraries in

Paris to only two days. Moral and political disorder, he implied, threatened to tarnish the city's reputation in places like the United States and England, a development insupportably bad for business. To restore the confidence of American sojourners and other foreign customers, Chiappe averred, "the hour to act had come."[7]

Raids on nightclubs like the American-run Le Grand Duc, investigations into books sold at Brentano's, the padlocking of jazz pianos in Montparnasse cafés popular with expatriates—such scenes vividly contradicted American myths about laissez-faire Gay Paree. Americans' relationships to these police efforts, however, proved even more complicated. The prominence of Americans in Paris—their participation in the cities' industries of pleasure and the ways in which they construed that participation—presented Chiappe's campaign with one of its greatest ironies. Many of those very same visitors for whom Chiappe purported to clean up Paris were instrumental in keeping the capital's nightlife, including its seedier side, going strong. At the same time, Americans frequently used their confrontation with the city's risqué sights as an occasion to hone their own sense of moral correctness and national superiority, doing so, invariably, at Parisians' expense. In the final estimation, the arrival of the Legionnaires had only been a convenient pretext for Chiappe's measures, for it would be the venues and purveyors who catered to the whims of these veterans and their compatriots that became his primary targets. Conflicts over public morals became inextricably linked to notions about national prestige and the role played by Americans and other foreigners in the postwar capital. Americans who sought out the pleasures of Parisian nights inserted themselves, even if often casually or unintentionally, into these dramas, drawing complex responses from their hosts.

Interwar Paris, from many angles, appeared to be a city sexually out of control. Women wore makeup and flirted with men on the street; couples danced provocatively in bars and made out openly in the corner booths of restaurants. The semiprivate encounters of assignation rooms for hourly rent spilled out into the streets of the postwar city. "Everywhere lovers," the American writer Sherwood Anderson had recorded in his Paris notebook; "The lovers are in all the little dark places, on the bridges, on the stairway leading down to the dark river." Public places suited all manner of sexual expressions, both furtive and uninhibited. Students paraded naked but for glitter and cardboard accessories to wild saturnalias that lasted until dawn. Nudists plied through the parks by the light of the full moon. Subtle men with tailored vests and eye-catching handkerchiefs cruised the promenades of the Champs-Elysées, scanning other men for knowing glances. The impulses of some exceeded all standards of acceptability. Pests of the boulevard, exhibitionists exposed themselves unduly. Nuisances of the garden, voyeurs ogled petting couples from nearby bushes. Parisian women came to dread lecherous *frôleurs* who rubbed up against strangers in crowded places. They feared even more the infamous *piqueurs* who purportedly trolled the lingerie sections of department stores and the depths of the Métro, pricking women with large needles through their clothing. For all tastes, the city had its hot spots and modus operandi, and after the war thousands, from gigolos to topless chorus girls, made their living by the capital's elaborate and booming industries of pleasure. Particularly tenacious guides lingered in front of train stations and hotels, offering to escort visitors to brothels and sex shows. Near the esteemed place Vendôme, postcard sellers accosted passersby with whispers of titillating photographs tucked under their coats. In the arcades behind the Opera, tawdry little shops stocked *films galants*, which could be viewed through stereoscopes for a franc.[8]

The capital, of course, had long been a place for sexual indulgences, but their availability blossomed after the war. It was not sex per se that would dismay Jean Chiappe and so many other Parisians, but those aspects of sexuality that carried over into public and seemed to be troubling by-products of a new stage of urban modernity in which cosmopolitan foreigners and other ascendant figures played a greater part. Since the second half of the nineteenth century, Paris, like other industrial centers, had served as a destination for young single laborers, both male and female, who traveled outside the home for work and increasingly turned to the city's commercial amusements for relief from the drudgery of the day. Away from traditional arbiters of community values, dance halls, theaters, and amusement parks promoted social and sexual experimentation just as they did in other modern capitals such as Berlin, London, or New York.[9] In Paris, such venues flourished in the years following the Armistice, when, as one witness attested, the capital's "number of establishments devoted to the service of the devil has tripled, at least."[10] The dislocations of the war and the influx of soldiers, conferencegoers, manual laborers, and others had unleashed on the capital more patrons for its pleasure grounds as well as a rising pool of workers to cater to them. The city's bawdy reputation soared. From the songs of homecoming veterans to Hollywood movie scenes, depictions of the French capital solidified, the world over, its status as a mecca of sensual delights. "Even in the remotest village the word 'Paris' is spoken with a wink," as one chronicler put it. At the same time, the crowds that flocked to the city's music halls, *boîtes de nuit*, and more illicit establishments had become increasingly heterogeneous.[11] They included once reticent elites, tourists in search of enjoyment more than refinement, black immigrants, and other "exotic" newcomers. With their motley clientele, these venues promoted all kinds of novel interactions and vibrant subcultures—changes that set the stage for Chiappe's purging of Paris.

If any of the capital's industries of pleasure did seem redolent of prewar days, they were the *maisons de tolérance*. These legalized brothels, characterized by their resident *filles*, who faced the scrutiny of doctors and policemen, continued to be a staple of the city's sexual stock-in-trade. In the nineteenth century, such institutions, with their unobtrusive, shuttered exteriors, did not reflect French permissiveness, as many Americans believed, so much as Victorian impulses to protect hygiene and the sanctity of bourgeois family life. Opulent *maisons d'illusions*, complete with Turkish salons or medieval dungeon rooms, continued to thrive near the Opera and the Palais Royal, but the majority of Parisian brothels were family-run, neighborhood affairs, designated outside only by their illuminated address numbers and distinguished inside by their heavy drapery and half respectable-looking parlors. By the 1920s, these places seemed almost dowdy. More indicative of the times were the no-frills "slaughterhouses" or "dimestores of sex," as the night photographer Brassaï called them, where workers paid their fees at a till and received towels and partners with modern assembly-line precision. Other new varieties called café-bordellos catered to a more leisurely clientele, admitting women as well as men into their chrome-plated front rooms, where couples indulged their curiosities over pricey drinks. The most famous of such venues, the Sphinx, opened in the late twenties around the corner from the Dôme in Montparnasse, boasting some of the city's first air-conditioning.[12]

Despite novelties like the Sphinx, traditional *maisons de tolérance* fell into decline after the war. In the early twenties, Paris officials counted only thirty left in the entire city. In their place, however, sprouted a host of unregulated *maisons de rendez-vous* in private apartment buildings and hotel suites. Of the capital's 270 known establishments of this kind, the more daring ones clustered behind the Opera and the Madeleine, where the wildest tableaux vivants and fantasy acts were acted out for audiences recruited by guides, taxi drivers, and others who received commissions for their efforts.[13] Affording mobility and anonymity, the automobile made possible a host of other new practices, not least notorious *partouzes* in the forest clearings of the Bois de Boulogne. Furtively, the sexually adventurous drove to these prearranged meetings, where swingers swapped partners between parked cars. These backseat encounters with strangers perfectly captured, according to one French chronicler, "the feverish, anxious, wearied, a bit morbid character of the big city today."[14] The proliferation of taxis and chauffeured cars after the war also gave rise to barhopping and slumming tours, allowing pleasure seekers to travel to several different parts of the capital in the course of a single night. Guides, too, took to soliciting pedestrians from slow-moving vehicles. Not inappropriately, alarmists regarded the automobile as a "moving house of debauchery."[15]

Almost as jarring were the thousands of prostitutes who strutted down the avenues with a sense of impunity they had not had before the war. Troupes of women violated laws prohibiting them from congregating in groups of three or more or soliciting in the vicinity of schools, churches, and principal thoroughfares. Their ranks swelled around the Pigalle region of Montmartre, where they propositioned patrons leaving nightclubs, and around the cafés of Montparnasse, where they posed as friendly artists' models. To observers, their inundation of the grand boulevards took on the scale of an invasion. High-class call girls known as *ces dames de la Madeleine* lingered by the Café de la Paix and in nearby hotel lobbies where big-spending foreigners could be found. Less extravagant girls crowded the alleys by the central markets of Les Halles, hoping to catch the eye of farmers and butchers. Male streetwalkers—*petits messieurs* with powdered faces—fought their female counterparts for the attention of potential johns.[16]

Women of all kinds stood out noticeably on the postwar street. The war had brought proper Parisian girls and middle-class women out of their homes to work in jobs abandoned by conscripts and to staff hospitals and schools. After the war, new technologies freeing housewives from time-consuming household labors and the rise of tertiary-sector work continued to draw *Parisiennes* out into the workaday world of the city. From society ladies to fashion models and garment workers, women casually sampled the boulevards' shopping and dining, eagerly searching for thrills. Suddenly, one exasperated Frenchman claimed, "The women were everywhere." The growing independence of young single women—styled as *femmes modernes* or *garçonnes*—seemed in particular to herald the demise of traditional gender roles. Striving to be openly flirtatious and intentionally alluring, they made it increasingly difficult to tell, some chided, if prostitutes had indeed overrun the boulevards, or if the streets had just been occupied by those who looked and acted like them. In the city's bustling nightlife, even in its dicey parts, many women now staked claims to a new and, for many, troubling sexual license that had begun to overturn time-honored protocols and the delicately balanced differences between the sexes.[17]

Nothing seemed to capture women's new, directive role in the capital's social life like the proliferation of those controversial figures, the gigolos. In their basic capacities, gigolos were professional dancing partners in the nightclubs of Montmartre or the cafés on the Champs-Elysées, who, like their female counterparts, received a fee for drumming up customer enthusiasm and showing unescorted ladies a good time. Such characters lived off the tips of wealthy women who paid to be tangoed and fox-trotted around the dance floor by slick-haired men with ingratiating manners and exotic good looks. Their ranks included many foreigners, Argentines, Spaniards, and Greeks among them, whose presence seemed all the more alarming in light of how many young French men had been lost in the war. These professional dancers' services often extended beyond the bounds of the nightclub. Many offered simulations of courtship and even sexual relationships in exchange for gifts or money. For out-of-town visitors, male escorts could be commissioned for an entire stay—recommendations could be found at travel bureaus, bank counters, and through reputable agencies advertised in newspapers. Beholden to the wishes of their female bosses, the gigolos offered a "decorative accessory," one writer suggested, for the smart woman's "turn-out."[18] Not only, then, had boundaries between women of good and bad repute dissolved, but the lines separating the proper roles of women and men had also blurred.

Striking public displays of homosexuality only compounded this sense of the breakdown of gender conventions in interwar Paris. Designated spots to search out partners for same-sex acts—like the Palais Royal—had long existed in the capital, and by the end of the nineteenth century a modern homosexual milieu had begun to take shape around a small cluster of taverns, brasseries, and baths.[19] After the war, however, both a lesbian community and a gay male world, rich with cultural codes and well-known meeting grounds, grew rapidly in size and diversity. The contours of these emergent subcultures extended well beyond the elite coteries of Jean Cocteau's club Le Bœuf sur le Toit or the celebrated salons of Natalie Barney and Gertrude Stein. The spaces men sought out for same-sex encounters included certain bathhouses, the promenading galleries of a handful of cinemas and music halls, as well as a plethora of sidewalk urinals—the ones with three stalls, called "teapots" or "teacups." The world of gay men stretched into the working-class district of the Bastille—to restaurants by the Gare de Lyon, known for their homosexual camaraderie, and to *bals musettes* on the rue de Lappe, where men danced with men, rubbing shoulders with neighborhood workers, colonial soldiers, and middle-class slummers. Lesbians frequented not only private salons and bookstores, but also bars in Montmartre and tearooms in the vicinity of the Madeleine. Entrées into this world of women could be made through contacts with salesgirls in the fitting rooms of lingerie boutiques and glove shops or the bathroom attendants of certain big restaurants. Few bars or nightclubs catered exclusively to lesbians or gay men, but many garnered reputations as homosexual hangouts. In Montparnasse, lesbians frequented the Monocle not far from the Sphinx, where shorthaired women in crisp tuxedos romanced their more feminine partners, cigarettes dangling from the corners of their mouths. Men who might have been called fairies in New York often congregated around the corner on the terraces of the Select and the Dôme. Montmartre harbored the greatest density of such places, however. Late at night the place Pigalle bristled with activity: male prostitutes leading clients into the Métro Blanche, men dressed as women emerging from parties in the backrooms of bars, sailors loudly cruising the crowds.[20]

Homosexuals' greater visibility in postwar Paris underscored the ways in which many had begun to take liberties and challenge older patterns of behavior that had yet to completely disappear. As one Frenchman later recalled, the twenties stood out as an "epoch of provocation," a period characterized simultaneously by continuing conversational taboos about homosexuality and an emerging, demonstrative frankness about same-sex desire. Because "one did not speak of homosexuality, it had to be shown," he explained.[21] Indeed, gay men staged lavish, well-attended masquerade balls at the Salle Wagram or the dance hall Magic-City, and one of the most popular entertainment acts in interwar Paris was that of Barbette, the transvestite trapeze artist who triumphantly revealed his masculine gender at the climax of his acrobatic show. Gay culture flourished in part because in France, unlike in Germany, Great Britain, and the United States, laws did not prohibit homosexuality or sodomy. Nevertheless, provisions against public sex acts, molestation, and cross-dressing were often employed against those of both genders engaging in same-sex activities. During these years, when access to the city's public spaces seemed at a premium, men still risked up to two years' incarceration for indecency if caught in flagrante delicto in a public urinal, and the publishers of homosexual material faced hefty fines and prison sentences. Popular wisdom and police logic alike continued to paint homosexuality as criminal and immoral; emerging medical discourses defined it as pathological. For this reason, the gay world in postwar Paris, like that of New York, remained clandestine even as it also sometimes appeared startlingly obvious and well integrated into public life.[22]

The arrival of new immigrants—not least those from France's colonies— also helped to change the perimeters of public sexual expression. Paris had long been home to elite, well-educated emigrants from the French territories, but not until the wartime migration of colonial subjects, drafted in special military regiments or recruited as factory workers, would the capital draw significant numbers of people of color. Together with a few dozen resident African Americans, *"exotiques"* from Senegal, Algeria, Indochina, and the

Antilles contributed appreciably to the city's commercial entertainments. By 1926, the new Grand Mosque, with its adjoining café, and a busy Chinese restaurant garnered a kind of cachet for their foreign novelty in the Latin Quarter. The vogue for jazz and dances like the Charleston and the beguine ensured that African American and Caribbean nightspots became especially important spaces to try out new poses of what passed for raw sensuality. To many, black performers seemed unburdened by the formalities that fettered traditional European musicians and dancers. Jazz orchestras, one French writer characteristically imagined, "wreathed their hot and deliquescent fantasies" in Parisian *dancings* flush with gyrating couples monopolizing the dance floors.[23]

As popular entertainers, black people in Paris became widely admired sex symbols. Their successes on stage evoked the crumbling of racial hierarchies even as they also hinted at the continued objectification of the black body. Offstage, people of color also flouted conventions about interracial sex. Such taboos in Paris paled next to American prohibitions, but mixed couples holding hands or dancing closely still presented jarring sights, and, judging from the sex acts between black men and white women regularly featured in the performance lineups of clandestine *maisons*, such encounters continued to exude an aura of transgression. Opportunities for interactions across the color line excited female socialites, wanting to shock and be shocked, and white gay men, for whom the colonial soldier in uniform became a particularly coveted partner. Whereas some Montmartre nightclubs turned black patrons away to please their American customers, others, including the Bal du Moulin Rouge and the Paradis, built their reputation on the free circulation of their mixed-race clientele. For same-sex interracial encounters, the dives on the rue de Lappe in the Bastille area became legendary.[24] Along with all the other new urban types crowding the clubs and cafés, people of color helped to shape a postwar nightlife that revolved around dancing, drinking, and promiscuous mingling, a world definitively shaken loose from nineteenth-century prescriptions about public propriety, which had begun to break down in the preceding decades. It was a place hundreds of thousands would want to come to witness for themselves.

Americans imagined Paris as part of a string of enticing, wide-open towns beyond their own borders, and they had good reason to believe that such destinations offered liberties that had been suppressed at home. The late nineteenth and early twentieth centuries represented a heyday for moral policing in the United States. Looking on the rowdy, bawdy places that American cities had become, elites sought ways to curtail urban underworlds that seemed rife with suspicious immigrant practices, debasing entertainments, and subversive radicalisms. Growing out of Victorian convictions about distinctive male and female sexualities and the imperatives of self-restraint, reformers mobilized a mix of Protestant beliefs, middle-class pretensions, and racial assumptions about their own fitness to determine moral standards for all. By the first decades of the twentieth century, such antivice activities shaded into progressive programs to remake cities into more efficient and healthy places. Pushes for child labor laws, garbage collection, and other social hygiene measures dovetailed with other bids to clean up theaters and circuses, to stamp out the excesses of gambling rooms, beer gardens, or the dens of cockfights. Forming temperance and purity groups, middle-class women targeted individual failings and inadequate laws, preaching the evils of alcohol and other corrupting indulgences that tempted fathers away from family duties. Middle-class male reformers, often stoked by journalists' muckraking, threw their energies instead into vigilance societies, combating corrupt municipal governance and organized crime through aggressive, extralegal forms of surveillance and suppression. For increasingly proactive vice committees, tackling the problem of prostitution during the 1910s proved an entrée into attacking all kinds of other indiscretions—dance hall temptations, unedifying nickelodeon fare, suggestive advertising, and so forth.[25]

To many other Americans, these campaigns felt increasingly repressive, the mark not of engineered progress but rather what the journalist Herbert Croly called "illiberal puritanism." The battle against the brothel and the saloon produced especially impressive results during the 1910s. Red-light districts, a staple of the urban landscape before, were shut down across the United States. During World War I, infamous quarters, such as Chicago's Levee, New Orleans' Storyville, and San Francisco's Barbary Coast became only shells of their former selves. At the same time, government agents and moralizing critics hounded modernist writers and other freethinkers, using the Comstock Law to prohibit the dissemination of their journals and other works through the mail. Then, at the start of 1920, Prohibition descended on the land. Antivice crusading peaked just as middle-class Americans were becoming more interested in "steppin' out" and enjoying cities' restaurants, theaters, and nightclubs. For these new pleasure seekers, American life appeared newly bound by all kinds of restrictions, which, by hampering their own freedoms and not just those of the working classes, had gone too far. Those who fancied themselves savvy, urbane types chuckled at the mayor of one city, who decreed that department store mannequins must remain fully clothed, and balked at the leaders of another town, who declared making "goo-goo eyes" at women a misdemeanor. Less funny were the Ku Klux Klan's speakeasy raids and whippings of "loose" women.[26]

By contrast, going abroad promised a respite from all these judgments and forbiddances—from the perceived narrow-mindedness of Sinclair Lewis' Babbitts and H. L. Mencken's booboisie. It was to Europe that Margaret Sanger fled to avoid prosecution for sending birth control materials through the mail; and it was there, too, that little-magazine editor Margaret Anderson retreated after her defeat in court for publishing installments of James Joyce's *Ulysses*.[27] Increasingly, destinations overseas catered not only to such exiled intellectuals and activists but also to common tourists in search of casual thrills. Places like Tijuana, Havana, and Shanghai were fast developing reputations for their libertine nightlife, and in Europe, Weimar Berlin set the pace for stylized debauchery. As a destination for thrill seekers, 1920s Paris was almost as notorious as Berlin, only more accessible and more popular.

Drawn in by the promise of Paris as a visitor's delight, Americans made up a sizable portion of those cosmopolitan crowds helping to remake the capital's pleasure industries between the wars. Ascertaining the nature and extent of Americans' participation in the city's amusements, however, proves difficult. The novelist Henry Miller's braggadocio aside, most Americans hesitated to reveal details about their own indulgences in the city's sexual underworld. They did, however, gleefully enumerate the pursuits of their compatriots in letters and travelogues, a convention that allowed visitors to discuss potentially controversial topics without admitting personal involvements. American guidebooks also contained an overabundance of detail about the city's nocturnal entertainments. Moreover, next to the selective absences in American writings are clues to their actions found in a wealth of French materials, from newspaper editorials and the sociological sketches of urban chroniclers to the files of the Paris police.

As a group, Americans, it seems, played a significant and conspicuous part in the pleasure grounds of Paris. One English chronicler, for example, attributed the striking transformation of postwar nightlife in large part to American and British women now "claiming a share in nocturnal dissipations which would have horrified many of them in the years before 1914." In the late nineteenth century, respectable female visitors did not dine without male escorts, but by the twenties, they went as they pleased to shops, restaurants, theaters, and bars. Embracing new fashions and fads, American women in Paris became prime customers, too, for the city's gigolos. All kinds of American "sex-adventurers," male and female, who were "willing to try anything once," inundated the city's fabled quarters by the mid-twenties, one bartender popular with such visitors reported. Those who passed for "stable citizens at home," he marveled, "went completely berserk the minute they hit Montparnasse."[28] So many of these arrivals became avid participants in the city's newly expanded homosexual subculture that one resident depicted an entire "American sissy world in Paris." This world encompassed not just writers and artists on the Left Bank, but also transient participants, who were drawn by internationally renowned baths and masquerade balls and who came and went with the tourist tide. Rich foreign men, including Americans, also fed the market for male prostitutes. Police roundups regularly included a considerable proportion of foreigners—individuals who sometimes claimed that they had been assured that homosexuality and male prostitution were not only permitted but also freely practiced in Paris.[29] Simply out of curiosity, other Americans fueled the city's sexual underworld, too. Americans sought out clubs known for their cross-dressing clientele. Places like Fétiche and La Petite Chaumière in Montmartre and the dives on the rue de Lappe became standard stops for gawkers on the nightlife circuit. Guidebooks featured such places as tourist attractions. One such work listed city addresses where readers could go to see "*fairy*-nice boys" and watch "Freaks cavort around and swish their skirts and sing in Falsetto and shout, 'Whoops, my dear.'" Even Barbette, the transvestite trapeze sensation, actually hailed from Texas.[30]

With their weighty dollars, Americans contributed greatly to the financial success of the city's commercial amusements. Kiosk owners and other news vendors did a brisk business in racy sheets designed for English-speakers. Americans also muddled their way through bawdy French stories in *journaux humoristiques*, glancing across the illustrations, which needed no language skills to decipher, and advertisements in the back for places they might go, which repeated the refrain "English Spoken" and also "Man Spricht Deutsch" and sometimes "Se Habla Español." Illicit books from the capital became prized souvenirs. The famous Obelisk Press not only published serious literature in English by authors like Henry Miller and Frank Harris but also put out erotic works without literary pretensions, catering to the city's Anglophone residents and visitors. Sales of volumes bearing the inscription "Not to be sold in England or U.S.A." skyrocketed during the tourist season—works ranging from James Joyce's *Ulysses* to *The Hindu Art of Love* and the sadomasochist *Stays and Gloves*.[31] "The idea that Paris is a museum of improprieties, a pornographer's paradise, dies hard," one writer related.[32]

Writers commonly observed that it was the "dazzled Americans, and not only the tourists but the residents, who keep the night life of Paris going." Sojourners from across the Atlantic became the proprietors of some of the city's most famous nightclubs—places like Florence's, Bricktop's, and the

This kiosk specialized in foreign periodicals as well as illicit literature, draped provocatively around its concessions window. Topped by a *Chicago Tribune* ad and flanked by magazine racks stuffed with everything from *Arts & Decoration* to *Yachting*, newsstands like this one reinforced common associations between Americans and the city's salacious entertainments. Brassaï (Gyula Halász), Kiosk, 1930–1932, Musée National d'Art Moderne, Centre Georges Pompidou, Paris, France. ©Estate Brassaï-RMN. Photo credit: CNAC/MNAM/Dist. Réunion des Musées Nationaux/Art Resource, N.Y.

Jockey—and they furnished a substantial bulk of their patrons. All kinds of establishments catering to visiting Americans cropped up in the nightlife districts during the annual tourist migration, when, as one journalist reported, "every cubit space" of Montmartre "became a night club, a hotsy-totsy, a gambling joint or a peep show."[33] The area around the place Pigalle, observers repeated endlessly, had been manufactured for Americans. It had the quality, one thought, of "Cedar-Rapids-let-loose." Another visitor marveled at all the "'booby traps' set by astute showmen to catch the expectant and willing tourist who is out for what he calls a 'good time.'"[34] Americans eagerly supported of all kinds of venues that one guidebook writer summed up as the "Hot Patootie places"—not only the music halls, their stages overflowing with half-naked girls, but also even more risqué destinations not advertised by big posters on the boulevards. Recruited by guides hovering around train stations and hotels, they formed a steady stream of patrons for the city's *maisons* where "la livre, le mark, le dollar" ruled. American visitors, one memoirist recalled, "didn't like the respectable family places," meaning the *maisons de tolérance*. Instead, he revealed, "you'd see good decent Americans shiver with awe and a fine delight" as they sought out the naughtier clandestine establishments and live sex shows.[35]

The city's street hawkers made their living, too, off affluent visitors. Dirty-postcard sellers and guides trailed Americans practically everywhere they went. At the Café de la Paix, men in straw hats sidled up next to Americans promising to show them the city's secrets. Itinerants living off tourist trade included a disproportionate number of foreigners—Russians, French colonial subjects, Poles, and even Americans themselves. Americans were often most successful at gaining the trust of their compatriots, steering them to places where they received commissions. Blackmailers and conmen also loitered at popular American bars. Others peddled saucy souvenirs among their countrymen, like one Pennsylvanian who sold illustrated maps of Paris condemned by French officials for their immorality. Many newcomers found the constant attention menacing. "The parasites of the streets are innumerable and they have an unerring eye for the visitor's nationality and all," said one Ohio man, capturing the sentiments of many. The resilience of these practices suggests that, despite Americans' reticence to detail their own illicit encounters in their letters and diaries, the demand for such services remained high well into the thirties.[36]

Prostitutes, too, were encouraged by the influx from across the ocean. American men often sought out erotic encounters in Paris without drawing too much of a distinction between women who were prostitutes and those who were not. One guidebook captured many visitors' assumptions about French girls' availability and habitual recourse to sex for money, venturing that "these little Hotsy-Totsy French Mamas are as plentiful in Paris as Shamrocks in Ireland. . . . Toss one a 100 franc tip and you will have to plead to the French Parliament to call out the entire standing army to help you get rid of her." To take advantage of this demand, women who did trade sex for money gravitated to where American men and other foreign visitors could be found. Ladies took great pains to learn English, pacing the promenading galleries of music halls like the Folies Bergère. Henry Miller described the walk from there down to the grand boulevards as "like running the gauntlet." Prostitutes "attach themselves to you like barnacles, they eat into you like ants, they coax, wheedle, cajole, implore, beseech, they try it out in German, English, Spanish, they show you their torn hearts and their busted shoes."[37]

Americans of all kinds relished experiences in the capital's underworld of vice: prodigal college boys seeking sexual initiation, fearless new women determined to be worldly, war veterans remembering leaves from the front, middle-aged divorcées with notions about Latin nightclub dancers, upstanding leaders of their communities taking a hiatus from their heterosexual, everyday lives—all "nookie hunters," in one writer's estimation, whose heads were "filled with images of sleek Parisian tarts and hustlers."[38] It was amazing, another observer remarked, "how many persons who are staid and respectable in their own home town insist on 'making the rounds' of the peep-shows . . . as a regular part of their visit to Paris." After just two weeks, he claimed, the average American "knows more about that side of Paris than do the residents of the city."[39] Many Americans had embraced the city's new world of modern sexuality; indeed, they had helped to fuel it. To be sure, similar pleasures could be had in the booming nightlife districts of other major cities, but Paris loomed in contemporary mythology, in the words of the journalist William Shirer, as a special place where "you could lead your own life, do as you pleased, get drunk or make love, without Mrs. Grundy or the police or the preacher or the teacher breathing down your neck."[40] Visions of Paris as a sanctuary free from petty policing brought more and more Americans each year to confirm the city's sultry reputation with their own eyes. Americans' raucous outings in the capital in turn reinforced truisms about the greater freedoms to be had abroad. Still, all this needs contextualizing. The French capital's thriving sex industries and bawdy image would not be universally welcomed. There would be serious policing of the city's risqué spectacles after all—and plenty of local Grundyism.

The French capital delivered on the fantasies of those who came from far and wide, but it was not filled only with pleasure seekers and those who ministered to them. Despite its reputation, the city was populated, too, by staunch moralists and zealous patrolmen, outraged parents, inconvenienced shopkeepers, and various other Parisians fed up with all the unruliness and vulgarity. Belying the stereotypes about them, residents and business owners continually protested—about lewd displays and morally dubious interlopers, about noisy altercations that forced them to keep their children off the streets and caused customers to complain. From the vicinity of the Gare Saint-Lazare to the narrow alleys behind Notre Dame, Parisians demanded action, showering neighborhood commissariats with letters sometimes signed with multiple rows of signatures. In the interest of morality and security, almost twenty put their names to one typical petition, detailing their neighborhood's "flood" of prostitutes and their clients, loud and drunken people giving rise to "vile scenes that the pen refuses to describe." Such scenes of intrigue cropped up in shopping districts and along major thoroughfares. Their businesses were suffering, dozens of proprietors wrote in desperation. Another man vented common angers about the *bouquinistes* who stacked their riverside bookstalls with "garbage with meaningful titles," designed, no doubt, to pervert the spirit of youth. In the interest of "the cleanliness and the aesthetic of the quarter," he hoped the area would be "purified of this rot."[41]

Parisians found even more cause for complaint when they encountered shady characters selling obscene postcards in the city's most reputed sections. From his establishment near the place Vendôme, one rare-book dealer witnessed this regrettable practice in front of the Hôtel Continental— "schemes incompatible with the good manners of PARIS, absolutely harmful to the renown of our country." These acts only added to exaggerations about the capital perpetuated by foreign newspapers, he thought. All along the boulevard des Italiens, street vendors thrust shameful postcards at strollers, even in front of women and young girls, another communicant informed the prefect. "For the respect of our guests," he wrote, the prefect should get rid of these scandalous doings "*en plein boulevard*, at the center of Paris." Yet another similarly deplored the presence of those selling overpriced "artistic" photographs. "What an unfortunate impression this produces on foreign visitors who immediately draw their conclusion about the morality of the capital," he wrote. This was happening, no less, for maximum offense, "*in proximity* to the Tomb of the Unknown Soldier!"[42] The city's public byways appeared to such apprehensive strollers like a minefield of obscenities. Women half undressed seemed to leap off of their Morris column music-hall posters; models in pornographic photographs flashed their naughtiness openly from kiosk racks in spite of bans against such displays. The young man no longer finds himself "*en sécurité* in the street," said one letter writer. These provocations, he thought, overstimulated the imagination and the body, reinforcing unhealthy appetites for sexual pleasure and, no doubt, contributing to the current economic and social instability of the capital.[43]

Parisians feared for the children, too. In quiet, bourgeois quarters, parents banded together in associations with solid-sounding names like the Federation of Associations of Large Families and the "Respect Our Children" League. The prospect of "shameful advertising" poisoning the city's youth struck a particularly raw nerve in light of postwar natalist fears about declining population numbers. Concerned citizens who signed their letters "A Good Frenchman" or "The Father of a Family" enclosed samples they had collected from the streets' all-too-accessible offending displays. One man sent in the dirty magazine he confiscated from his son. Another "good Frenchman" doing his patriotic duty collected twenty-seven different advertisement clippings as evidence for the police. Many complaining groups, such as the Association of Fathers of Catholic Families, were religious ones, but they made their objections on worldly grounds rather than in terms of sin. Pleas to protect the young were in fact overshadowed by demands to defend the capital's international reputation. References to the beleaguered "*bon renom*" of France and Paris echoed over and over in the letters. Surely, correspondents assumed, all these debaucheries dealt a blow to the "dignity of our country," marring the capital's image and lowering France's standing among other nations. Parisians interpreted all kinds of scenes as poor reflections on the city's integrity. Despairing of the obscenity at the *bouquinistes'* booths, one man exclaimed rhetorically, "If we think of the foreigners who visit Paris . . . all these provocations to vice!" More than a dozen others regarded the spread of prostitution near the place Clichy, even in broad daylight, as "the Shame of the quarter"—it was a practice, they said gravely, that "Dishonors the city of Paris."[44]

Jean Chiappe would not be the first to act on such fears and angers. The entire span of the Third Republic included purges like Chiappe's—from Marshal MacMahon's quest for a "moral order" in the 1870s, when Paris police not only routed out political radicals but also targeted gay men and other perceived offenders against decency, all the way to the dark days of the late thirties and the years of Vichy, when such campaigns escalated to horrifying levels.[45] Periodic police sweeps ebbed and flowed according to the whims of prefects and the national authorities who appointed them. Cleanup campaigns were often sparked by rousing press editorials or letters sent to the prefecture. In 1923, for example, complaints lodged by morality groups about objectionable scenes staged at music halls led to proceedings against at least two establishments and the American performer Harry Pilcer, whose revue "All Women" had been deemed in particularly bad taste.[46] In April 1924, officials—spurred on by American residents tired of the harassment— also passed an ordinance against the swelling ranks of guides infecting the better parts of the city. Prohibited from offering services to visitors in front of historic monuments, train stations, and entertainment venues, guides now had to obtain official status from the prefecture, which reserved such designation only for French citizens and subjects whose morality had been verified by investigators.[47] Later that same year, Chiappe's predecessor undertook a series of vigorous raids in Montmartre and Montparnasse, arresting scores of night revelers and confiscating five truckloads of obscene drawings and texts in one bust alone.[48]

Campaigns against regulated prostitution also redoubled after the war. Since the turn of the century, progressive spokesmen had begun to see regulation not as forward-thinking policy but as the backward remnant of an older system of exploitation, exposing the capital as behind the times when other places had already expunged their red-light districts. During the interwar years, abolitionists organized meetings that drew a mix of religious leaders, feminists, and doctors who pushed for the end of the city's officially recognized sex trade. One pastor called *maisons de tolérance* "the ruin of present-day society." The president of the League of the Rights of Man reminded a thousand listeners at another gathering that regulated prostitution was referred to overseas as the "French system." At another impressive meeting in early 1931, speakers held forth against this immoral and unhealthy blight on the city, this "monstrous commerce." "France alone remains backward in the civilized world," one activist regretted."[49]

The city, thus, may have appeared to Americans as a libertine oasis, far removed from the puritan domain of Mrs. Grundy, but in French forums, its world of illicit pleasures had legions of critics. Despite their contrariness on other matters, communists, too, joined others in abhorring the liberties some were taking on the Paris streets, backing proposals to suppress prostitution and close the city's *maisons de tolérance*—a product of bourgeois excess, *L'Humanité* ventured, that exemplified the "odious slavery" of women. Many communists expressed a similar antipathy toward the practice of homosexuality, maintaining that it, too, represented a decadent luxury of the rich. Daring departures from moral conventions, like Victor Margueritte's controversial novel *La Garçonne* (1922), which included lesbian themes, received lukewarm or even hostile reviews in the leftist press. Furthermore, many activists continued to view homosexuality as a vice naturally foreign to the working classes and only developed under the corrosive influence of alcohol and contact with the upper classes.[50]

Parisians of various political outlooks made stronger and stronger connections between a perceived increase in immorality and the simultaneous influx of foreigners. Immigrant communities—insular *îlots* packed with single men—represented to right-wing critics pockets of moral and medical contagion. Newcomers, isolated and uprooted, were particularly susceptible to the temptations of the street, moderates and conservatives alike believed. Supporters of this argument pointed to statistics. Between 1926 and 1931, foreigners comprised just over 9 percent of the city's population, but 25 percent of its arrested, 15–20 percent of its jailed, and, perhaps most distressing, 20 percent of those treated for venereal disease at Saint-Louis hospital.[51] Foreigners also made up a disproportionate number of those who serviced the capital's nightlife—its waiters and taxi drivers as well as its illicit dealers, street hawkers, and prostitutes. Affluent foreigners, for their part, constituted a large proportion of their customers.

Parisians credited Americans in particular with importing distressing tastes and behaviors. Whereas in the United States, risqué acts were often labeled "French," in Paris off-color magazines or sensational theater shows were increasingly referred to as "American." Commentators bemoaned that *"influence américaine"* had informalized courtship routines, driving young women to adopt the aggressive styles of Hollywood actresses and other American idols—to attract men with *"le sex appeal,"* as critics called it by the early thirties. Others prophesied the advent of modern, casual forms of marriage modeled after the American concept of "companionate marriage." Particularly troublesome was visitors' use of Paris as a "divorce mill." Drawn to the capital's private court proceedings with requirements more lenient than those in New York and other states, hundreds of Americans set up residence in Paris each year to dissolve their unions. The same year Chiappe's purge began, scandal erupted over Americans' use of street-corner agencies marketing quick and easy divorces. French officials rushed to stop the practice, fearing the damage it would do to the city's reputation and worrying that Americans' supposedly cavalier disregard for the institution might spread to Parisian households.[52]

By spring 1927, as Chiappe settled into his post, more and more Parisians had come to believe that public morals were in a state of rapid dissolution. Newspaper editorialists clamored for action against the "wave of indecency" at the city's music-hall revues. A critic for Le Petit Parisien called for the elimination of these shows' "stupid situations, unsavory expressions, and double meanings." Frenchmen might avoid such entertainments "like the plague," he argued, but masses of overseas visitors attended them and then went home with notions about the corruption of Paris. During the unrest of the Sacco-Vanzetti affair that summer, many residents' tolerance for the city's cosmopolitanism and freedoms completely evaporated. Immediately after the riots, outcries in the press about public indecency collided with other kinds of worries about order and security. Reports piling up at the police station about the Sacco-Vanzetti case got mixed up with protest letters about sexually deviant behaviors. Complaints about foreigners and political agitators abusing their stay emanated from the offices of the

In a popular racy magazine that would be prosecuted for immoral content, Pem envisions the harried, modern methods of lovemaking Americans brought to Paris. Only after nursing their hangovers and soaking their tired dancing feet do two lovers find the time to kiss. "Baiser à l'américaine" *Le Sourire*, c. 1930. Private collection. ©The Advertising Archives/ The Bridgeman Art Library

Ministry of the Interior. People began talking about, demanding even, a purging of the capital.[53] With the weight of many citizens behind him, Jean Chiappe was poised for action.

Americans had become important participants in the city's amusements, many of the same ones Parisians had become increasingly impatient to suppress. But sojourners did not come all the way across the Atlantic just for fun and freedom, as is often claimed. Many of them set out to experience Gay Paree not only to be titillated but also to disapprove. Sampling the sights abroad often had different implications than enjoying the same activities back home. There was a complex psychological payoff in going to France for pleasure, and this must have been one of the reasons Americans indulged in

Parisian nightlife so avidly. Otherwise, they had little reason to travel all the way to Paris, at least a six-day trip, when its offerings were not so different from what could be found in any large American city, even in the face of all those antivice measures, if only one went looking for them.

Despite their best efforts, vice committees discovered with alarm the enduring possibilities for sexual trysts in American cities during the 1920s and 1930s—the back rooms, excursion boats, and darkened movie theaters that could be put to subversive uses. New York, Chicago, and other towns offered the same opportunities as Paris. By the mid-twenties, audiences enjoyed topless girls at Ziegfeld's Follies and strip teases at burlesque theaters. Clandestine "French circuses" or "freak shows" copied the performances of the *maisons*. Vibrant gay neighborhoods flourished in the midst of wider urban landscapes brimming with homosexual spaces, and the "black and tan" cabarets and "buffet flats" of Harlem and Chicago's South Side facilitated interracial encounters. Indeed, versions of the gigolo, called "tango pirates" or "social gangsters," even trolled New York's swanky afternoon cafés. Once edgy, rough-and-tumble enclaves, the bohemian and ethnic quarters of American cities had become tourist meccas, too, packaging "atmosphere" just as Paris did for visitors. The "Paris by Night" charabanc tours might well have been inspired by New York's "Seeing Chinatown by Night" excursions. Times Square and similarly glitzy destinations beckoned as well. Already in 1918, *Variety* magazine lamented, "Like Paris was framed for Americans, so is Broadway now staged for the country folks."[54] As middle-class Americans embraced the new cocktail culture and flocked to speakeasies, Prohibition also turned out to be more farce than moral elixir. Americans hardly needed to trek all the way to France for a drink.

Part of what made the world of pleasures in Paris so compelling was that it could be enjoyed as a lark and then disavowed as something foreign. American women never tired of "an occasion to comment on the moral depravity of European life," one traveler wrote: "Whenever you meet an American woman abroad you have to spend the night in the music halls and the dance halls so that she may verify her theory of Latin morals." Some of the city's most outrageous new venues and fads might have owed their popularity to Americans and other foreign visitors, but many participants would take the opportunity to confirm their expectations about French immorality and reaffirm in their minds their own standards of propriety. This ritual repeated itself almost nightly at the capital's famous music halls. These productions, one onlooker explained, were put on "entirely for the delectation of foreign visitors, who, after having made a point of taking seats, always declare they will never come again, or in some cases actually leave the theatre while the performance is going on—to show everyone how proper they are." Indeed, in their letters and diaries, Americans found much to comment on and disapprove of at these shows, their stages a bonanza of nudity and double entendres, their foyers crawling with prostitutes. And yet, they continued to flock to such spectacles. A detective visiting from New York thought that "it would not look well in print" to relate what he witnessed at the Casino de Paris—a market fair of itinerant traders plying sex, candies, and lottery tickets, along with Alec, "the wise guy," who passed out his card to potential thrill seekers. This, however, did not stop the detective from taking a similar excursion a few days later. "We thought the Casino show bold on Saturday night," he exclaimed after attending the Folies Bergère, "Some bird. A riot of nakedness. Many 'risque' situations." The infamous "Hootchy-Kootchy" entr'acte in the promenading gallery, he thought, "put in the darkest shade anything I have ever seen pulled." He could not bring himself to describe it in "cold type." This travel-writing convention—the practice of indulging and disavowing, of detailing and censoring—appealed to many. In 1925, William Faulkner wrote home to his mother: "Went to the Moulin Rouge last night. Anyone in America will tell you it is the last word in sin and iniquity. . . . They have plays here just for Americans. . . . Nasty things. But Americans eat it up, stand in line for hours to get tickets." Indeed, they did, just as the young novelist had himself.[55]

Trips to ogle the city's cross-dressers and bohemian eccentrics, its legions of sex workers and immodest chorus girls, helped Americans to contemplate their own attitudes about gender roles and sexuality. As they worked to shore up their own sense of moral prestige, they often did so loudly and at the expense of Parisians' reputations. One letter written by four Americans to Prefect Chiappe illustrated perfectly the double purpose of Americans' surveys of the city's nightlife. Addressing him as "Excellence," the visitors penned their note in awkward French just before they returned to the United States. It had the subtlety and purpose of a backhanded compliment. They had wanted, they said, to express their admiration for Chiappe's *épuration*, which he had undertaken with such zeal and authority. Just one thing, they felt obliged to add with a hint of condescension: perhaps monsieur could attend to the "exaggerated nude of women in the 'Music-Halls' of Paris, which we do not believe good for the education of the people."[56] There was nothing like a dose of the capital's risqué fare to convince Americans of the superiority of their own ways.

During their stays in Paris, Americans actively sought out evidence of French depravity and criminality. At no time was this more the case than during slumming excursions into the city's poorer regions. Americans in

Miguel Covarrubias sketches "Some Americans Abroad Doing Bohemia in the Modern Way" for *Vanity Fair* in August 1928. After nightfall, its caption related, travelers such as these yearned to "look over a few live ones" in the city's "dark spots." Two summers before, customers for these Paris by Night tours had incurred the wrath of residents protesting the unfavorable exchange rate. Now they faced the scrutiny of Paris police. Vanity Fair/Miguel Covarrubias ©Condé Nast Publications

fact participated so avidly in the tradition of touring the underbelly of the metropolis after dark that what was once called the *Tournée des grands ducs* was rechristened in the twenties the *Tournée des américains*. For the less adventurous, "Paris By Night" tour buses hauled spectators fifty per car on a commercialized route beginning by the Opera and ending at prearranged Montmartre cabarets staffed by actors portraying gangsters, their girlfriends, and other stereotypes of the Paris underworld. Such theme bars multiplied after the war, capitalizing on night revelers' desires for a carefully mediated taste of danger. There were places like the Buddha Drug Parlors, where it cost fifty francs to gain admission to the "Outer Temple" alone and where girls in exotic costumes circulated among the low divans and tiger pelts selling pricey liqueurs and pinches of "snow." Even Prefect Chiappe himself—or rather an actor impersonating him—became part of the spectacle put on for tourists at another faux shady dive, the Assassins' Bar. Here, bouncers frisked guests for weapons as they passed a heavily bolted door to find a smoky room, stinking of garlic and stale beer. After entrants purchased their overpriced champagne, the dreaded Chiappe burst in on the scene and eyed everyone with dramatic suspicion.[57]

Searching for less premeditated glimpses of depravity, the more adventurous set out into the eastern working-class neighborhoods on their own or accompanied by plainclothes officers who could be commissioned for such an undertaking. Invariably, such excursions into the city's lower depths concluded at the central markets of Les Halles. Parties in their evening finery arrived in the quarter around three in the morning, zigzagging their way past beggars and trash scavengers, stepping over indigents sleeping on the sidewalks and street urchins in search of a meal. The markets were in preparation at this hour. Drivers with whips and broad-shouldered porters cluttered up the walkways outside the iron and glass pavilions with mounds of cabbages and cauliflower. The area stank of cheese and packing straw, freshly slaughtered meat and urine. The cries of market women, the echoes of profanities, and earthy jokes carried across the square. People drinking wine and smoking cigarettes leered at the parade of prostitutes who straggled past. It was a spectacle of "real moral and physical danger," according to dozens of residents who complained to the prefecture about it. Americans and other tourists made their way to well-known destinations for onion soup—Le Chien qui Fume or Le Père Tranquille—rubbing shoulders on the way with workers and working girls, getting a rush from their proximity to such lusty humanity. As they passed, one chronicler related, "hulking market porters glare at the décolleté and jewels of the women and mutter *sale bourgeois* under their breath." Visitors carefully recorded such hostilities in their travelogues as titillating proof of their own privileged position.[58]

The *Tournée des américains* in its various degrees of authenticity represented urban slumming in a new key.[59] Steeped in long-standing ideas about urban class relations, these after-hours tours also offered prime occasions for propagating theories about French degeneracy and American superiority, all while being entertained. In their evening wear, making their way through the dirty throngs, all Americans stood in as class elites, and all French residents could be lumped together as inferior immoral masses. Americans were not innocents who ventured abroad, as the famous Mark Twain phrase had it. Narrowly escaping the wrath of the virile porters of Les Halles and the pestilential charms of its fallen women, visitors *became* innocents abroad by exposing themselves to but ultimately overcoming the temptations of Paris. Sex tourism, the voyeuristic contemplation of the other—these were well-established traditions in France and her colonies.

But Frenchmen no longer commanded a monopoly on the gazing and judging, and this is what would most necessitate a rigorous purging of the capital.[60]

Jean Chiappe had a wealthy father-in-law who owned the reactionary *Gringoire* and ardent right-wing supporters like the publicists Léon Daudet and Charles Maurras, so his connections granted him entrance into the private circles of Parisian high society. But it was the public street that proved Chiappe's constant preoccupation. Reading the dailies in his office, entertaining the rumors of seditious doings that wafted in with the carbon-copied reports of undercover officers, he plotted his next moves against those who troubled the pleasant and orderly conduct of the *pavé parisien*.[61] Attuned to local challenges, Chiappe also developed a keen sensitivity to wider connections and ramifications. The prefect's campaign showcased possibilities for a new right-wing approach to the city between the wars—a perspective driven by familiar animosities toward communists and working-class foreigners, and yet also by an emerging form of reactionary cultural politics, which entailed bolder claims to the use of state power and expanded associations between traditional political subversion and more diffuse forms of moral subversion. Through such a politics, right-wing activists like Chiappe could hold together in their minds a cluster of enemies including foreigners, homosexuals, Jews, Americans, and other purported undesirables, all imagined as agents of an economic and cultural liberalism that would undermine the health of the nation. This panoply of threats seemed to be most acute in the capitalist, cosmopolitan, overly permissive streets of the metropolis. The Nazis, of course, would best exploit popular correlations between social, sexual, and political degeneracy attributed to urban modernity, but others, too, shared such concerns, not least Chiappe and his supporters.

The administrative structures of Paris bestowed upon Jean Chiappe enormous clout to pursue this agenda, powers far more expansive than those possessed by American sheriffs or police commissioners. After the excesses of the Commune, the French government had stripped the capital of its mayor in order to limit the sway Parisians had over the course of national politics. Thus for more than a century the capital's two highest officials—the Police Prefect and the Prefect of the Seine—reached their posts not through democratic election but by appointments made by the Minister of the Interior. With no set term limit, prefects like Chiappe were charged with policing the Department of the Seine in an incredibly broad sense of the term. During his seven-year tenure, Chiappe's tasks included not only fighting crime, controlling traffic, and maintaining civil order but also protecting public health, regulating commerce, assisting the needy, and preserving monuments. The prestige accorded to the prefect and the manpower at his disposal vastly outstripped those of his counterpart, the director of the Sûreté Générale, charged with security throughout the rest of France. These disparities became especially pronounced after World War I, when the Paris police employed roughly three times as many men as the Sûreté. Despite a stagnating population in the capital, the staff of the Paris Prefecture rose from just under 9,000 in 1920 to almost 15,000 by the mid-thirties. Already impressive police resources surged in the wake of the Sacco-Vanzetti riots, thanks to Chiappe's lobbying. The city's Municipal Council, a bastion for right-wing politicians, rewarded the prefect with budgetary increases and discretionary funds to pursue his cleanup of the city. By 1934, the prefecture operated on a budget of 546 million francs, compared to the Sûreté's 47 million. Better staffed, better trained, and better financed than the Sûreté, the Paris police formed a formidable corps of armed forces, which the prefect did not hesitate to use for secret assignments, personal vendettas, and illegal gain. Not without reason, he earned from Paris communists the epithet "Benito Chiappe."[62]

During his tenure as prefect, Chiappe courted royalists and other reactionaries for support and influence, and at the same time nurtured advantageous alliances with members of the centrist Radical Party (like Minister of the Interior Albert Sarraut, who appointed Chiappe), whose commitment to republican values had become increasingly tempered by the exigencies of nationalism and anticommunism. Chiappe claimed to accord more tolerance to foreigners than did many of his extremist supporters, but still, in his capital, newcomers' freedom came with very important limits. Paris, he promised, would welcome with open arms those who obeyed without question, keeping the capital's industries running, raising families cheerfully, and deferring to the rules as prescribed by those in power. To Paris, however, arrivals must not bring their conflicts or convictions. They must not read or write for contentious newspapers or publications of dubious moral worth. They must not attend raucous political meetings, indulge in provocative entertainments, or even participate in strikes and labor causes. According to Chiappe's doctrine, immigrants must be nonpolitical, and essentially nonpublic, people, doing nothing to "trouble public order." These were not the prefect's own personal expectations. They were shared by almost all but those on the far left. Parisians' widespread concerns about foreigners and their perceived hand in the recent unruliness had validated these policies, making them seem proactive and mainstream.[63]

Actions against working-class immigrants and political activists began even before the official start of Chiappe's épuration on September 1. In late

August, police stormed hundreds of rented rooms, apprehending the *"indésirables"* believed responsible for the Sacco-Vanzetti riots. For the first several months of Chiappe's campaign, agents' special night rounds included tours through the city's working-class neighborhoods. Telegrams passed to the prefect after midnight relayed news of vigorous descents on boarding houses and suspected gambling dens, of impromptu pedestrian searches for weapons and identity papers, of interrogations of Italians, Spaniards, Hungarians, Algerians, and Chinese. Arrests, fines, and expulsions abounded.[64] Early one September morning, police arrested sixty militants from the Communist Party's foreign-language sections in their homes. By January, Deputies Paul Vaillant-Couturier and Marcel Cachin, stripped of their parliamentary immunity by a Chamber vote, would be in jail. Three other major Communist leaders went into in hiding. A proxy would have to speak on Vaillant-Couturier's behalf during the upcoming government investigations into the Sacco-Vanzetti affair.[65]

At the same time, police also stepped up their surveillance of immigrant newspapers—Russian, German, Vietnamese, Arabic, and Polish sheets oriented toward proletarian revolution or colonial independence as well as those loyal to foreign fascist movements. Press freedoms in France had always come with qualifications, but the number of interdictions against foreign periodicals practically tripled the year Chiappe took up his post— from eight in 1926 to twenty-three in 1927.[66] Chiappe vowed never to allow leftist agitators access to the streets again. Their words would be censored from kiosk racks, their persons swept from squares and sidewalks. To thwart mass protests, he instituted a practice of preventative arrests. His agents routinely rounded up protesters exiting the Métro or alighting from buses before they had a chance to reach appointed gatherings. For no other offense than planning to demonstrate, or looking like a worker at the wrong place at the wrong time, individuals were detained at police posts long enough to defuse the possibility of political assembly in the city center. These tactics proved highly effective. The Communist Party's response to them had been "pitiful," in the estimation of one of Chiappe's assistants. "Its militants deserted all by themselves this street that they had wanted to conquer," he bragged.[67]

Chiappe's purge, however, would go far beyond these standard anti-left measures, and, like other new right-wing urban movements, it was not simply backward-looking. The prefect was a forward thinker, unafraid to harness the powers at his disposal to affect dramatic change. His aggressive use of force brought to mind the efforts of one of his role models, Prefect Louis Lépine, turn-of-the-century modernizer of the Paris police. Yet Chiappe harbored little if any of his predecessor's loyalty to republican institutions. His efforts diverged, too, from those of conservative critics who worried that signs of Americanization threatened their tradition and who pined for a return to the glorious days of the Second Empire. Not an antiquarian, the prefect did not see eye to eye with urban preservationists, for whom the city's monuments and picturesque details offered its greatest treasures. In many ways, Chiappe was an innovator of the progressive right, willing to sacrifice the city's quaint anachronisms in order to make the capital cleaner and more orderly. He banned, for example, housewives' morning ritual of beating carpets and bedsheets out their windows. He felt no sentimentality toward the city's few remaining goatherds, who steered their flocks through car pileups to sell their milk and cheese door to door. He banned them as traffic and noise nuisances. He raided the city's celebrated street fairs, too. Those found harboring illegal activities were shut down. Others became subject to a host of new regulations, promulgated in bulletins pasted along the outer fortifications: no more games of chance or scantily clad dancers; no more fortunetelling, female wrestlers, or animals.[68]

While he was of course a nationalist, Chiappe was also internationally minded, working against a backdrop of thick municipal-policy networks that helped to circulate all around the world a variety of urban regulations and reforms, from state-of-the-art policing techniques to transportation designs and antivice experiments. Like city officials elsewhere in the early twentieth century, Chiappe exhibited a sharp awareness of how the claims to world-city status of a metropolis depended on its ability to appear to outsiders as a showcase of both distinctive national culture and modern innovation— an achievement accomplished by borrowing and competing with other cities.[69] In the realm of traffic control, Chiappe embraced this task. Studying methods of regulation in London and New York, he introduced to Paris designated parking spaces, one-way streets, crosswalks, and traffic lights with red and green indicators.[70] In the interest of noise abatement, the prefect became an innovator himself. He ordered motorists to flash their lights rather than blow their horns to signal approach at intersections late at night and in the early morning. During these hours, he also outlawed streetcar bells, train and tugboat whistles, household phonographs, and orchestras without late-night permits. He asked milkmen to wrap their cans in felt and cautioned garbage men and ragpickers to work quietly. Chiappe's night patrolmen crouched in the shadows of doorways to catch renegade horn honkers and other disturbers of the peace. During the six months prior to April 1933, Chiappe's war on urban racket generated a reported 8,200 citations— violations by those who had not greased their car brakes adequately, people who had honked their horns "too assiduously" during the day, and other scurrilous folk who shattered the silence of now quieter Parisian nights.[71]

Chiappe, of course, would not win all of his battles, especially when they encroached on French residents' own day-to-day habits. Some Parisians decried the prefect's draconian use of police power, while others worried that his measures would turn the capital into a "Puritan desert." One pedestrian objected that the prefect's obligatory crosswalks forced one "to think like the Americans." Others thought Chiappe's "drill sergeant bent," as one English resident put it, would rob the city of its quaint anachronisms and time-honored rituals. Protests against the demise of the goatherds ultimately led to their reinstatement. Chiappe's ban on carpet beating, too, drew the ire of housewives, who flung their rugs out windows just the same (almost 4,000 of whom were fined for the act in 1932 alone), purportedly arguing "Everybody can't have vacuums." A Court of Appeals ruling allowed for a compromise of one designated carpet-beating hour each morning.[72] Nevertheless, with all kinds of worries about foreigners, radicals, and moral decline, many Parisians applauded Chiappe's initiatives, and some even insisted that they did not go far enough.

Buoyed by such public support, the prefect's offensive moved beyond traffic and noise regulation into far-reaching, in many ways even unprecedented, territory. Thousands would be subject to interrogation, embarrassment, and the loss of their livelihood. Describing his measures as a comprehensive *épuration* allowed the prefect to cast a wide net, ensnaring both political and social subversives at the same time. Since 1880, it had been forbidden to shut down an establishment for political reasons, but authorities retained the right to close places that harbored prostitutes or other perpetrators of "disturbing" behaviors.[73] Thus, in coming years, all kinds of police surveillance would be done under the guise of policing morals. In mid-December 1928, for example, descents into cafés and hotels near the place Pigalle had been officially organized as a drive against homosexual activities. Police, however, took the opportunity to monitor soldiers and sailors in uniform, inspect foreigners' papers, and arrest a known drug dealer—all in all, a well-rounded moment of *épuration*, illustrating the flexible purposes to which it could be put as Chiappe labored to restore Paris to order.[74]

Lesbians and gay men became particular targets for Chiappe's men, because the display of same-sex desire and an assumption of outward markers of the opposite gender challenged like few other activities the public sexual order believed to be among the most distinguishing features of French *civilisation*. Opponents of gay culture charged that homosexuals' claims to the city's streets signaled the end of an era when the heterosexual Frenchman had commanded the boulevards as singularly his own. Not surprisingly, then, Chiappe pledged to chase after such troublemakers "relentlessly."[75] Police kept special folders for well-known "pederasts" of various nationalities, and authorities prosecuted those who allowed their establishments to become habitual stomping grounds for "individuals of special morals." Controlling this milieu proved an immense challenge, however. Couples found performing sex acts in public could be charged with indecency, and those engaged in such activities with individuals under twenty-one could be charged for corrupting a minor, but otherwise the law provided few recourses to discourage the growth of a vibrant homosexual milieu. For this reason, Chiappe and his men had to get creative with statutes against cross-dressing. The prefect determined that anyone found in the dress of the opposite gender would be hauled without delay to the nearest police station. Detainees would only be released after their identities had been verified and their offending ensembles confiscated. Countless "*travestis*," sometimes more than a hundred at a time, were rounded up this way, nabbed upon exiting *bals* or netted in the course of nightclub raids—scenes that mirrored the roundups in 1930s New York.[76] One descent on the Montmartre *boîte* Au Moustique proved typical. From the outside, the club seemed unassuming, like an American speakeasy, with a bouncer ready to sound an electric buzzer at any sign of trouble. In early December 1933, police caught the Moustique's lookout off guard. Rushing inside, agents discovered a dimly lit room crowded with couples dressed with "vulgar elegance" and moving to the music of a phonograph—young men in makeup with "ambiguous appearances," a smattering of bob-haired women in semimasculine attire, and a formidable number of men dressed up as women. Police invited everyone to present their papers and submit to searches. They carted every man found in women's garments off to the police station.[77]

Policemen traveled all over the city to places signaled as homosexual rendezvous—to baths near the Champs-Elysées, dives on the rue de Lappe, and the *bal musette* on the rue de la Montagne Sainte-Geneviève immortalized by Ernest Hemingway's *The Sun Also Rises*. Montmartre, however, drew the bulk of their efforts. Perhaps even before the brasserie Graff's owner had replaced the light bulbs in his sign, smashed out by Sacco-Vanzetti protesters, he witnessed another dramatic invasion of the area around the place Pigalle. Establishments like the Graff, a popular homosexual hangout, fell under constant surveillance by undercover inspectors, and after midnight police forces descended on area streets and flophouses. Sometimes the scene was calm. In November 1932, one commissioner reported, "only a few *pédérastes* paced melancholically up and down the sidewalk in search of clients." They were scooped up and taken in. Also, he

added, "I sent a Chinaman to the depot for breach of an order of expulsion."
But more likely the area teemed with the activities Chiappe determined to
suppress—men in dresses, women soliciting, tourists coming to ogle the
strange world they had read about in guidebooks and magazines. To drive
away offending establishments' customers, Chiappe refused music and after
-hours permits and stationed policeman at the doors of popular resorts to
demand the identity papers of every entrant. He ordered, in addition, the
installation of supplementary lighting along the promenading galleries of
cinemas and music halls, ending their status as premier cruising grounds.
Popular bars folded under the weight of raid after raid.[78]

Upon close inspection, Chiappe's campaign did not constitute an indiscriminate attack on the city's sexual underworld. The prefect focused especially
on purging those "merchants of noxious or degrading pleasures" whose activities reflected poorly on the capital's legitimate business, and he combated
those who challenged traditional gender roles. The prefect vowed not to

A flock of bicycle cops, or "swallows," carries out the work of Chiappe's *épuration*.
Brassaï (Gyula Halász), The police force during a raid in Montmartre, 1931, private
collection. ©Estate Brassaï-RMN. Photo credit: Réunion des Musées Nationaux/Art
Resource, N.Y.

support overly "puritan" measures (like one Municipal Councilor's call for the suppression of public kissing).[79] Unlike those who crusaded against the city's brothels, Chiappe did not oppose prostitution—so long as it was the prostitution of women for the sake of men in regulated *maisons de tolérance*. His police could be extremely lenient in individual cases and toward those they did not consider recidivists. In their quest to rehabilitate the streets, Chiappe and his men imagined that they navigated a treacherous course between the machinations of perverts and prudes alike. As he worked to protect the prerogatives of heterosexual Frenchman above all, the prefect sensed that these privileges were not simply under siege by domestic threats. Rather, they seemed to face their most serious challenges from those elite foreign visitors, so integral to the city's nightlife.

Early on in his campaign, Chiappe had come to see the problem he faced as highly specific. "The real Paris, the Paris that thinks, that works and that produces is above reproach!" he exclaimed. This was not a case of a "general contamination of the organism," but of an "abscess" in need of "urgent intervention." Even more than those working-class districts full of unpredictable agitators, Chiappe argued that the capital's modern quarters, packed with Americans and other foreign visitors, seethed with a "cosmopolitanism in turmoil" that demanded "special vigilance." Certain parts of Montmartre and Montparnasse in particular, he attested, had become "true centers of debauchery." The prefect's severest sanctions, therefore, would target the night establishments of these districts, "well known for the disgraceful acts of their clientele and where champagne is sold for 250 to 300 francs a bottle"—against those places, in other words, where he estimated that affluent foreigners made up 70 to 75 percent of the regular patronage.[80] Of all his justifications for the campaign, wrenching back from tourists control of the city's reputation would be Chiappe's most persistent and forcefully argued one. Like noise and traffic nuisances, cosmopolitan excesses were imagined as noxious outgrowths in need of excising.

As the Legion convention approached, the purge escalated and became more obviously focused on areas and establishments frequented by Americans—bars by the places Pigalle and Blanche and the grand boulevards. The *New York Times* marveled at the alacrity of the police, reporting that a few Americans had already been detained and that many more, no doubt, would be swept up in the coming weeks. The *Chicago Tribune* noted that, to Americans' discomfort, the police had started "raiding not only the low dives, as heretofore, but some of the best known cabarets on the famous hill of Montmartre." The paper added incredulously that recent descents on area clubs, packed with dancing Legionnaires and other Americans, narrowly missed visiting New York mayor Jimmie Walker, amusing himself at a place just around the corner. Word of a raid on the famous Le Grand Duc shot across the newswires and filtered into regional newspapers across the United States. At this "dive operated by an Alabama negress," Americans read with interest, "several youths in women's clothing were arrested along with a group of girls in boys' clothes."[81]

During their campaign, policemen's field of action overlapped to a remarkable degree with the circuit Americans made for themselves through the city. Police investigations accumulated in the vicinity of the Opera and the Madeleine (thick with *maisons*, dirty-postcard sellers, and kiosks and stores selling illicit publications) and even included inquiries into the anglophone bookstores Brentano's and W. H. Smith. Police relentlessly raided Montmartre as well as outlying districts like the rue de Lappe, popular with American slummers. In Montparnasse, beat cops became a fixture on the sidewalks, scanning the terraces of the Dôme and the Rotonde. The celebrated Jockey Bar not far from there received nightly surveillance. Because it was frequented by "undesirable individuals" and run by a Californian who had yet to secure permission for the alcohol he was selling or the late nights he was keeping, the local *commissaire* determined that it deserved constant scrutiny. In his quest to quiet the city, Chiappe even ordered men to padlock pianos in Montparnasse cafés like the Select and the Dingo if they did not have proper music permits. What a different image this presented than the common picture of these bars as free zones! A writer for the African American *Pittsburgh Courier* tried to dispel his readers' illusions about Paris as a wide-open town. "The fact is that all these 'joints' in Paris are under strict police supervision," he explained: "The least winking at disorder, and bang! would go up the shutters of the proprietor, perhaps forever." The French only "*pretend* to take sex lightly," the writer Claude McKay similarly apprised a friend.[82]

Chiappe's police especially disapproved of those who served as handmaidens for this cosmopolitan subculture. Officers were on the lookout for taxi drivers, guides, and others who piloted foreign visitors to clandestine places. As men who simultaneously preyed on affluent women and seemed to signify emasculation, gigolos stoked the anxieties of authorities so much that they provoked a formal government inquiry into the urgent need for surveillance of this "very 'special' profession of the society dancer." With the cooperation of the Minister of Labor, Chiappe forced gigolos to obtain identity cards and administrative permission before practicing their trade. Lesbians and gay men, too, whose social worlds had become so thoroughly integrated into the city's commercial nightlife, faced a disproportionate level of police harassment, in part because their presence drew a flood of "indirect clientele"—the prefect's term for Americans and other gawkers making the rounds to the capital's curious sights.[83]

Mining the layers of logic Chiappe used to justify his measures reveals that many of those targeted, even if only in oblique ways, were suspected precisely for their connections to affluent foreigners. More than an interest in public health, for example, motivated the prefect's drive against street-walkers. If the prerogatives of Parisian men had been undermined by the appearance of manly women and womanly men, the reputation of proper *Parisiennes* was also in peril. Prostitutes had soiled the boulevards with their "cynical appearances," and the vast majority of them, Chiappe argued, were not Parisian at all, but immigrants, drawn to the city to ply their trade. These interlopers had transformed the boulevards into fleshpots, he insisted, and, more importantly, they made it difficult to judge those one encountered on the streets. "Anglo-Saxon" visitors in particular, onlookers often surmised, "misrepresented and maligned" French ladies by approaching them and making improper suggestions. Chiappe shuddered to think about how many "real *Parisiennes*" had been wrongly propositioned as prostitutes by tourists. Dramatizing the unequal standing between affluent foreigners and their hosts, when visitors judged women indiscriminately as sexually available, they not only assaulted the French woman's propriety but hinted at the Frenchman's inability to protect her from such actions. To ensure that *Parisiennes* could again traverse the boulevards without having to endure unwanted attentions or "clumsy confusions," the prefect declared himself the express enemy of women who solicited sex in tourist districts. In 1932 alone, Chiappe's police would fine an astounding 57,000 prostitutes.[84]

Concerns about visitors sullying the reputation of Frenchwomen also framed protests about images and objects created expressly for tourists. The day after the Sacco-Vanzetti riots, the Paris press exploded with anger when sample copies of an ashtray designed for sale during the Legionnaires' convention began to appear at grand hotels and other places frequented by Americans. *L'Œuvre* printed a large photograph of the offending item—"an intolerable insult to France"—on its front page. The trinket pictured a dancing Legionnaire holding up a glass of champagne in one hand and dipping a naked woman (taken to be French) with the other. The ashtray intimated that, like a souvenir, *Parisiennes* could be bought and enjoyed by visitors. Officials banned its sale and drew up an order of expulsion for the enterprising American who had designed it.[85] Just in time for the Legion-naires' arrival, the September issue of a periodical called *Paris-Plaisirs* featured a sketch that similarly outraged authorities—a blatant depiction of the sexual availability of Parisians for the well-heeled American. The illustration pictured a man (taken to be an American) grabbing a partially naked women from behind while showing her a sack full of dollars. In the eyes of the police, this was not lighthearted fare that might be permitted in Gay Paree, but a graphic and symbolic act that assaulted the propriety of all Parisian women. The day before the Legion parade, the owner of the journal and its illustrator were each sentenced to the maximum 500-franc fine. In coming years, Chiappe's police would remain vigilant in the night-clubs of Montmartre, watching for peddlers making their rounds with ribald cigarette cases, lighters, and other souvenirs besmirching the good name of *Parisiennes*.[86]

The reputation of the city and its citizens seemed, perhaps, most at stake in the proliferation of obscene publications. Much has been made of the fact that writers like James Joyce could publish their works in Paris without hassle, unlike in Great Britain or the United States. Indeed, authorities did not set out to ban all books with provocative content. But publishers and distributors faced far more repression than readily admitted in the memoirs of American expatriates whose gaze fixed back on Comstockery. Chiappe, in particular, became determined to root out the printed avalanche of "laborious indecency" that littered the streets, vowing that he would not be afraid to "seize all obscene publications, the largest number of which moreover are foreign." Each year of his reign, dozens of books and magazines were banned, bookstore inventories were seized, and the purveyors of publications deemed immoral were fined up to 500 francs and imprisoned for up to six months. Police especially targeted *bouquinistes* and stores openly displaying illicit works, banning volumes with informative titles like *Les fiancés en folie, Les 32 propositions amoureuses*, and *Ménages modernes*. Chiappe waged his battle, too, against pesky kiosk proprietors who ceaselessly hawked inappropriate materials. Paperwork piled up at the prefecture about permit suspensions, especially for stands on the inner Right Bank. Between the end of April 1926 and June 1930, authorities temporarily shut down eighty-eight offending kiosks. "Messieurs," he addressed the Municipal Council, "you will reason like me that the freedom of the press must stop where the exploitation of bad instincts begins."[87]

Judging from the materials that most outraged Chiappe, such bad instincts had to do not only with the ways in which publications contained graphic depictions of sexual acts, but, even more importantly, the ways in which they reflected on the city of Paris itself. This was true of actual literature, like Victor Margueritte's *La Garçonne*, set amidst the capital's sexual underworld, as much as it was true of the *journaux humoristiques*—racy tabloids, some of the same ones that had been clipped apart and sent to the prefecture by outraged parents. With names like *Gai Paris, Paris-Flirt*, and *Paris Sex Appeal*, these journals offered, like music-hall productions, provocative representations of urban modernity. The problem was not that they were about sex but that they equated Paris with sex. They portrayed the capital as a theater of erotic encounters and served as guides to its illicit pleasures. Among those Chiappe singled out as most scandalous was an unnamed foreign magazine edited in Paris, very likely an American magazine, which, to Chiappe's horror, could also be found in the readings rooms of transatlantic ocean liners. Following its defamatory descriptions of visitors "doing" Paris, the paper's editors requested its readers to write in and share their own titillating experiences. Never mind its admirable luxury trades, never mind its glorious history, the sum total of the capital's virtues, according to works like this one, was its nightlife and fleshpots. "You can guess easily what evil it could have done to our beautiful and great city of Paris," Chiappe told the Municipal Council.[88] With the prefect's prodding, the Minister of the Interior banned it. If *Ulysses* had been about Paris instead of Dublin, quite likely it would have received greater scrutiny from the French authorities, too.

Chiappe's police scrutinized the racy tabloids every day. Surprisingly, it was not the articles and illustrations that most piqued investigators' attention but the announcements featured on their back pages. In these sections, advertisements literally mapped the city's sexual underworld. Bookstores by the Madeleine tempted readers with photographs of "very audacious realism" depicting very Parisian themes: orgies in the Bois or the city's *maisons des rendez-vous*. There were notices from the peddlers of sex toys and aphrodisiacs. One lingerie store ad pictured a topless model from the back, wearing sheer underwear and nylons rolled just above the knees: "Lingerie Diana Slip, *des habillés de jolies parisiennes*, 9 rue Richepance, English Spoken, Man Spricht Deutsch." These sheets also printed the addresses of clandestine places where sex was sold in notes which only thinly veiled their true purpose behind code words (like "Beauty Salon," "Private hotel," or "Discreet entresol") and euphemisms for sex acts and shows (phrases like "Marriages all situations," "Novel curiosities," "Visions of Art,' "Innovations," and "Transformations"). Even more troubling, police discovered on these back pages *petite correspondance* sections that served as mediums for arranging encounters between readers. Here were the early, scandalous beginnings of the modern-day personals. Flagellants placed classifieds for "energetic mistresses," and organizers of *partouzes* recruited people of "very modern tastes." There were predatory men scouting for young women, individuals the police referred to as *"vicieux."* There were notices, too, from professional call girls with ostentatious names like Zibeline or Azuréa, agencies promising "matrimonials," and sadists offering initiates an "English education."[89]

These *petites annonces* served as some of the most damning pieces of evidence weighed against journal editors facing legal prosecution. A November 1927 issue of the weekly *Gens qui rient: Journal d'humour et d'amour* contained the following incriminating tidbits in its "La Petite correspondance et les bonnes addresses":

Monsieur 30 years old, very affectionate, rather free, seeks affectionate lady for loving relationship.

Good female typist of 30 years—single—timid—shapely, modern sentiments, seeks very loyal, honest, kind partner—to initiate him into love.

Married man 36 years, truly sensual... enemy of banality... desires to know young girl or young woman... searching without hesitation or reluctance the fulfillment of her desires—if not truly sensual, pointless to write.

The judge in this case determined that, although explicitly obscene terms had not been used, simply reading such texts provoked readers' imaginations and gave rise to notions that were contrary to good morals. Similarly, charges against the popular magazine *Le Sourire* in 1932 were upheld largely based on its notices for assignation houses, massage parlors, and bookstores. Because these announcements furnished readers with information about "houses of debauchery" and persons engaging in prostitution, the courts ruled, they qualified as "immoral advertising." The fate of the founders of *Inversions*, the first short-lived French homosexual journal, also hung in large part on the *petites annonces* columns featured at the back of its debut issue—entries from those interested in finding pen pals among readers in other European cities and classifieds like one from a man seeking another man who loved literature and long walks. The paper had become, the court determined, "the organ of liaison between homosexuals in all countries," a sinister propaganda aimed at the "glorification of homosexuality and the recruitment of new followers." The founders were condemned to six months in prison and 200-franc fines apiece.[90]

These deliberations did not simply belong to now curious-sounding, localized battles over definitions of obscenity. They were indicative of an international wave of campaigns to cleanse interwar cities of moral and political subversion. Previously, moral reform had been undertaken most vigorously by self-appointed groups who sought to make up for police and government inability or unwillingness to suppress objectionable activities, which were often identified through the prism of class antagonisms. By the 1930s, police chiefs, mayors, and other government officials more often assumed such crusades. Purifying the city had become a project of the state in a way it had not been before, and increasingly it was informed not simply by class tensions but also by desires to curb the influence of tourists and other outsiders helping to reshape the representation and tempo of city life and encouraging the growth of whole districts that catered to their desires. This was evident in Europe, in cities such as Rome, Berlin, and Paris, as it was in other politically charged metropolises where moral and political surveillance overlapped, such as Nationalist Shanghai.[91]

In the United States, too, federal prohibition agents stepped up their policing of Chicago and New York nightlife during the same years as Chiappe's campaign, raiding rowdy cabarets and padlocking black and tans. Mayors and other city reformers also periodically launched crackdowns on bohemian enclaves or clubs popular with slummers, and after Prohibition's repeal, they used licensing laws to roust gay men from their public gathering spots. Mayor Fiorello La Guardia's wide-ranging efforts to clean up Manhattan perhaps most echoed Chiappe's plans. Chiappe and La Guardia shared not only a progressive yet authoritarian leadership style but also their ambition to stamp out subversive activities as well as backward, "purely sentimental" traces of the old city. Like Chiappe, La Guardia trained his sights on "nuisances" and "undesirables." He lamented that hot spots in Harlem had been "staged" for tourists the same way, he said, resorts in Paris had been for gullible visitors. La Guardia did battle against organ-grinders, gambling rackets, and burlesque houses the way Chiappe had gone after carpet beaters, drug dealers, and dirty-postcard sellers. These parallel techniques suggest that La Guardia, despite his leftist leanings, may have been inspired by Chiappe's campaign. New Yorkers, like other Americans, followed the municipal politics of Paris, reading periodic news about Chiappe's cleanup measures, and the city's Committee of Fourteen regularly surveyed vice conditions and reform efforts in Europe. Certainly La Guardia's aggressive antinoise campaign had been explicitly modeled on the Paris Prefect's measures as well as those implemented in Mussolini's Rome. Like Chiappe, La Guardia insisted he was "not a prude." "I have traveled all over Europe," he lectured a group of smutty magazine publishers, "and I am sure that no one will say that I am either soft on this matter or unduly alarmed."[92]

By the close of 1933, Chiappe's battery of raids had combated the city's homosexual subculture with an exacting severity. Communists had been

dealt a crippling blow. *Partouzeurs*, those night denizens of the Bois de Boulogne, had been hunted down by patrols. Arrests in the park were so vigorous
that even the most adventurous abandoned it in a matter of months. As the
city sank into economic depression, its nightlife had already taken on a more
sedate rhythm and a dimmer glow. Before the approving faces of municipal
councilors at the Hôtel de Ville, the prefect detailed the fruits of his battle
against the clandestine *maisons*, the streetwalkers, and those vexatious street
guides—431 of whom had been arrested that year so far. To be sure, the
prefect admitted, the boulevards appeared less vivacious than they had once
been. The crowds exuded less excitement, and the streets had lost some of
their cutting edge. With the coming of hard times, foreigners were beginning to sail home, and the resorts that catered to them had closed. But the
city left behind, Chiappe rejoiced, more accurately reflected the values of an
honest, noble, and well-balanced people, those Parisians who had weathered
the wave of hedonism without being demoralized. "It is to prove to be worthy
of them," Chiappe orated, "that I will continue to mercilessly pursue all that
attacks or could attack the health of Paris, its radiance, its age-old prestige."
Better to risk losing the patronage of Americans and all the other foreign
visitors who made the capital prosperous, his speech suggested, than to relin-
quish Frenchmen's control of the Paris streets. The Hôtel de Ville erupted in
prolonged applause.[93]

As Chiappe and his officers ensured, Paris was not simply the carefree
playground Americans made it out to be. More importantly, it offered a
terrain for some of the central struggles that animated urban cultural politics
on both sides of the Atlantic between the wars. For many Parisians, public
morality, political stability, and the international reputation of the capital
had become bound up together and in urgent need of protecting against the
claims and impositions of foreigners. As a vanguard among these imposing
newcomers, Americans carved out a place and purpose in the postwar capital
that proved more complicated and controversial than it seemed on the surface.
They had used their time abroad not simply to cut loose but also to reinforce
their own sense of national and moral superiority, delighting in the evidences
they discovered of French immorality and delighting just as much in the
police scramble to eradicate it. Such American impositions were about to
take on an even grander scale. Only weeks after Chiappe launched his
*épuration*, Legionnaires arrived in droves to participate in what would prove
to be a startling parade down the Champs-Elysées.

PART III | # American Political Culture

*We also know what you did in Paris, Mr. Blaine.*
—Major Strasser of the Third Reich
to Rick Blaine, *Casablanca*

| Legionnaires on Parade

FOR PARISIANS ON BOTH THE left and the right, targeting Americans and the values they were perceived to embody had become one compelling way to assert their place in the city. Americans, however, were not simply the objects of controversy. They also drew on their overseas experiences to define their own politics. Americans' investment in foreign affairs during the interwar years would not be limited to monitoring the diplomatic wrangling over the debts and disarmament or following the dilemmas of the League of Nations. Nor was it solely a matter of going abroad, selectively picking up ideas and practices, and then importing them back to the United States. During these decades, politically engaged Americans saw themselves as world participants, their lives intimately tied up with the era's most pressing issues. Modern American political culture would be steeped in nationalist aesthetics and rhetoric, to be sure, but it was at the same time forged through transnational connections. This was true even for the most seemingly home-grown of patriotic groups, the American Legionnaires, who arrived in Paris just as police geared up to purge the city's nightlife districts. Mobilizing its members for a reunion of celebrated proportions, the Legion brought its ninth annual convention to the capital in order to showcase its power on an international stage.

Even before the debris had been cleared following the Sacco-Vanzetti riots, some Parisians began to protest, in shrill tones, the arrival of these American veterans. "Popular emotion, aroused by the execution of the unfortunate innocent workers, Sacco and Vanzetti," was "so profound," Communist deputies argued, that any American festivities during this "period of mourning" would be considered an insult by all workers in France. These celebrations would offend "sentiment, justice, and reason," echoed the novelist Michel Corday. "Humanity is in mourning," he declared, and "mourning precludes celebrations." Others, such as the prominent socialist lawyer Alexandre Zévaès, thought the scheduled demonstration "an intolerable provocation." If the government did not wish to incite "a formidable explosion of popular anger," he cautioned, it should prohibit the display of "Yankee fascism."[1]

To their dismay, twenty to thirty thousand American Legionnaires converged on the city anyway. Formed in 1919 at a caucus convened in Paris to address flagging morale among troops awaiting demobilization in the American Expeditionary Forces (AEF), the American Legion quickly became the largest and most powerful veterans' organization in the United States, with over ten thousand posts. Created ostensibly to address interests specific to soldiers and to promote bipartisan fellowship among survivors of the Great War, the American Legion rapidly broadened its ambitions. The association, almost from its inception, stood out as a forerunner among the patriotic groups that flourished amid the period's heightened nativism and antiradicalism—a climate laid bare by lynch mobs in Southern towns and race riots in Northern cities, by Mayor Ole Hanson's belligerent stance against the Industrial Workers of the World (IWW) in Washington State, and by the merciless raids and deportations instigated by Attorney General A. Mitchell Palmer in Washington, D.C. A heyday for vigilance societies, paramilitary community policing, and a reinvigorated, national Ku Klux Klan, the war years and their aftermath marked a zenith of state-sanctioned coercion combined with popular, extralegal forms of violence and intimidation across the United States. Seeking, like other nationalist organizations, to recapture the fervor of the war, and riding the crest of reactionary public sentiments in its wake, the Legion continued to increase its membership as its vanguard prepared to muster in Paris. With 609,000 subscribers in 1925, by 1931 1,053,000 veterans would align themselves with the ultrapatriotic group. "For God and country we associate ourselves together," their constitution's idealistic preamble ran in part, "to maintain law and order; to foster and perpetuate a one hundred percent Americanism; to preserve the memories and incidents of our association in the great war; to inculcate a sense of individual obligation to the community, state and nation . . . to promote peace and goodwill on earth."[2]

Dedication to these goals, bewildering in their breadth, provided the basis for an array of Legion initiatives during the interwar period. Its members piloted civic improvement schemes, contributing to child welfare services and disaster relief efforts. They commandeered community celebrations, jockeyed for control over school textbooks and curricula, and in some places even extracted mandatory loyalty oaths from instructors. At the same time they prevented, by violence or legal maneuvering, liberals' speeches and laborers' strikes. They intimidated inquisitive journalists, had bold teachers fired, ran radicals out of town. They attacked anything that even remotely smacked of communist affiliation. During the 1920s and 1930s, Legionnaires lobbied successfully for veterans' benefits and severely restrictive immigration quotas, for congressional investigations of "un-American" activities, and for a strengthened FBI. They championed universal military training and a steep buildup of the nation's arsenal. They did battle against the release of conscientious objectors imprisoned during the late war and engaged in character assassination against spokeswomen for the peace movement.[3] Joining in the actions of the Legion during its formative years—finding purpose in its zeal for righteousness, duty, and militancy—exemplified one extreme, but by no means atypical, response to the social upheavals of the immediate postwar era. As they took leave for Paris, Legionnaires intended to show the world a model of upstanding Americanism and right-wing civic activism.

By relying exclusively on accounts from the mainstream American press and Legionnaires themselves, scholars have underestimated the Legion convention's significance as an episode in transatlantic political debate.[4] The controversy surrounding the forthcoming ceremonies, as told in French sources as well as American ones, reveals that the historical relevance of the American Legion was not confined to its members' communities or even the boundaries of the United States. Born in Paris amid global war, in 1927 the Legion returned to the capital, where it became a lightning rod for heated disputes about the nature of right-wing social movements and the limits of political expression in the modern metropolis. For Legionnaires, the center of Paris became a useful vantage point from which to broaden their political influence and cast their idea of Americanism in sharper relief. Their claims to stand for all veterans—indeed, to embody the American nation as a whole— gained force by taking their convention abroad and by welcoming sympathetic members of France's political and military elite into their official proceedings. At the same time, those who opposed these veterans regarded them not as harmless, casual visitors but as probable fascists who shared the outlook and goals of far-right groups on the rise in Europe. For these critics, the Legion convention provided something tangible to rally against and served to clarify the international terrain on which their opponents operated. Together, the conspicuous presence of the Legionnaires and the counteractions of their detractors would exacerbate the political fault lines that ran through Paris. Like the Sacco-Vanzetti riots and Prefect Chiappe's ensuing campaign for urban moral reform, the conflict that erupted around the group's visit would ultimately become a disagreement over the control of the city's streets.

During their stay in Paris, American Legionnaires exemplified the aspirations and characteristics of a new, modern American right, in tune with those new nationalisms taking shape in other countries, and one that pioneered a particular ideal of the American abroad—one example of how Americans, as they became bolder players in world politics, might look and act. As their opponents feared, the Legion exhibited more than a passing likeness to Europe's new right-wing movements, but the display veterans put on in Paris would turn out quite unexpectedly nonetheless. The Legionnaires proved adept, even confounding, participants in the public life of the French capital, a point that rankled their enemies even more. Deciphering the controversy surrounding the Legionnaires' stay, as well as the complex layers lurking beneath the surface of their festivities, highlights the interplay between nationalist politics and international maneuvering at the heart of American political culture between the wars.

Formally inviting the Legion years before, the French government set aside almost four million francs to regale their American guests. French officials presumed that goodwill toward the veterans would be reciprocated by American magnanimity on the issue of war debts. Paris shopkeepers and restaurateurs for their part fantasized about the profits to be made off so many spendthrift visitors. France's old guard—its conservative upper crust, its military elite—intended in turn to flog once more the glories of wartime allegiances in order to whip up support for French rearmament and continued German subjugation. Painstaking efforts, thus, would be taken to please the Legionnaires. France's vexatious travel taxes and visa fees were waived. Indeed, Legionnaires could travel to Europe without passports; American Legion identification sufficed at border checks. The railways offered train service to Paris at half price, and hotels took veterans' reservations at a "favored-client rate." Banquets and religious services were planned in their honor. Post offices staffed by English-speaking clerks established special telephone and telegraph assistance and sold commemoration stamps picturing Washington and Lafayette. To drive the good feeling home, the French Chamber designated September 19, 1927, the opening day of the convention, a national holiday.[5]

A variety of motives marked the decision to take the Legion convention to Paris. For one, the tenth anniversary of the AEF's arrival in France seemed a fitting moment for veterans and their families to visit the battlefields and bestow honors on those buried near the front. Sincere wishes to consecrate the grounds where men had experienced the horrors of trench warfare and where loved ones had fallen were mixed with the curiosity of others who, though enlisted, never made it to Europe during the short duration of American engagement. Legionnaires, however, also seized upon this so-called Paris pilgrimage as a means to lengthen their own membership rosters, promising to bring the association not only more funds but more leverage as a lobbying force. The group's officials announced that only those fully enrolled for both 1926 and 1927 would be eligible to take advantage of this "life-long dream come true."[6]

The convention proved a stunning public relations coup in the United States. With incredible gusto that rivaled the advertising innovations of the late war itself, the staff of the Legion's news service generated more than two million words of copy and thousands of photographs, sending speeches to radio stations, convincing newsreel distributors to carry footage about the outing, and bombarding the press with all manner of stories designed to "supply the 'color' and emotional qualities needed to arouse in a man a desire to revisit France with the American Legion." The organization's national publication proclaimed, "The Legion is going to France conscious that the eyes of the whole United States are upon it. It will arrive in Paris knowing that the cables will be telling the nation it left behind its doings of every hour. . . . It will hold its deliberations," the magazine read, "visualizing the headlines in America's newspapers of the following morning." The pilgrimage would be, it rhapsodized, "one of the greatest news events in modern times."[7]

The Legion drummed up support from scores of national associations, like the American Federation of Labor, as well as leading corporations, such as AT&T and the Commonwealth Edison Company. Conservative public figures, too, endorsed the veterans' plans. President Calvin Coolidge pledged that the government would do anything in its power to assist the "worthy undertaking." Charles Lindbergh thought that the event would make permanent the spirit of camaraderie forged between the French and the American doughboys in 1917. Elected officials—perhaps with both authentic goodwill and future votes in mind—treated the Legionnaires generously. Congress enacted a law permitting ex-servicemen postal workers extra vacation time to make the journey. The Iowa State Legislature appropriated $50,000 to enable three prize-winning bands from its state to make the trip, and New York State Governor Al Smith signed a bill giving $10,000 to the Oneida Post Drum and Bugle Corps to go, expenses paid. Cottage industries sprang up to take advantage of interest in the pilgrimage. Advertising campaigns wooed Legionnaires with the perks of language courses, traveler's cheques, and extended European tours; banks underwrote special savings clubs; railroad agencies granted round-trip services to ports of embarkation for the price of a one-way fare. All this positive publicity magnified the significance of the convention to something beyond the routine meeting of a private group.[8]

Most importantly, the convention extended a chance to reinvigorate memories of war and nostalgia for a time "when America was blazing with a spirit which surprised herself"—romanticized notions that aided the political ambitions of the Legion leadership. "Listen, buddy," beseeched a supplement to the *American Legion Weekly*, "don't let the years draw a curtain between you and your experiences during the days of reveille, slum, K.P., allotments and all the rest of it. Don't outgrow the memories you wouldn't sell for a million." Embarking on the junket, the pamphlet claimed, presented an opportunity to renew confidence and credence—"to show your wife, mother or children," in other words, "just how and where you won the war." "The city of Paris," the supplement assured, "will be ours." The sense of pride, mastery, and manliness drawn from wartime experiences informed the convictions of the Legion's most active members and fueled the organization's various campaigns to purify American society and restore it to past glories. Viewing once again "the battlefields where they fought to establish the guiding principles of the Legion," one of the group's past commanders ventured, would reinforce Legionnaires' sense of purpose and privilege as veterans. Taking control of the French capital would, in turn, offer to the entire world a show of the strength and resolve of these fighting men, so quick to claim credit for winning the war. "We shall renew our life pledge to our Legion and revel again in the glory of our Allied victory," the Texan hard-liner Alvin Owsley swore: "In mass formation the Legion will advance on Paris."[9]

Coordinating the "lines of advance" of what would come to be known as the Second AEF fell to the French Convention Travel Committee, organized in 1925. Mapping out routes to the continent on twenty-eight liners from eight North American ports, the committee arranged for special health and accident insurance as well as optional tours to battlefields and cemeteries. The trip, the committee estimated, could be had for as little as $175 plus meals and spending money and completed in as little as twenty-three days. The five-day program of the convention itself was packed with speeches, memorials, and band contests—all in addition to the Legion's formal proceedings, booked for the majestic halls of the Trocadéro across the river from the Eiffel Tower. The highlight of the convention, though, would undoubtedly be the parade, slated for the afternoon of September 19. An elaborate affair scheduled to wind through the famous thoroughfares of the city center, the procession would file past review stands in the place de la Concorde, where General Pershing, Marshal Foch, Legion Commander Howard Savage, and other military notables would sit in tacit approval. Marchers planned to rendezvous at noontime in the place d'Iéna near Washington's statue and the American embassy—the same square that had been barred to Sacco-Vanzetti supporters so forcefully only weeks before. At the appointed moment, tens of thousands of American Legionnaires would kick off the parade by marching through the Arc de Triomphe and triumphantly down the Champs-Elysées.[10]

Despite its torrent of ballyhoo, the Legion could not insulate its grand demonstration in the French capital from bitter opposition. In France, criticism of the parade came from trade unionists and moderates in the League of the Rights of Man as well as from more radical leftists, still smarting over the Sacco-Vanzetti affair. The anarchist Comité Sacco-Vanzetti, carrying on after the executions, refused to have further contact with Prefect Chiappe after he bragged that he had "wiped the floor" with the demonstrators during the recent unrest. They considered the possibility of a Legion parade in Paris "like a second assassination of Sacco and Vanzetti." The Socialist Party likewise directed its members to avoid the Legion's ceremonies in protest against the event's "clearly Nationalist and reactionary character" and, given its timing, its assault on the "universal conscience" of those mourning for the two Italian anarchists. Legionnaires had been among those who most loudly called for Fuller to carry out the death sentences. For this reason, detractors situated the Legion parade at the center of a host of concerns. The procession, they believed, threatened to dramatize all at once the celebration of judicial murder and police brutality, the looming presence of the United States as a world power, and the bourgeoisie's odious tolerance for the militant reactionary groups thought to serve as handmaidens of the capitalist system. The Communist veteran leader Henri Barbusse stormed that the upcoming *"fête"* had been arranged to honor "a fascist American group," which had formally egged on the Boston officials who assured the deaths of Sacco and Vanzetti. "We must protest with all our forces," he thundered, "against this offensive of the executioners."[11]

Heeding calls from CGT spokesmen, various labor organizations refused to have any part in the celebrations. Activists for the CGTU also plastered up giant posters, denouncing the event in bold lettering: "In the service of international capitalism," the French government, they said, intended to impose upon Paris "the parade of the 'American Legion,' *organisation fasciste* that congratulated Governor FULLER" for refusing to stay the executions. The poster decried the loss of workers' wages on this unwanted national holiday. Forced already to pay a $250 billion debt to American bankers, it charged, Parisians would now be forced to bankroll the Legionnaires' revelry, too. "Down with the American executioners," concluded the sheet, "Down with *la répression capitaliste internationale*." Subsections of the CGTU—unions comprised of dockers and railway laborers, metalworkers and electricity men—urged members to boycott the parade, to boycott American movies, and to refuse to transport or sell American merchandise. Labor representatives suggested that acts of sabotage by those who worked in places selling American goods or receiving American customers would register proper contempt for the "Yankee plutocrat accomplices of the assassination." One union devilishly called on cooks and waiters to make all necessary arrangements to see that the Legion would be received in their establishments with the comfort befitting of "accomplices of assassins."[12]

Socialists and anarchists employed almost as brazen language, but for communists, fighting the Legion became a veritable obsession. Communist mayors of working-class suburbs rejected the government's plans, refusing to shut down municipal services or decorate public edifices for the proclaimed holiday. Others drafted rancorous editorials and held meetings. At dozens of well-attended rallies sponsored by the PCF in late August and early September, firebrands held forth on the evils of the Legion. One speaker told an audience of more than three hundred that the prelude to future revolution would be the "gesture of contempt that you will throw in the face of the American Legion, representative of international fascism." At an assembly of some two hundred people, the secretary of the Paris branch of the Secours Rouge insisted that when the time came, workers must take to the streets and stand up to the "*insulte*" of the American veterans. At another gathering, one activist invited guests to defy the "fascists of the American Legion," calling on them to "throw their lashing scorn in the face of these American executioners."[13]

*L'Humanité*, the PCF's official organ and the most widely read leftist journal in Paris, proved a consistent forum for anti-Legion invective. Even before Sacco and Vanzetti died, its contributors had campaigned against the "reactionary and chauvinistic veterans," these "accomplices of murder," these "fascists of the American Legion."[14] Paul Vaillant-Couturier—the ebullient leader whose treatises had played such a pivotal role in stirring up emotions about the Sacco-Vanzetti case—began denouncing the Legion in his front-page columns as its advance guard rolled into the capital in early August.[15] Shortly after, the paper printed a telegram from the American novelist John Dos Passos, reporting the Massachusetts Legion's compliments to Governor Fuller and preparations for maintaining order during the executions. Once the death sentences were carried out, Vaillant-Couturier and others resolved that the insensitive conventioneers must be stopped in their bid to "dance on the corpses of Sacco and Vanzetti." To convince their hundreds of thousands of readers of the Legion's crimes, the editors of *L'Humanité* painted an ugly picture of these "white terrorists," whose misdeeds rivaled the actions of the Ku Klux Klan. The group was a battle brigade "for the defense of capitalist privilege," explained one article; "the American Legionnaires are fascists, direct and brutal agents of imperialism and Yankee usurers." Like Italian Fascists, the piece continued, they followed military-style organization; with officers, barracks, and fighting posts, the Legion thought of everything "in terms of war," right down to their very name, borrowed from the Roman army. Writers for *L'Humanité* scoffed at Legionnaires' portrayal of themselves as peaceful pilgrims. They offered instead a counterportrait of a bunch of bloodthirsty wayfarers on a tactless mission of self-congratulation. "America warlike and fascist, America of lynching, of electrocution, of the fussy puritans and the brutal drunks spilled out . . . on the quays of Cherbourg," the paper relayed days before the convention. The article deplored the group's arrival as an occasion for waxing poetic about heroic death on the battlefield while cookies and champagne were passed around. "Enough! . . . Pouah! What stench of mass grave and fire rises up in our throat."[16]

Communists—and other leftists who shared their disgust, if not their predilection for hyperbole—could be viewed, as they were at the time by others, as opportunists using the parade as a pretext to censure their own government, to sustain popular discontent left over from the Sacco-Vanzetti affair, and to stir up more turmoil in the capital. To some, the ceaseless repetition of the same epithets—fascists, assassins, imperialists, agents of capitalism—seemed to float like sensational catchwords detached from any real analysis of the Legion's politics. Many thought that leftists' diatribes, in other words, had very little to do with the actual Legionnaires themselves. Broadcasting lurid warnings, casting themselves as hapless victims in mourning, activists no doubt hoped to parley their way into greater political influence. But these domestic ambitions unfolded against a backdrop of intense international debate about the nature and potential consequences of postwar right-wing social movements. Local aspirations, underwritten by manipulative sensationalism, certainly fueled French leftists' campaign against the Legion, but real and serious fears about the organization's intentions came into play as well.

French critics were indeed participating in a transnational conversation about the objectives of the Legion and not just flexing their political muscles. Their most damning evidence against the group, in fact, came funneling across the Atlantic from informed Americans eager to spread the word. One activist in Boston, for example, composed a hasty telegram to a contact in Paris immediately after Sacco and Vanzetti were executed, reporting on how the Legionnaires had counseled the governor not to overturn the death sentences. They have murdered Sacco and Vanzetti tonight, he relayed: "Hyenas plan to banquet together. You have the American Legion there. Make them understand what has happened." Following the dispatch from Dos Passos, widely commented on in France, the editors of *L'Humanité* ran bombastic criticisms of the Legion from H. L. Mencken and Upton Sinclair. The paper also received lengthy letters from an unnamed New York correspondent who, over the course of the first weeks of September, related how "slowly but surely," the Legion had transformed into "a sort of super-government," a "fourth power" after the three traditional branches prescribed by the U.S. Constitution. In story after story, the correspondent tapped information about the Legion's regional activities clearly drawn from reports by liberal American journalists and scholars who shared French leftists' suspicions about this powerful veterans' group. The resulting serial exposé unfolded like an ominous map of the Legion's wide-reaching political influence stretching from Oakland, California, through Little Rock, Arkansas, and Detroit, Michigan, to Bogalusa, Louisiana, and Bridgeport, Connecticut. Implicit in the coverage was the suggestion that this growing menace could soon spread beyond American borders, that the Legion's first of many forays abroad would begin when its members filed through the Arc de Triomphe and down the Champs-Elysées.[17]

By the time French leftists became involved, American critics had already amassed an impressive dossier on the veterans' group. The American Civil Liberties Union (ACLU), created in the same tumultuous postwar atmosphere as the Legion, zeroed in on the organization immediately as a threat to political rights and personal expression. As part of its drive against the suppression of free speech, the ACLU published a record of fifty acts of violence perpetrated by members of the Legion prior to 1920, including the razor-blade castration and lynching of the IWW activist Wesley Everest in Centralia, Washington. During July 1921, Arthur Warner similarly chronicled for readers of the liberal *Nation* "the truth" about the Legion in four incriminating installments, reports which appear to have been among the sources for *L'Humanité*'s New York correspondent. Piling anecdote upon disturbing anecdote, he recalled that Arthur Clark, a newspaper editor, had been whipped with rawhide for articles he wrote about the group in Carpinteria, California, and that Frederick Reis, a lawyer subpoenaed as the witness of a raid on a Communist Labor Party headquarters, was thrown from a bridge in Dayton, Ohio. Warner pilloried the Legion's "bigoted, business-controlled, undemocratic leadership"; he inveighed against the "illegal" and "ridiculous" laws they encouraged, the "insidious methods" to indoctrinate school children they proposed, and the attempts to "hamstring and terrorize the alien" they pursued. He mocked the organization's conception of a "strait-laced, self-sufficient nationalism which takes as its physical standard the young men who exhibit union suits in the advertising pages of our magazines, and as its mental guides our Coolidges and Ole Hansons." In "the spirit of repression and coercion, of prejudice and unreason," he charged, the group had "out-Palmered our former Attorney General himself in identifying Americanism with absolutism."[18]

The year of the Paris convention, the Legion earned from the ACLU the label of "most active agency in intolerance and repression in the United States today." Only months before the group's overseas pilgrimage, it received an equally unflattering portrayal in the progressive journalist Norman Hapgood's study, *Professional Patriots*, which, under the endorsement of almost one hundred professors, congressmen, reformers, and religious leaders, concluded that "for real action against radicals in the name of patriotism," the Legion had outdone all other extremist organizations. Hapgood discussed the tarring and feathering of two men who attended a Farmers' Non-Partisan League meeting in Kansas, the prevention of peace signs being raised in an Armistice Day parade in Boston, and the throwing of eggs, stones, and stink bombs at students trying to hold a Fellowship of Youth for Peace conference in Concord, Massachusetts. "The spirit behind these evidences of patriotic zeal is not far removed from the Italian Fascisti," he ventured. Indeed, Hapgood had hit on a central point of contention about the Legion—the question of the group's comparability to the budding fascist movements of Europe, a question that would be central to the conflict that unfurled around their plans to parade in Paris.[19]

Historians have often identified the Legion's actions with homespun conservatism, but such a characterization underrates the complexity of the organization's politics. Conservatives in the early twentieth century remained suspicious of new social initiatives, particularly those initiated by the government, so, in a strange way, the group owed more to the tradition of progressive reform. The charitable activities of its local posts mirrored the altruistic impulses in social welfare projects like the settlement house movement. The organization's quest to promote "100 percent Americanism," though ill defined, similarly paralleled coercive attempts by various authorities to "Americanize" immigrants. Its readiness to harness the powers of the state to mold society to its own prescriptions, too, echoed recent progressive undertakings of the more obdurate sort—racial segregation in industrializing Southern towns, imperialist ventures in the Caribbean and Pacific, the Taylorist regimentation of factory work, and the harsh wartime measures of the Wilson administration.[20]

Categorizing the Legion as conservative similarly elides what was so new about the organization and how much it was enmeshed in an international context of political crisis and ideological polarization. The Legion had been modeled, to be sure, on past veterans' societies—most notably on the Grand Army of the Republic, the Civil War fraternity of Union soldiers—and it inherited from patriotic orders of the nineteenth century many of its rituals and symbols. But veterans also quite consciously created the Legion in reaction to transatlantic events during the war and its immediate aftermath—to revolution in Russia and short-lived soviet republics in Germany and Hungary, to the manifest restlessness of Allied troops in France, and to mounting labor activism throughout Europe and North America. Seattle's explosive general strike, an uprising in Winnipeg, the Spartacist insurrection in Berlin, the mass factory occupations in Turin during Italy's *bienno rosso*, and more—all these leftist revolts, snowballing in 1919 and 1920 as the Legion was being formed, had been lumped together in the minds of the group's leaders under the banner of Bolshevism. Vowing to check such widespread threats, Legionnaires, like other right-wing activists, did not forgo international engagement for their nationalist convictions. Indeed, they displayed a surprising degree of interest in overseas developments, apprising themselves of the details of municipal affairs in Paris and other European capitals, of communist plots in China, strike attempts in India, or police raids in Bulgaria. It was this interconnectedness of world events that Legion officials acknowledged by taking their convention abroad in 1927, and the same sense of global urgency that guided French leftists' opposition to that visit.[21]

French leftists regarded the Legion's coming not only with that group's powerful place in the United States in mind, but also in the context of mounting right-wing action across Europe. Reaction and repression in postwar Europe paralleled or even surpassed that which shaped American society in the early twenties. While self-appointed patriots policed American communities—while hooded Klansmen rode through the night—hundreds of antisemitic societies and nationalist militias sprouted up across Poland, Romania, and Hungary. In northern Italy, middle-class defense squads, often headed by veterans, led assaults on socialists instead. In Germany, roving Freikorps of disgruntled ex-soldiers lashed out against the terms of the Treaty of Versailles, terrorizing their opponents and helping to occupy Berlin in 1920 during the Kapp Putsch, an attempt to overthrow the new Weimar

Republic. On the brink of power in 1922, Mussolini had observed with something more than wishful thinking, *"il mondo va a destra"*—the world is turning to the right. By the mid and late twenties, this chaos and grassroots violence of the immediate postwar years had consolidated into more organized, permanent right-wing movements. By then, Paris itself had become a haven for antiparliamentary *ligues* staffed by paramilitary youths and veterans bent on street violence and the demise of the Third Republic. Across Europe, liberal governments would topple like dominoes in the coming years. The seemingly unstoppable spread of military coups and fascist-style corps, the proliferation of repressive regimes under motley despots and dictators, have led scholars to question how suitable legislative compromises and democratic self-rule really were at the time for this brutalized "dark continent."[22]

Amid this international insurgency of right-wing politics—especially in the years before Hitler's rise—considerable confusion surrounded the exact nature of fascism. Until the Popular Front reappraisals in the mid-thirties, when communists began to ally with other leftists, the Communist International regarded fascism as simply an expression of capitalist power at its most extreme and imminently doomed state. In France during the late twenties, political affiliations of all sorts were liable to earn competitors the title "fascist" from the PCF, including socialists with shared reverence for Marxist doctrine, who French communists routinely dismissed as "Social Fascists." During the same period, when Mussolini's government still stood as the only fascist regime in power, many American liberals, too, misdiagnosed the import of such a political movement. Mussolini's Fascism even appealed to many pragmatic progressives who, for a while, admired the regime's adventurous social engineering experiments and redemptive campaigns for national unity. In forums such as *The New Republic*, some American liberals' openness to, or flirtation with, this emerging ideology reflected how permeable progressive thought could be and foreshadowed how flexible—as its style and tenets were co-opted by various groups—the nature of fascism once was.[23] Warier segments of the American left—contributors to *The Nation*, members of the ACLU, liberal academics and journalists—drafted forceful arguments against fascism and highlighted the American Legion's allegedly fascist tendencies. But these would largely come only later during the 1930s at the height of antifascist campaigning in the United States, years after the salvos volleyed by French radicals angry over the planned Paris convention.

Some Americans, however, saw the Legion's fascist connection almost immediately. They were the Legionnaires themselves. During his stint as National Commander in 1923, the Texan Alvin Owsley assured the press that "if ever needed, the American Legion stands ready to protect our country's institutions and ideals as the Fascisti dealt with the destructionists who menaced Italy!" Suggesting that the veterans' group would even take over the government if necessary, Owsley blustered, "Do not forget that the Fascisti are to Italy what the American Legion is to the United States." The Legion's regard for the Italian political experiment was further intimated by formal invitations to Mussolini to appear at their conventions and by readings of the dictator's salutations at annual proceedings well into the 1930s. In one glowing eyewitness account of Italy under the repressive regime, the Legionnaire B. M. Roszel could not applaud enough the miracle, the "wonderful thing," of Mussolini's new state. In a paean to the dictator's "guiding genius," he tried his hand at recent Italian history: "After the war, the danger of Communism and Bolshevism startled the nation. Patriotic Italians waked up and acted. Benito Mussolini organized his 'black shirts.' . . . The King wisely made him Premier, and a new spiritual order arose all over the land." Roszel praised the Duce as "the guiding spirit of the time," who "led, or forced his people to think as he thinks, to act as he acts, to hope as he hopes, to serve the State and to sacrifice self if necessary." The dictator had been "called the foe of democracy," the Legionnaire admitted. "Perhaps he is," Roszel mused, but "he has pulled together the men of Italy until . . . Italians think and feel and act alike." If only, the subtext of the report implied, the American Legion could do the same for the people of the United States.[24]

Taking into consideration the confusion surrounding fascism before the advent of German National Socialism and Legionnaires' own willingness to draw a likeness, parallels between the American organization and other new right-wing mass movements should not be dismissed outright. During the past few decades, scholars of comparative fascism have worked to bring cogency and historical specificity to a term that had been used loosely to describe all kinds of people and behaviors. The growing precision of this historiography, however, has set indisputably fascist groups off from other right-wing radicals, making it more difficult to theorize relationships between them. American groups, moreover, have been largely excluded from the scope of this debate among European historians. Nevertheless, just as scholars of the United States have explored the "family resemblance" between the second Ku Klux Klan and fascists overseas, so too the common ground shared by the Legion and Europe's far right should be addressed.[25] Crucial differences might have ultimately distinguished the Legion from fascism proper, but the veterans showed very real affinities with fascists and paramilitary groups in 1920s Europe. Recalling the international political context in which the Legion flourished helps to explain its particular success between the wars and, more generally, the nature of American popular politics on the right.

First and foremost, Legion efforts diverged in important respects from those of clear fascists. Significantly, many distinguishing features of the Legion also set the Klan apart from European groups, a coincidence perhaps not unrelated to the fact that membership between the two American organizations strongly overlapped in many locales. Like the Klan, the Legion encouraged a diffusion of power rather than the cultivation of a *Führerprinzip*. Many Legionnaires revered authority and hierarchy, but the Legion's structure, spread out geographically as well as administratively, allowed room for competing voices rather than concentrating leadership in the hands of a permanent figurehead. Also, like the Klan, the Legion declared reverence for the laws of American government. Its lack of overt intentions to overturn the framework of constitutional democracy sharply distinguished its pronouncements from the revolutionary rhetoric of groups like Mussolini's Blackshirts and Hitler's SA. It might be more accurate to compare the Legion to the Arditi in Italy and the Stahlhelm in Germany— right-wing veterans' organizations whose members often but not always crossed over to political party work for the Fascisti and the National Socialist German Workers' Party (NSDAP). Furthermore, the Legion drew its membership from the same kinds of middling classes that filled the ranks of fascist movements, but its leadership hailed from the more privileged rungs of society—ex-officers, educated and professional elites. These men brought to the organization a preference for the economic status quo rather than new plans to subordinate industry to the exigencies of the state, which scholars have attributed to fascism. The Legion, in sum, sported less of the bloodlust for violent change and the total authoritarian worship that historians have pinpointed as defining features of fascist movements.[26]

Fascism, however, inspired political manifestations of enormous variety, and scholars regularly admit that it remains one of the most contentious terms in historical discussion. The incredible diversity of such movements derived in part from the fact that, as expressions of nationalism above all, each garnered its legitimacy not from a shared text or doctrine but from interpretations of local traditions. Tapping into their own communities' patriotic references, fascist groups necessarily appeared different from each other in their symbols and pronouncements. For this reason, the outward trappings adopted by separate groups often effectively masked underlying affinities shared across national or regional lines. Focusing more on these surface displays than on underlying convictions, American historians looking for fascism in the United States most readily point to a small set of extremist organizations such as the German American Bund and the Italian American Blackshirts, which made frequent and obvious claims about their fascist intentions. With unabashed loyalty to overseas leaders, however, these groups that have seemed to historians most overtly fascist were less true to the creed than others who paraded as the leaders of homegrown, mainstream movements. True American fascists, burning with nationalist pride, would have appeared firmly grounded in their own culture even if also simultaneously inspired by the claims and actions of right-wing movements elsewhere. It was this contention of being free from foreign corruption that all fascist groups needed to cultivate to translate their small-time beginnings into a basis for more substantial power. Understanding this dimension to fascism leads to the startling sense that in its more subtle and purportedly indigenous forms fascist-style American political culture had the most potential—that fascism, whether wholly subscribed to or not, found an intriguing amount of traction even beyond the extremist margins.[27]

The American Legion indeed shared several prominent traits with fascist groups overseas. Like European fascisms, Legion politics relied strongly on the historical fact of World War I and its aftermath—on the disquiet of decommissioned soldiers facing unsettling new economic and political realities. The war effort on both sides of the Atlantic had raised the need for states to drum up unprecedented national mobilization, but in the United States, as elsewhere, government officials struggled to control the outpouring of patriotic energies they solicited. Like militants in Europe, Legionnaires gained footholds in their communities as citizens began to fear that the state had not gone far enough to ensure order. Through its vocabulary, insignia, and military training camps, the Legion sought to normalize the martial experience to fill this gap. The group's Armistice Day speeches revealed many Legionnaires' desire to perpetuate what they called the "splendid and essential virtues" awakened by the war. Similarly, the Legion's devotion to the Boy Scouts paralleled European fascists' interest in youth groups as means to inculcate an appreciation for armed conflict early. "Our boys are going to shoot," the Legion argued in favor of its sponsorship of Junior Rifle Clubs, so "the training will make the lads worth a little more to our country."[28]

Like European fascisms, Legionnaires' activities flourished in direct proportion to labor activism and left-wing radicalism. The group attacked liberals, communists, and immigrants using language designed to dehumanize its enemies as "vermin" and "swine." In November 1919, for example, Los Angeles Legionnaires proclaimed a "war of extermination" against the IWW and Bolshevism. An official resolution at the organization's first national convention similarly called for action "to rid our country of this scum who hate our God, our country, our flag." The Legion sought total exclusion of some groups from the political arena, advocating a complete halt to immigration, vigorous deportation campaigns, and the outlawing of the Communist Party. Like European fascists who became successful enough to seize power, the Legion manipulated traditional conservative groups to gain their support. Deputized by police chiefs and mayors, given information about so-called subversives by federal officials, holding joint meetings with groups like the American Defense Society and the National Security League, the Legion emphasized law and order despite its members' frequent resort to extralegal actions. Like European fascists, Legionnaires obfuscated class divisions by emphasizing the bonds of national community in a manner that was both populist and—by forcibly expelling some groups from that utopian vision— exclusive.[29]

The Legion's kinship to the new far-right groups of Europe seems clearest, however, when fascism is analyzed as a cultural movement.[30] The group's central doctrine of Americanism mirrored fascist belief systems by promoting an acute form of nationalism, designed to rouse initiates' emotions to new heights. In its broadest conception, Americanism "embraces every phase of an individual's relation to the community, state and nation. Primarily it begins in the home," explained the commission charged with publicizing the ideal. Like fascist ideologies, the Legion's Americanism appealed to notions of loyalty and sacrifice in order to convince followers to position all aspects of their lives in relation to the interests of the state. Like European nationalists, the group dictated precise choreography for official demonstrations as well as the use of lighting, music, banners, and other crowd-pleasing props. Their manual of ceremonies contained meticulous instructions on the positioning of speakers in relation to their audiences, the role of firing squads, and the proper timing of momentous silences, recited oaths, and ritualized salutes, all geared toward imparting the sacredness of the proceedings. Such ritualistic display and patriotic liturgy sought to engender in participants an almost religious experience that captured both the urgency and the grandeur of the cause of national survival. Americanism, one sermon for such an event assured, was "that spirit of patriotism which shall ever preserve our land from that stagnation which is the death of peoples."[31]

Propping up this all-encompassing, energizing national orientation, the Legionnaires' rhetoric also paralleled that used by fascists—a political language full of ideas about cleansing and redemption combined with constant reminders about enemies and threats. Self-consciously dedicated to the "purity and permanency of America," Americanism highlighted the way to better community life through adherents' contributions to the nation's "well-being." At the same time, the Legion viciously opposed competing visions for the future of the United States. California Legionnaire Frank Belgrano proclaimed, "there is room in this country for only one ism. That is Americanism": a blunt statement in an era of socialism, communism, trade unionism, feminism, and so many other isms. On another occasion, Belgrano similarly urged that "the duty of implanting the spirit of true Americanism in the heart of every citizen belongs to us [Legionnaires]. . . . We propose to wage this battle in every field in which the enemies of America operate." "We have declared war," he insisted. The group's official speeches for Armistice Day ceremonies underscored many Legionnaires' sense that they were waging an epic struggle for a reinvigorated American culture, and they promoted a worldview loaded with theories, borrowed from Madison Grant or Oswald Spengler, about the threat of national or racial decline. "History shows how often civilization has sapped the manhood of a race," prepared words for the holiday ran, "how often conquerors have in turn been conquered by the culture they overcame, how difficult it has been to achieve culture without decay." Americanism, tempered by the lessons of war, served as the Legion's road map for such a culture, untainted and without decay. War bred "contempt of softness," a "spirit of obedience," the "necessity of discipline," "self-sacrifice," and "the bigness to recognize that . . . for the good of us all, some of us must exercise authority over the rest of us, and that the rest of us, for the good of all, are bound in honor to obey them." Advocating the conversion of "martial courage into civil courage" and praising the "valor of clean, uncompromising lives lived in common honor and devotion," the Legion seemed to be primed for fascist commitments should conditions in the United States unravel as they had in many parts of Europe.[32]

Legionnaires' Americanism was instantly recognizable. Its symbols and practices appeared comfortingly familiar, gathering together the surface components of Americana but cultivating beneath them unseen depths that might be plumbed for radical use. Nowhere was this clearer than in the group's regard for the American flag, the primary weapon in the Legion's stockpile of patriotic hardware. In 1923, Legionnaires had led the effort to standardize the flag code, determining the fine points of Old Glory's place-ment in churches and schools, ruminating over the appropriate times to fly it, and cautioning that it "should be hoisted briskly but should be lowered slowly and ceremoniously." The Legion then broadcast the resulting "rules of heraldry" in millions of pamphlets and managed to enact laws dictating the flag's use in several parts of the country. Reverence for this national symbol, from the perspective of many Legionnaires, remained noncontroversial but also nonnegotiable. The flag served as a rallying point for the organization as a whole even as it became a convenient cover for the more extreme actions of some. In March 1924, for instance, a group of Legionnaires broke up a memorial for Lenin at a hall in Wilkes-Barre, Pennsylvania, forcing each attendee, as they exited, to salute the American flag at gunpoint. The display of the Stars and Stripes signified adherence to a whole cluster of cultural and political beliefs with implications beyond simple patriotism. But the Legion's ability to market its views through traditions and beloved national icons allowed the group to pass off its politics as unproblematic expressions of love for country.[33]

The Legion, then, though by no means a clear-cut example of fascism, exhibited key fascist elements. A large organization with a diverse membership, it housed a few outspoken members who were inclined toward explicitly fascist thinking and may have been, if the situation arose, open to fascist-style rule. The cultural tactics of the Legion suggest that it might be regarded as a distant relative of the more flagrantly fascist groups across the ocean—one softened around the edges and better suited to the American landscape. In a country where no serious crisis of constitutional democracy occurred, where the impact of the Great War was least, where conservative elites were too powerful and the political left too weak, there was less of an opening for the kinds of strident fascism that infested war-torn Europe. The Legion owed its rise to the same concerns and convictions that animated Europeans on the far right, but the group also adjusted itself to the specific political climate of the postwar United States.

The Legion's ability to downplay any suggestion of revolutionary intent while at the same time highlighting its extreme cultural imperatives—this unique mix of attributes was, arguably, the key to the organization's efficacy as a social movement. The Legion was adaptable enough to accommodate Northerners and Southerners, demagogues like Owsley and Belgrano as well as others devoted simply to the joys of fraternity and community service. The group's professed respect for the law and simultaneous unwillingness at National Headquarters to reprimand excessive actions taken by local posts lent a dynamism to the organization. It thrived by cultivating a respectable façade that obscured some of the more serious implications of its nationalist ideologies. Indeed, the fact that the group did not align itself with the Democratic or Republican parties and the fact that its most apparent innovations fell into the ambiguous realm of cultural practices emboldened its spokesmen to claim that the Legion was not political at all. Commander Savage, leading the charge to Paris, denied that the group harbored any political agenda at all: "It is the duty of the legionnaire to play his part as the citizen. But his politics should be apart from the Legion. Our program is a different one from political control. Our work is in the civic upbuilding and bettering of our nation." To the contrary, the tensions surrounding the Legion's upcoming parade in Paris offered a reminder of just how politically fraught the Legion's cultural demonstrations actually were.[34]

The Legion's curious blend of uncompromising, righteous chauvinism and ambiguous political intent became a beacon for conflict in France in 1927. In the weeks before the parade, French troops dispersed a rowdy crowd before the American consulate in Cherbourg, the seaside town where thousands of Legionnaires were due to disembark. In Marseilles, heeding calls to boycott, dockworkers refused to unload the American freighter *Liberty Bell*. In Paris, rumors circulated about communist plots to blow up buildings occupied by the Legionnaires, and on the Riviera someone did explode a bomb in a night-club popular with Americans. Eleven days before the convention, an anarchist in Lyon lobbied for his peers to show up at the parade and infiltrate the Legion's ranks. He imagined a scene in which police would be forced to intervene and, in the confusion, Americans would receive blows aimed at the protesters. With nine days to go, the anarchist *Le Libertaire* announced that "no consideration of international political order must suppress the popular protest." Huge headlines to the left of the paper's masthead suggested that all along the Legion's parade route *"Tomatoes will be* de rigueur. *But, WATCH OUT!"* its editors added sardonically, *"Don't mix them up with grenades!"*[35]

Authorities, not waiting around for events to unfold, reacted forcefully. While Chiappe campaigned successfully for more resources and men, conservative journalists and politicians delivered tirades on the foreign "peril" and the invasion of "undesirables"—immigrants and activists accused of fomenting revolution in a besieged capital. Minister of the Interior Albert Sarraut instructed Chiappe to "make all dispositions" to see that the convention would not be disturbed, and Chiappe complied zealously, beginning his campaign of *épuration*, scouring working-class neighborhoods and popular nightlife districts in an effort to impose greater moral and political discipline on the city's unruly spaces.[36]

City officials' crusade for order found support from many war victims' and veterans' groups who vowed to receive the Legionnaires "like individuals particularly loved, like brothers-in-arms who, on the battlefield, fought for the same cause, for the same ideal." Support from France's handful of veterans' groups, even from its right-wing ones, was no foregone conclusion. Only a year before, in July 1926—in one of those exceptional moments when the police approved a procession through the city center—veterans had paraded to the George Washington monument in the place d'Iéna to protest the debt accords. But the Sacco-Vanzetti riots solidified the proclivity, especially among veterans who belonged to groups on the right like the Union Nationale des Combattants (UNC), to regard the Legionnaires as renewed allies, this time in a war against the left. Demanding that the government "take all the necessary sanctions" to ensure order and to expel "the undesirable foreign elements," the UNC publicly promised to receive its American confreres in a dignified manner. Still seething over the attack on the Tomb of the Unknown Soldier, members of the Committee of the Flame under the Arc de Triomphe similarly joined the growing coalition of those determined to defend the Legion's visit. Despite the "menaces of the extremists and *métèques* against our American brothers," the committee resolved, it would "assure to the American veterans perfect tranquility at the ceremony under the Arch."[37]

Parisians on the far right especially extended friendship to the enemies of their enemies. The paramilitary Jeunesses Patriotes promised that "disdaining the communist menaces, a cordial reception will be reserved for the members of the American Legion." "At a moment when centers of unrest light up across all of Europe," they fulminated, it was the duty of "all men of order to organize themselves in order to check the progress in France of the *mystique révolutionnaire.*" The group called on those who desired to preserve "their liberty and their property" to stand by "ready to translate their resolution into actions." The previous July—when veterans marched to Washington's statue—groups like the Jeunesses Patriotes had targeted Americans in a string of mob attacks protesting the record plunge of the franc. In one harrowing incident, rightists descended on six loaded "Paris by Night" tour buses, swinging their canes through windows, shouting "Vive la France!" But the subsequent Sacco-Vanzetti affair unsettled the city's political balance, and those anti-American sentiments that had been simmering on France's far right would be put on the back burner. As the convention approached, their editorialists cooked up an impressive feast of flattery for the latest wave of American visitors.[38]

If correspondence sent to the central police station indicated at all the polarized state of public opinion in Paris at the end of that summer, it did not bode well for the scheduled parade. Hate mail—scribbled hastily to Chiappe—suggested that popular indignation over police actions during the recent unrest would play into opposition to the Legion's appearance. One citizen chastised the prefect for his "*banditisme*" during the Sacco-Vanzetti demonstrations, behavior, he wrote, that dishonored the nation's democratic principles. "*Au revoir* old Chiappe," he concluded, "we will perhaps see each other again the 19th of September." Threats peppered the letters. "You have massacred the workers well," one Parisian penned on a tiny note card, "the blood of the workers costs dearly do not forget it." "An eye for an eye, tooth for tooth," read another missive signed by a "leader of the revolution." "The anarchist union casts you a mortal challenge. *A bientôt*, I hope," he sneered, "*Prenez garde!*" Chiappe's men were labeled *abominables*, the Americans bandits, and all of their bourgeois allies she-asses. "You are all with a bunch of whores," wrote a professed anarchist; "down with the fat-cats." Chiappe himself was called a lying dog, a stupid bastard, a miserable assassin of a brute well fed from the sweat of the worker. "It will be extremely bloody for your little belly and your carcass, napoleon," raged one anonymous correspondent.[39]

Chiappe received letters of support as well, notes equally disturbing in their implications. Writers vituperated against the *"manifestations imbéciles,"* some calling for the expulsion of all foreigners, others clamoring for the destruction of *L'Humanité*, "a true center of pestilence," an "impassioned sheet that perverts [workers'] conscience and pours class hatred into their heart." Communists were branded traitors to the *patrie*, the "bloody claws" of Soviet operatives, and instigators of mobs "guided by instinct." "The whole of Europe and our sister America," wrote one concerned citizen, "will have to join hand in hand and on a single front combat . . . this vermin." "Force must be opposed with force!" cried another, offering his own personal services to the prefect. Recruit, he said, among the "good French," some "100,000 men in Paris for the *Défense de la capitale* in case of danger ready to sacrifice all" in order to oust "these looting hordes and criminals." It would be a civilian corps, this volunteer envisioned, but with armbands and revolvers and grenades. *"Monsieur,"* another timid "young patriot" wrote, "I desire simply that you know that at no matter what hour of the day or of the night, you could have me at your disposal." He added that the prefect could easily muster "a voluntary militia composed of a large number of young Frenchmen who like me love their country and place the interest of the State above all." Calls for vigilantism resounded through the letters. Against undesirable masses, ventured one person concerned about future revolutionary crowds, "you would need healthy elements of the population," of the kind the English government used in Ireland against the Fenians, he suggested. Oblivious to the ironies of ultranationalists banding together with foreign nationalists, he championed the role of French veterans' organizations in the upcoming Legion festivities, assuring the prefect, "you will find among us your collaborators—you will need us in order to protect your friends of the American Legion believe me!"[40] Letters to Chiappe, brimming with extremism, may not have represented average Parisians' sentiments, but they did point to just how inflamed passions had become in the city and how far political convictions stretched to the left and the right. Intensifying and reshaping preexisting local political animosities, the veterans' arrival attracted some while repelling others with equal force.

Sensing these mounting popular grievances, many Americans, too, questioned the wisdom of holding the convention in the French capital. Some of those who lived in the city tried to distance themselves from the parade's potential fallout. "Paris Americans had been looking forward with dread to the coming of the Legion[n]aires for months," remembered the *Paris Herald*'s night editor Al Laney. Many left the city. Others avoided visiting at all. One resident who stayed, Howard O'Brien, wrote to an associate in the United States that he was "sorry the affair was ever planned" and would "breathe more easily when the 19th has come and gone." Discerning "an ugly undercurrent of feeling," he could "hardly see how trouble can be avoided." With only days to the parade, tensions were palpable. The doctor-poet William Carlos Williams happened to arrive in Paris just before the convention. "We [Americans] were in a fair way to being hated," he admitted "I could feel it everywhere." Another American, a resident businessman and Legion member himself, recalled that on the 19th he awoke at dawn, his heart "filled with a dread and uncertainty, shared by his countrymen here, that he had not known since the days of the war itself."[41]

The surfaces of the city, awash in overtones of conquest, did not reassure such skeptics. The streets, the *New York Times* reported, gleamed with "unmistakable signs that the French capital is going to be 'taken over' by the thousands of former doughboys." Extra electric lights and welcome signs illuminated the pro-American district near the Opera. Southern California Automobile Club placards, reading "City Limits of Los Angeles," hung along the boulevards—a jest, one Legionnaire figured, "enjoyed perhaps by everybody but the French." Department stores hoisted above their doors giant spread eagles and other regalia in deferent surrender to the coming troops. The sacrosanct Notre Dame even suffered the indignity of red, white, and blue bunting. A brave few pasted pictures of Sacco and Vanzetti in their windows. Most glaringly, though, American flags saturated the streets. That preeminent emblem of the American Legion credo draped central avenues and waved from lampposts, gracing the façades of banks and government buildings, even topping the Eiffel Tower.[42]

The planned parade route through the Arc de Triomphe itself evoked invasion and occupation. Only twice had processions passed under the arch before—first the Prussians in 1871 and then the victorious Allies in 1919. After the Legionnaires, the next to file through would be the Nazis in 1940. A military procession through the arch made a bold, unmistakable claim to the city even in what was technically peacetime. The statement was not lost on many observers who saw in it the blurred boundaries between the Legion's professed innocuous pilgrimage of remembrance and its more troubling political innuendo. Even the veterans themselves sometimes became confused over their own distinctions between military and civilian excursions abroad. One Iowa Legionnaire, for example, touted the trip as the "greatest peacetime overseas movement since the time of the crusades." Many worried that the Legion's arrival would be about as peaceful as the crusades had been. Thus, the *Paris Herald* announced in bold type with approval what some would have read with a chilling sense of foreboding: "Paris Capitulates Joyfully to the Invading Hosts of Yankees," it claimed, "Paris Will Echo Once Again to Martial Tread of American Fighting Men as Thirty Thousand Vets Swing Impressively down Champs-Elysées Today."[43]

On sidewalks, the morning of the parade, Vaillant-Couturier's headlines for *L'Humanité* blared forth: "Paris will respond tonight by a demonstration of revolutionary force." Americans had to know, he argued, "that the Legion will only march in Paris thanks to a true state of siege, under the protection of truncheons, rifles, and automatic machine guns!" Along the line of the march, despite bursts of rain, onlookers arrived early. "Held back by more than ten thousand French soldiers standing at gun salute," one Legionnaire described, "by noontime the streets were literally alive with humanity." For the readers of *The Nation*, Ida Treat—Vaillant-Couturier's American wife—surveyed the forces of order amassed to protect the marchers. "All down the Champs Élysées," she took stock of the "double line of soldiers. *Agents de ville*, holster on hip. Plain clothes men, moustached and derby-hatted, circulate uneasily through the crowd." Red Cross staffers and Boy Scouts with stretchers camped out at thirty first-aid stations along the parade route, as mounted Republican Guards with glinting brass helmets trotted past the throngs, followed by French infantry divisions with bayonets fixed. By the start of the parade, hundreds of thousands had amassed on the sidelines, ten people deep in places, to see what would happen when the Legionnaires came stomping through the Arc de Triomphe and down the Champs-Elysées.[44]

The buildup to the Legion's controversial march raised difficult questions about the group's place along the period's spectrum of far-right politics. It also rekindled concerns about who would be afforded the freedom to demonstrate in the French capital and whose protests would be muted, or even suppressed with force. Choosing, quite literally, to parade their views before the world, the Legionnaires sought to show that "the city of Paris will be ours." Their assertions would be challenged by some of their hosts, as well as by other Americans who took issue with Legionnaires' claim to be the sole

As the parade begins, militant Legionnaires advance through the Arc de Triomphe. Stock footage courtesy of the WPA Film Library.

arbiters of patriotic loyalty, but one momentous fact loomed: that September day the Legion had been accorded privileged access to the city, a right that only weeks before had been violently denied even to France's own citizens. The day of the parade was a day that clarified the international terrain on which nationalist movements operated, a day when squabbles between the political left and right—in all their obstreperousness—were mapped out across the city's streets. But it was also a day when pinpointing the nature of right-wing American political culture was about to get even more confusing, as anticipations about the Legionnaires' arrival gave way to the sight of actual veterans moving through the city in ways that flew in the face of expectations. "It was a gray day, sprinkled with little gusts of rain," one correspondent cabled to the *Chicago Daily News*. As the first Americans appeared through the hollow center of the Arc de Triomphe, he reported, "it seemed that the war itself had returned to Paris—the war in all its somber glory. Closely packed, rank on rank, the Americans came—. . ."[45]

"Showmanship is fundamental to the fascist strategy," observed the cinema virtuoso Orson Welles after years of thinking about the aesthetics of mass politics, "and the chief fascist argument is the parade."[46] Yet the performance put on by Legionnaires that gray September day in Paris was not what most had in mind. It began with an air of solemn discipline, as Legionnaires trod past the Tomb of the Unknown Soldier. The participants' resolution at first suggested that this would be a formidable demonstration of right-wing street politics, reminiscent of the marches and rallies that had become familiar in recent years. But as Legionnaires cleared the arch and descended the Champs-Elysées, the parade's semblance of seriousness gave way to the festive and the bizarre. Grouped according to their states of residence, marchers in whimsical accessories sallied forth, swaying to the peppy tunes belted out by thirty-odd bands interspersed among their ranks. Onlookers—who had heard so much about the Legion's convictions and far-reaching power—stood flabbergasted. Accompanied by a woman impersonating the Statue of Liberty and sixteen Native Americans in their traditional war regalia, the Legionnaires appeared in cowboy outfits, New York cop uniforms, Zouave costumes, and Revolutionary War apparel. They donned sombreros, Hawaiian leis, steel helmets, ten-gallon hats, and billowing blue tunics. The Legionnaires waved sloppily to the crowd and burst spontaneously into song. The Legionnaires did not look fascist at all.[47]

Observers, like one writer for *L'Œuvre*, characterized the parade as "a veritable innovation for the Parisian population." The French, a *New York Times* correspondent reported, "did not expect to see great brass bands dressed in white and gold. . . . Neither did they expect to see women with rifles on their shoulders, and silk stockings on their shins. They did not expect to see a duck led by a string down the Champs Elysées." One American hazarded that Parisians who saw the visiting veterans "must have felt that America, though perhaps more than ever incalculable, was no longer quite so perilous; what was anticipated as something like a reconnaissance in force, a spying out of the land presently to be conquered, turned out to be much more akin to the Sunday-school picnic." The French magazine *L'Illustration* called it a strange cortege, with perplexing brass instruments and banners and badges. "Did it surprise us at first?" *L'Œuvre*'s reporter asked rhetorically, "Obviously!"[48]

The Legion parade contrasted sharply with the uniformity and restraint of traditional European military processions. Drawing comparisons with the Victory celebration on July 14, 1919, the last great parade to pass through Paris—an occasion marked by joy, but also by dignity and gravity—viewers reportedly wondered out loud if the Legion parade deliberately parodied European militarism. "The marchers did not indeed answer closely to the French conception of war heroes or pious pilgrims," noted the *English Review*, and members of their brass bands "looked as if they had just marched off the musical comedy stage." Recalling that for the French the war had not been a grand parade or a circus in motion, some critics found the demonstration offensive, given French suffering during the recent conflict. They questioned, as one reporter relayed, the "holiday gaiety" of the former doughboys, since the war was "invested with a sad sacredness in the French mind." "It's not a march," someone in the crowd remarked incredulously when the event began, "it's Carnival."[49]

Bystanders scrutinized the Americans intensely. Spectators crowded against the soldiers guarding the line of the parade, peered out of upper-story windows, and scaled lampposts and store awnings. Staunch opponents of the Legion largely stayed away, leaving others to fill the sidelines: middle-class shopkeepers, fathers with children on their shoulders, government clerks and single working women free for the day, American tourists and day-trippers from the nearby countryside. Beyond widespread curiosity, reactions along the parade route proved mixed. One Legionnaire recalled that the cheering was "occasional and mild, usually started by other Americans on the scene." But another veteran insisted on the friendliness of the crowd. Some reportedly gazed at the parade "ironically." Communists, of course, mocked "la 'parade' stupide," sneering at its ranks of "pseudo-héros" and labeling "Average Joe of Carolina" and "maniacs from Texas" and "anthropoids from Illinois" as the world's most eccentric barbarians. Others were far more forgiving of the Legionnaires' originality. The moderate paper Le Matin called the parade "unique, majestic, and funny," a window that opened onto a horizon at which Parisians had not guessed the immensity. Le Figaro praised its joie de vivre and youthfulness, which aroused "joyous emotion" along the route.[50]

Indeed, many onlookers appeared to have been genuinely entertained by the procession. A relieved American diplomat relayed to Washington that the event "passed off successfully and with considerable cheering." Onlookers shouted "Vive la Légion" and "Hurrah Amérique" and called out the names of the states as their divisions came into view. Whatever ill will some might have had, concluded a French professor from Cornell University, "was dispelled by this unique spectacle." For those who opted not to read too much into the public performance, the parade served as an afternoon diversion that reinforced impressions of the United States as a land dominated by grown-up children and idiosyncratic millionaires—a race, as one Frenchmen put it, of "joyeux garçons, jovial and jokey in their way, simple, childish, gay." Those who cheered, most likely, were those who also thronged cinemas to see American films, the same young people who followed American dances and music, the same curiosity seekers who marveled at the strange American bohemians who congregated in Left Bank cafés. These casually approving bystanders must have experienced the parade as part of the era's string of public demonstrations of Franco-American amity, from the feting of President Woodrow Wilson and the celebrated return of Ambassador Herrick just after the war to the rapturous reception given to Charles Lindbergh just that spring.[51]

With surprisingly few disturbances along the route, police arrested only a handful of people for blocking traffic, using seditious speech, or tearing down American flags from apartment windows and taxicabs. One individual on the boulevard Victor-Hugo, spotting an American flag waving from the façade of a furniture boutique, took a revolver out of his pocket and blew a hole through the window. He fled, but was apprehended. Most conflicts, though, seem to have been unexpectedly elided by incidents of miscomprehension between the marchers and their audience. Watching from the place de la Concorde, for example, the American playwright Elmer Rice noticed that when the Massachusetts delegation appeared, the crowds began, "with savage delight," to shout *"Où est la chaise électrique?"* But the marchers, who mistook the yelling "as some special tribute, beamed and waved in grateful acknowledgement." A similar misunderstanding occurred near the steps of the Madeleine where Howard O'Brien witnessed what he identified as a band of communists, encircled by alert policemen. When the veterans swung into view, he recounted, "the Reds began to whistle." The Legionnaires, unaware that whistling in France signaled disapproval, "thought they were being applauded, and whistled back! The French suddenly burst into laughter— and the last fear of 'trouble' was dissipated." The parade's gaiety, and the Legionnaires' own blissful ignorance, effectively defused much of the apprehension that had preceded it.[52]

With little overt animosity from the sidelines, the parade's apparent triviality allowed Legionnaires a chance to pass off their definition of what it meant to be an American in the postwar world as politically innocent, a harmless burlesque. Showmanship, the parade suggested, was indeed fundamental to the argument put forth by the Legionnaires, but it appeared to be more of a throwback to the P. T. Barnum variety than a premonition of the Nazi-rally kind. Some, however, suspected with good reason that the Legion's superficial lightheartedness and the group's potential as a dangerous political force were really two sides of the same coin. Legionnaires paraded in Paris in the simple sense of the term, but also in its second sense—they paraded as disinterested visitors, when their intentions were actually more complicated.

Indeed, as Orson Welles intimated, a parade was a political statement in this era, no matter how colorful the uniforms. Parades served as shows of strength, and launching one, or prohibiting one from taking place, became a central drama in early-twentieth-century popular politics. Back in the United States during World War I, patriotic marches helped to compel civic compliance with the home front effort, and likewise they offered targets for antiwar radicals—it was a bloody attack on a Preparedness Day parade in 1916 for which Tom Mooney had been held accountable. Breaking up May Day parades and peace movement processions also became a staple practice of those on the right, who billed their own marches by contrast as legitimate expressions of the public will. Parading was serious business and functioned as a tool of intimidation that opponents well understood. The brutal conflict in Centralia, Washington, in 1919, which left several Legionnaires dead and led to the lynching of IWW leader Wesley Everest, began with the politics of parading—Legionnaires, in collusion with local businessmen and other patriots, had changed the route of their Armistice Day procession so that it would pass directly in front of the local IWW hall. Union men awaited their arrival, and when a flank of Legionnaires broke off from the cortege to storm the hall, they responded with gunfire. Such marches departed from the intentions of most nineteenth-century processions, which had served as celebrations of public consensus and American pluralism, solidifying democratic traditions in an era of widening political participation.[53] Parades in the age of world wars had different messages; buried beneath their revelry lay an ever-present threat of violence in the quest for political and territorial control.

A newsreel cameraman captures the Legionnaires' fanfare from the perspective of the marchers themselves. Here, veterans from North Carolina stride down the boulevards in silver helmets, scarlet coats, Sam Browne belts, and jaunty, white breeches. Stock footage courtesy of the WPA Film Library.

In Paris, the Legionnaires offered a corporatist vision of the United States, holding up an image of their national community as defined primarily by its subdivision into states and territories. The most pronounced aspects of the parade's iconography brought to mind regional cultures and natural resources: marchers from Maine in bright green blazers sported pine trees on their caps; men from Alabama carried fluffy bunches of cotton; and Kansans wore sunflowers. Such tokens of regional pride conveyed a sense of healthy, good-natured camaraderie, a spirit of cheerful rivalry reinforced by the songs crooned by marching units, from Montana's Powder River Yell to the Texas roundelay. Nominal differences between states, the parade's symbolism suggested, furnished the only form of suballegiance tolerated under the Legion's uncompromising conception of national loyalty. The parade referenced little of the vibrant urban cosmopolitanism fast becoming a defining feature of American culture. It offered little clue to the greater role of women in public and political life. In the Legionnaires' parade, women, Native Americans, and African Americans appeared in marginalized or mascot roles. In the Legion's orderly, hierarchical America, a form of paternalistic patriotism subsumed divisions of class and culture. Taking their parade to foreign soil emboldened the group to venture even more forceful claims about the veracity of this representation of the United States.[54] "America will see its own image reflected back three thousand miles," the Legion's magazine promised. Noting that the parade's ranks consisted of "just honest-to-God samples from every corner of the U.S.A.," the *New York Times* similarly passed it off as a display "purely American in every respect," showing "the Paris crowds a reflection of the American character that held them spellbound."[55] Reporters pitched the parade as a passive reflection, but it offered, more precisely, an active imagining of America and its people.

With all its whistles and bells, the Legion's march also dramatized that quality of festive cartoonishness that often gilded right-wing populist actions in the early twentieth century, from the charivari-style public humiliations of wartime nonconformists in New England to the spectacle lynchings in the New South. Like the blustering and buffoonery of Mussolini and his Black-shirts, the Legionnaires' rowdiness did not signal a momentary inversion of the social order, as carnivalesque demonstrations on the left often did. Rather, it hinted at a permanent disruption, a move toward a new order dictated solely by the marchers. Offering a colorful satire on their own bid for power, the Legionnaires' demonstration recalled just how powerful their organization had become. Only individuals firm in their beliefs and convinced of their control over the situation could cut loose this way during such an important event.

At the same time, the march's fanfare was meant to demonstrate just how much clout Legionnaires had, compared to their enemies. The veterans relished the outcry they drew from leftists—and relished even more that their plans had not been disrupted by them. Looking back on the extraordinary pilgrimage, one Legionnaire bragged that all the "perturbation" and "visible annoyance" leading up to the convention went "little heeded anyway," for when all was said and done, he noted, "we had escaped the rioters and had the extreme pleasure of doing Paris as an American likes to do it—top and bottom." At the convention's opening session on the morning of the parade, the department commander of the France division similarly gloated that among the "real patriotic French people" who mattered, they had been welcomed. "A hammer on an old empty boiler makes a lot of noise," he said, alluding to detractors, "but no soldier will be misled by the rumpus."[56] Dissension only fueled the Legionnaires' merriment. At the proceedings that morning, a lone voice had cried out in protest: "*Vivent Sacco et Vanzetti!*" It was the Comité Sacco-Vanzetti founder Louis Lecoin, who had stolen a Legion pass, shaved his moustache, and donned a pair of American eyeglasses to slip into the hall unnoticed. Audience members cheered as the anarchist leader was forcibly removed—and then promptly returned to the business at hand, renewing their motions for more vigorous deportations, the adoption of a universal draft bill, and the suspension of all immigration to the United States.[57] Regional American newspapers picked up news of the incident over the wires, reporting that "instead of causing a riffle in the enthusiasm of the meeting, [it] rather increased it."[58]

Legionnaires, like other politicized individuals, treaded a fine line between exaggerating at times the influence of their enemies and, at other moments, minimizing their importance. On the eve of May Day celebrations or the occasions of strikes, Legion leaders used fearmongering to convince Americans that stronger measures were needed to combat the rising radical threat. But shows of strength on the right presented occasions for demonstrating, quite to the contrary, how easily veterans and other patriots could crush the opposition. Of course, not all Legionnaires put on bow ties or silly hats as part of a sinister plot to disguise their intentions, but in the end such parade antics proved to be most effective popular political tactics. Disarming potential critics with unexpected zaniness, mistaking criticisms for support, and burying exclusionary political convictions under a veneer of burlesque, the American veterans suggested in defiance of their own violent history that they did not need guns and force to vanquish their foes; they had only to win them with banners and song.

A postcard commemorates New Jersey Legionnaires in motley suits and uniforms marching through the place de l'Opéra past crowds held back by French soldiers. The Café de la Paix appears on the left. New Jersey State Archives, Department of State.

Legionnaires maintained a high profile in the city during the entire convention week, indulging in some of the same rowdyism that had made their reunions back in the United States notorious. During the many hours not filled by official functions, Legionnaires flooded the hotels and shops in the Opera district and cut a conspicuous figure on the boulevards. "For the moment this city seems to belong to America," one American student studying at the Sorbonne marveled. Beyond the reach of the Volstead Act, veterans displayed a propensity for collecting cocktail shakers, pocket flasks, and other alcohol-related souvenirs, a practice many Parisians mocked and, considering Prohibition's toll on France's wine exports, also resented. More than a few must also have been irritated by the piercing honks of automobile horns Legionnaires snatched up in the hundreds and used throughout their stay. "When are they going home?" one editorialist demanded impatiently. The revelries tested the patience of many residents. Veterans milled around street corners, drank excessively at sidewalk cafés, and ogled passing women. They packed to capacity the nightclubs of Montmartre and the city's sex shows. "Loud, noisy, rampageous and occasionally violent from alcohol," the Legionnaires could be found, the budding American journalist William Shirer recorded, "occasionally breaking up the furniture in the night spots and in the hotel lobbies." Others mixed it up with taxi drivers, altercations the Americans blamed on chauffeurs' "ill-will."[59]

Legionnaires regarded this as harmless merrymaking, totally compatible with their image of themselves as exemplars of Americanism. Forging their brand of modern right-wing activism, the veterans also pioneered in Paris a model of American interaction abroad. They fancied themselves as goodwill ambassadors for the United States, their mission to remind the French of their part in winning the war. During commemorations at the Tomb of the Unknown Soldier and area cemeteries, they posed as semiofficial dignitaries, despite their insistence that their hosts not bring up the debt or other pressing international issues and despite their repeated habit of drowning out French officials' speeches with singing and carousing. They touted their importance in shoring up Franco-American amity, trudging out the old truisms about Lafayette and enduring friendship between the two republics as well as new efforts to liken themselves to Lindbergh. Ohio Legionnaires went so far as to claim in a subsequent recruiting campaign that "more has been accomplished toward the realization of world peace through the Paris convention of the Legion than any diplomatic conference since the signing of the Armistice." American lawyers, businessmen, and other conservative professionals residing in Paris staunchly supported the visitors, adopting the veterans' characterization of themselves as emissaries and praising the men, as the director of the American Hospital did, for their "diplomatic mission."[60]

Many excused the veterans' rough revelry in Paris as signs of Americans' good-natured temperaments, reinforcing Legionnaires' claims that their politics were mainstream and accepted—not controversial, just good clean American fun. Matching the veterans' overblown tone of self-congratulation, the *Paris Herald*'s editor remembered that the conventioneers "were out to have fun, roaring their exuberant Americanism in the fun center of the world." Supporters echoed veterans' claims that the parade and convention had taught the French "what real Americans are." Legionnaires set out to be the "showmen of Paris," one correspondent wrote. They delighted in orchestrating impromptu concerts and mock military drills that blocked traffic and attracted large crowds. They had something to show Parisians. Such performances on the Paris streets acted out many Americans' growing belief that Europe was stagnant and inefficient, a region weighed down by cumbersome traditions, spent by the war, and burdened by out-of-control radicalism. What a contrast the veterans offered—what vibrancy, what pep! "The French got a picture of American hustle," one reporter argued, intimating that Europeans might well draw lessons not only from Americans' assembly-line production methods but also from their energizing, youthful demeanor.

Stoking patriotic pride and a sense of Americans' growing cultural energies, the Legionnaires modeled a new, assertive worldview, a form of posturing abroad that helped to reconcile the official aloofness of the United States from international organizations such as the League of Nations and the World Court with simultaneous desires to champion Americans' ascendance in the world. An American student watching the parade had detected this growing confidence in the faces of those who filed past. "Each one," he wrote to his hometown paper, looked as though "he had been in the colonies and was returning to be feted as a Caesar or a Napoleon."[61]

If veterans and their supporters imagined the Legion as a leading force for international cooperation, others viewed it as damaging to Americans' standing in the world. American critics objected especially to the notion that the marchers typified the modern American abroad. "The ex-doughboy faces in a foreign setting looked almost depraved," the writer Elliot Paul argued with an expatriate's characteristic disdain. During the parade, he charged, "the costumes were ill-chosen; the average veteran wasn't drunk enough to be clownish or sober enough to be dignified." Some Americans were particularly sensitive to Legionnaires strutting about as if they owned the streets of Paris. They cringed at how veterans' intemperance and rambunctiousness were often taken as representative of all Americans' manners. William Shirer regretted scenes of Legionnaires cutting up, commandeering café terraces and Montmartre nightclubs, "bellowing their barbershop tunes on ancient street corners, slapping incredulous French men—and women—on the back." Ida Treat, too, scorned the conduct of the typical Legionnaire, who, "obviously arrogant" and "obviously drunk," vented the opinion "that all Paris is a bar and a brothel—and that the town is ours!" Treat loathed the common perception of the Legionnaires as "unofficial 'ambassadors.'" "But what America," she asked exasperatedly, "do they represent?"[62]

The Legionnaires indeed promoted a particular type of overseas engagement, one based on heightened self-confidence but also, simultaneously, a reluctance to move beyond familiar habits. The impressive resources of the American community in Paris were therefore mobilized to ensure that veterans would be adequately protected from cultural disorientation. English-speaking officials waited at their disposal, companies like American Express took care of travel details, and *Herald* editors printed a special "American Legion News" section with "Useful Hints" about getting around the capital in plain American speech. The group's temporary headquarters in a building on the Cours-la-Reine next to the Seine best embodied the visitors' social insularity, with its loitering crowds of Legionnaires and their wives, hesitant to leave the artificially familiar surroundings. Here veterans found various travel facilities, recreation rooms, and the immensely popular "Salvation Army Hut," where volunteers served up doughnuts and coffee donated by Maxwell House. Six days before the parade even took place, *Herald* headlines declared: "Doughnut Demand Proves Too Great." During the following week, the Knights of Columbus distributed more than a million free cigarettes, 30,000 soft drinks, and some 32,000 bars of soap—three of the most coveted comfort items from home.[63]

The Legion's Cours-la-Reine headquarters, especially the doughnut hut, infuriated critics such as Elmer Rice, who hated the thought that Legionnaires' comportment could be taken as evidence of all Americans' lack of taste. "Everywhere," he regretted, "one saw blowzy men in fatigue caps, drunk, boisterous, quarrelsome, trying to bargain with shopkeepers, drinking champagne at little bistros at eleven in the morning, lining up in the stifling heat and the stench of frying fat to buy doughnuts in the barracks which the Salvation Army had erected in the citadel of French cookery." Such bad behavior might be endured with resignation in American cities, he admitted, but on foreign soil, "the American who esteems his country and values its good name squirms at the antics of these ill-bred middle-aged adolescents." The Legionnaires' absence of decorum, he intimated, appeared especially obnoxious abroad, where it took place against a backdrop of suffering and instability—where debt and the deflated value of the franc caused a serious disparity of wealth between French citizens and their transatlantic guests, where amputees and black-clothed widows remained a common sight on the streets and a ready reminder that the war was more than a romanticized memory in France. What might have been tolerated as puerile rabble-rousing in Kansas or Kentucky, that is, became bellicose abroad. Rice thought this best illustrated by the ruckus that had first alerted him to the veterans' arrival. On a balcony across from his hotel room, the playwright saw one merrymaker wearing only his underwear, swigging from a bottle, and propositioning women in the street below. To passing men, he shouted, "What you make in francs I make in dollars." As few other moments did, this one made Rice wish he was not American himself.[64]

The ways in which Legionnaires construed their international participation and flaunted their views overseas was complex, even paradoxical. Legionnaires showed themselves to be immensely interested in world events, and yet even more resolutely "American" abroad. The extraterritorialization of justice accorded the veterans during their convention signified this most forcefully. French policemen had been instructed to overlook minor offenses, but for excessive situations, special tribunals headed by American judges arbitrated cases involving Legionnaires. One of the makeshift court's hearings

The cover of *Life*'s special Legion number features two American veterans who, judging from the pile of saucers on the table in front of them, have had quite a bit to drink. The "English Spoken" sign in the distance recalls the capital's new accessibility and intimates therefore that the book of French lessons tucked under one of their arms serves only to help the men hit on coquettish *Parisiennes*. One of the city's ubiquitous policemen looks on from the street. Courtesy of Harvard College Library, Widener Library, P267.2.

involved an Arkansas man who had hurled two tables through the plate-glass façade of a Montmartre establishment and assaulted a couple of its waiters. Before he had been informed that an American judge would hear his case, the former soldier bellowed, "I ain't goin' to tell my story to a lot of Frogs." Granting American visitors immunity from French laws may have averted awkward diplomatic incidents, but it also intensified Legionnaires' expectation of special treatment as American men no matter where they were in the world.[65]

The Legionnaires resolved to be subject to no one but themselves even as they became more assertive participants in foreign affairs. Years later, they would still be held up by critics as one negative but increasingly common model of American behavior abroad. "Too many Americans in foreign lands, from the American Legionnaires up and down," opined one *Nation* article in 1931, "have not troubled to acquaint themselves with the most dearly held customs of the countries they visited, have lugged out their American provincialisms, have been loud-mouthed, quarrelsome, vulgar, insistent on their 'rights' as citizens of the greatest little old country on God's green earth." Legionnaires' braggadocio likewise played into French commentators' deepening prejudices against American culture, fueling what would be enduring stereotypes about American people. Tarring the veterans with the kind of language that would become a staple in coming years, detractors such as Georges de la Fouchardière proclaimed them "grandiose Barbarians, brain-washed with patriotic pride and capable of the coldest atrocities in order to prove that their country is independent of the unanimous sentiment of humanity."[66]

Some Parisians sniffed at the veterans and their convention, but others rejoiced at the opportunity to promote an international alliance of right-wing groups. If the parade was a performance intended to bolster Legion-naires' standing as the leaders of a new American right, it also promised to assist their political allies in France who wanted to hold onto Paris, not only politically but also spatially and symbolically. Faced with a common crisis and common enemies, interwar nationalists often collaborated with each other across national boundaries, appreciating each others' missions, learning from each others' techniques, even benefiting from foreign financial support. Thus, French leaders who arrayed themselves against the left eagerly associ-ated with the Legion ceremonies, among them men such as Marshal Pétain, the future head of Vichy France; Louis Marin, a seminal figure of the French far right; and Police Prefect Jean Chiappe. As guest of honor, the conservative President Gaston Doumergue greeted the American conventioneers at their opening ceremonies, surrounded on the platform by most of his cabinet. Right-wing veterans' organizations crowded the parade's sidelines, and France's great military commanders appeared at Legion banquets. Sympa-thetic local newspapers for their part evoked scenes of joyous reunion between the French and their former allies on the boulevards.[67]

Like the Americans, their hosts hoped that celebrating the bonds of the late war and enjoining in another shared battle would strengthen the cause of order against what they imagined as the mounting forces of disorder. One French general applauded the Legion for coming "to renew a sacred union," by which he meant a different one from the mythologized *union sacrée* in which French people of all political persuasions had temporarily and tenuously joined forces during the Great War. The sacred *national* union of 1914—as the Legion's visit made clear—had given way to a new *nationalist* union, one that would grow in strength and international importance in coming years. Echoing the rhetoric that framed the Sacco-Vanzetti affair, another right-wing Frenchman declared that the "complete success" of the parade "proves that in spite of the noise that they make, the revolutionaries, all the same, are as yet the masters neither of the street nor of the spirit of Paris."[68]

For Legionnaires, this support from Parisians served as vindication of their own ideas and goals. When *Le Matin* declared that "the future" of youth and order had filed past at the parade, the *American Legion Monthly* proudly translated this reading of their display, asserting that such a notion would only grow stronger "now that the Legion is back home once more." "The parade will go on," it declared dramatically; "the Legion will march on from Paris with stronger steps through every city and town in its homeland." For the Legion, the French capital provided a springboard from which it could launch itself into even greater glory. Conquering the streets of Paris became a central battle won in the Legion's war to vanquish its enemies both at home and abroad. One veteran bragged after the visit that "all the r-r-red, red talk of the Reds came to nothing. It left them the color of a pale washed out pink." France, like the United States, "was strengthened against a danger," he thought, thanks to the accomplishment of the Americans' procession.[69] Casting their presence in the city as a bulwark against left-wing subversion, expiating the offenses perpetrated by Sacco-Vanzetti rioters, Legionnaires offered a beacon of hope for the triumph of nationalist politics in general.

Leftists well understood the Legionnaires' stay in Paris as an occasion for such alliance building on the right. Some of the most withering critiques of the parade revolved around this conception of it as a demonstration of the right's stake in the city center, a "mobilization day—for the church, the army, the fascists, the police, Montmartre, and Montparnasse," as Ida Treat saw it. Detractors thought that the parade especially highlighted the political rift between the capital's commercial, cosmopolitan quarters and its poorer outlying districts, marked by leftist leanings. "Aristocratic Paris puts on its party clothes," a writer for *Le Libertaire* pictured this political topography; "chauvinistic Paris puts on its makeup." Joining the Legion in its spirit of hate and repression, the paper charged, was the official Paris of the police and the government, "the contemptible Paris of the coat of arms . . . of high finance and industry . . . and the servile *patriotards*." "But what will the other Paris say and do," the same column inquired, "so that the guests of the fascist Paris know that the Paris of '93, of '48, and of '71 does not fraternize with the assassins of Sacco and Vanzetti?" As a counterpoint to the right-wing central Paris so despised by leftist writers, papers like *Le Libertaire* romanticized an alternative city of *faubourgs* and slums. In response to their alienation from the cosmopolitan, modern quarters of the city center, leftists increasingly turned to the cultural resources of the plebeian neighborhoods with few extravagances on the outskirts. These down-and-out districts of the capital would furnish the setting for the Popular Front as it was celebrated in famous songs and films of the mid and late thirties.[70]

In an effort to recover some of that lost association with Parisian public space, leftists staged a counterdemonstration the afternoon of the parade. In the northern working-class suburb of Clichy, protesters gathered to rename a neighborhood square the place Sacco-Vanzetti. The Communist committee that arranged the event declared it a "national day of revolutionary demonstration" to counter the national day put on by the bourgeoisie. They linked their local fight against the American Legion to a bevy of broader concerns, using the square's rechristening to call for amnesty for political prisoners and the abolition of all wartime debts, to protest against the consequences of capitalist rationalization and show support for the Russian Revolution and Chinese peasants' fight against imperialism. Roger Baldwin, head of the ACLU, appeared at the protest, joining Vaillant-Couturier and other French Communist leaders up on a dais flanked by giant pictures of Sacco and Vanzetti in order to speak to the thousands who had marched through streets decorated not by American flags but by red banners and black crepe. Crowds sang the Internationale and chanted *"Amnistie! Amnistie!"* In front of the photographs of the two martyrs, passersby doffed their hats and clenched their fists. *L'Humanité* lovingly recreated the gathering on its front pages, but the brief mentions of it in mainstream French and American newspapers paled next to the columns devoted to Legion activities. The square's dedication was a marker of Americans' impact on the city that would soon be forgotten. Indeed, it would be expunged on the eve of the Second World War, when rightists carried out systematic *"débaptisations"* to erase traces of communism in the Paris suburbs.[71]

The Legion's festivities effectively drowned out this suburban counterdemonstration. Marginalized in the press, it had also been pushed back physically to the edges of the city.[72] Despite activists' efforts to reverse the trend, the center of Paris had increasingly become the terrain of the right. The suppression of Sacco-Vanzetti demonstrations and the triumph of the Legion parade—those two heated collisions with American political affairs—represented important chapters in the gradual unmaking of Paris as the capital of leftist revolutionary traditions that had been evident since the era of the Dreyfus affair. With the undoing of the Third Republic itself, the next revolution the city would host would be a National Socialist one, announced fittingly by the installation of German street signs, the hoisting of Nazi flags, and a parade of storm troopers through the Arc de Triomphe and down the Champs-Elysées.

Paris in the end provided a ready battleground well suited to different ideologically motivated maneuvers, but it also highlighted just how paradoxical such actions could be. Sacco-Vanzetti internationalists who rioted with patriotic resentments against the city's American traces and military-minded Legionnaires who paraded around like jokers and clowns brought reminders of the flexibility and ironies that were hallmarks of popular politics in the late twenties, at a time when communism and fascism were not always what they seemed, and when both extremes appeared at moments to share more with each other than with the liberal center they opposed. As illustrated by Sacco-Vanzetti rioters' contradictory behavior, left-wing internationalism would increasingly depend on the articulation of rustic cultural nationalisms, culminating with the Popular Front politics of the mid-thirties. Alternately, as suggested by the Legionnaires' ability to use foreign territory and media to bolster their own nativist agenda, nationalism as a political force needs to be understood as a transnational enterprise that benefited from alliances and inspirations that stretched across borders. In their pilgrimage to Paris, Legionnaires exemplified this key element of right-wing American political culture during the early twentieth century—at once reactionary and progressive, nationalist and internationally minded. Peeling back the surface claim that the Legion was not "political" reveals beneath it the ambitions of a group primed for collaborations with simpatico organizations abroad. The Legion was not exceptional or less American for its affinities with extremists overseas. The far-right potential of the group and its sense of sharing in world events were part and parcel of the popular brand of Americanism it promoted.

## CHAPTER SIX

The Expatriates Reconsidered

IN LIGHT OF ALL THIS messy wrangling in the capital, the police presence, the skirmishes in the streets, what of those famous expatriate artists and writers? For historians, these figures have often seemed largely distant from the most pressing issues of the early-twentieth-century United States—from the struggles of laborers and immigrants, the enduring quests for civil liberties and rights, and the rise of nationalism and a modern state. Retreating, supposedly, into the life of the mind, sinking themselves into modernist esoterica, expatriates have appeared, frankly, just as narrowly focused—just as parochial in their own way—as the Legionnaires. And yet, seeing them, like seeing the Legionnaires, in the context of the period's polarizing politics shows just how compelling expatriates could be as international actors.

Myths and assumptions about the expatriates run so deep that it is difficult to dig out the urgent political passions that preoccupied many of them alongside their more famous artistic endeavors, and it is surprising to rediscover the grittiness and resolve that many exhibited on their travels. To recall American expatriates in the twenties is to conjure up instead the characters of *The Sun Also Rises* (1926)—a reckless, raucous generation lost to postwar cynicism, burning up their youth and burnishing their literary reputations in the alcoholic haze of Paris's late-night cafés. Ever since the publication of Hemingway's novel, expatriates have been stereotyped as escapists who selfishly renounced civic responsibilities, watching unscathed from afar the social conflicts of the postwar United States, while at the same time maintaining distance from the vagaries of European affairs. "The expatriate need not concern himself, living as he does in a foreign country, with injustice and stupidity in public life, with the incapacity and corruption of officials, the struggles of class and party," read one contemporary survey in *Harper's*.[1] Critics pilloried expatriates for suspending themselves between a rejected native land and an adopted culture never fully their own. As outcasts, many derided, they suffered from self-aggrandizing delusions, the squandering of talent, even neurosis. In forums such as *Literary Digest* and the *Saturday Evening Post*, unsympathetic portraits of those who spent too much time overseas abounded in the 1920s: long-haired sons not fit to take up dad's business, parasitic painters, overindulged flappers. The expatriate became a social type, as derogatory a model of the American abroad as the Legionnaires seemed to their critics.[2]

Expatriates' own efforts to explain their activities abroad only reinforced these myths. Rather than defend their movements, they began instead to atone for their foreign interlude by the early thirties, publicizing their repatriation with as much gusto as they had trumpeted their departures only a few years before. Harold Stearns, who had led the charge to France shortly after the war, penned his apologies in a series of popular magazine articles and began to reassess the state of American culture in more positive terms.[3] F. Scott Fitzgerald, who came closer than most to the sensationalized clichés about expatriate living, mulled over his regrets in "Babylon Revisited" (1931), a rueful short story about a man whose Paris dalliances cost him everything that mattered. Yet it was Malcolm Cowley's chronicle *Exile's Return* (1934) that best crystallized the enduring conventional wisdom about the expatriate experience. Paris, his memoir suggested, had been in the end largely a diversion for young intellectuals—a tangent into surrealist shenanigans. Cowley sketched the eventual return of his peers, friends who drifted back in the wake of the stock market crash to Manhattan jobs, sank their roots into New England farms, as Cowley himself had, and embraced the Popular Front ethos of the 1930s. The subject of youth spent in Paris became unfashionable to dwell on in activist circles like Cowley's, and those who succeeded in putting Paris behind, he intimated, were those who immersed themselves in domestic causes. Finally in the face of the Great Depression, Cowley believed, the nation's up-and-coming cultural leaders had come back to take up the mantle of American letters, to embrace public engagement— to return to, or discover at last, political commitments.[4]

Buried beneath Cowley's narrative and all the other stereotypes, however, lies another history of expatriation, one that does not hinge on a simple path of escapist exile followed by repentant return. Paris, after all, was a beacon for rebels, a hub of international news. It was a crossroads for the century's most powerful cultural and political forces, not least for visiting Americans. The capital's exciting mix of art and politics helped to shape expatriates' ideals and allegiances; its neighborhoods and institutions formed important training grounds where writers and artists honed their craft and sharpened their opinions about foreign affairs. In the city's churches and museums, young painters and photographers reached epiphanies. In its cafés and studios, American essayists, poets, and adventurers rubbed shoulders with fugitives from other nations, drawing on a range of cosmopolitan aesthetics and world-views. Saturated with the most intense social movements and theories of the day, Paris was an entrepôt of causes and connections where expatriates began to develop new forms of American internationalism.

Even more importantly, for several expatriates Paris was not a temporary overseas destination but rather a jumping-off point for a set of ambitious and global itineraries. Not all expatriates disavowed their time abroad—not all exiles returned by the 1930s, that is, turning inward to American national life, tracking back to their Midwestern hometowns, or retreating to those New England farms. Instead, as they developed their convictions, an impressive number of them moved even farther out into the world, traveling to Berlin, Madrid, Moscow, Shanghai, and other political hotbeds. They immersed themselves in the task of documenting colonial battles for independence, underground resistance to brutal dictatorships, or the bloody outcomes of civil wars. The political leanings of these Americans varied, of course, by person and over time, but many moved from anarchistic quests for individualism during the twenties toward a growing dedication to social democracy in the thirties. Expatriates' movements to and from Paris reveal that such intellectual trajectories did not derive solely from domestic responses to the Depression and the New Deal. Rather, they depended on years of overseas experience, stretching back to the First World War and forward to the Second. Theirs was a politics that took shape most clearly abroad, through firsthand encounters with the era's epic yet deeply personal struggles against fascism and imperialism.

Situating expatriates amid the tumultuous events of the interwar years—charting the places they went, the political movements they encountered—reveals that many of them were not just literary and artistic icons but also leading proponents of a new kind of leftism, infused with a sense of international obligations and fit for an age of tragedy, intrigue, and devastating wars. Traversing the globe, these intellectuals charged themselves with the important task of illuminating foreign affairs for Americans back home. By the 1930s, many of them in fact stood among the nation's leading overseas reporters and analysts. Their bestselling novels and memoirs, their popular poetry, and their investigative journalism offered key sources of information for Americans seeking to learn about world events. Expatriates' convictions presented a foil for the politics of the Legion. In their reports, they consciously countered the interpretation of global events offered up by right-wing patriotic groups and the conservative mainstream press. Casting themselves as radical sympathizers or noble partisans of democracy ready to take on the burdens and moral choices demanded by the period's popular politics, they modeled a deeply social and cosmopolitan sense of the engaged world participants Americans could be, an alternative to the bellicose versions of worldliness displayed in Paris by the veterans, casual tourists, or the Chamber of Commerce crowd. Expatriates' letters, memoirs, and other works are littered with hints of these often overlooked engagements. "I hope the communistas kick the asparagus out of the American Legion on the 19th which is tomorrow," John Dos Passos scribbled at the end of a letter to Ernest Hemingway in September 1927. "Want to go to Russia and China—Let me hear where you'll be this winter . . ."[5]

As Dos Passos wrote, Hemingway had already set off from Paris for a summer in Spain. The past few years had been busy, pivotal ones for both men as they began to garner recognition as novelists while traveling extensively, awakening to international affairs, and corresponding across the continents. The two writers had first met in Italy while serving as ambulance drivers in 1918, but they only became close friends when their paths crossed again in Montparnasse in 1924. Spending days at the races, trading literary confidences, the two bonded over a shared love of Spain and a skepticism about the motives of Europe's statesmen. In Paris, Hemingway talked "beautifully" about the international conferences he had attended, and Dos Passos concluded that he "had one of the shrewdest heads for unmasking political pretensions." They agreed on a "restrained heroworship" of the revolutionaries Karl Liebknecht and Rosa Luxembourg, who had been tortured and murdered by Freikorps soldiers in Berlin.[6]

Travel, too, filled their conversations. After relocating to Paris in December 1921, Hemingway sailed back and forth to North America twice and crisscrossed Europe indefatigably, taking assignments for the *Toronto Star*, and always, afterwards, returning to Paris as a beloved home port. In Genoa to cover an economic summit, he socialized with the inveterate leftists Max Eastman and Lincoln Steffens and toured the slums where the Italian communist movement was based. Only months before Mussolini's March on Rome, he pointedly dissected the phases of Fascist organizing and the capriciousness of Italy's street politics. In September 1922, he took the Orient Express to Constantinople, capturing in print that city's "tight-drawn, electric tension," with its dregs from various Russian armies and its trapped Greeks and Armenians, all dreading the coming Kemalist troops. Hemingway had an eye for telling detail, and his dispatches on the Greco-Turkish War not only developed the terse writing style for which he became famous but also some of the political themes that would prove so central to expatriates' travelogues. Watching the twenty-mile-long trail of displaced Christians evacuating eastern Thrace, Hemingway recorded the quiet desperation of individuals caught in the crossfire of power struggles larger than themselves. He sketched the heartbreaking cries of a young girl looking on as her mother gave birth in the rain and the stoicism of an innkeeper along the route, who had seen the ebb and flow of conquest all before.[7]

Dos Passos had ventured even more widely, always making "fitful stopovers in Paris" along his way. Like Hemingway, he had seen the "grubby little war" between the Turks and the Greeks while passing through Constantinople in 1921 en route to the regions of the former Transcaucasian Republic, under Bolshevik control by the time he arrived. Journeying through the Near East promised a graphic education in the Great War's fallout. Amid the rubble of the Ottoman Empire, the region erupted with ethnic hatreds, competing independence movements, and renewed imperialist ambitions. Georgia, he found, buzzed with excitement for the communist experiment. But terror lurked around the corner in back alleys, where, in scenes that would haunt Dos Passos in other countries as well, men bayoneted or shot alleged counterrevolutionaries, who, he thought, "didn't look any guiltier than anybody else." Training south through Armenia revealed a landscape even more ground "down into cinders" by famine and disease. Dos Passos watched from his railroad car as guards raided the trains looking for enemies and directionless refugees died of typhus and cholera on the sides of the tracks. He had been "scared pissless every moment," he admitted, since leaving Tiflis. Pressing on through Tehran just months after Reza Kahn's nationalist coup, broke and malarial, the writer bargained with an Armenian who owned a Ford Model T and spoke "missionary American" to drive him to the border of the new Iraqi state. From Baghdad, Dos Passos joined a camel caravan across the Syrian desert, bearded and disguised in Arab dress so as not to be mistaken for British by the various marauders and anticolonial insurgents along the way. Dos Passos subsisted for more than a month on a near-starvation diet, nursing chilblained feet, before making it to Damascus, where "mysterious people in courtyards" plotted against the new French order. Before long, he was back in Paris. Paris, he mused on the return, was a center for all this unrest, for "the building up and the tearing down of this century."[8]

Dos Passos and Hemingway were only two among scores of well-known Americans who found in Paris both inspiration and a gateway to exploring broader horizons. The postwar cohort of expatriates, whether or not they embraced that label themselves, included self-appointed spokesmen for the Left Bank scene, such as Hemingway and Cowley, who dipped into the city's avant-garde circles for a time and professed to speak for an entire generation, as well as others who stayed on for decades, sinking even deeper roots into the capital. Sylvia Beach saw Paris through both world wars and tended to her bookstore Shakespeare and Company for all the years in between. Janet Flanner faithfully captured the fads and foibles of the city for fifty years, beginning with her first "Paris Letter" for the *New Yorker* in 1925. Following her Paris debut that same year, Josephine Baker would make the capital her permanent home, even becoming a French citizen. The city furnished an important if far shorter chapter in the lives of other creative Americans who are better remembered for later accomplishments elsewhere, among them the composer Aaron Copland, the regionalist painter Grant Wood, the Harlem Renaissance poet Langston Hughes, the graphic artist Ben Shahn, and the foreign correspondents William Shirer and Martha Gellhorn.

A diverse lot, these expatriates nevertheless shared certain characteristics. They had been born around the turn of the century, mostly to middle-class parents: doctors, ministers, shopkeepers, and upright patrons of the arts. Growing up—a great number of them in the second-tier towns of the Midwest, only just opening up to the wider world of possibilities—they felt stifled by their families and communities. They lived through literature. Like Hemingway, who escaped his prim hometown of Oak Park, Illinois, in Rudyard Kipling's tales of empire, the future novelist and social critic Josephine Herbst fantasized about experiences beyond her lot as the daughter of a struggling Iowa hardware store owner. "As other girls packed lingerie and household linen in a hope chest," Herbst packed away into her notebooks "morsels from books that seemed to hold the sacred fire." Haunted by Chekhov's three sisters, who pined for Moscow the way she longed for New York and Paris, Herbst's encounters with distant heroines stiffened her resolve "to get beyond helpless yearning to the Real Thing."[9] Expatriates were intellectually curious, well read, and often skilled in several foreign languages. Several were the children of progressive reformers or suffragists, who cautioned against racism and intolerance and urged sympathy for the less fortunate. Frequently they were encouraged in their creative pursuits by mothers who chafed at their own domestic confines and hoped for bigger things for their children. Most received at least some college education or art school training, even at prestigious universities. Unsuited, however, to the regimen of formal studies or impatient to make a splash as artists and writers, a lot of them would drop out, more often than not to secure a position with some regional newspaper or magazine that promised both freedom and finances.

A great many expatriates (Dos Passos, Wood, Flanner, and Shirer among them) lost a parent at a young age, often forcing family moves and other sacrifices, which only compounded their growing sense of rootlessness. In his youth, Langston Hughes knew many homes in five different states across the heartland. Hughes's father, frustrated by racial barriers to lucrative employment in the United States, had abandoned the family for Cuba and Mexico. His mother was also often absent, looking for work and leaving her son with his grandmother in Kansas. Terribly lonely, "books began to happen to me," Hughes recalled. If people suffered in books, he thought, "they suffered in beautiful language, not in monosyllables, as we did in Kansas." For a time in high school, Hughes even lived by himself in a rented room, subsisting on mushy rice and hot dogs, reading himself to sleep with Schopenhauer, Nietzsche, Dreiser, and Guy de Maupassant in French. "I think it was de Maupassant," he later reflected, "who made me really want to be a writer and write stories about Negroes, so true that people in far-away lands would read them—even after I was dead." Poems came to Hughes spontaneously, which he began to compile into a notebook.[10]

Expatriates' upbringings left them with a taste for far-flung exploits. They spent a good portion of their lives in search of the next great place, the next eye-opening encounter—firsthand experiences that they believed would fortify their art. They were ambitious and adventuresome above all. The age that had brought farmers the Model T, Herbst explained, had also "opened the world to its literary young on a scale never before ventured." The future novelist and little-magazine editor Elliot Paul understood this quest for mobility well. Raised with the support of extended family following his father's death, Paul worked for the U.S. Reclamation Service in Montana, studied for a year at the University of Maine, then took a position as a city engineer in Louisville, Kentucky, before ambling through Idaho and Wyoming, playing piano in saloons and picking up odd jobs. By 1913, still only in his early twenties, Paul returned to his native Massachusetts, covering Boston statehouse politics for local newspapers. After serving overseas with the Signal Corps during the war, Paul quit journalism to concentrate on fiction. In 1923, following the modest success of two novels, he abandoned his first of five wives for Paris.[11] Decisions to embrace their wanderlust, to strike out rather than settle down, would not be without tradeoffs. The difficulties of keeping family ties together while traversing the nation and eventually the globe would be reflected in a string of failed marriages, spectacular fallouts with friends, and affairs that ended badly. Many would have few or no children at all.

For those who did finish their degrees, college often proved a critical turning point. Edward Estlin Cummings, for one, remained in his hometown of Cambridge, Massachusetts, all the way through university, studying Greek and English at Harvard, living at home under the watchful eye of his Unitarian minister father, and transcribing into his notebooks promises to shun temptation. "I am a young man living in an advanced and cultivated era," he wrote, with "a high reputation, everywhere I go, as a gentleman. My friends are pure, high-minded girls and clean, manly fellows." But by age nineteen, like his newfound college friend John Dos Passos and his classmate Malcolm Cowley, the aspiring poet began to reenvision himself as an irreverent outsider, skipping church, carousing with a small group of intellectual rebels who scoffed at their buttoned-down peers, devouring modernist art and music, and living a "double life" in the sawdust-strewn dives and burlesque theaters of Boston, "getting drunk and feeling up girls" while lying about it to his father. The young iconoclasts of the East Coast shared a common set of dreams with their restless Midwestern peers: to live by their creative talents, to be touched by the wider world, and to make their mark upon it. It was more than escaping something in the United States that would compel them to make their pilgrimages, Herbst and others would insist. Theirs, she said, was a "love affair with the world." "I was running toward something too," not just running away, Dos Passos echoed; "It was the whole wide world."[12]

In time, Asia, Africa, and Latin America would captivate their attention, but Europe loomed foremost in their young imaginations. Reading about the continent in books, those from more prosperous families also encountered it firsthand with their parents on tours that sparked earnest self-promises to return later on their own. Such exposure to the world across the Atlantic fired Sylvia Beach's imagination as a teenager. In 1902, her family temporarily relocated to Paris when her father took a position as associate pastor for the American Church. Upon returning to staid Princeton, New Jersey, Beach found ways to make repeated trips back in coming years, living for a year in Italy, immersing herself in French opera and theater, and moving to Spain at the end of 1914, despite the war, where she picked up her fourth language. By the summer of 1916, she relocated to Paris, intent on studying experimental poetry. Soon goaded by her father into service for President Wilson's emerging crusade, she volunteered as a farmhand in the French countryside, picking grapes and bundling wheat twelve hours a day, feeling healthier and more useful than she ever had at home. For the first half of 1919, Beach also worked as a translator and secretary for the Red Cross in Serbia. Struck by the subordination of women in the organization and by the postwar desolation of the region, her time in the Balkan Peninsula awakened her to socialist and feminist inclinations. Taking the Orient Express back to Paris, she determined to remain in Europe. "I should like to get into a publishing house or newspaper office over here and perhaps sometime a little book business of my own," she wrote home to her father, who did not approve. After all, her preference for Europe, she reasoned, had been her parents' fault. They had given her and her sisters "a taste of it when we were very young."[13]

For expatriates like Beach, Europe was not the feudal holdover often imagined by older intellectuals and social reformers but a region pulsing with the era's most vibrant expressions, a chaotic continent, Cowley reported, "feverishly seeking the future of art, finance and the state." It demanded their attention, especially after the outbreak of the Great War. Several aspiring writers—among them Cowley, Hemingway, and the novelist Louis Brom-field—volunteered as ambulance drivers, seeing the conflict as an occasion to come of age amid history. Imbued with pacifist notions but also jumping at the prospect of adventure, both Dos Passos and Cummings signed up with the Norton-Harjes Ambulance Service for Harvard graduates in 1917. To his disappointment, Cummings would be posted to a dreary section of the front with little fighting, dashing his hopes for the stimulus of a "wholly new environment" in contrast to the "unchanging scene" back home. Yet, just as it would for others, the war opened a deeply international chapter in Cummings' life and provided fodder for some of his best early work. Mired in mud and mundane maintenance work, he and his new friend William Slater Brown openly derided the rules of their unit and tried to outwit the censors by writing home in French, calling the war a "chimère abominable."[14] Both were interned for suspected espionage. Sketching his fellow inmates and compiling notes for what would become *The Enormous Room* (1922), Cummings reflected on how the conflict laid bare the social mechanisms that pressed against the freedoms of the self, stripping away participants' self-respect and forcing them, no matter what their nationalities or sensibilities, into blind obedience. Already many young intellectuals like Cummings did not share elder progressive reformers' confidence in the positive good of the state. The war reinforced their suspicions of government and sparked soft forms of philosophical anarchism and pacifist internationalism.

For Dos Passos, too, the war unfolded like a youthful lark set against a slowly encroaching backdrop of horrors that forced him into more nuanced political thinking. Dos Passos was no stranger to Europe. The illegitimate son of a prominent New York lawyer, he had spent a "hotel childhood" on the continent with his mother, learning French as his first language, attending

English boarding school, and traveling as far as Egypt and Turkey before enrolling at Harvard. Back in France for the war, holed up in dugouts under intense shelling and poison gas at Verdun, Dos Passos poured into a notebook his contradictory moods. "But gosh," he exclaimed, "I want to throw the dice at every turn with the old roysterer Death . . . and through it all I feel more alive than ever before." Mixed in with these excitable, even hackneyed, impressions, however, appeared the statements of disillusionment for which expatriates would be renowned. Cursing the military leaders and the Morgan banks, as he had seen Emma Goldman and Max Eastman do at antiwar rallies back in New York, Dos Passos jadedly pronounced in letters to his friends that the war was "utter damn nonsense." "Of all the things in this world," he decided, "a government is the thing least worth fighting for." Transferred to the Italian front, he, like Cummings, ran afoul of authorities for his insubordinate manner and the contents of his intercepted letters. The Red Cross deported him back to the United States at the end of his enlistment, but nevertheless he returned to Europe in a matter of months, laboring to strip all that "twentyone-year-old rhetoric" out of his writing, to really show how the war's frightening absurdities undermined for good the old cherished ideals. Anticipating Hemingway's more famous invocation against "abstract words" such as courage and honor, now "obscene beside the concrete names of villages, the numbers of roads," Dos Passos wrote in *Three Soldiers* (1921) that the conflagration's "gigantic phrases" and glittering promises rose like "soap bubbles to dazzle men for a moment" before shattering. "This was his last run with the pack," Dos Passos' protagonist John Andrews decides. "He would be recklessly himself" and "proclaim once more the falseness of the gospels."[15]

Those who did not make it abroad during the war followed yet another well-trodden path out of the United States from the bohemian enclaves of Chicago and New York. Early-twentieth-century Chicago was in the midst of a cultural renaissance, its universities overflowing with scholarly and social innovation, its downtown quarters humming with cutting-edge journalism and literary pursuits. Yet it seemed not enough. Those who made their way to the Midwestern hub from their smaller hometowns would not stay long, usually pressing east. The influential Left Bank publisher Robert McAlmon had spent his childhood moving from place to place in South Dakota, withdrawing from the University of Minnesota after only one semester and then shambling across the region harvesting grain and working as a reporter and copywriter. Following his father's death, McAlmon accompanied his mother west, enrolling in but never earning a degree from the University of Southern California. Restive, McAlmon enlisted in the army in early 1918 but never

Shortly before running afoul of Red Cross authorities, John Dos Passos stands at attention, fourth from the left, as an ambulance corps volunteer in Milan in December 1917. As it did for others, the Great War would catalyze the young American's interest in exploring the intersections between politics, travel, and art. Papers of John Dos Passos, Accession #5950, Special Collections, University of Virginia Library, Charlottesville, Va.

made it past San Diego. Encouraged by the publication of his first poems, he traveled to Chicago in 1920 and then on to New York. Posing nude for Cooper Union art classes, McAlmon made ends meet in Greenwich Village.[16]

By the early 1920s, the Village's status as a mecca for cultural and political rebels had been well established. The neighborhood bristled with condemnations of mainstream culture—the laments of Van Wyck Brooks about the absence of robust, indigenous American traditions; H. L. Mencken's caustic denunciations of middle-class prudishness; Sinclair Lewis's and Sherwood Anderson's gentler satires of the quiet desperation on the Main Streets of the Midwest. Future expatriates waded into the quarter's talk of the corrosive effects of a modern society given over to crassly profit-driven capitalists. Poring over the latest literature, they reiterated "the old things over again," Cowley explained, with a "clever and apologetic twist" of their own. Nevertheless, as much as upstarts like Cowley inherited such well-rehearsed complaints, they also wanted to strike out beyond what Dos Passos called the "smug repudiation" of the Village critics. Expatriates did not buy the contentions of Brooks, Waldo Frank, and others who believed that living abroad was deracinating, although a few would certainly blame it later for their failures. Almost as soon as they had arrived to New York, these young pathfinders itched to move on. Greenwich Village itself, battered by the reactionary political climate, now felt, as McAlmon explained, "postwar despairing." It, too, increasingly functioned as a steppingstone to destinations further afield. Like so many others, McAlmon would depart within a year for what became a twenty-year exile in Europe.[17]

If expatriates' paths abroad proved fairly predictable, the routes they took to Paris, by contrast, were often circuitous. Some planned extended travel or took up temporary residence in other capitals before settling in France—Herbst to Berlin, for example, and McAlmon to London. Langston Hughes left the United States just after the war to visit his father in Mexico, staying for months on end, practicing Spanish, learning German from an immigrant housekeeper, frequenting the bullfights in Mexico City, and beginning to write prose as well as poetry. Dreaming of Harlem, he arrived at Columbia University in 1921 for study, but he disliked the curriculum. Leaving for a job as a mess boy on a freighter bound for West Africa, Hughes fantasized about the lush climes of his black ancestors. Instead, in the outposts along the Congo, its riverbanks and "Europeans Only" taverns patrolled by white men with whips, he got an up-close introduction to the horrors of colonialism. Hughes next set sail on a freighter making rounds between New York and Rotterdam. In the middle of his second run, he abandoned his position on the ship on a whim and caught the night train for Paris with little more than the clothes on his back. The young writer determined no longer to live only through the literature of others. On that first voyage to Africa, he had tossed all of his books overboard into the night waters off the New Jersey coast. "It was like throwing a million bricks out of my heart," he rhapsodized. "I felt grown, a man, inside and out. Twenty-one. I was twenty-one."[18]

Many others had not been intent on Paris at the start either. Thinking back to his ambulance service, in 1921 Hemingway was buying up lira and making preparations to move to Italy with his new bride Hadley before suddenly changing course on the eve of departure and heading to the French capital instead, where he could keep his correspondent job with the *Toronto Star*. Cummings, back in New York that year talking revolution with Dos Passos and Yiddish journalists on the Lower East Side, only decided on Paris after a scheme to go to South America with his former fellow internee William Slater Brown fell through because the two could not secure shipboard work to finance the passage. Even Sylvia Beach, once she had resolved to stay on in Europe, had originally intended to open a French bookstore in London, only settling on an English-language "poetry center" in Paris after her scouting trip across the Channel failed to turn up adequate leads.[19]

From all sorts of directions, then, Americans trickled into the French capital. The city's accessibility by boat and train and its extensive opportunities for social and professional networking had made it Europe's most convenient and attractive base for Americans abroad. Easy friendships were struck up on café terraces. New collaborations were hatched in the workrooms of local newspapers, and reunions among old travel companions or acquaintances from college or the war were celebrated over cheap bistro meals. By contrast, Weimar Berlin was too volatile and only sparsely settled with American institutions. Rome and Venice were too remote and, before long, too fascist.[20] London, which held great potential for prewar exiles such as Ezra Pound and T.S. Eliot, seemed after the war, like Greenwich Village, past its glory days. Pound himself relocated to Paris during the early twenties. Paris had the advantage of proximity to these intriguing destinations, along with Spain, a perennial expatriate favorite, but it had far more amenities and key liaisons to ease arrivals into the city's intellectual life. Gertrude Stein, a fixture in Montparnasse since 1903 and much older than the postwar group of exiles, inducted neophytes into the aesthetics and philosophies of modernism. As proprietor of Shakespeare and Company, a beacon for newcomers, Sylvia Beach took great pleasure in introducing talented Americans to each other and to other artists in the quarter. Among the several able literary brokers and publishers in the neighborhood, Robert McAlmon, blessed by family money, helped struggling writers find audiences for their experimental work. With its wealth of presses and journals, its cluster of renowned salons and galleries, Paris simply was, Sherwood Anderson assured Hemingway, the place aspiring writers went if they were serious about their work.

In Paris, thus, expatriates came together. But, just as importantly, it was also the place from which they scattered to the winds. Many became seasoned birds of passage, traversing the Atlantic again and again. Grant Wood took four extended trips across the ocean during the 1920s, staying mostly in Paris. George Antheil and Aaron Copland, who both spent apprenticeship years in the capital in the early twenties, also returned habitually over the next decade. E. E. Cummings's primary Paris years fell between 1921 and 1923, but he, too, would voyage back roughly every other year into the mid-thirties. Like Hemingway and Dos Passos, expatriates became avid travelers. Using Paris as a trusty base camp, they set off for the trenches of France or the devastation of Serbia, to witness the political uncertainties of Italy, Austria, and Germany or the unrest in Ireland and Morocco. "In those days," Cowley recalled, expatriates "waved to each other from the windows of passing trains." More and more, these young Americans, out to discover themselves and the world, began to realize their potential as interpreters of the mounting international tensions in the wake of the Great War. "Feeling ourselves actors in a rare moment," Herbst later wrote, "we seemed to have gained an insight into the creative fissures of the world."[21]

The comings and goings of the novelist and journalist Vincent Sheean attested to just how far beyond idle café life the possibilities of expatriation extended. A bookish youth already with some knowledge of three foreign languages, Sheean had enrolled at the University of Chicago, a place, he regretted, full of "nincompoops" striving to make the right fraternities. Founding a poetry club and consorting with the school's handful of eccentrics, Sheean could not afford to finish his degree anyway after his mother died in 1921. One day on a whim he boarded a train bound for New York. Immersing himself in the Greenwich Village scene, he took a job as a *Daily News* reporter, but within the year moved on to Paris, where he secured a post as a political correspondent for the *Chicago Tribune*. Intended at first as a means of income to supplement his novel writing, the position grew on Sheean. In the postwar "hothouse of Europe," Sheean could not help but "take sides." Reporting the effects of inflation on Rhineland farmers in the winter of 1923, he grew critical of the French occupation of the Ruhr, a presence as odious, he surmised, as the British in Ireland or the Americans in Haiti. From there, he made his way to Italy to cover the murder of the outspoken deputy Giacomo Matteotti by Mussolini's minions, his affinity for the socialist left growing along with his abhorrence for Fascism. He disapproved of Primo de Rivera's rule in Spain, too, where that spring he was followed by secret police and jailed briefly for the content of his dispatches. Crisscrossing the continent, Sheean regrouped back in Paris, scrounging up funds and awaiting further assignments. The capital, he said, was his "hideout." Fired by news of the Rif War in Morocco, Sheean ducked off from Paris again in 1925, twice crossing French-Spanish lines through a series of cloak-and-dagger arrangements, slinking across the desert past suspicious tribes, cursing double-crossing guides, and sleeping in ditches, all to get his audience with the colonial rebel Abd el-Krim. Straggling back barefoot, covered in lice, Sheean was rescued in the middle of seemingly nowhere by an African American from California, who had defected from the French Foreign Legion to fight on Krim's side.

Back in Paris the following year, now tailed by a police detective, Sheean lost little time before setting his sights on other hot spots. Departing for Persia, where Reza Shah Pahlavi was solidifying his rule, Sheean hopscotched through Cairo, Beirut, and Baghdad on the way, before returning to Paris via

Russia in late summer. Tiding himself over with work for the local *Paris Times*, Sheean next lobbied the North American Newspaper Alliance to send him to civil war–torn China in 1927; perhaps Dos Passos's urge to go there that year had been piqued by Sheean's cables. In Shanghai, only just purged of the Guomintang's leftist faction by Chiang Kai-shek's Nationalist forces, Sheean grew to detest the exploitative but fearful foreign elites who sequestered themselves from the deteriorating conditions outside their quarters. In Hankou, crawling with Chiang's detractors, Comintern agents, and sundry Asian anticolonial nationalists, Sheean flirted with the ideas of his communist contacts and saw what he thought was the world's hope for revolution. Sheean had come to care "nothing about" ephemeral stories with only local resonance—sensational murders or the small-time political elections that saturated the American press. What he wanted to understand, he realized, was how "a fundamental idea—an idea of race, class or even nation" could move masses. All the while, Paris served for Sheean as vital "background." It was, he said, the "place to go away from."[22]

In 1925 William Shirer was on a train speeding east from Chicago when a headline in that morning's paper caught his eye: "FRENCH DRIVE REPULSES RIFFIAN TRIBES WITH MANY DEAD. TRIBUNE MAN ALMOST SHOT AS SPY." Glancing across the article, detailing how Vincent Sheean had narrowly escaped a Moroccan rebel firing squad in his quest to interview Abd el-Krim, Shirer daydreamed about such adventures "so terribly distant from the placid Iowa cornfields" in which he grew up. Shirer, freshly graduated from a small college in Cedar Rapids, had arranged to work his way across the Atlantic for the summer on a cattle boat before returning to solid job prospects and a fiancée back home. Yet correspondents like Sheean impressed Shirer greatly as a "romantic tribe, dashing from one battle to another, from one revolution to another." Already, the young graduate's vocabulary had been stocked with the requisite expatriate barbs about the "cultural poverty" and "preachy" boosterism of the American Midwest. And already he had a keen, if still underdeveloped, interest in history and politics, underscored by his parents' tales of Haymarket and the Pullman Strike and by the "real education" he received harvesting wheat alongside IWW migrants in Nebraska after his freshman year. Talking books with these autodidacts who rode the rails had convinced Shirer that to find fulfillment, "you didn't have to live conventionally, settle down . . . join a church, a lodge, Rotary." Now, as he trained east, Shirer recalled that Sheean worked out of the *Chicago Tribune*'s Paris office. Perhaps when he got there, he reflected, he could talk his way into a job. Shirer had expected to be in Europe for two months. Instead, he would stay on for two decades, chronicling the disintegration of peace and the spread of dictatorship. That position with the *Tribune* miraculously materialized just as he was packing to leave. He never saw his girl back in Iowa again.[23]

As veterans of war, bohemia, or the farmlands of the American interior, most expatriates came to Paris with an inchoate leftist orientation, a cultural politics arrayed against bourgeois elders or warmongering authorities and devoted above all to individual expression—a politics of youth, to be sure. Expatriates like Shirer would be remembered best for contrasting a life overseas, full of inspirations, with the blandness of the life they had left back home. The unorthodox living arrangements and career paths expatriates opted for, the lovers they took, amounted to so many private choices, but they also doubled as protest gestures flung at the sexual and racial taboos, the bigotries and narrowness of American society as expatriates saw it. Fancying themselves as trailblazers, expatriates also reserved special contempt for the growing boatloads of their compatriots making the ocean crossing along with them. Other Americans in Paris were "the most abhorrent human tripe ever spilled from the swill-can, tout et seul," Cummings wrote home to his parents during his first stay in the capital; "How we flee them!" Expatriates mocked casual visitors' simple "Stars and Stripes-ism" and scoffed at the glum faces of those who collapsed into café chairs after whirlwind days of Paris sightseeing with nothing but thoughts of their own comforts on their minds. "They are thinking about Sacco and Vanzetti," went one joke. Whereas common tourists blundered their way across Europe in a blaze of ignorance and faux pas, expatriates insisted that they had made the effort to "get to know the values," as Hemingway's Jake Barnes put it. Whereas the Legionnaires had lined up for fried doughnuts at the edge of the Seine, they made a point of eating like the locals.[24]

In Paris and elsewhere, expatriates were looking for alternative, more worldly ways to be Americans abroad. They were sometimes far from enlightened in their social politics. Slurs and prejudices sometimes slipped into their private letters and notoriously colored the fiction of Fitzgerald and Hemingway.[25] Most nevertheless prided themselves on their cosmopolitanism—not the old oversophistication of writers like Edith Wharton or Henry James, but a grubbier kind that sunk them into motley collections of seekers and wanderers as restless as they. During his wartime internment, E. E. Cummings admired his multilingual, multiracial fellow inmates, "hideous and authentic" men possessing a "certain insane beauty." They made, he told his mother, "splendid comrades." Langston Hughes, who had learned his cross-ethnic sympathies attending high school with Jewish and Catholic immigrants in Cleveland, similarly rejoiced in the oddballs and outcasts he crossed paths with as he made his way in the world: the Mexican Indians living in poverty near his father's ranch; the lone Chinese boy he befriended at Columbia; the diverse assemblage of workers on his boat to Africa, as colorful as the crew of the *Pequod;* the down-and-out Russian dancer with whom he shared his room in Montmartre.[26] Paris—with its international cast of abstract painters and sculptors, *négritude* writers, irreverent surrealists, and avant-garde theater people—would famously nurture this appreciation for foreign cultures. Yet the lessons of expatriation would not be limited to artistic cross-fertilization, which has received so much attention from scholars.[27] When they went abroad, Americans discovered more than the life of the mind. Amid the turmoil of interwar Europe, many quickly moved beyond the simple judgments against boobs and Babbitts for which they have been remembered, engrossing themselves in far more ambitious and more explicitly political critiques, interests which they nurtured alongside their more famous artistic preoccupations. For them, the 1920s was "not the museum piece it has since become," as Herbst later insisted, but instead a moment of "flux and change, with artistic movements evolving into political crises."[28]

Shirer's social contacts in Paris illustrated these deepening commitments. Upon arrival, he headed straight for the famous Dôme, but like other new residents, he soon uncovered a richer expatriate subculture than the one imagined by visitors who only flitted across the surface of Montparnasse's legendary sights. Near the Luxembourg Gardens, Shirer took a room at a simple boarding house with stand-up toilets and coal-burning fireplaces, and from there he would set off to stroll this city of parks, markets, and bookstalls before work. Shirer went to churches for their chamber music and sat in on free lectures at the Collège de France. Like so many other young Americans in the quarter, he tried with some difficulty to write poems and short stories. Baudelaire and Verlaine had once lived at his hotel. Now it housed fellow *Tribune* staffers who aspired to emulate the great French poets and held late-night bull sessions, criticizing each other's writing or arguing passionately about current events. Working the night copydesk of the *Tribune*'s local edition, Shirer befriended Elliot Paul and Eugene Jolas, who would soon found the influential little magazine *transition*. Haunting the Closerie des Lilas and the café Les Deux Magots, he met literary celebrities like Hemingway and Pound and debated the future of American art with his hometown acquaintance Grant Wood. When Vincent Sheean was in town, the two adjourned to the Left Bank's best Italian restaurant for spaghetti and Chianti.[29]

Shirer, however, would also feel the pull of the capital's longstanding tradition of mixing art with politics, just as his role model Sheean had. Like

other Americans, he shared his café terraces with a growing number of refugees and revolutionaries, hiding out amid the starving poets and artists'
models. At Isadora Duncan's crowded Sacco-Vanzetti protest meetings, he was
introduced to French Communist leaders, including Paul Vaillant-Couturier
and his American wife, Ida Treat. Frequenting one popular restaurant near the
Sorbonne, oddly packed with university faculty, White Russians, and leftist
Hungarian exiles, the young writer "first began to grasp the meaning of what
was brewing in Europe. Ruthless men, ruthless gangs, who knew what they
wanted, were beginning to take over, or were waiting in the wings." Gaining
experience as a reporter for the *Tribune* kept Shirer "digging away at these
matters." Scouring the capital's spirited daily press and the Left Bank's circles
of dissenters, covering the Sacco-Vanzetti riots and the American Legion
parade, Shirer took note of the central controversies of the day: the power
struggle in Russia following Lenin's death; the light sentencing of Matteotti's
murderers in Italy, signaling the hardening of Fascism; the 1926 general strike
in Britain; the crisis of the franc and the rise of antiparliamentary movements
right there in Paris. "I was beginning to turn outward—after a year of trying
to write poetry and short stories—to what was going on in the world," Shirer
related.[30] Americans like him would not have to wait for the 1930s or return
home to become politically engaged.

For others, too, the trek across the Atlantic offered not so much an escape
into freedom as an initiation into the continent's social ills, problems in
some cases even more serious than those back home. Any notions E. E. Cummings had entertained about the superiority of Europe to the United States
died with World War I and its aftermath. During his wartime detention, the
young writer graphically learned that all the restrictions and historical forces
aligned against the individual could not simply be blamed on American
puritanism or backwardness. In his criticism of the conduct of the war,
Cummings showered as much, if not more, sarcasm and abuse on the "great
and good French government" as he did on the "great and good American
government."[31] After the war, the more familiar Cummings became with
Europe, the more it seemed to suffer from the same mob mentality he had
found so unpalatable in the United States. In 1919, back in New York
during the Red Scare, the young poet had been greatly disturbed by khaki-
clad "hoodlums of our well-known Uncle," who attacked socialists on the
streets and tried to storm a Mooney protest meeting Cummings attended at
Madison Square Garden. Traveling through Italy and Austria during the
early twenties, chillingly similar scenes dampened his spirits. Shoved off the
sidewalks by Blackshirts in Rome, the "fascist louts" plagued the poet's conscience. Recalling, not fondly, the patriots at home, he described to his

mother these "hollow-chested, knock-need sneering lopsided betassled youths crying 'For God for country and for Yale.'" In Vienna, he discovered only more "fascisti" hunting down Jews and picking fights, scenes that made him "feel weakly in my liver or lights." Questions of state power and the dynamics of mass politics would be too important to ignore. Cummings often concluded letters to his family with commentary about them. Reflecting on Mussolini's temporary occupation of Corfu, he wrote to his father that "Fiume looms, Poincaré wrangles. As usual, I admire Russia."[32] Expatriates' struggles against oppression and small-mindedness, then, did not conclude upon arrival in European ports, as myths often imply, but rather had only just begun.

Expatriates may have sometimes downplayed Europe's troubles as a rhetorical strategy to make their critiques of American culture sharper, but as they made their way out into the world, few romanticized foreign lands for long. "I fail to discover fewer morons and bigotries in other countries than in the United States," Robert McAlmon summed up flatly. As avid travelers, expatriates came face to face with the continent's mounting radicalism, its simmering nationalisms, its stubborn class pretensions and resentments. Europe's bigotries, its fears—they had a way of intruding on even the most charmed of expatriate stories, pushing some toward more resolutely political stands. Amid rising unemployment and surging racism, Josephine Baker's 1928–1929 continental tour attracted violent protests. In Vienna, right-wing students and Catholic groups denounced her as degenerate and immoral, hounding her wherever she went under police escort. Her show was banned by the Munich police. In Budapest, detractors set off ammonia bombs inside the theater, and in Zagreb, Croatian clerico-fascists heckled her and threw projectiles at the stage. Devastated to discover the same raw feelings when she sailed to Latin America, Baker angrily wrote back to Paris newspapers that she would give up dancing. No longer regarding racism as a distinctly American problem, she now saw its global ramifications. Memories of the ill-fated trip, etched into her mind as starkly as those of the St. Louis race riot, inspired her to write a novel against intolerance. Back in Paris, the music-hall star began French lessons and transformed her public persona. The pandering to audiences' convoluted and sexualized fantasies about black life, the banana skirts, were "finished."[33]

Paris was not Vienna or Zagreb, but still it was no haven from the interwar years' festering conflicts. In 1922, Hemingway included the city's bloody May Day riots in a six-sentence distillation of the most important incidents he had witnessed during his first five months of residence there. Cummings, too, noted the frequent, violent altercations between demonstrators and the

Paris police, valorizing the city's outnumbered communists and deriding its arrogant *flics* in his poetry and letters home. Like slummers caught up in Chiappe's dragnets, expatriates harbored no illusions about the power of the police or their role in the capital's factious political battles.[34] Robert McAlmon ranked them high on his list of things he "deplored," next to Prussians, Italian Fascism, and "New Englanders with their 'conscience.'" In *Banjo*, the Harlem Renaissance writer Claude McKay pronounced the French police "the rottenest of the whole world." Over the years, expatriates often chafed at France's crackdown on leftists, its reactionary movements and xenophobic paranoias, its steadfast dreams of empire. French liberty, so touted back home, sometimes amounted, they thought, to the same kinds of false promises as American freedom. "America beats your brains out with a policeman's billy," Dos Passos had written in *Three Soldiers*, but France would get you, too: "It stifles you very slowly, with beautiful silk hands."[35]

Arriving from Rotterdam in 1924, Hughes would have understood this sentiment. With no contacts in the city, he wandered Paris excited but tired and hungry until the American Express office's African American doorman pointed him toward Montmartre. Established black musicians in the quarter scowled at his desire for any kind of work: "There ain't no 'any kind of job' here." Hughes spent more than a month looking unsuccessfully for employment, selling off his clothes, starving and freezing in a barren rented room. "But about France! Kid, stay in Harlem!" Hughes implored Countee Cullen, "do they like Americans *of any color?* They do not!!" The city's American banks and businesses turned him away; French workers chased him off job sites, calling him a dirty foreigner. Retreating into the "Parisian world of color," Hughes began to reflect on the troubled position of colonial subjects— and by extension his own place—in the metropole, a subject to which he would return in coming years. Like others driven from their colonial homelands, he explained in the poem "Lament for Dark Peoples," he felt himself trapped, herded by the modern world's civilizing imperatives. For Hughes, as for other well-traveled black artists, the Harlem Renaissance represented more than an aesthetic movement celebrating African American arts and history back in New York. It was also a political project, buttressed by the anticolonial critiques of other people of color, fired by injustices overseas as well as at home. After a season of grunt work in the nightclubs of Montmartre, Hughes drifted south to the Mediterranean, where he had his pocket picked. Destitute, he begged on the beaches of Genoa, slept in its municipal flophouse, and was chased by Fascist police. Waiting far too long for a ship that would employ a black crewman and take him back across the Atlantic, Hughes composed his famous retort to Walt Whitman, "I, Too, Sing America."[36]

Disheartening as these lessons could be, expatriates were frequently inspired by their travels. They found purpose in the causes they encountered, the people they crossed paths with, the troubles they saw. Art, politics, and travel could be tremendously complementary. "Poetical" vacations, as Claude McKay put it, often had a way of turning into political educations.[37] This was certainly the case for the painter Ben Shahn, who embarked on two tours through North Africa and Europe during the twenties, culminating in extended stays in Paris. During his first sojourn in the capital, he took art classes, studied Picasso intently, and copied down French phrases he hoped to master. More than formal coursework, casual wandering through the city's streets and museums inspired Shahn to sketch. Drawing the crowds at the big Montparnasse cafés and digesting the quarter's bevy of manifestos, he began to develop a sense of his own artistic mission. Sailing home, his luggage stuffed with illustrated French magazines and African wood sculptures, Shahn immediately began planning another trip. When he returned to New York after his second crossing in 1929, Shahn dabbled in Cubist and Expressionist composition but struggled for more than competent craftsmanship. Beginning to incorporate themes of social justice into his illustrations, Shahn reached back to the lessons of the French capital. Turning to a book he had bought in Paris on the Dreyfus Affair, Shahn completed a series of watercolor portraits in 1930 depicting the major figures involved in the scandal. Two years later, he tackled the Sacco-Vanzetti case, producing a collection of compelling gouaches that would at last bring him widespread notoriety. Paris had fired his interest in contemporary controversies, the Sacco-Vanzetti trial in particular. During all those hours on the café terraces of Montparnasse, "I argued art and politics," he recalled, "as everyone did," and among the more vigorously debated subjects was the fate of the two Italian anarchists in Massachusetts. Like many of his compatriots, Shahn had not been fully aware of the case until his Paris sojourns, when he witnessed the city's vigorous activism on behalf of the two men and began to think about the affair as potential material for his art. "In Europe of course I'd seen all the demonstrations against the trial—a lot more than there were over here," he explained. "Ever since I could remember I'd wished that I'd been lucky enough to be alive at a great time—when something big was going on, like the Crucifixion. And suddenly I realized I was! Here I was living though another crucifixion. Here was something to paint!"[38]

Amidst the great affairs of the 1920s—the territorial conflicts not settled by the war's treaties, the birth of the Soviet state and Italian Fascism, the Sacco-Vanzetti affair, and more—many expatriates began to develop deeper, more socially engaged dimensions to the anarchistic, pacifist politics of their youth. Not for long, or only with great blindness, could they ignore the

Part of Ben Shahn's Sacco-Vanzetti series, this gouache recalls the artist's initial fascination with the case during his Paris days. Picturing Vanzetti's sister Luigia surrounded by protesters, the piece recreates the formidable Bois de Vincennes gathering on August 7, 1927, during Shahn's second residence in the capital. *Demonstration in Paris*, 1932, private collection. ©Estate of Ben Shahn/Licensed by VAGA, New York, N.Y. Photo credit: Scala/Art Resource, N.Y.

dramatic developments, the dire news, unfolding around them. "There were too many ways in which life intruded into the most defended drawing room," Vincent Sheean would recall. The newspapers, the radio, the "casual talk of casual comers" all brought word of suffering and disaster right into the "scented center" of company.[39] Looking forward to the central tenets of the Popular Front, some began to explore the potentially greater role artists and writers might play in social affairs. Art, Shahn and others increasingly recognized, could combat selfish indifference. It could help to clarify the profoundly complicated struggles consuming masses the world over. It could advocate for justice, distill truths, take its content from the ugliness and urgency of public affairs without necessarily compromising artistic form.

Especially by the early thirties, this emerging political culture would become hard to resist, even for those like Janet Flanner, who tried. Struggling with her father's suicide some years before, Flanner had moved east after failing out of the University of Chicago and rashly marrying a college friend who offered her an escape from her native Indianapolis. In Greenwich Village just after the war, she met Solita Solano. A confident woman, fluent in several languages, Solano had eloped at fifteen, fleeing with her new husband for four years in China, Japan, and the Philippines, where he worked as an engineer. But hers had been an unhappy marriage. Climbing out the window one night, she stole back to the United States, where she built up a reputable career as a journalist. In the Village, Flanner and Solano shared confidences about their attraction to women and their aspirations to write great fiction. Flanner agonized over her sense of feeling out of place in her marriage and in New York. Furthermore, she was pregnant. When Solano received an assignment to travel to the Mediterranean for *National Geographic* in 1921, Flanner reluctantly seized the chance to break off her marriage and get away. For whatever reason, the pregnancy never progressed. During several months of travel in Europe, Flanner began to think through the serious crises of the day and envision for herself a different kind of life. In Vienna, she observed antisemitic demonstrations and, on the city's outskirts, homeless women and children scavenging for food. In Greece and Constantinople, she witnessed some of the same strife Hemingway and Dos Passos had seen. The fervor for war, Flanner was coming to believe, was made by men—bureaucrats and demagogues who wrongly believed in their own superiority and righteousness.[40]

Still, as she and Solano settled in Paris to make a life together, Flanner intended to shrug off these themes, pouring her energies instead into a semi-autobiographical novel about love and betrayal. Conservative in temperament, Flanner wanted to lead a beautiful, civilized existence far removed from the unpalatable world of politicians and their power brokering. Writing her Paris column for the upstart *New Yorker*, Flanner turned out bantering, textured reports of the capital's eccentric fashions, socialite gossip, and theater debuts in keeping with the magazine's wry, urbanely detached tone. Turned off by the militarism and masculine bravado of the left, only sometimes disturbed by the violent intolerances of the right, she eschewed political labels and debates. Subsequent trips to Italy and Austria did not spawn the same disgust as they had for Cummings. During the Sacco-Vanzetti riots, she was vacationing in the Loire Valley. Yet by the late twenties, Flanner feared that her writing had become formulaic. Plans for a second novel went nowhere. To write her letters from Paris, Flanner read about a dozen French newspapers each day, so, hesitatingly, she began to slip economic and political subject matter in among her column's lighter fare. She studied France's political parties, took potshots at Prefect Chiappe in her articles, and joined in the conjecture, the amateur analyzing that had consumed her Left Bank friends long before her. Learning about politics, she wrote home to her mother in the early thirties, made life more exciting. With the deterioration of parliamentary democracy in France and elsewhere, with the rise of Hitler, Flanner saw no need to keep at her novel writing. "European and French politics, too," she reasoned, had their own "appalling capacity for sounding like fiction, for sounding like horrifying thrillers."[41]

Following the stock market crash, in the now famous formulations of Cowley and others, many American writers and artists traveled, both physically and mentally, from the cosmopolitan excitement and modernist experimentation of postwar Paris to the rustic, Depression-era realism of the United States. In light of expatriates' assessments of European affairs during the 1920s, however, their political engagement did not always originate with the economic collapse and the programs of the New Deal as often claimed. The events of the thirties would change expatriates' politics, but they did not create politics where there had been none. Hemingway for one pushed back against this misconception, perpetuated by "recent converts" like Cowley. The political conversion stories so popular in the early thirties, he thought, denoted a form of fashionable fellow traveling, which came at the expense of nuanced thinking and integrity in art. Even worse, he believed, they generated myths that artists and writers had been in the dark about social issues before. In 1932, he railed against these "boys who had no kick against the system" back in the wake of World War I in a series of letters to Dos Passos. "Remember how nosepicking all those twirps were when we were all out seeing the bloody world?" he asked. "It's damned funny when I used to get the horrors about the way things were going those guys never took the slightest interest nor even followed it," he wrote exasperatedly. They, too, "were all in Europe," but frittered away their time with Dadaist experimentation "when the god damndest things were happening." But now, Hemingway noted incredulously, "when you've gotten as hot about something or as burned up and finally completely disillusioned on the *working* of anything but intelligent political assassination then they start out and say, 'Don't you see the injustice, the Big Things that are happening'"?[42] For Hemingway and many of his peers, the thirties would signal not a turn to the politics of the left, but a shifting of interpretations, a refining of criticisms and convictions—and for many, a deepening of disillusionments.

Honing their preexisting leftist sympathies, former Paris residents, like other artists and writers, benefited from the expanding cultural initiatives and Popular Front institutions of the 1930s. Grant Wood, Walker Evans, Berenice Abbott, Ben Shahn, and Stuart Davis found jobs with the Public Works of Art Project or the Farm Security Administration. Others, such as James T. Farrell and Aaron Copland, devoted themselves to creating and composing for the masses beyond the auspices of New Deal support. Under all kinds of government and private patronage, journalists and photographers journeyed through the back roads of the American South, as foreign to most of them as any European village had been, where they hoped to capture the plain truths of the unprecedented economic catastrophe. Unsettled, like others, by the grimness of the situation, many returning exiles set out to raise awareness about worsening conditions and inequalities while also capturing an uplifting sense of American perseverance. Championing the common people, producing iconic images of the nation in peril, such intellectuals embraced the period's progressive strain of Americanism, a rugged and deeply patriotic aesthetic, infused with themes of egalitarianism and social justice. Their craggy pioneer portraits and plebeian parables, in fact, often seemed so culturally nationalist that they suggested a profound new introspection among those who had once been so outwardly focused.[43]

And yet, expatriates were not simply homeward bound. Their intensified focus on American places and people during the thirties did not preclude an equally serious and enduring interest in foreign affairs. For example, Aaron Copland's excursions abroad, beginning with his stay in Paris in the early twenties, complemented his growing political activities at home. The son of Jewish immigrants, Copland had been drawn to socialism long before the Depression, defending the Bolshevik Revolution to his disapproving father during his youth in Brooklyn. By the late twenties and early thirties, he grew even more dedicated to reading socialist classics, attending communist rallies, and participating in the productions of the Popular Front Group Theatre, organized by his former Paris roommate Harold Clurman. At the same time, he traveled widely in Europe, Morocco, and Latin America. Plans to visit Russia never panned out, but like Hughes and others, he became enamored with the political and artistic vibrancy of Mexico City. He resolved to create an American music informed by world events and international trends. Politicized by the Sacco-Vanzetti affair, Josephine Herbst followed similar trajectories that took her both deeper into national politics and at the same time farther out into the world. Analyzing the Farmers' Holiday move-ment, the Scottsboro case, and the Flint sit-down strike for the nation's leftist journals in the early thirties, she also traveled to Russia for a conference on revolutionary literature. In 1935, she dispatched reports on civil liberties battles in Cuba, attended the Communist novelist Henri Barbusse's funeral in Paris, and searched for anti-Nazi resistance in Germany. Contrary to the stereotypes, Paris had readied many expatriates not simply for a return to their own nation but also for a new international participation. Some expatriates may have reoriented themselves around domestic issues, but for an important contingent—for the wanderers like Herbst—travel would continue to define their politics.[44]

Langston Hughes, who began celebrating the nation's "low-down folks" years before the Depression, sharpened and renewed his commitments to leftist politics by seeking out more experiences overseas after his Paris residence. The poet's next serious traveling, in classic Popular Front fashion, took the form of two extended tours through the American South, first with Zora Neale Hurston in 1927 and again in 1931, using his "poetry as a passport" to meet locals and visit the Scottsboro boys in jail. Like others, however, he also set off for the Caribbean, sending the New Masses incisive accounts of the region's class inequalities and colonial oppressions. In U.S.-occupied Haiti, he "first realized how class lines may cut across color lines," and in Cuba he was charged with trespassing and disorderly conduct for protesting his exclusion from a beach reserved for white Americans. In 1932, he traveled to Russia, taking a year to trek from Moscow, the center of Bolshevik power, to the fascinating Soviet peripheries to the south and east, reveling in foreign customs and the ways of the poor, celebrating the end of segregation on the trans-Siberian railroad under Communism, and writing the most radical poetry of his career. Pressing on to China, Hughes toured factories in Shanghai full of laboring children. Seeing the gutted remains of the Zhabei neighborhood, bombed and brutalized by invading Japanese troops the previous year, would later haunt him in Spain. Next passing through Japan in mid-1933, he was deported for suspected radicalism. After returning to the States, he dabbled in California labor politics, by then nearing the point of class warfare. Threatened by Legionnaires and other local patriots, Hughes was run out of there, too, pushing on to Mexico in 1935, where he spent much of his time translating short stories by local leftists.[45]

Far from forsaking international ideals for nationalist allegiances during the depths of the Great Depression, expatriates demonstrated how the two had become for them deeply intertwined. The parched desolation of the Great Plains, the blustering antiradicalism of Hearst's newspapers, the lynchings of the South—such cornerstone Popular Front issues, many former expatriates imagined, not only spoke to the situation of crisis and political polarization in the United States, they could also be viewed as local

Langston Hughes poses with locals at a farm collective in Turkmenistan during his journey through Central Asia in 1932. Langston Hughes Papers, James Weldon Johnson Collection in the Yale Collection of American Literature, Beinecke Rare Book and Manuscript Library, Yale University.

outcroppings of a drama being played out on a global scale. There would be not only Harlan County, the San Francisco docks, and the rallies of Madison Square Garden, but also Jim Crow in Haiti, the tightening clamp on the press in Berlin, purges in Moscow, fascist atrocities in Spain, and betrayals of the people in embattled China. For them defining a new, vigorous Americanism to face the nation's greatest challenges could not be separated out from the task of understanding Americans' relationship to these developments overseas. Like European activists, expatriates believed the fate of one cause was tied to others. They saw forging international links not as supplemental but vital to their mission, chronicling the erosion of freedoms elsewhere to convince Americans that their plight could be the same. "What was going on in the world" would not be decided by the literati in New

York, Josephine Herbst realized: "That's why I was always leaving for Germany, Cuba, Mexico, Latin America, the Midwest, and Spain."[46]

The future war correspondent Martha Gellhorn shared these convictions. Raised in a gregarious household by progressive parents, Gellhorn could not wait to return to Europe, where she had spent several summer breaks as a child. Dropping out of Bryn Mawr, she set off for Paris in 1930; it was the place, she later recalled, where her "real life" began. She took a wire-service job with the United Press to support her novel writing and immersed herself in local pacifist politics and a tumultuous affair with a married, leftist French journalist. "I wanted to go everywhere and see everything and I meant to write my way," she declared. Only a year later, however, Gellhorn returned to Chicago to terminate a pregnancy. She next headed west, writing reportage, hacking away at her fiction, reading *The Enormous Room* and *A Farewell to Arms*, and crossing over into Mexico alone with no vaccinations or passport to track down Diego Rivera. Soon she was back in Paris. Feeling poorly informed about European affairs compared to her French friends, she sought out a political education in the meetings of the capital's working-class neighborhoods. But by the autumn of 1934, she, like so many other Americans in Paris, felt the pull of the Depression at home and returned once again. Wangling a position as an investigator for the Federal Emergency Relief Administration, Gellhorn documented social conditions across the United States, sending back to Harry Hopkins penetrating letters that captured widespread demoralization "through the eyes of the people" and laced with Gellhorn's own outrage. Still, this New Deal work represented an interlude rather than an end point for her expatriate story. Gellhorn, like others, shuttled back and forth across the Atlantic incessantly during the 1930s. For her, so much lay ahead: civil war in Spain, deteriorating democratic resolve in France and Great Britain, invasion in Czechoslovakia and Finland.[47]

All this movement overseas would give wanderers like Gellhorn a particular vantage point from which to refine their political thinking. Expatriates' evolving commitments derived foremost from their up-close encounters with the interwar period's starkly different models of state organization: those communist, fascist, and liberal regimes locked in fierce competition. Each promised its own seductions, and each, many decided, was fundamentally flawed. Clearly, expatriates' left-leaning accounts of global affairs for American audiences contributed to the Popular Front cause, but their messages would not simply reiterate progressive politics back home. They had eyewitness knowledge of those places where, in Hemingway's phrasing, "revolutions have gotten past the parlor or publishers' tea and light picketing stage," knowledge which led these traveling intellectuals to modify the certainties that their counterparts in the United States often clung to.[48] Out in the field, optimism about the New Deal's domestic reforms paled beside the deadly consequences of the policy of neutrality. Sentimental allegiances to "the people" were undermined, over and over again, by the sight of the horrific acts of which ordinary people were capable. The slogans and party lines peddled at fundraising rallies in the United States, the clear notions about battles between good and evil in Spain or China and elsewhere, fell apart upon closer inspection of the world's war zones. Attempts to come to terms with complexities on the ground would lead expatriates to nuanced, sometimes even capricious, positions. A few would even abandon their leftist allegiances altogether. Through their insights as well as their shortcomings, however, these wanderers pioneered a compelling strain of American internationalism.

As expatriates combed the world's empires and hinterlands, some of the most trying tests of their principles would come out of trips to Russia. Purporting to transform an autocratic land of serfs and tsars into a modernizing, emancipated confederation of republics, the world's first socialist state enthralled expatriates just as it did most Americans on the left. In the footsteps of other journalists, scholars, and advisors, expatriate writers and artists scrambled to secure clearances to travel to "the future" Lincoln Steffens had so famously touted in 1921. Expatriates' interest in communism ultimately would have little to do with the finer points of Marxist doctrine or even the dilemmas of industrialization and political economy that roused the attention of the nation's new Soviet experts. Like other leftists, they typically advocated a progressive redistribution of wealth and even socialist reforms, but their attention to economic issues remained curiously vague, even into the thirties, when class analysis moved to the center of intellectual debates in the United States. Rather, to them, the greatest attributes of the Soviet experiment lay in its cultural initiatives, ranging from its sponsorship of the arts to its pledges to dispel anti-Jewish prejudice and respect the traditions of the various ethnic groups living under Bolshevik rule. Recalling the fascinating people he had encountered in the Caucasus after the war, Dos Passos, for example, applauded these policies and found everywhere, during his stay in Leningrad and Moscow in 1928, an encouraging "enthusiasm for social betterment." The Kronstadt massacre had bothered him, but now, he told himself quite wrongly, the terror was "fading." Things in Russia, he wrote in letters to Cummings and Hemingway, were "pretty darn swell."[49]

People of color felt even more the pull of these promises. Visiting in 1922, Claude McKay insisted that only a "soulless body" could not have been "stirred to the depths" by the headiness of progressive change in Russia's leading cities, filled with liberated women and men and a harmonious mix of polyglot peoples from the state's diverse republics, now social equals. A decade later, Langston Hughes echoed McKay's assessments of the Soviet territories as wonderfully, nobly populist. Able to make a living by his writing for the first time, Hughes declared that Moscow had supplanted Paris as the "greatest city in the world." Lighting out for the republics of Central Asia, Hughes swore he saw the "new life" of socialism sweeping away illiteracy, concubinage, and "Allah-worship." In his newspaper articles and memoirs, he offered no hint of Stalin's state-driven famine or the liquidation of kulaks, millions of whom were killed in the early thirties. Instead, the Soviet Union's "concrete modern social achievements"—eradicating antisemitism, segregation, prostitution, and unemployment while bringing medical care, electricity, and culture to the masses—"seemed almost like miracles." Like others, expatriates at times overlooked the complexities of Russia's domestic and foreign affairs, championing its egalitarian and anticolonial rhetoric while turning a blind eye to the horrors perpetrated under Bolshevism.[50]

For some, however, hesitations, questions, and growing uncertainties began to supplant these initial enthusiasms. It was hardly surprising that nonconformists like E. E. Cummings would find the collectivizing impulses of the Soviet experiment unbearable in person. In the early twenties, Cummings had characterized himself as a "good (if innocuous) Leninnite or Trotskyite or what-you-like-it." The "pro-Bolshevik," he also told his sister, was someone whose mind remained "unclouded by 'The N. Y. Times' and kindred bullshit." And by the late twenties and early thirties, composing the powerful conscientious objector poem "i sing of Olaf," Cummings seemed headed for the same kinds of Popular Front commitments his friends would make. But a six-week Russian tour, courtesy of a visa secured by Dos Passos, would lead the poet dramatically away from the politics of his peers. Plans for the trip transpired while Cummings was again living in Paris at the end of 1930, socializing with Russian artists, who piqued his interest in their language, and "pro-communist" Americans who extolled the state-sponsored cultural programs and the way the Soviet Union seemed to have escaped the Depression. In the spring of 1931, Cummings instead found a land where demoralizing demands for regimentation were only matched by the life-draining details of eking out a daily existence. Followed by undercover police, Cummings kept a secret diary recording his disappointments with everything from propaganda-spoiled theater to overflowing, "too comrady" streetcars. Returning to Paris via Istanbul, Cummings expanded his notes into the autobiographical narrative *Eimi* (1933), an even blacker comedy than *The Enormous Room*, tracing his Dantesque journey into a drab and punishing underworld, where men were "shadows," women were "nonmen," and in restaurants one struggled through meals of "unmeat." "To open the prizepackage of Marxism," Cummings concluded dourly, "was to find a joyless experiment in force and fear." Russia served as a profound political and intellectual turning point for Cummings. Renouncing even moderately leftist positions, he retreated into increasingly brittle defenses of his own individualism.[51]

Driving some to tortured apologies for Stalinism and others to reactionary reversals, communism proved impossible to ignore and yet also exceedingly difficult to come to terms with in a satisfying way. Many tried to toe a line between the two extremes. Impressed like Dos Passos with Moscow in the late twenties, Vincent Sheean confessed a "half-conscious emotional sympathy" for the Bolsheviks and reassured himself that this did not equate to condoning their "methods or results." Moving in revolutionary circles in China, however, he became more circumspect. Communists were too pat in their thinking, he suspected. More and more, he found himself "disturbed" by the "precision" with which Bolshevik intellectuals explained the all-important relationship between the individual, society, and the state. With too great ease, communists answered questions Sheean "had begun to think unanswerable." Communism highlighted an uncomfortable tension at the heart of expatriates' evolving quests to be both artists and political actors: how to respect the integrity and individuality of art, the subtleties of intellectual argument, while also advocating for collective social change?[52]

Encounters with Comintern operatives, expanding their influence around the world during the early and mid-thirties, only reinforced these dilemmas. Communists shrewdly, and often convincingly, cast themselves as inheritors of the democratic revolutionary tradition and visionary leaders in the fight against fascist aggression. For this reason, those who criticized communist ideas or tactics risked being denounced as profascist. And, to American intellectuals, like many of their European counterparts, communists seemed to be on the right side of history, standing up for the Scottsboro boys, fighting off Japanese invaders in China, coming to the rescue of Spanish Republicans. They displayed much-needed organizational energies and helped to shine a light on repugnant injustices. They had a "nuisance value," as Dos Passos conceded in retrospect.[53] Still, with its propensity for using people as pawns and its dogmatic, top-down party culture, mired in behind-the-scenes motives and confounding policy reversals, the communist movement would be a perennial stumbling block for expatriates' political identifications, checking the degree to which they were willing to move to the left. Although many expatriates closely aligned themselves, at least for a time, with communism, almost none became party members.

Expatriates found it far easier to orient their political views in relation to fascism, the era's other great new political force. For those who spent so much time overseas, fascists on the make constituted the most important story of the interwar years. The paramilitary leagues, the takeovers and occupations, the insidious intention to "send the human race back to the dark ages," as Langston Hughes put it—all of which began in the twenties—would be more mobilizing, more defining, than the Depression back home. Unlike the prewar exiles Ezra Pound and Gertrude Stein, who had little trouble making peace with the far right, most postwar expatriates were deeply disturbed by their face-to-face encounters with dictatorship and right-wing populism. In 1934, still hopeful about the chance for rapprochement, Martha Gellhorn had traveled with her French pacifist friends to a youth conference in Germany, only to be greeted upon arrival by unctuous Hitler Youth with "one parrot brain among the lot." Witnessing the "bullying Nazi louts" and what they were "up to" fired Gellhorn's resolve in coming years as she renounced her pacifist associations. The rise of the far right would edge expatriates away from their antiwar sentiments and toward more militant engagements. Opposing fascism, unlike coming to terms with communism, did not present a difficult moral decision. In fact, fascists helped expatriates to simplify their allegiances. "The Nazi papers had one solid value," Martha Gellhorn discovered during one stay in Germany in the mid-thirties: "Whatever they were against, you could be for."[54]

As part of a vanguard observing the world's trouble spots with their own eyes, these writers often diagnosed the emerging threat to democracy earlier than those who learned of such developments through the filter of mainstream American news syndicates, frequently biased in favor of right-wing order for fear of leftist revolution. Still, some were slow to report on the true depths of the period's challenges to liberal government. Stretching back to Hemingway's jabs at Mussolini as "Europe's Prize Bluffer" in the early twenties, expatriates often expressed their scorn for fascists through easily misconstrued caricature. Mocking fascist leaders risked underestimating them. Embracing the New Yorker's breezy style, Janet Flanner's profile of François Coty soft-pedaled the activities of the French perfume mogul and fascist financier as essentially harebrained political scheming. Her tone came across as flip. Flanner's three-part feature on Hitler in 1936 similarly emphasized the Führer's personal idiosyncrasies. To write the feature, Flanner read Mein Kampf three times and cultivated contacts in Hitler's inner circle. Dissecting the convoluted points of Nazi ideology and the calculations that brought Hitler to power, she touched on the Nuremberg laws, the purges, and the SS, but what stood out was Flanner's evocation of Hitler's odd eating habits. Flanner argued that she had been striving for respectable detachment, but other American journalists had already pronounced objectivity unsustainable with so much at stake. For her equivocation, Malcolm Cowley would denounce her as a fascist to her face.[55] Yet Martha Gellhorn, who had pitched her own stories on "France's Mussolinis" and "pseudo-Mosleys," defended this kind of ridicule as prevention against defeatism. Readers needed to know, she argued, about the buffoonery that underlay fascists' all-powerful façade to believe in the effectiveness of resistance. Echoing French leftists' sense of the slippery slope that led from Legionnaires' antics to more serious actions, she noted that only a year before they seized power, Nazis in the Sudetenland, like others, had been running around "wearing white stockings and behaving like Peck's Bad Boys."[56]

Others by contrast risked being branded as "prematurely antifascist" for their exposés of the hysteria and terror descending on fascism's epicenter, Central Europe. Since the late twenties, William Shirer had spent hours hashing out theories about the looming threat with other correspondents in Paris, Vienna, and Berlin, and by 1934, when he accepted a job with Universal Service, dissecting the ruthlessness of National Socialism became his main preoccupation. Shirer moved to Berlin just as Dorothy Thompson, another former Paris resident and the first American journalist expelled from the Reich for her outspoken criticisms, had been given twenty-four hours to clear out. Until he was also forced to flee, Shirer diligently recorded the whispers of torture and murder as well as the overt and systematic ways in which the Nazi regime ate into the region with lies and hate. The "crazed expressions" of Hitler's admirers reminded Shirer of the "Holy Rollers" he had once seen in the Louisiana backcountry, and the annual Nuremberg rallies offered more than a "gorgeous show" to mask followers' maniacal antisemitism, he argued forcefully in his widely read analyses of the region. Their "pageantry and colour and mysticism" injected crowds with "religious fervour," sweeping away individuals' critical faculties, so that delusions would be accepted as "high truth." Warding off censorship, arrest, and the random violence and pitfalls of a region unglued, Shirer broadcast back to the United States warnings that fascism was nothing but political gangsterism of a most horrible kind, robbing and intimidating and blasting away at what was good and noble.[57]

Expatriates like these did not agonize over precise definitions of the new political ideology as scholars later would. They thought it more important to draw connections between putatively fascist groups like the Nazis and broader threats to freedom cloaked in all kinds of guises. Fascists were those who waged a wholesale assault on the principles of local political and cultural self-determination, which expatriates valued above all else. They burned books, bombed museums, and subordinated those who were different or who dissented. For travelers like Hughes, fascism was what happened when local intolerances took on a grand, new scale. It was, he explained, "what the Ku Klux Klan will be when it combines with the Liberty League and starts using machine guns and airplanes instead of a few yards of rope." During the 1930s, Hughes had discovered its operatives skulking all over the world: in Germany, with its abolition of unions and "tyranny over Jews"; in Italy, with its shrill nationalism and "expedition of slaughter in Ethiopia"; in Japan, a "Fascist country," lorded over by secret police and bent on colonial ambitions and the "savage treatment of Koreans and Chinese"; and in Cuba and Haiti, with its "American-made tyrants" presiding over "semi-fascistic" puppet dictatorships. Expatriates' analysis of fascism may have been speculative, but it could also be quite powerful. In a rousing speech in Paris in 1937, Hughes warned that fascists aspired to remap the globe along devastating lines of "blood and color" and "poverty and power."[58]

These mounting concerns about right-wing insurgency went hand in hand with more difficult assessments of the liberal governments of the United States, France, and Great Britain—the "dilapidated and uncertain," the "trembling democracies," as Vincent Sheean branded them. If the crimes and rigorism of communism tempered most expatriates' affiliation with the radical left, the inability of the Allies to solve the period's most pressing problems made equally difficult a strong identification with liberalism. In the United States, under the electoral realignments of the late twenties and early thirties, liberalism increasingly denoted a certain kind of center-left politics, affiliated more and more with the Democratic Party's New Deal coalition and pitted against an increasingly conservative Republican opposition. For expatriates, however, arguing about these domestic distinctions amounted to so much hairsplitting. Progressives and conservatives were all liberals in the broader context of world affairs, brimming with communist- and fascist-style alternatives to republican forms of government. And, for critics like Sheean, they both suffered in essence from the same shortcomings; next to the more aggressive, decisive moves of radicals and reactionaries, they hesitated, equivocated, and made excuses. Although many supported the Roosevelt administration and other left-leaning governments such as Léon Blum's Popular Front coalition in France, expatriates detested the leading democracies' ineffectual diplomacy and appeasement of dictators, their un-willingness to stand up for the Ethiopians, Spanish Loyalists, Chinese, Czechs, and Jewish refugees. "One could not give one's undivided loyalty to our leaders, not by a long shot," Gellhorn regretted. "We were full of shams and expediencies," she charged, and two cheers for democracy, as E. M. Forster suggested, "was all one could manage." As independent agents in the field, expatriates saw themselves as far wiser than the diplomats and politicians. "Nothing seems urgent to these people with stiff white shirts and double chins; they will meet and discuss, and meet and discuss," Sheean charged, while "the bones of our dead are strewn from China to Spain on fields where Fascism has conquered." With Spain in mind and still months before the Munich Agreement, Hemingway echoed: "The fascist nations act while the democratic nations talk, vacillate, connive, and betray."[59]

Frustrations with liberalism ultimately cut deeper and mattered more than disillusionments with communism, because although expatriates often scorned liberals as lacking resolve, they were, at heart, liberals themselves who believed in what Dos Passos in 1934 called "old time Fourth of July democracy." Looking back, Gellhorn later described her young self as a "Liberal-reformer," and William Shirer conceded that he and his peers had been "little more than Jeffersonian liberals." Yet they hesitated to label themselves as such between the wars. Liberals, Dos Passos and his friends had judged, were "oldfashioned," annoyingly "educationist," and devoted to "dogoodism." They had, he said, merely "tea-table convictions." Expatriates preferred people with stronger tastes, bolder morals, sharper tongues. This explains why, well into the 1930s, Martha Gellhorn remained friends with the French fascist Pierre Drieu La Rochelle, whom she found "sexy as a satyr," and why, covering the Soviet invasion of Finland at the end of 1939, she chose the company of two Italian Fascist journalists, who had fought on the other side in Ethiopia and Spain, over that of English and American diplomats. At least the Fascists, like her, did not run to the woods each night under the threat of bombs.[60]

The democracies, critics like Gellhorn sensed, had compromised their moral high ground, not only by appeasing dictators but also by perpetuating their own class and racial inequalities, which undermined liberal promises of progress and fairness. For expatriates, nowhere was this more graphically displayed than in the far-flung reaches of the French and British empires. Expatriates reserved special contempt for English administrators in the colonies, who imposed all kinds of censorship and travel restrictions and who cultivated a particularly unpalatable form of racist condescension toward natives. On his second trip to witness the anticolonial movement in India in the early 1930s, for example, William Shirer seethed at the British officials who cautioned him not to socialize with the locals and who denied him passage to Afghanistan. Determined to subvert them, he befriended a sixteen-year-old Afghan prince, delighted to find someone to talk to in French about Paris, who helped him cross the treacherous Khyber Pass to

Kabul, the first correspondent in more than a year to break into the war-ravaged buffer region between the British and Soviet empires. Trips like this opened travelers' eyes to the "awful stupidity" of empire, as Vincent Sheean put it. In his bestselling *Personal History* (1935), Sheean similarly detailed the ways in which travel, from the Middle East to China, had led him to his staunch anticolonial politics. "That Imperialism was murderous and hypocritical was no discovery," he admitted, but until his forays into the Rif in the mid-twenties, he had not realized "the ghastly wrong-headedness" of the enterprise. Through tortured arguments and "guns big and little," imperial powers "sacrificed the time and the lives of its best men for the enrichment of its worst," he told his American readers. Colonial subjects were rewarded for their strength and industriousness with "economic enslavement," Sheean wrote, while troops brought to compel their labor were "fed on patriotic lies until they thought they were accomplishing something for their native country by murdering the inhabitants of another." In their foreign affairs, fascists may have taken what they wanted unapologetically while liberal governments concocted high-minded pretexts for their imperial plunders, but eyewitnesses in the colonies like Sheean thought the distinction a fine one. Fascist aggression in Europe, many would venture, was merely imperialism coming home to roost. If expatriates were searching for heroes in this world of "international brigandage" and disappointing statesmen, they found them in those who challenged this system head-on, from Abd el-Krim to Éamon de Valera and Gandhi—bold and original leaders with the "mark of greatness," observers like Sheean and Shirer decided, who accomplished more than tea-table talk.[61]

Black expatriates, of course, also condemned imperialism. Much more than their white compatriots, who often talked about colonialism in terms of economic exploitation and obstacles to self-determination, African American travelers recognized the special and pervasive role of racism in the structures of modern empire. Whereas white expatriates often sympathized with colonial populations as bystanders, people of color felt more personally their plight, sensing that in many ways they, too, lived under the weight of imperialist policies. One of their first travel lessons, after all, had been that American segregation, which they knew so intimately, had its corollaries all over the world. Nevertheless, African Americans were not inherently critical of the colonial powers. Josephine Baker, who portrayed herself as an embodiment of France's *mission civilisatrice*, delighted in the 1931 Colonial Exposition in Paris and publicly supported Mussolini's invasion of Ethiopia, since he promised to stamp out its slave trade. Back in the United States, African Americans often overlooked French colonial practices, preferring to focus on the metropole's relative freedoms—especially after 1923, when African American newspapers gave favorable coverage to French officials who had forcefully denounced the racist behavior of American tourists.[62]

Descents into the colonies, however, disabused others of any sympathies for French imperialists. Claude McKay, spending time among colonial peoples in Marseilles and North Africa, saw the French as "the cleverest propagandists in the world," who compared themselves favorably with discriminatory Americans as a calculated bid to project themselves as liberal benefactors rather than exploiters. Cordial treatment in Paris, he argued, often blinded black intellectuals to the forced labor conscription and pauperization of tribes in Senegal, policies no less "barbarous" than the infamous abuses in the Belgian Congo. For Langston Hughes, too, scathing attacks on imperialism sat at the center of his deepening antifascist and antiracist politics. His trips to Africa, France, the Caribbean, and beyond formed the basis for a collection of astute essays and poems in the early thirties, which evoked the powerful forces sustaining the formal and informal empires of the world: the dehumanizing racism, the mocking promises of Christian salvation, the economic scheming, the pretenses to more civilized comportment. If in the United States the politics of the left seemed to revolve unendingly and unprofitably around the role of communists and communism, for those who developed their political stances in international contexts questions of fascism and empire could be even more defining.[63]

Expatriates' desire to find a middle ground that respected their ambivalence about communism, their abhorrence for fascism, and their frustrations with liberal democracy—these intellectual struggles helped many to avoid rigid dogma, but also suspended their political views uneasily between liberal and radical impulses. Sometimes slow to recognize the severity of the human catastrophes before them, they were more likely taken in at times by the big ideological clashes of the day, sensing that the new forces on the left and right had proven much more compelling than the long-established democracies, compromised by their capitalist and imperialist agendas. At odds with their professions of pacifism, they found themselves uncontrollably drawn to the spectacle of war and political extremism. Scouring the globe for evidence, searching for answers in their own creative work, expatriates tried to chart a course through these difficult principles, alliances, and moral quandaries. Theirs was a politics not programmatic or easily encapsulated by party affiliations and party lines, but one undergirded by adventure and personal agency.

In many ways, this expatriate politics would both culminate and falter in Spain. Between the wars, American writers and artists adored this country to the south of France and the values of anarchistic individualism and separatist autonomy they thought it embodied. Spared the devastation of World War I, it was a region, frequent visitors like Hemingway and Elliot Paul imagined, passed over by modern industrialism and its false promises of progress—a place that was, if not timeless, still grounded in organic, localized traditions, or what Dos Passos called the unchanging "foundations of life."[64] After civil war broke out in July 1936, Spain dramatized even more the world as expatriates had come to see it: a contest between an authoritarian right propped up by fascist aid and a diverse Popular Front left abandoned by the liberal democracies but supported, though at great cost, by the communists. For Loyalist sympathizers, Spain had become an inspiring terrain where volunteers—those Hemingway called the "clear thinkers"—had lighted out in defiance of their own governments to stand up against the forces of intolerance. Italians striving to weaken Mussolini's grip on their country; Jews who battled on behalf of Hitler's victims; the "wide-awake Negroes," as Langston Hughes dubbed them, coming from across the Atlantic world to wage their surrogate war against the invaders in Ethiopia—all saw Spain as the front lines of a looming global crisis. Civilization was "not divisible into water-tight compartments," Martha Gellhorn reminded a sympathetic Eleanor Roosevelt. Spain, she repeated the popular refrain, sacrificed itself "fighting our battle."[65]

Armed with this thinking, expatriates converged on the region. Traversing the mountainous border in cars or on foot, they hopped in and out of the embattled country as roving reporters, taking periodic breaks from the carnage back in Paris. First and foremost, they wanted to get to Madrid. Surrounded on three sides by Franco's forces since the early days of insurrection, the rubble-strewn holdout stood for the hope that the Republic might still prevail, while also symbolizing the terror of modern urban warfare. After an extended stopover in Paris in 1937, Langston Hughes spent six months in Spain, crossing paths with Hemingway, Gellhorn, Cowley, Sheean, Paul, and other expatriates. In Madrid, he chronicled for the *Afro-American* the shape of life under food shortages and intensive shelling, drowning out the bombs with music from swing records he had improbably carted with him. That fall, Hemingway, Dos Passos, Herbst, and Gellhorn were all staying nearby at the famous Hotel Florida, braving the mortar attacks to inspect the picked-over inventories of the city's shops and the dangling contents of its façadeless apartment buildings. Amid the grisly civilian casualties, against the constant crackle of gunfire, notions about home fronts and war fronts ceased to make sense. The capital's streetcars ran all the way to the barricades. War, Hughes marveled upon seeing this, was "only a few blocks away." The unsettling existentialism that governed daily life under these conditions—the chilling usualness of activity going on as in a nightmare—this would be one of the enduring themes of expatriate war reporting. Writers sketched for their readers back home the charwomen who each morning scrubbed blood off the floors and the plasterers who repaired holes in the walls, the unflappable office workers who kept watering the plants. World War I had cured most expatriates of their desire to fight in the trenches among the ranks, but Spain rekindled the dreadful excitement of being at the center of events. Smuggling a carload of supplies across the Pyrenees with Hemingway in 1938, Vincent Sheean admitted that one did not have to be a fascist or glorify war to recognize that diving into danger brought "a definite exhilaration."[66]

Wanting to capture the war's urgency and significance, in Spain expatriates perfected their immensely successful style of political travel writing. Aiming for something more than "blood-and-thunder stories," as Herbst explained, they brought poetic and novelistic sensibilities to the task of capturing complex situations from the ground up, evoking a grim aesthetic to bring to life a set of soon-to-be-stock scenarios: the small but telling atrocity, the last stands of stalwart underdogs, the futile bids for normalcy. For Martha Gellhorn, who went to Spain "with the boys" four times, the war marked the start of her celebrated career as a war reporter. The conflict also solidified Hemingway's standing as a leading foreign correspondent. At the height of his engagement with social democracy and antifascism, Hemingway found in Spain material for perhaps his greatest and most popular novel, *For Whom the Bell Tolls* (1940), and the setting for his affair with Gellhorn, shortly to become his third wife.[67]

For the novelist Elliot Paul, the war was also a turning point, inspiring his engrossing bestseller, *The Life and Death of a Spanish Town* (1937). Far more compelling than Paul's mystery capers set in Montparnasse, this work offered a case study in how political polarization tore communities apart. Recounting what was to be a routine vacation to his favorite island, Ibiza, Paul arrived from Paris in the placid village of Santa Eulalia only days before civil war broke out on the mainland. As the mail and supply boats stopped coming and the island descended into isolation, an all-too-common chain of events pushed his village toward bloodshed: a local coup in support of Franco emboldening fascist youths, who paraded down the roads, tripping over their guns and playing with politics and authority like children playing with fire; communists huddling secretly in consultation; Catholic reactionaries stockpiling weapons in ancient hillside tunnels; small injustices mobilizing those who had vowed to stay out of it; tip-offs and arrests; busybody informants casually playing with neighbors' lives; rumors of the killing of a priest; and murderous reprisals. Paul and his family remained longer than the island's other foreigners but at last made a hasty and risky departure on a passing German destroyer only a day ahead of invading Italian forces, who would round up and slaughter some four hundred of the island's remaining Republicans. A touching if at times maudlin homage to lost friends, his book aimed most of all to sway Americans to the *Causa*. Paul portrayed the villagers, whose complicated dialect he had learned, as people who shared reassuringly familiar values. The island's handful of "reds," he claimed disingenuously, had scarcely heard of Moscow or Marx. Its Republicans, he insisted, only sought, like Americans, freedom of thought and action, separation of church and state, and the "abolition of special privilege." In bids to bring to life unfolding tragedies like this one, expatriates had to battle against a range of censorship issues abroad, against conservative publishers and press syndicates insisting on superficial "hijinks," and against the complacency or disparagement of some Americans back home, who, like one reader of the *Saturday Evening Post*, dismissed them as "those journalists of discontent who make a living scratching at the dunghills of the world."[68] But through creative, interpretive reporting for leading magazines and newspapers and bestselling books like Paul's, they had good reason to believe they could move minds and turn the tides of war.

Nevertheless, the heroic posturing and high hopes did not outlast the Spanish Civil War's harsh and murky realities. Even aside from its particularly gruesome violence, the conflict did not live up to the political or personal romance that some, like Hemingway, made it out to be. Too many had acted against their interests or stated principles. How could Léon Blum's Popular Front government, Gellhorn and Sheean raged, let a fellow republic die its slow and bloody death? How could North Africans, Langston Hughes wondered, fight on behalf of the rebels, their colonial oppressors? Even more discouraging were the on-the-ground disputes tearing apart the Loyalist side. If, from afar, Spain seemed to crystallize interwar politics in their simplest, clearest terms, up close the nation's unraveling showed just how convoluted the factions and their motives really were. Liberals and communists accused the anarchists of being too undisciplined, vulnerable, even, to becoming dupes of Franco's side. Anarchists and socialists in turn feared that Communist operatives were beholden to Moscow's complicated geopolitical objectives, stymieing the genuine groundswell of revolutionary sentiment that made the Republican effort possible and worth fighting for. Far too often, the Loyalists turned on each other, waging a civil war within a civil war. Gellhorn and others wanted not to see this treachery on the Republican side, a dilemma that would recur elsewhere. Trying to preserve what they felt to be the war's higher truths, they censored from their reports the behind-the-scenes torture and executions, the outrages George Orwell was quietly documenting in Barcelona.[69]

John Dos Passos would be deeply disturbed by these dynamics, however. Since 1916, he had traveled outside the United States every year, taking stock of the era's various new regimes and rebel forces, always aligning his sympathies with local leftists. He picketed and went to jail for Sacco and Vanzetti in Boston, fraternized with agrarian radicals in postrevolutionary Mexico, and found Leningrad "breathlessly exciting" even on the eve of Stalin's terror. Yet Dos Passos had been suspicious of Communists' handling of the miners' strike in the "war zone" of Harlan County, Kentucky, in 1931, and even more so of their disruption of socialist events in New York in 1934.[70] Now, returning to Spain in spring 1937—his eighth extended stay in the country—this author of the recently completed *U.S.A.* trilogy encountered a landscape given over to "confusion and crosspurposes and illusions." No longer would he give Communists the benefit of the doubt. "Hogtied" by the Kremlin's agendas, the party's duplicitous scheming in Spain seemed no less sinister than the Nationalists' power grab. Particularly devastated by the Communist execution of his friend, the scholar José Robles, Dos Passos judged the costs of "partisan fanaticism" too great and began whittling away his leftist affinities, just as E. E. Cummings had. Viewing the food-strapped towns, the sandbagged roads, the foreigners with dynamite in their pockets, Dos Passos, like Orwell, who he met in Barcelona, thought the Republican movement undone by the "ruthless forces of world politics too big for it." Underneath the "hurray-for-our-side aspects," he wrote with Robles in mind, lay the "bloody tangle of ruined lives."[71]

Despite the heartbreaks of Spain, there would be still other places for political engagement. The Spanish Civil War, if anything, inaugurated the worldwide struggle that would send expatriates to even farther reaches of the globe. Many spent more and more time in Central Europe after the Anschluss in 1938, watching as persecution descended on the Jewish population of Vienna, witnessing sorrows in the streets of Prague as loudspeakers announced Hitler's determination to annex Czechoslovakia, and trying to stir Americans back home with tales of the desperate gestures, the orphans, the suicides. These events, despondent observers such as Sheean insisted in their final dispatches from the region, were the fascist fruits of that long rise of intolerance and brutality that had been brewing since the early years of Mussolini's reign. Shaken by her trip into the abyss of Nazi-controlled territories in mid-1938, Janet Flanner dropped her pretense of cool in her subsequent reports. Soon she would be arguing forthrightly that "we must be ready with the deep feeling and the real conviction that democracy is worth dying for, as our ancestors did." William Shirer, who lingered longer than most, burned some of his notes and dared not write other things down, but in 1940 he smuggled out what evidence he could of the pogroms and monstrosity for his landmark *Berlin Diary*.[72]

Early the following year, when continental Europe had become an Axis stronghold and Britain battled under siege, Ernest Hemingway and Martha Gellhorn set off for the South China Sea. In Hong Kong, while Gellhorn investigated opium dens and trinket sweatshops, Hemingway dove into its local customs and gathered intelligence from contacts of shadowy nationality and purpose on the region's economic and military situation, information he would pass along to U.S. government officials. On the mainland, they met with Chiang Kai-shek and his wife and, through a series of underground channels, the Communist organizer Zhou Enlai, drawn to the party during his own Paris residence in the early twenties. But China tested both travelers' resolve to play the role of political globetrotters. Trailing down cholera-infested rivers to take stock of the Canton front, sleeping on wooden boards in rooms given over to bedbugs as they pressed on toward Nationalist head-quarters, the two authors regretted their sojourn in this "awful" place, as Gellhorn groaned, "where the poor literally never straighten their backs, and seem to be born, live and die in mud." At the outset of their expedition, the battle in the East had seemed the same as in Europe—a story about little people fighting for democracy against big-time aggressors, one that begged to be told. Yet it was even more like Spain than the two realized when they set off. More concerned about domestic challenges to his own power than the threat of Japan, Chiang was siphoning off funds and hardware to fight the Communists, and they in turn through boasting and deception were seeking to manipulate outside aid. Hemingway and Gellhorn admitted in private that China, more dictatorship and colonial quarry than democracy, was plagued by internal intrigues and oppressions. Yet bound by the region's censorship and their own allegiance to the war against the Axis, both quashed these insights in their public writings. To a journalist friend, Gellhorn pleaded: "If you can just tell me what stands firm and is absolutely decent and good, so that I can trust in it, and believe that the future will not be as filthy as the past and the present, I will be very grateful."[73] But events would get no better. In a few short years, Gellhorn would be among the first journalists to view the camp at Dachau.

Trips like this stung so much because travelers like Gellhorn and Heming-way had come to see themselves not just as the arbiters of American art and the creators of American idioms but also as knowing interpreters of the hot

Martha Gellhorn and Ernest Hemingway confer with Chinese officers in Chongqing during their survey of the Sino-Japanese War in early 1941. Ernest Hemingway Collection, John F. Kennedy Presidential Library and Museum, Boston.

spots, the disaster zones, of an impending world at war. Tacking back and forth between American and distant shores, expatriates popularized a new ideal of the American abroad: worldly and steeled, neither a parochial Babbitt or bumpkin on tour, nor a Legionnaire blustering through foreign capitals, but rather an intrepid observer able to weave through the complicated and cosmopolitan milieus of Europe or North Africa or Asia. They promoted intellectual but hard-hitting speech and a devil-may-care attitude about danger and daily hardship. To stomach all the indescribable atrocities, there was the world-weary stoicism of a Hemingway character or the wisecracks of Martha Gellhorn. To survive the political insanity, there was the playful defiance of Cummings, the introspection of Dos Passos, or the genuine sympathy for common people of Hughes. Expatriates like these purported to be pacifist yet engagé, close to the action but above the fray, looking for answers in a lawless and corrupting world. They posed as reluctant heroes, and in this way expatriates' romance with international engagement was not so different from those stories about American innocence abroad that had been told by others in interwar Paris.

Yet by forging new social and artistic paths abroad, by searching out positions not bound by allegiances to either communism or the New Deal, expatriates enriched the political culture of the American left in distinctive ways. For all their self-righteousness, blind spots, and occasional naiveté, these travelers who had set out for Paris in their youth became important liaisons between their audiences back home and the wider world, challenging Americans to consider roles in foreign affairs that transcended patriotic categories and interests. Their textured travel dispatches wove together diplomacy lessons, political commentary, and personal interest, mixing the art of novel writing and poetry with the intensity of history, all to convince Americans that they were part of the world and not separate, that people suffering and enduring elsewhere were like Americans rather than innately other, that their lands were not timeless but now, not fatalistically doomed but savable. Americans such as these plunged into important questions about rights and responsibilities on the world stage long before the Atlantic Charter or the bombing of Pearl Harbor.[74] For them, World War II would not denote a new, internationalist departure but the culmination of much longer histories of adventure, discovery, and slowly dawning commitments, stretching back to childhoods spent in books, travels to the fronts of the Great War, and those first exciting evenings spent in heated debate about art and politics on the terraces of the Left Bank.

# Epilogue
*The Beginning of American Innocence*

ON FEBRUARY 6, 1934, THE American journalist William Shirer—no longer an awestruck Iowa boy but a savvy, globetrotting political reporter—witnessed from a Hôtel Crillon balcony the violence that almost toppled the Third Republic. Back in Paris after his travels through Central Asia and a temporary residence in Spain, Shirer pressed against the railing overlooking the place de la Concorde to watch as thousands of demonstrators amassed below. From the embankments of the Tuileries, mobs showered the police with stones, garden chairs, and iron grilles. Nervous mounted guards barricaded the bridge to the Chamber of Deputies, weathering civilian attacks and periodically charging the crowd. From the square, rioters threw marbles and firecrackers at the hooves of policemen's horses and slashed at their legs with razors. As the animals collapsed, they mauled their riders.

Order in the capital had unraveled following the scandal surrounding Serge Alexandre Stavisky, a denizen of the fast Parisian world of gigolos and cocaine dealers whose shady dealings, ironically, would end Jean Chiappe's tenure as the capital's police prefect and chief moral crusader. Stavisky, Jewish and foreign-born, had evaded prosecution for fraud on numerous occasions, presumably with help from his government and police connections. When, in January 1934, he was found dead, rumors that it had been staged as a suicide to cover up official involvement caused an explosion of public outrage. The Stavisky affair fueled already smoldering resentments in the capital. The Great Depression had come late to France, but its effects, combined with incendiary press commentary, chronic government instability, and revelations about widespread corruption, had conspired to create a situation of almost nightly unrest on the streets of Paris. By the end of the month, demonstrations in the city center, especially by those on the right, had become extremely volatile. "I have not seen *cette ardeur* since the Sacco and Vanzetti demonstrations in 1927," admitted the director of the Municipal Police.[1]

In order to restore public confidence, Edouard Daladier's new cabinet removed Chiappe from his post as prefect at the start of February. His enemies rejoiced. "Finally Paris delivered from its coup d'état prefect," a headline for *Le Populaire* exclaimed. Chiappe's supporters, by contrast, were scandalized. The government had sacrificed "the leader of the army of order to the elements of disorder," claimed almost half of the capital's municipal councilors. Then on February 6, Chiappe's supporters, fascists, and other malcontents attempted to storm the Chamber of Deputies in protest of its ineffectual liberalism. Under street lamps that had been shot out, and by the light of a bus on fire next to the Obelisk of Luxor, fifteen people would die and fifteen hundred would be wounded as Shirer and others looked on from their balconies.[2]

That evening Dr. Charles Bove of the American Hospital had just left the bedside of Mrs. William Randolph Hearst in the Hôtel Crillon when the first battery of shots sprayed the hotel's façade and the adjacent premises of the new American embassy. He emerged onto the rue Royale amid rioters belting out the Marseillaise and terrified people banging on the doors of shops and apartments, begging to be let in. Bove made his way to the Café Weber, where stretcher-bearing waiters transported the wounded and managers passed out brandy shots. In the elegant dining room of that Paris institution, the doctor made bandages out of restaurant linens and performed emergency procedures atop dinner tables. From his balcony far above the chaos, William Shirer hadn't heard the initial gunfire that sent Bove in the direction of the Café Weber. As he stood there watching tensions mount, a woman to his left silently slumped to the floor. "When we bent over her," Shirer related, "blood was flowing from her face from a bullet hole in the center of her forehead. She was dead."[3]

The proximity of Bove and Shirer to these bloody events offers a graphic reminder that the politics of Paris had an immediacy and relevance to many Americans that have often been elided in subsequent accounts of the interwar capital. Yet the moment William Shirer found himself standing over the corpse of a Hôtel Crillon chambermaid also serves as a fitting omen for the demise of the Paris of Americans that had flourished for more than a decade. The Hôtel Crillon itself provided an appropriate site for the end of that era. Once a popular spot for Americans—first with AEF personnel, who came for home cooking in the army's basement kitchen, and then with journalists and dignitaries—the building now stood scarred by the bullet holes of civil unrest, a testament to the dangers posed even to bystanders in a capital that had changed rapidly for the worse. Lilian Mowrer, an American journalist's wife, described the new tenor of the streets around the Crillon after the riots. Around midnight, she had made her way past crackling street bonfires to the shuttered entrance of her nearby hotel, flanked by armed infantrymen in steel helmets. For several nights, she relayed, the boulevards of the inner Right Bank were not alive with leisurely crowds, but, dark and deserted, rang out with the "sound of splintering glass and scampering feet." In the wake of the shootings, another visitor reported that thoughts of revolution preoccupied people everywhere in the city, recording ominously that young men of both political extremes were busy "buying cheap revolvers."[4]

By the mid-thirties, Americans like Shirer would still be caught in the crossfire of Parisian conflicts, but no longer would they play such an important role in the capital's social struggles. More pressing preoccupations, ranging from antifascism to antisemitism and made urgent by the rise of the Nazis, had begun to eclipse Parisians' concerns about modern American culture and power, which were so intensely debated between the close of World War I and the early 1930s. By the unrest of winter 1934, the trajectory of Parisian politics had shifted eastward toward "the German problem," and there would be a diminishing place for Americans amid the strident nationalisms to come—even though the presence of Americans had helped to define those nationalisms. A resident of Montparnasse remarked on the escalation and sea change of public passions after February 6: "Everyone talked politics," she stressed, "The wildest kind of politics." Dr. Bove and many of his successful compatriots regarded the situation as "ugly" and began to contemplate returning to the United States.[5]

The world of the mid-thirties was a different place, and not just in Paris. Both Adolph Hitler and Franklin Delano Roosevelt had risen to power. Japan and Germany had withdrawn from the League of Nations. At mid-decade, the Stalinist purges began in Soviet Russia, and Mussolini's Fascists invaded Ethiopia. Parisians, like others, became transfixed by the growing brazenness of these factions in search of national strength and empire. To make sense of it all, they began to recite, as Elliot Paul put it, "a modern Mother Goose in which the words 'communism' and 'fascism' fitted into all the rhymes."[6] Even more than the stock market crash of 1929—the ending usually chosen for stories about Americans in Paris—these international realignments between 1933 and 1935 and the reorientation of Parisian affairs around them marked a turning point when Americans began to feel like outsiders in a city where they had once seemed like central players.

The arrival of economic depression in France and the demise of the gold standard exacerbated the difficulties travelers faced abroad and decimated the American community in Paris. By mid-1933, the capital's resident American population had plummeted to 13,500; the following year less than 100,000 Americans would arrive during the tourist season. American churches, offices, and schools shuttered their windows. Their staff and clientele filled boat trains headed out of the capital. "Gone were the harassed patrons of cheap tours" milling around the Opera area, the visitor Philip Gibbs wrote. Revealingly, business dragged, too, for the sellers of "unpleasant postcards." By 1934, the Montmartre jazz scene appeared to have all but vanished as African Americans, hit by quotas against foreign musicians, drifted elsewhere looking for work. Across the river at the Dôme, Gibbs discovered, the bohemians had also been "swept away, poor wretches, by the brutal force of an economic crisis."[7] Once-conspicuous Americans—the capital's former "principal characters," according to one writer in the *Saturday Evening Post*—had grown conspicuously absent from the Paris landscape of the mid-thirties. The French seemed suddenly "everywhere," and, if only for a short while, "Paris ha[d] been given back to its original owners."[8]

During the late 1930s, some Americans stayed on, of course, most notably expatriates like Shirer who periodically returned in the course of their travels, but the Paris moment headed for certain conclusion when Nazis marched into the city in June 1940. The writing room at the Ritz, which Americans had patronized in such numbers, was converted into a checkroom for pistols, and the entire Hôtel Crillon was transformed into a headquarters for German officers. Publishers could no longer distribute books by Jewish, Communist, or American authors. Other items were restricted amid grave shortages. Milk was now only sold for pregnant women, infants, and the elderly. Housewives began planting *potagers* in the city's public gardens and renting babies to stand in line for rations. To Janet Flanner, who left just ahead of the invasion, reports of the occupation revealed a chillingly clinical takeover. German accounting for the city's population fastened each individual's fate to a piece of paper "the way an entomologist pins each specimen insect, past struggling, to his laboratory board." Devastating things were happening with disquieting ease. "In the old days," Flanner surmised, soldiers had "looted with disorderly enthusiasm—raping, robbing, staggering down roads with booty and with blood on their hands." Now, she discovered, "Nazis ring the French front-door bell while an Army truck waits in the street, and soldiers do the job of fanatical moving men." The fall of Paris had been "pure T. S. Eliot," Vincent Sheean echoed, a world that expired "not with a bang but a whimper."[9]

In the wake of the occupation, many Americans aborted plans to return to the capital, and those already in Paris began looking for ways out. Sheean, who kept a room at the Crillon, could not get back in time to secure his belongings. They had been pilfered, he assumed, by German officers.[10] Robert McAlmon, who had spent the 1930s roaming across Europe, the United States, and Mexico, was back in the city when the Nazis arrived. Suffering from tuberculosis under the severe food and fuel shortages, he finally secured passage out via Lisbon with the help of family connections. All of his books and papers, too, were lost. A few others stayed. A committed activist and member of the League against Racism and Anti-Semitism, Josephine Baker rallied French troops with concerts following the declaration of war and volunteered to help refugees. After France fell, she joined the Resistance, slinking across North Africa and Spain as a messenger, work that would earn her several formal commendations. Under the occupation, Sylvia Beach struggled at first to keep her library afloat for those members who remained in the city, but following a German officer's threats to confiscate her books, she closed up shop. After the United States entered the war, Beach would be hustled away to the internment camp at Vittel, where she spent six desperate months scrounging for supplies and trying to locate disappeared friends. She never reopened Shakespeare and Company.[11]

With Paris gone, expatriates' mental map of the world, as they leap-frogged from London to Moscow, Shanghai to Los Angeles, Kentucky mining country to New York City, lost a vital center. Not even the city's liberation would change that for this aging group of artists and writers, shocked at the utter brutalities of World War II. Hemingway, who spent the first years of American engagement gathering intelligence on Axis spies around his home in Cuba and prowling for Nazi submarines on his fishing boat, returned to Europe for *Collier's* in 1944. Heading toward Paris with a ragtag outfit of resisters and GIs that August, he helped to reclaim the Ritz as the Nazis retreated from the capital. But the inveterate war writer was not well. Tormented by the aftereffects of a concussion, his rash acts in the field would lead to a military investigation; those in private would seal the fate of his marriage to Martha Gellhorn. Misery greeted Janet Flanner, too, as she returned to the capital shortly thereafter. With a stash of wool underwear and a hot plate, Flanner holed up in the Hôtel Scribe with Hemingway and other foreign correspondents, taking trips out into the nightmarish corners of the slowly pacified continent. Touring liberated camps with the dead still piled high, passing through Warsaw and other gutted sites of urban warfare, Flanner felt disgusted and confused. "Europe has been the victim of cannibalism," she lamented. "The half-consumed corpses of ideologies and of the civilians who believed in them have rotted the soil of Europe." She gasped at how the inhabitants of the region's great cities had been "reduced to the primitive problems of survival, of finding something to eat . . . of hiding, like savages with ration cards."[12] For these expatriates, liberation would be an ending as well as a beginning.

After World War II, new stories about Americans in Paris would arise in place of the old, and the tropes established at that time are the ones that have endured to this day. Beginning with MGM's *An American in Paris* (1951), Hollywood paid tribute to the French capital in a series of lavish musicals and other successful movies that painted the city in spectacular wide-screen Technicolor. These films showcased a Paris of timeless appeal and stock clichés: boulevard cafés, neighborhood bistros, and—now the most important icon of the city for Americans—the Eiffel Tower. In many of these works, elaborate references to impressionist and postimpressionist masterpieces by Manet, Degas, or Toulouse-Lautrec became crowd-pleasing vehicles for celebrating the capital in purely aesthetic terms.[13] Between the wars, impressionist painting had seemed passé. Now it enjoyed renewed appreciation for its visual sumptuousness. It had the virtue of not being cubism, social realism, or those other avant-garde movements that smacked of the factious interwar political scene. On this stage set, the Americans in Paris premise was remade as an overseas romp. The portrait painted by films like *An American in Paris* offered up, in the words of one French reviewer, "a crazy salad of frenzied American gaiety" set against a romanticized urban backdrop. This image of Paris, he predicted, would be "fixed for generations to come of an old-fashioned and delightful toy that the American tourist can play with for a while longer, as long as it doesn't break."[14] Gone was a sense of the city's political edge. Awash in white faces, it gave little hint of the city's anticolonial rebels or even the new generation of African American intellectuals gathering there to combat racism with their writing. Nor were there any maniacal communists or marching fascists, only petty con men and surly waiters who caused minor inconveniences. Any remaining trouble derived from the romantic dilemmas of Fred Astaire in *Funny Face* (1957), or, in a television version, the comically botched communications of Lucille Ball on holiday.

Soon, a cleaned-up vision of 1920s Paris found its cachet in print, too, as former expatriates, now growing old, published their memoirs. In nostalgic autobiographies such as Sylvia Beach's *Shakespeare and Company* (1959) and Kay Boyle's revised and supplemented reissue of Robert McAlmon's *Being Geniuses Together* (1968), former Paris residents reflected back on the twenties in the French capital as a golden age of creativity. Thick with homages to James Joyce, details about publishing concerns, or anecdotes about drunken escapades, such accounts largely ignored the broader political dimensions to Americans' stays in the capital. Downplaying the great social conflicts of the day, they dwelled instead on petty gossip and rivalries between former friends. Connections between art and politics were recast at greater distance. "It was an easy, adventurous age, good to be young in," Malcolm Cowley wrote in a new, depoliticized epilogue for the 1951 edition of *Exile's Return*. Replacing the tone of urgency and partisanship which had infused his original conclusion, Cowley insisted that American writers went abroad during the 1920s "in search of treasure and then came back like grown children to dig for it at home." If Cowley thought of Paris in terms of buried riches, Ernest Hemingway recreated it as a "moveable feast." Looking to settle old scores and to memorialize his apprenticeship years shortly before his death, Hemingway stripped the city of its shrill newspaper headlines, its refugees, its rampaging policemen. It became instead a deeply personalized space. Regretting the failure of his first marriage during that time, he wrote that "All things truly wicked start from an innocence." With its charming cold-water apartments and hospitable cafés, Paris had become synonymous with that innocence for Hemingway, before life grew complicated, "in the early days," he wrote, "when we were very poor and very happy."[15]

This sanitized version of Americans' place in the capital appealed at mid-century, because it resonated so well with the intellectual and social preoccupations of the age. After the horrors of World War II, the steadfast ideological commitments of the recent past now seemed to have been but misguided idealism, leading ultimately to totalitarian nightmares. Under the cloud of McCarthyism, many quietly buried the past associations of their more adventurous days of youth. Politics now was not to be an uncompromising clash of wills and morals but something less all-encompassing, a practice of give-and-take over clearly definable issues undertaken on common ground. Art was to occupy its own space for its own sake, as critics and others concentrated on symbols, language, and experimentation with form, just as the modernists of the 1920s had. The study of history, too, was to shy away from extreme positions, to chart incremental progress and shared traditions, and to capture the pitfalls of noncentrist belief. A view of interwar Paris as a site of charmed artistic and literary innovation, disconnected from any weighty political terrain, correlated well with these intellectual sensibilities after World War II. The artistic endeavors of expatriates no longer seemed so esoteric. Novels by Ernest Hemingway, F. Scott Fitzgerald, Henry Miller, and other Paris veterans were reissued to growing popularity and critical acclaim.[16]

This selective portrayal of Paris flew in the face of actual Franco-American relations at the time. Animosity toward Americans and their foreign policies peaked again during the decades following the institution of aid under the Marshall Plan in 1948 and the signing of the NATO pact in 1949. Communist militants, established intellectuals, and right-wing statesmen alike chafed under American leadership of postwar reconstruction in Western Europe. Diplomatic tensions arose over crises in Indochina, Algeria, and Egypt. French journalists and their readers feared American control of the bomb and the materialization of the Cold War on their own soil in the form of American troops, CIA operatives, and rapacious capitalists intent, some said, on the *coca-colonisation* of France. Paris erupted with anti-American movements. In May 1952, riots left one dead and some two hundred wounded when protesters came out against the arrival of the American general and NATO commander Matthew Ridgway, regarded by leftists as a war criminal for his actions in Korea. While some Paris moviegoers delighted as Gene Kelly traipsed around his faux fountain at the Colisée theater, other residents mobilized in opposition to the conviction of the Rosenbergs. After their executions in June 1953, activists massed in front of the American embassy. Some eight hundred arrests and one shooting followed. Passions against Americans still ran high during the 1960s, when Charles de Gaulle provoked his allies from the presidential palace and Vietnam War protesters attacked the American Express office that had been more effectively guarded during the Sacco-Vanzetti campaign years before. Next to these gritty realities, the world conjured up by Audrey Hepburn ingénues and can-can numbers unfolded on screen like a parallel universe. Such depictions of American experiences abroad in no way helped viewers come to terms with the rising tide of popular anti-Americanism bubbling up from the streets of Paris, Beijing, or Caracas, as crowds around the world grasped for ways to understand and critique American power.[17]

This glamorized image of Paris stood at odds not only with contemporary evidence but also with history. More than the site of café terraces and haute couture, Paris served as a junction for international exchanges, a stage for capricious street politics and bitter disputes of all kinds. Especially by the 1920s, it had become the locale for a particularly volatile and diverse cosmopolitanism. Arrivals to the city then looked out on a strikingly new urban landscape—an electric terrain with signs and automobiles, foreign faces and languages, one marked by widening perimeters of permitted public behaviors, but one, at the same time, imposed upon by new levels of surveillance and control. Although many of these changes traced their roots back to the turn of the century, Paris was not the same place it had been during the

Belle Epoque. A devastating war had come and gone. The advent of communism and fascism, compelling alternatives to democracy and capitalism, had renewed battles over the city's spaces and representation, infusing older class politics with new forms of cultural politics. And recent arrivals from the colonies, the United States, and many other places had become key participants in public life.

Whether they came for simple amusement or for more serious pursuits, Americans had found this bustling metropolis a place of great consequence. In Paris, Americans gained a clearer sense of themselves as Americans even as they were forced to confront some of the implications of their growing contacts abroad. In the early twentieth century, American people, things, and ideas—once so tightly tethered to transatlantic traditions and assumptions—came to be more sharply distinguished from European ones. Out from under the shadow of Europe, Americans began to display more confidence, even bravado. At the same time, people both inside and outside the United States developed an increasingly coherent if still multifaceted picture of what modern American culture looked like, or what it stood for: the fast-paced tempo, jazzy sounds, and bright neon colors of its cities and the peppy derring-do attitude its citizens celebrated, as well as the more serious political and economic aspirations that came along with these features. In this context, new ideals of the American abroad flourished, from the enterprising daredevil Charles Lindbergh or the commanding, backslapping Legionnaire to the sensational and brave Josephine Baker or the fast-quipping, jaded Ernest Hemingway character—social types each in their own way resolutely American but at home in foreign lands. Many travelers learned while abroad to cast themselves in roles that emphasized their own integrity in a treacherous and tumultuous world. They believed themselves innocents abroad—tried and tested by others' sexual and political excesses but ultimately escaping unscathed, a worldview immensely serviceable for masking Americans' growing interests overseas. The Americans in Paris story played a crucial part in promoting these ideals, since for a time that city had been a primary gateway to destinations overseas.

Defining the nature and consequences of Americans' increasing involvements abroad, however, would not be left up to Americans alone. Just what Americanness entailed became clearer as it was defined in conflicts over its traces in the French capital. Parisian critics, politicians, and protesters keenly debated the extent of the American impact on their city, and they employed anti-American slogans as rallying cries to mobilize others and claim their place in urban life. Such oppositional sentiments proved incredibly adaptable across the political spectrum. These campaigns and struggles may have foreshadowed the more widespread concerns about Americanization and the fitful bursts of anti-Americanism that would help to define popular European politics in the second half of the twentieth century, but even more importantly, they revealed the extent to which "America" had become a potent international symbol during the interwar period itself. Beyond the trails forged by capitalist missionaries searching for new markets, outside the movie theaters beaming forth Hollywood dreams in the dark, a broader, more subtle array of encounters in Paris revealed how national identifications were formed and contested.

Rethinking the history of Americans in Paris opens up a window onto how, in the twentieth century, Americans carved out for themselves new roles in the world, both formal and informal. As they extended their political reach and held up their cultural models for emulation abroad, Americans struggled more and more with the desire to see themselves as the architects of a different kind of empire than the collapsing colonialisms of Europe, and at the same time, they increasingly sought to distinguish their world order from a Soviet empire in the making. The stories Americans had been telling themselves since the 1920s about their triumphs abroad, their admirable pep and ingenuity, and their offerings of hope for a troubled world had congealed by midcentury into a powerful national mythology about enlightened empire builders, sensible idealists, and reluctant heroes. This theme of American innocence in the world, emphasizing noble intensions, seemed ever more resonant as citizens of the United States worked to justify their expanding activities overseas. It helped to drown out dissenting interpretations of American motives by others and to paper over the tensions that often arose between Americans' aspirations to promote democracy and individual rights beyond their own borders and their equally steadfast but often conflicting quests for profit. Only the perspectives of others can help tease out the omissions and inconsistencies.

Myths about Gay Paree matter because they belong to this larger set of ideas about American innocence in the world. Such reimaginings of Paris may have seemed on the surface politically benign, but they have served to condition Americans to their growing relationships overseas, obscuring the ambiguity and conflict that often accompany such worldly participation. Myths about Paris have presented the history of Americans abroad as a one-way adventure, when really the making of American culture and influence has been a two-way street. Twentieth-century Americans were made by the world they lived in just as much as they helped to make the twentieth-century world. Both processes lay at the heart of Americans' experiences in interwar Paris, even if that story has been as much a history of forgetting as it has been one of remembering.

ABBREVIATIONS IN THE NOTES

| | |
|---|---|
| AFP | Aldino Felicani Papers (Sacco-Vanzetti Collection), Ms. 2030. Boston Public Library. |
| *ALM* | *American Legion Monthly* |
| *AM* | *American Mercury* |
| APP | Archives de la Préfecture de Police, Paris |
| BHVP | Bibliothèque Historique de la Ville de Paris |
| CA/CPUSA | Files of the Communist Party of the USA. Microfilm edition. Moscow: Comintern Archives, 1999–2000. |
| *CD* | *Chicago Defender* |
| CMVP | Commission Municipale du Vieux Paris. *Procès-verbaux*. Paris: Imprimerie Municipale. |
| *CT* | *Chicago Tribune* |
| FCTC | American Legion France Convention Travel Committee |
| *HM* | *Harper's Magazine* |
| *LA* | *Living Age* |
| *L'AF* | *L'Action Française* |
| *LD* | *Literary Digest* |
| *Le Fig* | *Le Figaro* |
| *L'Hum* | *L'Humanité* |
| *L'Ill* | *L'Illustration* |
| *Le Lib* | *Le Libertaire* |
| *Le Mat* | *Le Matin* |
| *Le Pop* | *Le Populaire* |
| *LHJ* | *Ladies' Home Journal* |
| *L'Œ* | *L'Œuvre* |

| | |
|---|---|
| LT | *Le Temps* |
| MHP | Myron T. Herrick Papers, MSS 2925. Microfilm edition. Cleveland, Ohio: Western Reserve Historical Society, 1994. |
| NAR | *North American Review* |
| NR | *New Republic* |
| NY | *New Yorker* |
| NYT | *New York Times* |
| OI | *Outlook and Independent* |
| PH | *Paris Herald* |
| PP | Prefect of Police |
| RDS | *Records of the Department of State Relating to Internal Affairs of France, 1910–1929* (RG59). Microfilm edition. Washington, D.C.: National Archives and Records Service. |
| RR | *Review of Reviews* |
| SEP | *Saturday Evening Post* |
| SM | *Scribner's Magazine* |
| SRL | *Saturday Review of Literature* |
| SS | *School and Society* |
| S-V DC | Sacco-Vanzetti Defense Committee, Boston |
| TN | *The Nation* |
| VF | *Vanity Fair* |
| WHSL | Wisconsin Historical Society Library Pamphlet Collection |
| WP | *Washington Post* |

## Introduction

1. The classic articulation of this idea is Cowley, *Exile's Return*. Scholars have since made important discoveries about the capital's role in promoting feminist literary modernisms (Benstock, *Women of the Left Bank*) and the cultural politics of the Harlem Renaissance (Stovall, *Paris Noir*). Above all, however, works such as these tend to build on the old myths by concluding that Paris was not only an arena of artistic liberty and financial advantage for Americans but also a place of sexual and racial freedoms.

2. On Americans' dependence on European cultural models, see Levine, *Highbrow/Lowbrow*; Orvell, *Real Thing*; Rodgers, *Atlantic Crossings*; and Hoganson, *Consumers' Imperium*.

3. Scholars often cite Stead's book as a precursor to later literature on Americanization, and, released as the United States became a leading manufacturer, it does contain glimpses of the discourse that would characterize these subsequent debates, for example in the fanciful description of the average Englishman's day on pages 354–6. Nevertheless, a close reading shows just how different Stead's concerns are from those of future critics. His primary focus remained on production and trade balances, not consumption and culture.

4. For these themes, see Susman, *Culture as History*; Cohen, *Making a New Deal*; Igo, *Averaged American*; and Wall, *Inventing the "American Way."* Art historians, by contrast, emphasize the role of transatlantic exchanges in the creation of modern American art: Corn, *Great American Thing* and Lévy, *Transatlantic Avant-Garde*.

5. Henry Luce, "The American Century," *Life*, Feb. 17, 1941, 61–5.

6. In transnational histories of the United States, certain kinds of people and cross-national activities have taken center stage. Charting transatlantic

relations in the early twentieth century, scholars of progressive reformers (Rodgers, *Atlantic Crossings*), commercial agents (de Grazia, *Irresistible Empire*), and African American intellectuals (Edwards, *Practice of Diaspora*) have led the way toward a richer, more international portrait of the period. Yet, beyond these subfields, more must be done to overturn long-ingrained notions about Americans' isolationist impulses.

7. On the resilience of isolationism as a framework for understanding the thirties especially, see Kennedy, *Freedom from Fear* and Herring, *From Colony to Superpower*, ch. 12.

8. Préfecture de la Seine, *Annuaire statistique: Années 1927 et 1928*; Burton Holmes, "The Streets of Paris," *Mentor*, Jan. 1928, 23–32.

9. Demangeon, *Paris*, 19–22; Wilson, *Paris on Parade*, 13–17, 90–112; Branguyn, *Everybody's Paris*, ch. 2; Bidou, *Paris*, 402–6; Chadych and Leborgne, *Atlas de Paris*, 170–1; Célati and Trouilleux, *Chronique de la rue parisienne*, 10–11, 64–5, 72–4; Jones, *Paris*, 358–9, 407.

10. Muriel Harris, "What is Background?" *North American Review*, July 1922, 53–62; Cummings, "selfdiscovery," 53.

11. On the "industrious revolutions" of the long nineteenth century, see Bayly, *Birth of the Modern World*.

12. Nevill, *Days and Nights*, 30.

13. Although outnumbered by a handful of other groups, Americans still ranked among the ten largest foreign populations in Paris. Statistics on the number of Americans permanently settled in Paris vary. French officials recorded 18,000 in 1926 (see the *Statistique générale de la France*), but many Americans circumvented the capital's registration processes. Considering the breadth of local American activities, Warren Susman's estimate of 40,000, drawn from the *Chicago Tribune*'s Paris edition, seems more accurate: "Pilgrimage to Paris," 164–5.

14. Brace, *Americans in France*; Brewster, *American Directory; How to Enjoy Paris and the Smart Resorts*; Josephy and McBride, *Paris is a Woman's Town*, 162–77, 205–6; Wilson, *Paris on Parade*, 291–315.

15. O'Brien, *P.S.*, 271.

16. Gertrude Stein, "An American and France" (1936), in Rahv, *Discovery of Europe*, 571–8.

17. The cultural impact of African American artists is particularly well developed. See Blake, *Tumulte Noir*; Archer-Straw, *Negrophilia*; Jackson, *Making Jazz French*; and Edwards, *Practice of Diaspora*. In another exception, Harvey Levenstein explores the conflicts stirred up by American tourists in *Seductive Journey*. Nevertheless, Levenstein's interwar research draws almost exclusively on American media, and he minimizes what was at stake in Americans' presence in Paris by emphasizing only that they came for the purposes of "having fun."

18. Vincent O'Sullivan, "The Yankee in Paris," *AM*, Oct. 1924, 160–2; "'Hundred Per Cents' Abroad," *Outlook*, 11 Aug. 1926, 498–9.

19. Martin, *France in the Après Guerre*; Weber, *Hollow Years*.

20. On immigrants and reactions to them, Rosenberg, *Policing Paris*, esp. 27–36 and Schor, *L'Opinion française*. On tourism, Levenstein, *Seductive Journey* and *We'll Always Have Paris*.

21. On exiles, Kaspi and Marès, *Paris des étrangers*. On the Red Belt, Stovall, *Rise of the Paris Red Belt* and Fourcaut, *Banlieue rouge*. On right-wing municipal politics, Rosenberg, *Policing Paris*, 36–40.

22. Préfecture de la Seine, *Annuaire statistique: Années 1927 et 1928*; Paul, *Last Time I Saw Paris*, 104–5; Wilson, *Paris on Parade*, 9–11; Brassaï, *Secret Paris of the 30's*; "clamorous hell" from Bertaut, *Paris*, 284.

23. Morand, *Paris to the Life*, 10–13.

24. Manela, *Wilsonian Moment*; Furet, *Passing of an Illusion*, 29–33; Ferguson, *Paris as Revolution*.

25. On creative dialogue and travel as an impetus for self-reflection and sharpening social critiques, see Edwards, *Practice of Diaspora* and Campbell, *Middle Passages*.

26. Hobsbawm, *Age of Extremes*, 22, 52. More and more, scholars are uncovering the tensions and overlap between nationalist convictions and international interaction, particularly as these forces were experienced and shaped by those struggling against imperialist control (Manela, *Wilsonian Moment*; Stephens, *Black Empire*; Perez, *On Becoming Cuban*). As the drama surrounding Americans in Paris shows, those at the center of world power as well as at its peripheries developed their nationalist ideas and practices in international contexts.

## Chapter One

1. Louvrier, *Guide du chauffeur de taxi*; André Salmon, *L'Ame des gares*, trans. as "The Soul of Paris Railway Stations," in Griggs, *My Paris*, 10–12; Le Gallienne, *From a Paris Scrapbook*, 58–9; photograph, "Départ des américains," in Augé, *Paris années 30*, 526.

2. Photograph, "Place de l'Opéra embouteillé (1928)," in Lanzmann, *Paris des années 30*, 24–5; "raging, disputing" in Wilson, *Paris on Parade*, 5–9; Préfecture de la Seine, *Annuaire statistique: Années 1927 et 1928*; Miquel, *Main courante*, 274, 283–4; Alexander Woollcott, "The Paris Taxi-Driver Considered as an Artist," *SM*, June 1921, 643–51.

3. Lewis, *Dodsworth*, 114; Gibbs, *European Journey*, 13.

4. J. C. Furnas, "The Vanished American," *SEP*, Dec. 8, 1934, 88–93.

5. Matthew Arnold, *Culture and Anarchy* (London: Smith, Elder, 1869), xxx; Rudyard Kipling, *American Notes* (Boston: Brown, 1899), 102; Rydell and Kroes, *Buffalo Bill in Bologna*, 105–17, 142–63.

6. Josephy and McBride, *Paris Is a Woman's Town*; Wilson, *Paris on Parade*, 34–112; photograph of Harry's New York Bar in Lanzmann, *Paris des années 30*, 48; Christopher Morley, "Paris Crowd," *SRL*, Sept. 13, 1924, 109. On looking for the Opera if lost see, for example, Reynolds, *Paris with the Lid Lifted*, 152–3.

7. Stowe, *Going Abroad*; Levenstein, *Seductive Journey*, 93–106, 125–75; Anne Herendeen, "Bon Voyage—If Any," *Everybody's Magazine*, Sept. 1919, 29, 79; "Paris Is Still Fascinating, But Getting There Is Difficult," *LD*, Dec. 13, 1919, 78; "Traveler's Paris of To-Day," *RR*, June 1920, 625; "Passport Adventures," *LA*, June 26, 1920, 787–9; Kathleen Howard, "Paris—Changed and Unchanged," *LHJ*, Sept. 1920, 28–9; Kenneth Roberts, "Trial by Travel," *SEP*, Sept. 4, 1920, 18–19.

8. Ogilvie, *Tourist Movement*, 208–18; Mead, *Atlantic Legacy*, 160; Susman, "Pilgrimage to Paris," 176.

9. "Swelling Tide of Foreign Travel," *NYT Mag.*, May 6, 1928, 77; James Whelpley, "American Travelers in Europe," *Fortnightly Review*, Aug. 1922, 330–8; Katherine Anthony, "Over the Summer Sea," *Bookman*, Aug. 1928, 677–80; Mary Heaton Vorse, "Tourist Third," *HM*, March 1929, 508–15; "Young America to Invade Old Europe," *NYT*, April 5, 1925, SM6.

10. T. R. Ybarra, "Turistus Americanus," *OI*, April 24, 1929, 647; Chauncey Leake, *1938 Travelog*, 12.

11. P. J. Philip, "Step by Step Paris Becomes American," *NYT*, July 8, 1928, pt. 3, 1–3.

12. The local Chamber of Commerce's 1927–1928 *Directory* listed sixty-nine American periodicals either published or represented by offices in the French capital: Brace, 383–90, 420, 467.

13. Mowrer, *House of Europe*, 135, 553; Josephy and McBride, *Paris Is a Woman's Town*, 169–70; James T. Farrell, "Paris Scene: 1931."

14. "French Spoken in Paris," *NYT*, Aug. 26, 1928, pt. 2, 9. Even when tourism declined during the Depression, Americans continued to rank among the most numerous foreigners seeking accommodations in the capital: reports, Nov. 1933–March 1939, "Service de Garnis," and "Direction de la Police Judiciaire graphique du mouvement des 'entrées' dans les hôtels de Paris par nationalité" in APP B^A 2255, dossier Statistique Touristique.

15. T. R. Ybarra, "America's Conquest of Paris," *NYT*, July 31, 1927, pt. 4, 1–2, 21; Hotel Astoria ad in Brace, *Americans in France*, 453. See also Janet Flanner, "Paris Letter," *NY*, July 21, 1928, 34, 36–7; Golda Goldman, "Paris Is Not America," *OI*, 5 Nov. 1930, 372–3, 395–6 and Woon, *Paris That's Not in the Guide Books*, 44, 127–35.

16. Brace, *Americans in France*; Reed, *"American Express"*; Miller and Hill, *Giant of the Western World*, 76; Brassaï, *Henry Miller*, 27; Emma Goldman, letters from Paris, March and April 1928, in Candice Falk et al., eds., *Emma*

*Goldman Papers: A Microfilm Edition* (Alexandria, Va.: Chadwyck-Healey, 1990). American organizations facilitated visitors' stays, partly because the French government was slow to promote or regulate tourism until after World War II: Frank Schoonmaker, "The Tourist's Dollar," *OI*, July 23, 1930, 460–1; Reginald Kauffman, "We Get the Glad Hand," *Collier's*, July 11, 1931, 26, 52; Endy, *Cold War Holidays*, 58–9; Levenstein, *We'll Always Have Paris*, 7–10.

17. Susman, "Pilgrimage to Paris," chs. 2–3; Levenstein, *Seductive Journey*, 93–106; Brace, *Americans in France*, 11–14; Katz, *From Appomattox to Montmartre*, 26–9; Wharton, *Backward Glance*, 257–92.

18. Wharton, *Backward Glance*, 281–2, 320.

19. Rosenberg, *Spreading the American Dream*; Herring, *From Colony to Superpower*, ch. 11; Dos Passos sketch in *Fourteenth Chronicle*, 405.

20. Boucher and Huard, *American Footprints in Paris*; Brewster, *American Directory*, 209, 268; Brace, *Americans in France*; "The American University Union in Europe," *SS*, Feb. 7, 1920, 164–5; Dos Passos, *Best Times*, 76–7. On raucous military men—those James Thurber dubbed the "good bad boys"—see Miquel, *Main courante*, 249–52 and Thurber, "First Time I Saw Paris."

21. Hawkins, *Hawkins of the Paris Herald*, 117; Seldes, *Lords of the Press*, 283–93; Laney, *Paris Herald*; Susman, "Pilgrimage to Paris," 181–206; Heald, *Transatlantic Vistas*; Weber, *News of Paris*.

22. Miller and Hill, *Giant of the Western World*; Rosenberg, *Spreading the American Dream*; de Grazia, *Irresistible Empire*.

23. Brace, *Americans in France*, 4–10, 21–4, 253–380, quotation p. 7; Brewster, *American Directory*; Josephy and McBride, *Paris Is a Woman's Town*, 165–6; Adams, *Family Sees France*, 61–2; James Lebensohn, "The American Student in Paris," *Educational Review*, April 1923, 232–6; Southard, *American Industry in Europe*. Statistics on American expenditures from Mead, *Atlantic Legacy*, 165.

24. Phelps, *Foreign Expansion of American Banks*; Rosenberg, *Spreading the American Dream*, 63–75, 122–5, 136–60; Boucher and Huard, *American Footprints in Paris*, 124–5; Brace, *Americans in France*, 421–8. Overseas banking reforms came under the Federal Reserve Act (1914), the Export Trade Act (1918), and the Edge Act (1919).

25. Address at the Independence Day Banquet of the American Chamber of Commerce, July 3, 1926 in MHP, folder 65. See also speeches in folder 136.

26. Weinberg, "Lure of Paris for American Painters"; Susman, "Pilgrimage to Paris," 76–82; Hanna, "French Women and American Men"; "American Soldiers and French Universities," *SS*, May 24, 1919, 629; George Boas, "A Soldier at the Sorbonne," *NAR*, Jan. 1920, 36–43; "Americans in French Universities," *LD*, May 1, 1920, 43; Frank Aydelotte, "Educational Foundations with Special Reference to International Fellowships," Dec. 26,

1925, *SS*, 799–803; Frances Warfield, "Innocence Abroad," *SM*, Oct. 1928, 457–64. *School and Society* reported in detail on fellowship opportunities and overseas programs. See also pamphlets of the Institute of International Education in New York, esp. Feb. 10, 1923; April 1, 1923; Dec. 1, 1925; Dec. 31, 1926; and Oct. 1, 1930.

27. Josephy and McBride, *Paris Is a Woman's Town*, 166–75, 195–228; Lebensohn, "American Student in Paris"; Stephen Duggan, "Observations of an American Educator Abroad," *SS*, Dec. 26, 1926, 803–9; Boucher and Huard, *American Footprints in Paris*, 47–54, 66–7; *How to Enjoy Paris and the Smart Resorts*, 44–59; Loud, *Elegant Time*, 50, 81–3, 89.

28. Wilson, *Paris on Parade*, 193–4. See also Ford, *Published in Paris*; Putnam, *Paris Was Our Mistress*; Beach, *Shakespeare and Company*; Hemingway, *Moveable Feast*; and McAlmon with Boyle, *Being Geniuses Together*.

29. J. A. Rogers, "The American Negro in Europe," *AM*, May 1930, 1–10; Bennett quoted in Fabre, *From Harlem to Paris*, 121. On the African American community in Paris, Stovall, *Paris Noir* and Shack, *Harlem in Montmartre*. On the capital's importance to the rise of black internationalism, albeit one inflected by enduring national differences, Edwards, *Practice of Diaspora*.

30. Baker and Bouillon, *Josephine*, 48, 50, 63; Rose, *Jazz Cleopatra*, 81, 105–7; Jules-Rosette, *Josephine Baker in Art and Life*, 53; Hughes, *Big Sea*; Carisella and Ryan, *Black Swallow of Death*; Bricktop with Haskins, *Bricktop*, 86; Bechet, *Treat It Gentle*, 149–50.

31. Garey, *American Guide Book*, 11.

32. "Liberal-developmentalism" in Rosenberg, *Spreading the American Dream*, 7–13.

33. Charles Merz, "Never Again—Till Next Summer," *Independent*, Oct. 2, 1926, 383–4; Bromfield, "Expatriate—Vintage 1927," *SRL*, March 19, 1927, 657–9; Fitzgerald to Edmund Wilson, May 1921 in *Letters*, 326–7.

34. Bender, *Nation Among Nations*, 140; Wyman, *Round-Trip to America*; Wiebe, *Search for Order*, 9, 14.

35. Levine, *Highbrow/Lowbrow*, ch. 3; Beckert, *Monied Metropolis*; Hoganson, *Consumers' Imperium*.

36. Butler, *Critical Americans*, including Curtis quote, p. 167; Sidney Smith, ed., *Edinburgh Review*, 33 (Jan.–May 1820), 79; Brooks, *America's Coming-of-Age*, 43; Levine, *Highbrow/Lowbrow*, 214–15. American progressive reformers felt a similar sense of lagging behind in social policy innovation: Rodgers, *Atlantic Crossings*, 69–75.

37. Cowley, *Exile's Return*, 78. On Stearns, Ford, *Four Lives*. On the "problem of the intellectual in America" as a foundation for expatriation, see Susman, "Pilgrimage to Paris," 7–62 and Earnest, *Expatriates and Patriots*, 3–12, 251–75.

38. Draft speech, May 24, 1914, memo for Foreign Press Bureau of Committee on Public Information, July 1918, and remarks to the New Haven Chamber

of Commerce, Dec. 6, 1919 in MHP, folders 128–9; Trachtenberg, *Incorporation of America*; O'Leary, *To Die For*; Capozzola, *Uncle Sam Wants You*.

39. Susman, *Culture as History*, pts. 3–4. On French views, see ch. 2.

40. Josephson, *Life among the Surrealists*, 155; May, *End of American Innocence*; Dumenil, *Modern Temper*; Denning, *Cultural Front*.

41. Copland in Pollack, *Aaron Copland*, 113–14; Hughes, *Big Sea*, 162; Gilbert Seldes, *The 7 Lively Arts* (New York: Sagamore, [1924], 1957), 4; Matthew Josephson, "The Great American Billposter," *Broom*, Nov. 1922 in Strout, *American Image of the Old World*, 188. See also Josephson, *Life among the Surrealists*, 121–6, 155–6, 188–90; Lévy, *Transatlantic Avant-Garde*.

42. Stein, *Paris, France*, 2; Hemingway, *Moveable Feast*, 5, 7; Earnest, *Expatriates and Patriots*, 251–75; Mellow, *Walker Evans*, 38–60; Shirer, *20th Century Journey: The Start*, 56–7, 186–9, 273–8. See also Susman, "Pilgrimage to Paris" and Corn, *Great American Thing*, ch. 2.

43. Irwin Edman, "On Meeting Americans Abroad and Discovering One's Own Country There," *Century*, March 1927, 536–42; Samuel Spewack, "Four Years in Europe Made Me an American," *SEP*, May 29, 1926, 27, 91–4, 99; Bromfield, "Expatriate—Vintage 1927."

44. Morley, "Paris Crowd"; Brand Whitlock, "Modern Innocents Abroad," *Collier's*, April 18, 1925, 5–6.

45. Wilson, *Ladies Third*, 46, 70, 81–2, 105; Edwards, *Paris*, 92–3.

46. Herald, *Doing Europe*, 21–2; Garey, *American Guide Book*, 32–5; Greer, *What a Buckeye Cover Man Saw*, 63–8; Merz, "Never Again—till Next Summer"; O. O. McIntyre to Myron Herrick, July 13, 1926, in MHP, folder 64.

47. The central place Paris assumed in American popular culture was strikingly new. As recently as the eve of World War I, the intellectual Randolph Bourne mused at how Americans routinely overlooked Paris in favor of London, "an enormous mistake," he thought. Succumbing to influenza, Bourne would not live to see the end of the war, when Paris began to do an enormous amount of cultural work for his compatriots: Bourne to Carl Zigrosser, Paris, Dec. 13, 1913, reprinted in Rahv, *Discovery of Europe*, 416–17. See also Susman, "Pilgrimage to Paris," 71–5, 92–102.

48. Lebensohn, "American Student in Paris"; Wilson, *Ladies Third*, 105. Paris became such a frequent subject for Hollywood after the war that one critic declared, "Never more than today . . . has there been in America such an infatuation with French atmosphere, above all Parisian": Valentin Mandelstamm, "Le film parlant international," *Ciné-magazine*, April 1930 in Jeanne and Ford, *Paris vu par le cinéma*, 212. At the same time, Paris scenes figured in close to one hundred Broadway shows, including at least thirty hits. The city also assumed an important place in American literature. Jean Méral calculated that two-thirds of the works for his sweeping study of Paris in American novels were written during the 1920s: *Paris in American Literature*, 136.

49. Loos, *Gentlemen Prefer Blondes*, 69–96. For typical timetables, see Woon, *Paris That's Not in the Guide Books*; Milton, *Paris in Seven Days*; and Reynolds, *Paris with the Lid Lifted*, 60–83.

50. Brassaï, "The Last Bum of the Cour des Miracles" and photographs in *Secret Paris of the 30's*, n.p.; photographs in Célati and Trouilleux, *Chronique de la rue parisienne*, 20–7; translations of *L'Humanité* articles in "Immigrants in France," *LA*, Nov. 1, 1926, 226–33; photographs in Beaumont-Maillet, *Atget Paris*, 629–45, 727–9, 774–7; Madeleine Leveau-Fernandez, "La zone et les fortifs," in Fourcaut, *Banlieue rouge*, 56–65; Evenson, *Paris*, 206–7.

51. Reynolds, *Paris with the Lid Lifted*, 204–5; "American Blight on Artistic Montparnasse," *LD*, Oct. 22, 1927, 28–9; Stewart, *Mr. and Mrs. Haddock in Paris, France*, 278–9.

52. Newman, *Seeing Paris*, 219–24. In *The Sun Also Rises*, Jake Barnes similarly quipped, "No matter what café in Montparnasse you ask a taxi-driver to bring you to from the right bank of the river, they always take you to the Rotonde": 49.

53. Wilson, *Paris on Parade*, 278; Homer Croy, "Americans Abroad"; Ybarra, "America's Conquest of Paris"; Philip, "Step By Step Paris Becomes American."

54. Cornelius Vanderbilt Jr. to Myron Herrick, July 27, 1926 in MHP, folder 63; Joel Cook, *A Holiday Tour in Europe Described in a Series of Letters Written for The Public Ledger* (Philadelphia: J. B. Lippincott, 1879), 143; Keely, *Paris and All the World Besides*, 6–13, 78.

55. Deems Taylor, "Pages Out of a Paris Sketch-Book," *VF*, Aug. 1928, 46; Goldman, "Paris Is Not America"; Acheson, *Password to Paris*, 80; T. R. Ybarra, "Words and 'Ads,'" *OI*, July 16, 1930, 424; "Papers in English Aid in Americanizing Paris," *NYT*, April 11, 1927, 38; Mildred Kearney in *Paris Comet*, trans. as "Les Américains en france," *L'Ill*, Oct. 26, 1929, 458–9; Wilson, *Paris on Parade*, 276; Croy, "Americans Abroad"; Edwards, *Paris*, 400. For an example of a multilingual music-hall program, see *Bonjour Paris: Revue du Casino de Paris: Saison 1924–1925* (Paris: Devambrez), BHVP, In-F° 95 087. On postings of taxi rates in English, see Commissaire Général au Tourisme to PP, July 29, Sept. 28, and Oct. 29, 1936 in APP B^A 2255, dossier Haut Commissariat du Tourisme.

56. "Americans Take Hate to Paris," *Chicago Defender*, Aug. 11, 1923, 1; Muller, "Ever Thine," 37; Loud, *Elegant Time*, 107–8.

57. O'Sullivan, "Yankee in Paris"; Nunnally Johnson, "France on Two Words," *SEP*, April 26, 1930, 29, 149–50. See also C.M. Webster, "French in One Easy Lesson," *AM*, Nov. 1936, 301–6. In his jovial guidebook *Paris with the Lid Lifted*, Bruce Reynolds included an appendix of translations for visitors: "Carry this: pohrtay se(r)-see," "Hurry up: day-pay-shay-voo," and "Go away (clear out): ahl-lay-voo-zau(ng)." Clearly, Reynolds regarded French primarily as a means to bossing around hired help and, more importantly,

as "the Golden Key that opens the Pearly Gates" to sexually available Parisian women: 36–41, 262–81.

58. Edwards, *Paris*, 91–2; Hughes to Countee Cullen, March 11, 1924, quoted in Fabre, *From Harlem to Paris*, 64–5. See also Wilson, *Paris on Parade*, 17–18 and Norman Fitts, "Vignettes Parisiennes," *Unpartizan Review*, Jan. 1920, 17–23.

59. Eleanor Kinsella McDonnell, "Plain Tales From the Tourists," *SEP*, April 19, 1930, 10–11; "Outwitting European Bandits," *LD*, Oct. 8, 1921, 46–9; and George Nathan, "The Evacuation of Paris," *AM*, Nov. 1929, 370–1.

60. APP C^B 2.48 Quartier Saint Georges, juin 1927–avril 1928; Acheson, *Password to Paris*, 77.

61. Adams, *Family Sees France*, 45–6; Garey, *American Guide Book*, 18; Hemingway, "Living on $1,000 a Year in Paris," *Toronto Star Weekly*, Feb. 4, 1922 in *Dateline: Toronto*, 88–9.

62. Reynolds, *Cocktail Continentale*, 37–8; Herald, *Doing Europe*, 35, 48; Mowrer, *House of Europe*, 537; Nevill, *Days and Nights*, 38–9. See also Ring Lardner, "The Other Side" (1925) reprinted in Rahv, *Discovery of Europe*, 539–70; Cummings, *Him*, 104.

63. Wilson, *Paris on Parade*, 278–9; Hiram Motherwell, "The American Tourist Makes History," *HM*, Dec. 1929, 70–6.

64. *American Magazine* in Ward, "Meaning of Lindbergh's Flight"; W. J. Carpenter to Myron T. Herrick, May 22, 1927 in MHP, folder 198.

65. Herrick rehearsed his portrait of Lindbergh as an innocent and brave youth, an "example of American idealism, character, and conduct," in letters and press releases before finalizing it in his preface to Lindbergh's memoir of the flight, *"We"* (1927). See drafts in MHP, folder 200.

66. Speech, Josephine Baker, Keil Opera House, Feb. 3, 1952, Western Historical Manuscript Collection, University of Missouri St. Louis, UMSL Black History Project online: http://www.umsl.edu/~whmc/. Lindbergh actually grew up in Minnesota, but he was running mail between St. Louis and Chicago on the eve of his historic flight. His plane had been named for the St. Louis businessmen who funded the trip. On Lindbergh's reception in Europe, see Eksteins, *Rites of Spring*, ch. 8; Chiappe and Pierre Godin quoted in Eksteins, 266; clipping, "Out of the Ashes of Hate," n.d. and gift lists in MHP, folders 200–201.

67. "Americans Take Hate to Paris," *Chicago Defender*, Aug. 11, 1923, 1; Shack, *Harlem in Montmartre*, ch. 4; speech, Baker, Keil Opera House.

68. On Americans' sharp divisions over the Sacco-Vanzetti case, see Laney, *Paris Herald*, 240–1. On Americans' protest meetings, see "Les Américains de Paris tiennent un meeting," *L'Œ*, Aug. 10, 1927, 1 and "Une belle réunion des Américains libéraux de Paris," *L'Hum*, Aug. 10, 1927, 2. On Duncan, see Shirer, *20th Century Journey*, 312–14 and Desti, *Untold Story*, 200–1.

69. Huddleston, *Paris Salons, Cafés, Studios*, 190; Laney, *Paris Herald*, 149; Seldes, *Lords of the Press*, 195–6; Hawkins, *Hawkins of the Paris Herald*, 210–11; *Herald* circulation from Hansen, *Expatriate Paris*, 24; Herrick to Sec. of State, June 7, 1924, folder 113 and conversation notes, July 16, 1923, and memo, Feb. 13, 1929, in MHP, folder 129; Mott, *Myron T. Herrick*, 290.

70. Haney, *Naked at the Feast*, 155; Rose, *Jazz Cleopatra*, 110–16; Jules-Rosette, *Josephine Baker in Art and Life*, 219–28.

## Chapter Two

1. Robert de Beauplan, "Au Paris du dollar," *L'Ill*, Oct. 23, 1926, 443–6, trans. as "The Paris of the Dollar," *LA*, Dec. 15, 1926, 507–11.

2. T. R. Ybarra, "'Americanization' Again," *OI*, Nov. 6, 1929, 382.

3. To compare French and German attitudes toward American economic models, see Strauss, *Menace in the West* and Nolan, *Visions of Modernity*.

4. Excerpts from the French press in T. S. Wauchope, "What the French Think of Us," *AM*, Dec. 1925, 479–86; André Tardieu, "What France Thinks of Her War-Time Allies," *Harper's*, May 1926, 670–5. Americans, for their part, believed their favorable interest rates, debt reductions, and investment in France's devastated regions more than generous. While the United States pursued peace and a stabilized postwar Europe with a balance of power, many argued, the French had been misled by their own blustering politicians bent on imperialism and revenge. See Blumenthal, *Illusion and Reality* and Costigliola, *Awkward Dominion*.

5. Siegfried, *America Comes of Age* (1927) and Duhamel, *America the Menace* (1931). For more on this genre, see Strauss, *Menace in the West*.

6. Lacorne, Rupnik, and Toinet, *Rise and Fall of Anti-Americanism*; Kuisel, *Seducing the French*; and Pells, *Not Like Us*.

7. Kuisel, *Seducing the French*, 1–2.

8. de Grazia, *Irresistible Empire*, 10.

9. Branguyn, *Everybody's Paris*, 85–6, 92–3, 97; Wilson, *Paris on Parade*, 11–13; photographs of gas company employees in Brassaï, *Secret Paris of the 30's*, n.p.; photograph of a bus queue in Lanzmann, *Paris des années 30*, 27.

10. Martin, *France and the Après Guerre*, 105–10; Préfecture de la Seine, *Annuaire statistique: Années 1925 et 1926* and *Années 1927 et 1928*.

11. Martin, *France and the Après Guerre*.

12. Rosenberg, *Policing Paris*, 8, 28–33, 65–6, 130–3; George Mauco, "Le problème des étrangers en France," *La Revue de Paris*, Sept. 15, 1935, 375–406; Schor, *L'Opinion française*, esp. 35–63; Dewitte, *Mouvements nègres*.

13. Quotes from Mauco, "Problème des étrangers." See also Ralph Schor, "Le Paris des libertés," in Kaspi and Marès, *Paris des étrangers*, 13–33; Schor, *L'Opinion francaise*, ch. 2; Rosenberg, *Policing Paris*, 49–50, 73–5; and Bidou, *Paris*, 407–9; Noiriel, *French Melting Pot*.

14. Rosenberg, *Policing Paris*, 38–9, 49, 64–8; Martin, *France and the Après Guerre*, 112.

15. Rosenberg, *Policing Paris*, 141–3. On the *tumulte noir*, see Blake, *Tumulte Noir* and Archer-Straw, *Negrophilia*.

16. The phrase is Maurice Muret's: *Le crépuscule des nations blanches* (Paris: Payot, 1925). See also Strauss, *Menace in the West*, 81–5, 158–60; Ezra, *Colonial Unconscious*; and Philippe DeWitte, "Le Paris noir de l'entre-deux-guerres," in Kaspi and Marès, *Paris des étrangers*, 157–69.

17. Levenstein, *Seductive Journey*; Stansell, *American Moderns*; Cocks, *Doing the Town*; Schwartz, *Spectacular Realities*; and Walz, *Pulp Surrealism*.

18. Wilson, *Paris on Parade*, 278–89.

19. Georges Lecomte, "The New Paris Emerging Since the War," *Current History Magazine*, Sept. 1925, 924–35.

20. "A Rebel Host in Montmartre," *Christian Science Monitor*, May 5, 1920, 3; Émile-Bayard, *Montmartre*, 100–34; "Montmartre Assumes Dignity of a Republic," May 14, 1921, 10, "Montmartre Marks 'Republic's Year Two,'" Dec. 19, 1921, 16, and "Paris Artists 'Rout' Stingy Barkeepers," Jan. 28, 1929, 5, all in *NYT*. Hostile to American encroachments, such rebels, curiously, were also inspired by them, as evidenced by their references to Woodrow Wilson as well as their advocacy of mechanical escalators—the invention of an American corporation, first exhibited at the 1900 Paris Universal Exposition: Rydell and Kroes, *Buffalo Bill in Bologna*, 101–2. On these neighborhood groups more generally, see Jackson, "Artistic Community and Urban Development."

21. Mac Orlan, *Aux lumières de Paris*, 139. See also André Vaillant, "I Thought I Knew My France," *AM*, March 1937, 286–90.

22. Warnod, *Visages de Paris*, 323.

23. Warnod, *Plaisirs de la rue*, 60–4; Munholland, "Republican Order and Republican Tolerance"; Chevalier, *Montmartre du plaisir et du crime*, esp. 129–216, 226–39, 293–306. The literary critic Elisabeth de Gramont also recalled the conspicuousness of American soldiers, claiming that after midnight it was impossible to cross the place Pigalle without hearing gunshots fired off by drunken doughboys: *Souvenirs du monde*, 320.

24. Gravigny, *Montmartre en 1925*; Montorgueil, *Vieux Montmartre*; and photograph of place Pigalle in Bucovich, *Paris*, 181.

25. Nevill, *Days and Nights*, 33. See also Mac Orlan, *Lumières de Paris*, 46; Bertaut, *Belles nuits de Paris*, 35; and Carco, *Images cachées*, 18–19.

26. Cohen-Portheim, *Spirit of Paris*, 92; Émile-Bayard, *Montmartre*, 143, 155. See also Richard, *Guide des grands ducs*, 197–8, 232; Bertaut, *Belles nuits de Paris*, 189–91; Sarti, *La Tribuna* (Rome), trans. as "Montmartre Is Dead!" *LA*, Feb. 2, 1924, 232–3; Daniel Halévy, "Pays Parisiens," *La Revue Hebdomadaire*, May 4 and 11, 1929, 33–53, 201–22.

27. Bertaut, *Belles nuits de Paris*, 81–3; Roubaud, *Music-hall*, 11–14. For a sense of these productions, see the annual programs, *Revue des Folies-Bergère* (Paris: Art Editions), BHVP In-4° 142 443.

28. Robert de Flers, *Le Fig*, Nov. 16, 1925 quoted in Kear, "Vénus noire."

29. Fréjaville, *Au music-hall*, 28; Jackson, *Making Jazz French*, ch. 4 and quote p. 79. See also André Rouveyre, "Music-Halls," *Mercure de France*, Sept. 1, 1926, 410–16 and André Levinson, "The Negro Dance Under European Eyes," *Theatre Arts*, April 1927, 282–93. On mongrelization, Strauss, *Menace in the West*, 48–9, 160.

30. Roger also makes this point in *American Enemy*, 167–76.

31. Ogilvie, *Tourist Movement*, 217–18; "Parade of Legionnaires Begins through Chic Shops of Paris," *PH*, Sept. 23, 1927, 9; Valentino, *Américains à Paris*, 2, 16–17.

32. Gustave Tery, *L'Œuvre* in Wauchope, "What the French Think of Us." See also "Tourists in Paris Will Be Protected," *NYT*, July 26, 1926, 6; and Schor, *L'Opinion française*, 410–13, 467–76.

33. Surveillance reports, July 21–24, 1926 in APP B^A 1851, dossier Manifestation du 21 juillet 1926. Americans were certainly aware of this animosity (as they were aware of broader debates about Americanization), since it received such extensive press coverage. See "Europeans That Hate Us," Sept. 18, 1920, 61 and "Our Tourists' Troubles in France," Aug. 14, 1926, 12–13, both in *LD*; "Paris Crowds Jeer Tourists in Buses," July 23, 1926, 1 and Edwin James, "Parisians Insult American Tourists," July 24, 1926, 1–2, both in *NYT*. One commentator surmised that his compatriots had in fact "inherited all the passionate hatred which was concentrated upon the German ten years ago": Frank Simonds, "Does Europe Hate Us and Why?" *RR*, Feb. 1927, 167–74.

34. G. de Villemus, *L'Echo de Paris*, trans. in "Tourists Welcome and Unwelcome," *LA*, Sept. 11, 1926, 586–8; Herrick to Frank Kellogg, July 16, 1926, in MHP, folder 64; Chancellor, *How to Be Happy in Paris*, 91–2; Raymond Recouly, "Social Upset in France After the War," *SM*, Dec. 1925, 609–15; Paul Morand, *L'Europe galante* in Wauchope, "What the French Think of Us"; de Beauplan, "Au Paris du Dollar." See also Georges Villa, "Paris Shrugs Its Shoulders at the Tourist Horde," *NYT Mag.*, May 30, 1926, 2; "Foreign Cartoon Fun," *LD*, May 12, 1928, 17; and Le Semainier, "Courrier de Paris," *L'Ill*, July 31, 1926, 118 and Aug. 28, 1926, 210.

35. Sieburg, *Dieu est-il français?*, 141–4, 285–6; Gisken Wildenvey, "Paris Without Parisians," *LA*, Dec. 1928, 298; Morand, *Paris to the Life*, 10–12; *Réaction*, July 1930 quoted in Roger, *American Enemy*, 340.

36. Sutcliffe, *Autumn of Central Paris*, 152–5, 161–4, 170–6; Nord, *Paris Shopkeepers*, 100–20.

37. Jacques Chastenet, *L'Oncle Shylock ou l'impérialisme américain à la conquête du monde* (1927) quoted in Strauss, *Menace in the West*, 99; Abel Hermant, *Le Fig*, trans. as "Dayton on the Boulevards II," *LA*, Oct. 24, 1925, 188–90.

38. Recouly, "Social Upset in France after the War"; T. R. Ybarra, "Words and 'Ads,'" July 16, 1930, 424 and Golda Goldman, "Paris Is Not America," Nov. 5, 1930, 372–3, both in *OI*; Roth, *Frankfurter Zeitung*, Aug. 26, 1925 reprinted in *Report from a Parisian Paradise*, 30–1.

39. Ann T. Leitich, *Neue Freie Presse*, trans. as "Mr. Babbitt in Paris," *LA*, Oct. 24, 1925, 190–2; *L'Œ*, July 20, 1924 in Schor, *L'Opinion française*, 352.

40. Photographs in the following: Collomb, *Années folles*, 41, 68–9, Bucovich, *Paris*, 12, and Lanzmann, *Paris des années 30*, 28–9; CMVP, Nov. 18, 1911, 121–4. For characteristic prewar discussions, see meeting minutes for Jan. 30, 1909, 4–5; June 16, 1909, 72–3, 79; and Oct. 26, 1912, 191–6, all in CMVP. The Commission, which operated as an advisory board for the city administration, began in 1897 as part of the preservation movement gaining ground in reaction to the drastic urban renewal projects under Haussmann and the prefects of the early Third Republic: see Evenson, *Paris*, 311–14 and Sutcliffe, *Autumn of Central Paris*, 179, 187, 197–210, 295–306.

41. CMVP, Jan. 26, 1929, Annexe no. 1, 13–24 and Nov. 27, 1926, 140–3; "Loi autorisant la Ville de Paris à percevoir à son profit une taxe sur les affiches," *Recueil de la Gazette des Tribunaux* (Paris: Rédaction et Administration, 1926), 76. This is not to say that posters did not elicit protest before the war, but that the scale of both abuses and complaints intensified after the war as other changes compounded the poster's appearance in the street. For a sharp analysis of the prewar association of the poster with urban problems and even *américanisme*, see Verhagen, "The Poster in *Fin-de-Siècle* Paris."

42. Roth, *Report from a Parisian Paradise*, 27; Mac Orlan, *Lumières de Paris*, 43; de Grazia, *Irresistible Empire*, ch. 5 and on the nebulous nature of national branding, 214–17.

43. CMVP, April 28, 1923, 91; Feb. 27, 1926, 43–4; Nov. 27, 1926, 140–3; June 25, 1927, Annexe no. 7; Dec. 17, 1927, 184–8; and Jan. 26, 1929, Annexe no. 1, 13–24.

44. Lecomte, "New Paris Emerging Since the War"; CMVP, Dec. 17, 1927, 184–8.

45. di Borgo, *Champs-Élysées*; Sutcliffe, *Autumn of Central Paris*, 170; Vernier, *How to Enjoy and Get the Very Best of Paris*, 53–7; *How to Enjoy Paris and the Smart Resorts*, 65–81; Sabatès, *Champs-Elysées*, 97, 126. Quote from Pollock, *Paris and Parisians*, 28. On prewar *café-concerts*, see F. Berkeley Smith, *How Paris Amuses Itself* (New York: Funk & Wagnalls, 1903), 17–39.

46. Henri Simon, "Les Champs-Elysées se transforment," *L'Œ*, Sept. 20, 1927, 4; photographs and text from di Borgo, *Champs-Élysées*, 29, 163; photograph "Coupé Panhard et Lavassor," in Augé, *Paris Anneés 30*, 414; Evenson, *Paris*, 36–7.

47. Miquel, *Main courante*, 253; Branguyn, *Everybody's Paris*, 99–100; Ybarra, "America's Conquest of Paris."

48. de Beauplan, "Au Paris du dollar"; di Borgo, *Champs-Élysées*, 110–11. On Fitzgerald, Bricktop with Haskins, *Bricktop*, 96.

49. Duhamel, *America the Menace*, 35; André Bellessort, "L'américanisme en france," *La Revue Hebdomadaire*, April 1928, 259–77. See also René Jeanne, "L'invasion cinématographique américaine," *Revue des deux mondes*, Feb. 15, 1930, 857–84; de Grazia, "Mass Culture and Sovereignty"; and Strauss, *Menace in the West*, 146–8.

50. Henri Duvernois, *Le boulevard*, trans. as "On the Boulevards," in Griggs, *My Paris*, 17–19; Lecomte, "New Paris Emerging Since the War"; Soupault, *American Influence in France*, 12–13.

51. Southard, *American Industry in Europe*, 93–102; Bellessort, "L'américanisme en france"; "Notables at Opening of Paris Paramount," *NYT*, Nov. 25, 1927, 25; Janet Flanner, "Paris Letter," *NY*, Dec. 24, 1927, 36–7.

52. Hayes, *France*, 183; di Borgo, *Champs-Élysées*, 47–51, 302–3.

53. Chadych and Leborgne, *Atlas de Paris*, 170–8; Flonneau, *Paris et l'automobile*, ch. 3; Studeny, *L'Invention de la vitesse*, 277–90; de Grazia, *Irresistible Empire*, 249. See also Marvin Black, "Americanizing Europe," *OI*, Nov. 13, 1929, 409–11; and Janet Flanner, "Paris Letter," *NY*, Oct. 27, 1928, 69–72.

54. Boyd Cable, *Observer*, reprinted as "Paris Revisited," *LA*, Dec. 20, 1919, 720–2. In similar terms Sisley Huddleston elegized the boulevardiers now "sadly submerged by the flood of hurrying folk who are on business bent. They are homeless on these boulevards of gorgeous shop-fronts and blinding lights": *Paris Salons, Cafés, Studios*, 18.

55. Herald, *Doing Europe*, 29; André Billy, *L'Œuvre*, trans. in Harold Callender, "Paris Finds Its Gayety Is Now Being Doubted," *NYT*, Dec. 16, 1928, pt. 10, 11.

56. Bellessort, "L'américanisme en france"; Ybarra, "America's Conquest of Paris"; Fegdal, *Fleur des curiositez*, 330–3; Gaston Rageot, "Les mœurs nouvelles," *L'Ill*, Aug. 7, 1926, 122–3; Bertaut, *Paris*, 283–4, 293–5. See also François Porché, "Idées et images du temps present," *L'Ill*, July 24, 1926, 74–5.

57. Slocombe, *Tumult and the Shouting*, 49–51, 234; photographs of Montparnasse at night in Cohen-Portheim, *Spirit of Paris*, 45; Nevill, *Days and Nights*, 300. See also W. Aldophe Roberts, "The Great Montparnasse Hoax," *SRL*, Aug. 30, 1924, 82; T. R. Ybarra, "Is Montparnasse 'Doomed'?" *OI*, May 8, 1929, 50; and Fegdal, *Coins curieux*.

58. Huddleston, *Back to Montparnasse*, 47; *London Graphic* in "American Blight on Artistic Montparnasse," *LD*, Oct. 22, 1927, 28–9. Jerrold Seigel also discusses the American eclipse of French bohemia after the war in *Bohemian Paris*.

59. Marchand, *Paris, histoire d'une ville*, 222–6; Hansen, *Expatriate Paris*, 121–5; photograph of the Dôme and blvd. Montparnasse, c. 1920, in Plazy,

*Paris, History, Architecture*, 414; Sabrié, *Nouveau Montparnasse*; quote from Stearns, *Street I Know*, 208.

60. For examples see Warnod, *Visages de Paris*, 313; Gonzagul Truc, "A Travers la Quinzaine Babel ou de la discourtoisie," *La Grande Revue*, July 1930, 139–41; *Guide des plaisirs à Paris*, 118–19; Cohen-Portheim, *Spirit of Paris*, 42–3; T. R. Ybarra, "A Bunch of French Worries," *OI*, June 5, 1929, 211; and Wambly Bald, "Montparnasse Today," *Vanity Fair*, July 1932, 31, 58.

61. Huddleston, *Paris Salons, Cafés, Studios*, 20–1, 25, 28.

62. Jules Bertaut's works are shot through with these themes; see *Le boulevard; Belles nuits de Paris*; and *Paris*, with quotes from 280–2.

63. *"Babel montparnassienne"* from Adolphe Basier, *Le cafard après la fête* (1929) quoted in Schor, *L'Opinion française*, 356; Mauclair quoted in Golan, *Modernity and Nostalgia*, 150–1.

64. *Le Petit Bleu*, May 9, 1932, and Louise Faure-Favier, *Blanche et Noir* (1928), both quoted in Schor, "Paris des étrangers," 28; *Le Petit Parisien*, Nov. 20, 1929 quoted in Schor, *L'Opinion française*, 348. On cosmopolitanism's association with Jewishness, see Lebovics, *True France*, 20. On its similarities with mongrelization, see Gilbert and Hancock, "New York City and the Transatlantic Imagination." On conflations of anti-Americanism and anti-semitism, see Roger, *American Enemy*, 318–19, 359–61.

65. Slocombe, *Paris in Profile*, 72.

66. In his discussion of foreigners at the center of Paris, the author does not refer to Americans by name, but it is clear—not least from his references to their propensities for mineral water and coffee with milk—that he is using foreigners as a synonym for Americans, a common conflation: Henri Duvernois, "On the Boulevards," in Griggs, *My Paris*, 20–2.

67. Richard, *Guide des grands ducs*, 3; Fegdal, *Dans notre vieux Paris*, 120; Warnod, *Plaisirs de la rue*, 9–11.

68. Bercovici, *Nights Abroad*, 211; V. Blasco Ibañez, "Night Life in Paris," *NYT*, Jan. 30, 1921, xxi.

69. "French Spoken in Paris," Aug. 26, 1928, pt. 2, 4; "Paris Cabaret Poets Told To Be Careful," Feb. 16, 1922, 2; "Freedom of Song," Feb. 17, 1922, 14; "Paris Roars at the Stage American," July 12, 1925, 22, all in *NYT*; Holland, *Things Seen in Paris*, 99–101; Nevill, *Days and Nights*, 134–6.

70. "Ile St. Louis," *TN*, June 11, 1924, 669–70; "Ile St. Louis Residents Band to Resist American Efforts to Modernize Paris," *NYT*, Feb. 24, 1929, pt. 3, 1. Among the invading Americans who lived for a time on the island were John Dos Passos and Caresse and Harry Crosby. Other expatriates, too, flocked to the Rendezvous des Mariniers restaurant on the quai d'Anjou (it is featured in Hemingway's *The Sun Also Rises*), since the offices of the *Transatlantic Review* and Robert McAlmon's Contact Editions were right next door: Hansen, *Expatriate Paris*, ch. 5.

71. Diana Bourbon, "'Paris by Night' is a Tourist Myth," *NYT*, June 20, 1926, SM12.

72. Weber, *Peasants into Frenchmen*; Golan, *Modernity and Nostalgia*; Lebovics, *True France*; Beale, *Modernist Enterprise*; Rearick, *French in Love and War*.

73. Erenberg, *Steppin' Out*.

74. Schwartz, *Spectacular Realities*; Abel, *Red Rooster Scare*.

75. Kear, "Vénus Noire"; Rearick, *French in Love and War*, 81.

76. Jean Guéhenno, *Revue de Paris*, Jan. 1, 1919, quoted in David Strauss, "The Rise of Anti-Americanism in France: French Intellectuals and American Civilization, 1917–1932," in Vaughan Baker and Amos Simpson, eds., *France and North America: L'Entre deux guerres* (Lafayette: University of Southwestern Louisiana, 1975), 79; Tardieu, "What France Thinks of Her War-Time Allies"; on the Paris Olympics, Roger, *American Enemy*, 202.

*Chapter Three*

1. Cmsr. Barthelemey to PP, Sept. 15, 1927 and report, "Manifestations pour protester contre l'exécution de Sacco et Vanzetti," Aug. 24, 1927 in APP B^A 1637; telegrams, Aug. 23–24, 1927, in APP B^A 1643; "Les bagarres à Paris," *Le Mat*, Aug. 24, 1927, 1–2; "Après l'exécution," *LT*, Aug. 25, 1927, 3.

2. Report, Brigadier Goret, Sept. 15, 1927 and Police Judiciaire report, "État des fonctionnaires et agents blessés grièvement," Sept. 15, 1927 in APP B^A 1643; "Police and Troops Repel Red Mobs," *PH*, Aug. 24, 1927, 9.

3. Avrich, *Sacco and Vanzetti*.

4. "La protestation mondiale," Aug. 9, 1927, 3 and "De suprêmes efforts sont faits," Aug. 23, 1927, 3, both in *L'Œ*; "L'agitation pour Sacco et Vanzetti," Aug. 9, 1927, 3, and "L'Affaire Sacco-Vanzetti," Aug. 10, 1927, 3, in *Le Fig*; "Le monde en révolte," Aug. 10, 1927, 2, "La protestation du prolétariat mondial," Aug. 20, 1927, 2, and "Pour sauver les deux martyrs innocents!" Aug. 22, 1927, 2, all in *L'Hum*; "L'agitation en France et à l'étranger," *Le Mat*, Aug. 22, 1927; numerous articles in *NYT*, Aug. 23, 1927, 1, 3, 5–6; "Protest Meetings for Sacco Held Everywhere," Aug. 23, 1927, 9, "Strikes in Argentina" and "Consul Hooted by Red Mob in Sydney," Aug. 24, 1927, 1 and 9, all in *PH*; "Dernière heure pour sauver Sacco et Vanzetti," *L'AF*, Aug. 23, 1927, 2; "L'exécution de Sacco et de Vanzetti," Aug. 24, 1927, 2–3 and "Les manifestations communistes," Aug. 27, 1927, 3, both in *LT*; Freda Kirchwey, "Some Mass Demonstrations," *TN*, Oct. 5, 1927, 337–8; Cannistraro, "Mussolini, Sacco-Vanzetti, and the Anarchists."

5. Memo, "Manifestation du 23 Août 1927," Aug. 29, 1927, report, "État Général . . . des dommages," Sept. 15, 1927, report, "État des fonctionnaires et agents blessés," Sept. 15, 1927, and Cmsr. Barthelemey to PP, Sept. 15, 1927 in APP B^A 1637.

6. Newton, *Tourist in Spite of Himself*, 70–1.

7. Clipping, Paul Faure, "Ni Sébastopol, ni le Moulin-Rouge," *Le Pop*, Sept. 3, 1927 in APP B^A 1637.

8. Martin, *France and the Après Guerre*; Rosenberg, *Policing Paris*.

9. "ECCI Appeal," *Inprekorr*, Aug. 9, 1927, in Degras, *Communist International*, 401–2; report, Oct. 14, 1921 and clipping, "Pour Sacco et Vanzetti," *Le Lib*, Oct. 21, 1921, 1–2 in APP B^A 1643; Cmsr. Barthelemey to PP, Sept. 15, 1927 in APP B^A 1637; Creagh, *Sacco et Vanzetti*, 173–6. On the bomb targeting Herrick see letters, Oct.–Nov. 1921 in MHP, folders 17–20. On other bombings in late 1921, see McGirr, "Passion of Sacco and Vanzetti."

10. For a discussion of these longstanding networks as they applied to the Sacco-Vanzetti affair, see McGirr, "Passion of Sacco and Vanzetti."

11. Berry, *History of the French Anarchist Movement*, 106–7, 149–50; Laurent Couder, "Les Italiens de la région parisienne dans les années 1920," in Milza, *Italiens en france*, 501–46; Wohl, *French Communism in the Making*, 394–5; Gautherot, *Monde communiste*, 195–203.

12. Data for 139 of those arrested allows only for informed estimates: report, Brigadier Goret, Sept. 15, 1927, and arrest records in APP B^A 1637; bulletins in the French press and *Paris Herald* for Aug. 25-28, Sept. 1 and 4, 1927.

13. "Art" to "Gene," Chicago, Nov. 18, 1921 in AFP, Series 8; Lyons, *Life and Death of Sacco and Vanzetti*; McGirr, "Passion of Sacco and Vanzetti"; Russell, *Tragedy in Dedham*, 107, 216, 222, 334, 408.

14. Eley, *Forging Democracy*, 123–38; Preston, *Aliens and Dissenters*; Becker and Berstein, *Histoire de l'anti-communisme*.

15. Correspondence and two-part report by Eugene Lyons, undated in AFP, Series 2B. Palmer Raid statistics in Topp, *Sacco and Vanzetti Case*, 17.

16. Kruse & Bosse, "Sacco-Vanzetti Case," reports to ECCI, Sept. 22 and 23, 1927 in CA/CPUSA, Reel 69, Delo 936. James Cannon of the New York Workers' Party tried to keep defense organizers on the line without committing too much: "Dear Comrade Lyons. . . . you seem to be under the impression that I was skeptical about our ability to accomplish anything by the use of our well-known party machinery. No, that was not it exactly. I didn't have it quite clear in my head just how we were going to accomplish it. I feel quite sure now that we will get results in most of these cases. . . . Yours in the fight": letter to Eugene Lyons, April 20, 1922 in AFP, unprocessed box.

17. McMeekin, *Red Millionaire*, 202; bounced checks in AFP, Series 2B.

18. Report, Eugene Lyons, undated in AFP, Series 2B. See also reports of American consulates and embassies in 1921, compiled in United States FBI files, Sacco/Vanzetti Case, Part I, available at http://foia.fbi.gov.

19. Resolution, May 10, 1925 in AFP, Series 8; Kruse & Bosse, "Sacco-Vanzetti Case."

20. Reports, "Le soir tribune des gauches," and "La journée nationale pour Sacco et Vanzetti," June 7, 1927 in APP B^A 1643; Lecoin, *Cours d'une vie*,

103–4, 116–20, 130–42; Garel, *Louis Lecoin*, 1–10; Creagh, *Sacco et Vanzetti*,
12, 197–200, 213–18; "Le mouvement pour Sacco et Vanzetti en France,"
Sept. 13, 1927 in CA/CPUSA, Reel 69, Delo 937.

21. Lyons, *Life and Death of Sacco and Vanzetti*, 171; S-V DC statement, June
1927 in AFP, Series 2B; Temkin, *Sacco-Vanzetti Affair*, 16–22.

22. Plans for fundraisers and S-V DC meeting minutes, esp. Dec. 1924–March
1925 in AFP, Series 2B; letter [Eugene Lyons], March 29, 1921, unprocessed box. Lists of amazing breadth on newspapers as far away as India and
Australia can be found throughout AFP. For these and frequent references
to Mooney, see Series 8. On tailoring correspondence to recipients' tastes,
see Series 2B.

23. On the involvement of the League of the Rights of Man and other French
moderates, see Temkin, *Sacco-Vanzetti Affair*, ch. 3.

24. Nicolas Faucier, "Souvenir d'un permanent anarchiste (1927–1929), " *Le
Mouvement Social*, April–June 1973, 47–56.

25. In December 1922, the Third International sanctioned cooperation with
other leftists. By July 1924, however, the Comintern increasingly pressed
national parties to conform to its own imperatives. This policy of "Bolshe-
vization" escalated during the mid and late twenties, by which point, as
Geoff Eley relates, Communist parties retreated "from broader Left arenas
into their own belligerent world": *Forging Democracy*, 228.

26. S-V DC meeting minutes, 1924–1927, and S-V DC statement, June 1927
in AFP, Series 2B; Federated Press Eastern Bureau, July 12, 1926 and Roger
Baldwin to E. G. Flynn, Sept. 2, 1926, unprocessed box. Sean McMeekin
corroborates that Communists withheld funds, suggesting that the ILD
collected nearly $500,000 but forwarded only approximately $6,000 to the
Boston Committee: *Red Millionaire*, 202 and 347 fn31.

27. Kruse & Bosse, "Sacco-Vanzetti Case."

28. Judt, *Reconstruction du parti socialiste*, 149–64; Selon Zyromski, *Le Pop*, Nov.
6, 1921, cited in Judt, 152; Berry, *History of the French Anarchist Movement*,
84–6.

29. Report, Service des Renseignements Généraux et des Jeux, Aug. 23, 1927
in APP B$^A$ 1643. It is difficult to accurately assess membership, but most
scholars suggest that Communist ranks during the mid-twenties remained
close to the party's initial size of some 50,000 members, albeit with
spectacular turnover. By one estimate, between the summer of 1924 and
the beginning of 1926, the PCF experienced a 70 percent turnover in
membership, but still counted some 75,000 members: Stephen Hopkins,
"French Communism, the Comintern, and Class against Class: Interpretations and Rationales," in Worley, *In Search of Revolution*, 108. Statistics for
crowd sizes are equally elusive. Invariably, *L'Humanité* overreported
numbers for communist gatherings, whereas others likely underreported
them.

30. On telegraph wires in Charlestown prison, see Russell, *Tragedy in Dedham*, 422.

31. "Nous voulons la paix des rues," *Le Fig*, Aug. 24, 1927, 1.

32. Russell, *Tragedy in Dedham*, 355, 380–4, 416; Creagh, *Sacco et Vanzetti*, 14, 167, 226; Temkin, *Sacco-Vanzetti Affair*, 38; "Anatole France to the People of America," *TN*, Nov. 23, 1921, 586; Simone de Beauvoir, *Memoirs of a Dutiful Daughter*, James Kirkup, trans. (New York: Harper & Row, [1958], 1974), 238; Seldes, *World Panorama*, 258. Copies of letters accompanying these petitions in AFP, esp. Series 8.

33. "Press Comment on the Sacco-Vanzetti Execution," Sept. 14, 1927, 252–3 and "World Opinion on Sacco and Vanzetti," Aug. 24, 1927, 174–5, both in *TN*; "Around the World," *LA*, Sept. 15, 1927, 471–7; "French Protests Made Calmly," *NYT*, Aug. 22, 1927, 3; report, "Le mouvement pour Sacco et Vanzetti en France," Sept. 13, 1927 in CA/CPUSA, Reel 69, Delo 937; Temkin, *Sacco-Vanzetti Affair*, 124–6; Seldes, *World Panorama*, 249–57.

34. Seldes, *World Panorama*, 249–57; Levinson, *Figures américaines*, 51; *Neues Wiener Tagblatt*, trans. in "Around the World"; H. G. Wells, "Wells Speaks Some Plain Words to US" *NYT Mag.*, Oct. 16, 1927, 3, 23 in *Way the World is Going*, 270–81. On comparisons to the Dreyfus Affair, see Temkin, *Sacco-Vanzetti Affair*, 3–7, 107–16.

35. Letters and telegrams to Fuller and Jane Addams's telegrams to Sen. Borah and Pres. Coolidge, c. Aug. 1927 in AFP, Series 8.

36. Seldes, *World Panorama*, 258–9; Sunday in Russell, *Tragedy in Dedham*, 385; on Legionnaires, see Lyons, *Life and Death*, 173–5. Borah's comments reappear in many accounts: see, for example, Shachtman, "Sacco and Vanzetti: Labor's Martyrs," 70. On the relationship between overseas protesters and backlash in the United States, see Temkin, *Sacco-Vanzetti Affair*.

37. Rosenberg, *Spreading the American Dream*, 38–86, 122–60.

38. Many articles, *PH* and *NYT*, Aug. 22–4, 1927; Russell, *Tragedy in Dedham*, 216–19.

39. Spivak, *Man in His Time*, 126–8.

40. Ruth Crawford, "On the Trail of Sacco-Vanzetti Abroad," *TN*, Oct. 5, 1927, 334–5; Cannistraro, "Mussolini, Sacco-Vanzetti, and the Anarchists"; "Europe on Edge," *NYT*, Aug. 23, 1927, 5; Vorse, *Footnote to Folly*, 339.

41. Annie Burger, "Paul Vaillant-Couturier," in Jean Maitron and Claude Pennetier, eds., *Dictionnaire biographique du mouvement ouvrier français: Quatrième partie, 1914–1939*, vol. XLII (Paris: Ouvrières, 1992), 389–94; "L'indignation universelle du prolétariat contre le crime!" *L'Hum*, Aug. 24, 1927, 2.

42. "Our Paris Embassy Heavily Guarded," *NYT*, Aug. 20, 1927, 4; "Les Mesures de précaution," *L'Œ*, Aug. 23, 1927, 3.

43. "En France, en Europe, dans le monde entier des protestations s'élèvent," *L'Œ*, Aug. 24, 1927; Cmsr. Barthelemey to PP, Sept. 15, 1927 and report,

"Manifestations pour protester contre l'exécution de Sacco et Vanzetti," Aug. 24, 1927 in APP B$^A$ 1637; telegram from Cmsr. Courbier, Aug. 23, 1927 in APP B$^A$ 1643. *Vache*, meaning cow, served as an epithet similar to *cochon* (pig) or *salaud* (bastard). In popular slang, *une vache* connoted a policeman or a police spy. Further, the phrase *"Mort aux vaches!"* was a motto criminals often tattooed on their bodies: Barrère, *Argot and Slang*.

44. "Hier, au Bois de Vincennes," *L'Œ*, Aug. 8, 1927, 1–2; Robert Chenevoix, "La manifestation pour Sacco et Vanzetti," *Le Fig*, Aug. 8, 1927, 1; Claude Jeantet, "Quinze mille révolutionnaires défilent," *L'AF*, Aug. 8, 1927, 2; telegrams from Vincennes, Aug. 7, 1927, and clipping, *L'Hum*, Aug. 7, 1927, 1–2 in APP B$^A$ 1643.

45. Omitting the *panthéonisation* of Jean Jaurès in 1924 (discussed below) and listing no protests for 1925, this report likely excluded demonstrations during the left-leaning *Cartel des gauches* government from May 1924 to July 1926: APP B$^A$ 1851, dossier Listes des Différents Manifestations, c. 1936; "Note sur les demandes d'Interpellation," Oct. 7, 1927 in APP B$^A$ 1637.

46. APP B$^A$ 1643 is flush with documents attesting to this game of cat and mouse.

47. "La lutte contre le communisme," Aug. 23, 1927, 3 and "Paris ouvrier maître du pavé," Aug. 24, 1927, 1, both in *L'Hum*; "Note sur les demandes d'Interpellation," Oct. 7, 1927 in APP B$^A$ 1637; report on Comité Sacco-Vanzetti plans, Aug. 22, 1927, report, "Assemblée d'information des cadres de la région parisienne du parti communiste," Aug. 23, 1927, and report, "Les dispositions prises pour ce soir," Aug. 23, 1927 in APP B$^A$ 1643; Sheldon Whitehouse to U.S. Sec. of State, Aug. 24, 1927, RDS, 851.00/926.

48. "Manifestation 23 Août—Service d'Ordre," and telegram from Cmsr. Gourbier, Aug. 23, 1927 in APP B$^A$ 1643; "Les protestations du monde civilisé," *L'Œ*, Aug. 24, 1927, 3; "Paris Mobs Loot Shops," *NYT*, Aug. 24, 1927, 1; letter, among others, to PP, Aug. 24, 1927 and clipping, *L'Intransigeant*, Aug. 24 or 25, 1927 in APP B$^A$ 1637; *Le Petit Journal* in "Sarraut voulait son 'émeute,'" *L'Hum*, Aug. 25, 1927, 1; "Police and Troops Repel Red Mobs," *PH*, Aug. 24, 1927, 9; "Une déclaration de M. Chiappe," *LT*, Aug. 25, 1927, 3; "Les manifestants assommés par les flics," *L'Hum*, Aug. 25, 1927, 1–2; "Sur les boulevards," *Le Fig*, Aug. 24, 1927, 1–2.

49. Clipping, "Discussion de plusieurs interpellations," *Journal Officiel*, Jan. 21, 1928, 206–22 in APP B$^A$ 1643.

50. Stearns, *Street I Know*, 213–14; Higonnet, *Paris*, 46–74; Ferguson, *Paris as Revolution*.

51. Rearick, *French in Love and War*, ch. 7; Tartakowsky, *Manifestations de rue*, pts. I–II. Geoff Eley similarly points to 1935 as a turning point when the language used by French communists "shifted dramatically from the class

struggle to 'people' and 'nation.'" In this, too, the Sacco-Vanzetti riots anticipated future developments: *Forging Democracy*, 264.

52. On the political associations inflecting the Paris east and west, see Maurice Agulhon, "Paris: A Traversal from East to West," in Nora, *Realms of Memory*, 523–52.

53. Cohen, *Paris dans l'imaginaire national*, 26–32; report, Gardiens de la Paix Gonnet and Gilbert, Aug. 23, 1927 in APP B^A 1643; report, Brigadier Goret, Sept. 15, 1927, Cmssr. Barthelemey to PP, Sept. 15, 1927, and CGTU poster in APP B^A 1637.

54. Paul, *Last Time I Saw Paris*, 116. Extensive coverage of these tributes appeared in French and American newspapers between Aug. 24 and Sept. 4. See, for example, "Après l'émeute," Aug. 26, 1927, 1 and "La souillure effacée," Aug, 27, 1927, 2, in *Le Fig*.; "Après l'insulte de la 'crapule' au Poilu inconnu," Aug. 25, 1927, 2 and "Après le Sacrilege" Aug. 28, 1927, 2, in *L 'AF*; "La cérémonie expiatoire de dimanche," *Le Mat.*, Sept. 1, 1927. *Gueules cassées*, meaning broken faces, referred to those disfigured during the war.

55. *Le Gaulois* in "Revue de la Presse," *LT*, Aug. 26, 1927, 3; clipping, "Le bilan d'une soirée d'émeute," *La Liberté*, Aug. 25, 1927, 1 in APP B^A 1643; Marcel Lucain, *Paris-Midi* in "Revue de la Presse," *LT*, Aug. 25, 1927, 4 and "Les grandes manœuvres de la révolution," *L'AF*, Aug. 25, 1927, 3.

56. Chevalier, *Laboring Classes and Dangerous Classes*; Higonnet, *Paris*, 75–85.

57. In the five years preceding 1927, the *banlieue* received almost 220,000 new residents. The city, by contrast, lost over 25,000. Blanc, *Ceinture rouge*, 7–9, 21–5; Demangeon, *Paris*, 19–22, 46–60; Fourcaut, *Banlieue rouge*, 12–37.

58. Eugen Weber, "France," in Rogger and Weber, *European Right*, 71–127; Gustave Hervé, *L'AF* in Weber, 104–5; Tartakowsky, *Manifestations de rue*, chs. 4–5.

59. Lhande, *Christ dans la banlieue*, 3, 12–13; Blanc, *Ceinture rouge*, 9, 12–13, 187–8, 192.

60. Rosenberg, *Policing Paris*, 63; Julián Casanova, "Terror and Violence: The Dark Face of Spanish Anarchism," *International Labor and Working-Class History*, 67 (Spring 2005), 79–99; support letters to Herrick, Oct.–Nov. 1921 in MHP, folders 17–20.

61. Articles in *L'AF* and *Le Fig.*, Aug. 7–12, 1927, 2–3; "De suprêmes efforts sont faits," *L'Œ*, Aug. 23, 1927, 3; "Protest Meetings for Sacco Held Everywhere," Aug. 23, 1927, 9 and "Bombs Thrown in Red Protests," Aug. 24, 1927, 1, both in *PH*.

62. "Le Parti de l'émeute," Aug. 25, 1927, 1 and "Politique et droit commun," Aug. 27, 1927, 1, both in *LT*; Albert Sarraut trans. in Sheldon Whitehouse to U.S. Sec. of State, Aug. 24, 1927, RDS, 851.00/926.

63. Of forty-seven arrested rioters whose addresses could be established, only eleven claimed residence outside the city walls.

64. "Paris Streets Again Quiet," *PH*, Aug. 25, 1927, 9; "Paris Police Crush New Red Outbreak," *NYT*, Aug. 25, 1927, 1.

65. Josephson, *Life among the Surrealists*, 346–8; Putnam, *Paris Was Our Mistress*, 116–17; damage report by Jules Veschambres in APP D$^A$ 434; "Paris Mobs Loot Shops," *NYT*, Aug. 24, 1927, 1.

66. Orders to Meyer, Peyrot, and Niclausse, Aug. 23, 1927, and Paul Guichard to district chiefs, Aug. 23, 1927 in APP B$^A$ 1643.

67. "Manifestations pour protester contre l'exécution," Aug. 24, 1927 in APP B$^A$ 1637; photograph of Fouquet's in Lanzmann, *Paris des années 30*, 173.

68. Photographs in *Illustrated War News*, Aug. 12, 1914, 16–18.

69. That a café patron fired the first shot was not as fanciful a claim as it sounded. Americans were known for packing and even on occasion brandishing guns in France. In the wake of the war, armed doughboys lingering abroad caused problems for French authorities. African Americans working in the tough neighborhoods of Montmartre also sometimes carried guns, and other visitors might have also brought weapons to the poorer parts of the city. Guidebooks sometimes recommended this precaution for tourists slumming in the east.

70. Telegram from Cmsr. Gaud, Aug. 23, 1927, and M. Bittard-Monin to the PP, Aug. 24, 1927 in APP B$^A$ 1643; Diamant-Berger to PP, Aug. 25, 1927, and report, "Manifestations pour protester contre l'exécution," Aug. 24, 1927 in APP B$^A$ 1637; damage report by Gino Casini of the Café Tortoni in APP D$^A$ 434; Diamant-Berger to Léon Blum reprinted in "Après l'émeute communiste," *L'AF*, Sept. 1, 1927, 2; "Police and Troops Repel Red Mobs," *PH*, Aug. 24, 1927, 9; "Des cafés Wepler et Tortoni des bourgeois ont tiré sur la foule," *L'Hum*, Aug. 25, 1927, 2.

71. Report, Service des Renseignements Généraux, Aug. 7, 1927, and clipping, "ASSASSINÉS! Tous à l'Ambassade américaine!" *Le Lib*, special ed., Aug. 23, 1927, 1 in APP B$^A$ 1643.

72. "Les bagarres à Paris," *Le Mat*, Aug. 24, 1927, 1–2; "Dans le quartier des boîtes de nuit," Aug. 24, 1927, 2 and "Des cafés Wepler et Tortoni," Aug. 25, 1927, 2, both in *L'Hum*; damage report by Gaston Namur of the Brasserie Wepler in APP D$^A$ 434, dossier Copie des Procédures constatant Bris de clôture, vols et dégâts . . . Automobiles; report, "Manifestations pour protester contre l'exécution," Aug. 24, 1927, and report, "État Général . . . des dommages," Sept. 15, 1927 in APP B$^A$ 1637; telegram from Brigadier Diolot, Aug. 23, 1927, and report, Cmsr. Siron, "Déprédations commises au cours d'une manifestation," Aug. 24, 1927 in APP B$^A$ 1643. On the Auto-Confort Touring agency, see Brace, *Americans in France*, 510 and Brewster, *American Directory*, 275.

73. "Police and Troops Repel Red Mobs," *PH*, Aug. 24, 1927, 9; damage report by Louis Soulages of the Brasserie Mikado in APP D$^A$ 434.

74. See Vaillant-Couturier's front-page articles for *L'Humanité* on Aug. 5, 8, 10, 22, and 23, 1927. The experiences of Paul, the boy, prefigured the urban political sensitivities of Vaillant-Couturier, the soldier, poet, and Communist militant. On bus rides as a child through the capital, his father had pointed out the scars of past sieges, the damage done by insurrections. "Decidedly, Paris is a battlefield," the young Paul concluded: Jean Maitron, *Dictionnaire biographique du mouvement ouvrier français: Quatrième partie: 1914–1939* (Paris: Ouvrières, 1992), 389–94; Vaillant-Couturier, *French Boy*, 96–101, 148–56.

75. Report, "État Général . . . des dommages," Sept. 15, 1927 in APP B$^A$ 1637; Cmsr. Siron, "Au sujet des manifestants . . . Boulevard de Clichy et au Moulin Rouge," Aug. 24, 1927 in APP B$^A$ 1643; report, Brigadier Diolot, "Coups de revolver et bris de glaces," Aug. 23, 1927, and damage reports by Alphonse Becquart of the Bal du Moulin-Rouge and Henri Schild of the music hall du Moulin-Rouge and brasserie Graff in APP D$^A$ 434.

76. Clipping, Vaillant-Couturier, "Avec les Martyrs Face au Dollar!" *L'Hum*, Aug. 24, 1927, 1 in APP B$^A$ 1637. *La noce* here refers to revelry or high life.

77. Clipping, "Sébastopol et Moulin-Rouge," *L'Hum*, Sept. 5, 1927 in APP B$^A$ 1637; Vaillant-Couturier, "Vont-ils tuer?" *L'Hum*, Aug. 22, 1927, 1.

78. *L'Humanité*, July 25, 1926 trans. in Levenstein, *Seductive Journey*, 269–70; ECCI meeting and remarks by Dmitrii Manuilsky, Dec. 1927, summarized in Degras, *Communist International*, 401. For more on the events of July 1926, see ch. 2.

79. Dos Passos, *Best Times*, 169; Miller, Pennybacker, and Rosenhaft, "Mother Ada Wright and the International Campaign to Free the Scottsboro Boys."

80. Paul, *Last Time I Saw Paris*, 131.

81. Taittinger, *Le National* in "L'affaire Sacco-Vanzetti," *Le Fig*, Aug. 23, 1927; Daudet, "Le communisme et les grands ancêtres," *L'AF*, Aug. 31, 1927, 1; Jacques Ditte, "Les leçons de l'émeute," *Le Fig*, Sept. 1, 1927, 1.

## Chapter Four

1. Historians sometimes mention Chiappe's purge in passing, although no one appears to have researched it specifically. Indeed, the files on which this chapter is based have largely been overlooked; they are dispersed in different boxes at the Paris Police Archives, many which were found in a box simply labeled "Various Reports."

2. Chiappe, *Paroles d'ordre*, APP, Livre n° 122, esp. 38, 40, 50, 62–7, 140, 203, 232; Zimmer, *Septennat policier*, esp. 92 and 117; Stead, *Police of Paris*, 155–6.

3. Sieburg, *Dieu est-il-français?*, 228.

4. "107—Question de M. Lionel Nastorg à M. le Préfet de police sur les mesures . . . pour opérer un nettoyage," *Supplément au Bulletin Municipal*

*Officiel du mardi 5 décembre 1933*, pp. 4345–51; "French Strongboy?" *RR*, July 1936, 58.

5. "Question de M. Fernand-Laurrent à Monsieur le Préfet de police sur l'épuration de Paris et plus particulièrement sur la surveillance de la profession très « spéciale » de danseur mondain," *Supplément au Bulletin Municipal Officiel du dimanche 18 mars 1928*, pp. 1437–41; report, Cmsr. Priolet, April 10, 1933 in APP B^A 1689, dossier Répression de la Prostitution sur la Voie Publique, 1906–1946.

6. Rosenberg, *Policing Paris*.

7. "Question de M. Fernand-Laurrent"; "Note sur les demandes d'Interpellation . . . au sujet des incidents du 23 Août," Oct. 7, 1927 in APP B^A 1637; "Paris Stifles Vice to Guard Legion Guests," *CT*, Sept. 10, 1927, 18; "Paris Cleans House for Visit of Legion," *NYT*, Sept. 10, 1927, 19; Georges de la Fouchardière, "Une idée de M. Chiappe," *L'Œ*, Sept. 17, 1927, 2.

8. Fanning, *France and Sherwood Anderson*, 44; Zimmer, *Septennat policier*, 92–3, 122–31; "Question de M. Fernand-Laurrent"; report, "Les outrages aux bonnes mœurs commis sur la voie publique," July 18, 1928 in APP B^A 2245, dossier Sécurité dans Paris et à la Morale Publique; Brassaï, *Secret Paris of the 30's*; "105—Question de M. Lionel Nastorg à M. le Préfet de police," *Supplément au Bulletin Municipal Officiel du dimanche 3 décembre 1933*, 4320–33.

9. For this development in New York, see Kathy Peiss, *Cheap Amusements: Working Women and Leisure in Turn-of-the Century New York* (Philadelphia: Temple University Press, 1986) and Erenberg, *Steppin' Out*. For Europe, see Erika Rappaport, *Shopping for Pleasure: Women in the Making of London's West End* (Princeton: Princeton University Press, 2000); Roberts, *Disruptive Acts*; and Katharina von Ankum, ed., *Women in the Metropolis: Gender and Modernity in Weimar Culture* (Berkeley: University of California Press, 1997).

10. V. Blasco Ibañez, "Night Life in Paris," *NYT*, Jan. 30, 1921, xxi.

11. Cohen-Portheim, *Spirit of Paris*, ix. A *boîte de nuit* was a nightclub or dive, often a tourist trap.

12. Corbin, *Women for Hire*; Boudard, *L'âge d'or des maisons closes*; Brassaï, *Secret Paris of the 30's*; Windstaff, *Lower Than Angels*, 114–16; Zimmer, *Septennat policier*, 124–30, 145–9; Hansen, *Expatriate Paris*, 153.

13. Valti, *Femmes de cinq heures*; Bizard, *Vie des filles*, 110–15, 157–8, 211–12; Morain, *Underworld of Paris*, 259–60; Windstaff, *Lower Than Angels*, 114–16; Zimmer, *Septennat policier*, 91–3, 124–30.

14. Bertaut, *Belles nuits de Paris*, 37–9. On *partouzes*, report, "Les outrages aux bonnes mœurs commis sur la voie publique," July 18, 1928 in APP B^A 2245, dossier Sécurité dans Paris et à la Morale Publique; Zimmer, *Septennat policier*, 92–3; and "British Spinster Sees Paris 'in the Nude' and Calls Cops," *CT*, Aug. 27, 1930, 8.

15. Corbin, *Women for Hire*, 136 fn17.

16. Brassaï, *Secret Paris of the 30's*; Miquel, *Main courante*, 250, 262, 265–7; Gravigny, *Montmartre en 1925*, 87–91; Corbin, *Women for Hire*, 332–7; "Rapport au sujet des filles soumises stationnant sur la place de l'Etoile," Nov. 11, 1921 in APP B$^A$ 1689, dossier Prostitution: Plaintes et Réclamations; report, Cmsr. Chain, Nov. 22, 1938 in APP B$^A$ 1690, dossier Rapports divers . . . Pédérastie.

17. Bertaut, *Paris*, 282; Roberts, *Civilization without Sexes*, 1–87; Chadwick and Latimer, *Modern Woman*, 3–19.

18. Cohen-Portheim, *Spirit of Paris*, 24–5; Gravigny, *Montmartre en 1925*, 50–3; Josephy and McBride, *Paris Is a Woman's Town*, 231–6; Morain, *Underworld of Paris*, 46–9, 283–5; "Question de M. Fernand-Laurrent"; "Paris Police Begin a Drive on 'Gigolos,'" *NYT*, Feb. 4, 1928, 3.

19. Michael Sibalis, "The Palais-Royal and the Homosexual Subculture of Nineteenth-Century Paris" and Leslie Choquette, "Homosexuals in the City: Representations of Lesbian and Gay Space in Nineteenth-Century Paris," in Merrick and Sibalis, *Homosexuality in French History and Culture*, 117–30, 149–68; Peniston, *Pederasts and Others*.

20. Reports, 1930s, in APP B$^A$ 1690, dossier Rapports divers . . . Pédérastie; Zimmer, *Septennat policier*, 112–17; Brassaï, *Secret Paris of the 30's*; Barbedette and Carassou, *Paris gay 1925*, esp. 15–38; Tamagne, *Histoire de l'homosexualité*, 48–9, 79–89. For a literary history of famous Left Bank lesbians, see Benstock, *Women of the Left Bank*.

21. André du Dognon quoted in Barbedette and Carassou, *Paris gay 1925*, 56–61.

22. Copley, *Sexual Moralities in France*, 135–6; Francesca Sautman, "Invisible Women: Lesbian Working-Class Culture in France, 1880–1930," in Merrick and Ragan, *Homosexuality in Modern France*, 177–201; Tamagne, *Histoire de l'homosexualité*, 83, 503–14; Chauncey, *Gay New York*.

23. Dewitte, *Mouvements nègres en France*; Report by Cmsr. Priolet, Aug. 25, 1931 in APP B$^A$ 1690, dossier Rapports divers . . . Pédérastie; Bertaut, *Paris, 1870–1935*, 272; Brassaï, *Secret Paris of the 30's*; Blake, *Tumulte Noir*.

24. Report by Cmsr. Priolet, *ibid.*; van Paassen, *Days of Our Years*, 101; Longstreet, *We All Went to Paris*, 234, 404; Reynolds, *Paris with the Lid Lifted*, 189–200; Goddard, *Jazz Away from Home*.

25. Boyer, *Urban Masses and Moral Order*; Gilfoyle, "Moral Origins of Political Surveillance."

26. Boyer, *Urban Masses and Moral Order*, esp. 203–19 and Croly quote p. 196; Erenberg, *Steppin' Out*.

27. Stansell, *American Moderns*, 76, 236, 326–8.

28. Nevill, *Days and Nights*, 14, 58–9; Charters, *This Must Be the Place*, 103, 162–3. On American women's new license abroad, see also Josephy and McBride, *Paris Is a Woman's Town*, esp. v, 231–8, 243–52; Williams, *Voyage to Pagany*.

29. Windstaff, *Lower Than Angels*, 100, 117; Bizard, *Vie des filles*, 212; report, Nov. 10, 1934 and two reports, "Cabinet de M. L. Lefebvre," March 20, 1936 in APP B$^A$ 1690, dossier Rapports divers . . . Pédérastie.

30. Reynolds, *Paris with the Lid Lifted*, 194–200; "Arrest 60 in Paris Raids," *NYT*, Oct. 31, 1924, 40; Bertaut, *Belles nuits de Paris*, 189–94.

31. Windstaff, *Lower Than Angels*, 124; Laney, *Paris Herald*, 159; Chancellor, *How to Be Happy in Paris*, 17; Longstreet, *We All Went to Paris*, 420; Pascal, *Les livres de l'enfer*; report, Cmsr. Priolet, Jan. 11, 1932 in APP B$^A$ 1689, dossier: Pièces et Rapports Divers; clippings from offending publications in APP B$^A$ 2242, dossier: Obscénités: Annonces Immorales.

32. A Paris Observer, "Visitors of Unclean Mind," *LA*, Sept. 11, 1926, 589–90.

33. E. Waugh, "Labels, an Essay on Travel," *Fortnightly Review*, April 1930, 485–99; van Paassen, *Days of Our Years*, 101–2.

34. Laughlin, *So You're Going to Paris!*, 73; Edwards, *Paris*, 84.

35. Reynolds, *Cocktail Continental*, 41; Windstaff, *Lower Than Angels*, 114–16. See also Bizard, *Vie des filles*, 157–8; Valti, *Femmes de cinq heures*, 155–85; reports by Cmsr. Caron, Dec. 10 and 11, 1923 in APP B$^A$ 1689, dossier Bastard, Eugènie; Dir. of Police Judiciaire to PP, July 19, 1928 in APP B$^A$ 2245, dossier Sécurité dans Paris . . . Attentats à la Pudeur; report, Cmsr. Priolet, Dec. 22, 1928 in APP B$^A$ 1690, Dossier: Rapports divers . . . Pédérastie.

36. Greer, *What a Buckeye Cover Man Saw*, 67–8; "Le service de la répression des ouvrages licencieux," March 19, 1931 and report, Cmsr. Priolet, Jan. 11, 1932 in APP B$^A$ 1689, dossier Pièces et Rapports Divers; "Des interprètes qui n'exercent pas sur la voie publique à proprement parler" in APP B$^A$ 2242, dossier Obscénités: Statistique sur l'Activité du Service de Répression; Dir. Police Judiciaire to PP, July 19, 1928 in APP B$^A$ 2245, dossier Sécurité dans Paris . . . Attentats à la Pudeur; Cmsr. Général au Tourisme to PP, July 29, 1936 and responses, Sept. 28, and Oct. 29, 1936 in APP B$^A$ 2255, dossier Haut Commissariat du Tourisme. See also Herald, *Doing Europe*, 21, 26, 48; Randolph Bartlett, "Paris Racket," *AM*, Aug. 1932, 412–20; and "Urban Vignettes," *LA*, Jan. 24, 1925.

37. Reynolds, *Paris with the Lid Lifted*, 38–9, 43–4; Miller, *Tropic of Cancer*, 158. See also Williams, *Autobiography of William Carlos Williams*, 252–7; Chancellor, *How to Be Happy in Paris*, 100–3; and Le Gallienne, *From a Paris Garret*, 56.

38. Windstaff, *Lower Than Angels*, 112. See also Longstreet, *We All Went to Paris*, 235; and Walter Havighurst, "Collegians in Quest of Culture," *NAR*, June 1930, 757–61.

39. Woon, *Paris That's Not in the Guide Books*, 257–60.

40. Shirer, *20th Century Journey: The Start*, 22.

41. APP B$^A$ 1689: Petitions and follow-up reports, 1920–1928 in dossier Prostitution: Plaintes et Réclamations; report, Cmsr. Priolet, April 10, 1933 in

dossier Répression de la Prostitution sur la Voie Publique, 1906–1946; Paul Piètre to Dir. Police Judiciaire, January 1934 in APP B$^A$ 2242, dossier Obscénités: Boîtes des Quais, Bouquinistes. See also complaints in APP B$^A$ 2245, dossier Sécurité en Général . . . Coupures de Journaux.

42. Complaints and follow-up reports in APP B$^A$ 2242, Dossier: Camelots, vendeurs de cartes postales obscènes.

43. M. Panabière to PP, July 3, 1935 and numerous other letters, esp. for 1930–1935 in APP B$^A$ 2242, dossier Outrages aux Mœurs: Affiches de Théâtre, Cinémas, Music-Halls. On the ban against immoral displays, see Paul Guichard to districts chiefs, Feb. 27, 1929 in dossier Camelots, vendeurs de cartes postales obscènes.

44. Letters and petitions, late twenties and early thirties, scattered throughout APP B$^A$ 2242.

45. Peniston, *Pederasts and Others*; Copley, *Sexual Moralities in France*, ch. 6; Stora-Lamarre, *L'enfer de la III$^e$ République*, esp. 88–95. On a renewed campaign of *épuration* in the late thirties, see clippings in APP B$^A$ 2249, dossier Epuration: Coupures de Presse.

46. "Would Clean Paris Stage," March 23, 1923, 17; "Bar Nudity in Theatre," March 24, 1923, 6; and "Paris, May 2," May 6, 1923, X2, all in *NYT*.

47. Ordinance, April 5, 1924 in APP D$^A$ 742; "Paris Sweeps Out All Unofficial Guides," *NYT*, April 11, 1924, 23.

48. "Arrest 60 in Paris Raids," Oct. 31, 1924, 40 and "New Prefect Wars on Vice in Paris," Nov. 16, 1924, 30, both in *NYT*.

49. Reports on anti-prostitution meetings in APP B$^A$ 1689, dossiers Répression de la Prostitution sur la Voie Publique, 1906–1946, Ligues—Associations—Congrès, and Pièces et Rapports Divers. See also 'Union Temporaire' contre la Prostitution réglementée et la Traite des Femmes, "Discours prononcés le 6 février 1931 à la Salle des Sociétés Savantes," BHVP, In-16° 619 608; E. Armand, "La prostitution et ses multiples aspects," pamphlet, 1933, BHVP In-8° 940 617; M. Le Grand-Falco, "Les rouages secrets du système de la prostitution réglementée," pamphlet (Paris: 'Union Temporaire,' 1935), BHVP In-16° 619 613. On prewar anti-prostitution campaigns see Corbin, *Women for Hire*.

50. Clipping, ". . . et l'on reparle de la prostitution!" *L'Hum*, Feb. 16, 1928 in APP B$^A$ 1689, dossier Pièces et Rapports Divers; clipping, Pepin, *L'Hum*, March 27, 1936 in APP B$^A$ 1690, dossier Rapports divers . . . Pédérastie; Sautman, "Invisible Women." On leftists' conventional views on sexuality and gender roles more generally, see Eley, *Forging Democracy*, 185 and 198.

51. Ralph Schor, "Le Paris des libertés," in Kaspi and Marès, *Paris des étrangers*, 13–33.

52. André Bellessort, "L'américanisme en france," *La Revue Hebdomadaire*, April 1928, 259–77; Leake, *1938 Travelog*, 12, 34; Rearick, *French in Love and*

*War*, 92–3. On divorce trends, see "Paris as Rich America's New Divorce Mill," March 10, 1923, 54–8 and "Blow to Easy Divorce in France," March 24, 1928, 34, both in *LD*; Frederic Can de Water, "Zip! Zing! Decree!" *LHJ*, Feb. 1925, 22; "Dorothy Dunbar Bromley, "The Market Value of a Paris Divorce," *HM*, May 1927, 669–81.

53. Charles Omessa, *Liberté*, c. spring 1927 in Barbedette and Carassou, *Paris gay 1925*, 18; "Cries Raised in Paris to Clean Up Stage," *NYT*, March 13, 1927, E7; letters to PP, late Aug. and early Sept. 1927 in APP B$^A$ 1637. On Minister of the Interior Albert Sarraut's concerns about politicized foreigners, see Rosenberg, *Policing Paris*, 7–8, 39, 80–81, and 96.

54. Boyer, *Urban Masses and Moral Order*, 207; Allen, *Horrible Prettiness*, 244–6; Heap, *Slumming*, 76, 106, 201 and *passim*; Erenberg, *Steppin' Out*, (tango pirates) 83–5, (*Variety* quote) 240.

55. Beach, *Meek Americans*, 19–27; Nevill, *Days and Nights*, 27, 153; Dougherty, *Exploits of a Detective*, 104–8; Faulkner, Sept. 22, 1925, in Gopnik, *Americans in Paris*, 304. See also Sheridan, *West and East*, 43–6; Flambeau, *Red Letter Days in Europe*, 60–1; Newman, *Seeing Paris*, 209–13; Shinkman, *So Little Disillusion*, 26.

56. Letter to PP, Dec. 12, 1927 in APP B$^A$ 1637, n564.

57. Paul Block, "Paris by Night," *LA*, Sept. 1, 1927, 432–6; Carl de Vidal Hunt, "Paris Traps for the 'Easy Marks,'" *WP*, May 27, 1928, SM4; Robert Destez, "Promenades pour étrangers," *Le Fig.*, July 26, 1926, 1.

58. *Guide des plaisirs à Paris*, 122–8; Richard, *Guide des grands ducs*; Woon, *Paris That's Not in the Guide Books*, 237–47; Andrews, *Innocents of Paris*, 51–7; Chancellor, *How to Be Happy in Paris*, 167–75; Le Gallienne, *From a Paris Garret*, 209–11; Fegdal, *Choses et gens des Halles*; letter from youth groups in the quartier des Halles Centrales to PP, May 24, 1935 in APP B$^A$ 2242, dossier Racolage sur la Voie Publique.

59. Seth Koven, *Slumming: Sexual and Social Politics in Victorian London* (Princeton: Princeton University Press, 2004) and Heap, *Slumming*.

60. The theme of Paris as a test of personal virtue also inflected American novels and films. Sinclair Lewis's *Dodsworth* (1929) provides a classic example. On Frenchmen's similar practices with respect to their colonial subjects, see Malek Alloula, *The Colonial Harem*, Myrna and Wlad Godzich, trans. (Minneapolis: University of Minnesota Press, 1986).

61. Zimmer, *Septennat policier*, 9, 49–50.

62. Jones, *Paris*, 330–2; Noël Pinelli, "Rapport . . . sur le fonctionnement des services de la Préfecture de Police au cours de l'année 1932," in Conseil Municipal de Paris, *Rapports et documents*; Carrot, *Maintien de l'ordre en France*, 49–54; Stead, *Police of France*, 80–3; "How Its Police Force Has Made Paris Safest City in World," *PH*, Aug. 28, 1927, pt. 2, 1, 4; press clippings, Sept. 1930 in APP B$^A$ 2245, dossier Sécurité en Général . . . Coupures de Journaux; "Benito Chiappe" in Berstein and Becker, *Histoire*

*de l'anti-communisme,* 220–1. On corruption under Chiappe, Martin, *Crime and Criminal Justice,* 97–102, 116–21.

63. Chiappe, *Paroles d'ordre,* 152–7; Rosenberg, *Policing Paris,* esp. 91–7.

64. "La police opère plusieurs descentes chez les étrangers," Aug. 28, 1927, 2; "De nombreux étrangers sont encore expulsés," Aug. 31, 1927, 2; and "De nouvelles operations de police," Sept. 2, 1927, 2, all in *L'Œ;* "A la recherche des étrangers suspects," *Le Mat,* Aug. 28, 1927, 2; "L'action des étrangers dans les troubles communistes," *L'AF,* Aug. 28, 1927, 2; "Police Round Up 400 Undesirables," *PH,* Aug. 28, 1927, 1; "Pour l'épuration de Paris," *Le Fig,* Sept. 14, 1927, 3; telegrams and documents on *rondes de nuit,* 1927–1928 in APP B^A 2245, dossiers Etats des rondes effectuées en banlieue and Sécurité dans Paris . . . descentes de police.

65. "A/S du débat sur l'arrestation des députés communistes," Paris, Jan. 13, 1928, "A/S de l'interpellation sur les incidents du 23 Août," Paris, Jan. 19, 1928, and clippings from *L'Hum* and *Le Mat,* Jan. 13, 1928 in Direction de la Sûreté Général, "Notes 'Jean' [1918–1936]" (Paris: Archives Nationales, 1984), Série F^7 12956; clipping, "Discussion de plusieurs interpellations," *Journal Officiel,* Jan. 21, 1928, 206–22 in APP B^A 1643.

66. Logbook in APP B^A 1714, dossier Etat des journaux ou publications interdits, 1922–1930.

67. Zimmer, *Septennat policier,* 27.

68. Berlière, *Préfet Lépine,* 263–5; "Paris Reform Drive Scope Is Extended," *WP,* July 8, 1928, 16; "Famous Night Fairs of Paris Now Are Curbed," *NYT,* Sept. 15, 1929, E3; Janet Flanner, "Paris Letter," *NY,* April 28, 1928, 64–7.

69. On municipal policy networks, Saunier, "La toile municipale aux XIX^e–XX^e siècles" and Rodgers, *Atlantic Crossings,* ch. 4. On the international resonance of vice reforms, see Andrée Lévesque, "Eteindre le *Red Light:* les réformateurs et la prostitution à Montreal entre 1865 et 1925," *Urban History Review* 17.3 (February 1989), 191–201 and Ian Tyrrell, *Woman's World, Woman's Empire: The Woman's Christian Temperance Union in International Perspective, 1880–1930* (Chapel Hill: University of North Carolina Press, 1991).

70. N. C. McLoud, "Paris Rules Traffic to Accommodate All," April 7, 1929, XX17; "London Traffic Rules to Be Tried in Paris," Nov. 1, 1931, 55; "Paris Will Synchronize Traffic, Adapting New York Control Plan," March 4, 1931, 1, all in *NYT.* On international traffic control generally, see Clay McShane, "The Origins and Globalization of Traffic Control Signals," *Journal of Urban History* (March 1999), 379–404.

71. "Paris Police Arrest 200 Auto Honkers," Aug. 20, 1928, 16; "Paris Orders 10 P.M. to 6 A.M. Ban on Noise," Jan. 28, 1931, 15; "Paris Wars on Noise," April 2, 1933, E3, all in *NYT.* On antinoise movements more generally, Thompson, *Soundscape of Modernity.*

72. *Le Petit Parisien*, Jan. 3, 1931, and photograph in Célati and Trouilleux, *Chronique de la rue parisienne*, 36; Le Gallienne, *From a Paris Garret*, 114–18, 152–3, 208–9 ("drill sergeant bent"), 115; P. J. Philip, "Police Clean-Up Annoys," Dec. 25, 1927, E1 and "Paris Police Head Hits at Tradition," Oct. 29, 1933, E2, both in *NYT*; Conseil Municipal de Paris, *Rapports et documents*, 184–9.

73. Munholland, "Republican Order and Republican Tolerance," 15–36.

74. Report, Cmsr. Priolet, Dec. 16, 1928 in APP B$^A$ 1690, dossier Rapports divers . . . Pédérastie.

75. "107—Question de M. Lionel Nastorg." Conjuring up such a spectacle, however, actually provided rhetorical means to reinforce heterosexual masculinity as a social norm. On the use of sexual crisis and regulation as a strategy to articulate and confirm heterosexual Frenchmen's prerogatives and duties in the Third Republic, see Surkis, *Sexing the Citizen*, esp. 10–12.

76. Personal files in APP B$^A$ 1690, dossier Rapports divers . . . Pédérastie; report, "Service de la brigade mondaine au parquet" in APP B$^A$ 2242, dossier Obscénités: Statistique sur l'Activité du Service de Répression; clipping, "Suivez nous—mesmoiselles!" *La Presse*, Nov. 12, 1927 in APP B$^A$ 2245, dossier Sécurité dans Paris . . . Attentats à la Pudeur; "107—Question de M. Lionel Nastorg"; Zimmer, *Septennat policier*, 112–17.

77. Cmsr. report, Quartier de Clingnancourt, Dec. 3, 1933 in APP B$^A$ 1690, dossier Rapports divers . . . Pédérastie.

78. Reports, Cmsr. Priolet, Dec. 1928–Nov. 1932 in APP B$^A$ 1690, dossier Rapports divers . . . Pédérastie; report, Cmsr. Priolet, April 10, 1933 in APP B$^A$ 1689, dossier Répression de la Prostitution sur la Voie Publique, 1906–1946; Slocombe, *Tumult and the Shouting*, 213. On lighting cinema and music-hall *promenoirs*, see report, M. Boulanger, Dec. 20, 1933 in APP B$^A$ 1690. In Hemingway's sketch of the wavy-haired gay men who arrive at the *bal musette* with Brett, he notes a policeman at the *bal*'s entrance, suggesting that this venue was under surveillance even before Chiappe's tenure: *Sun Also Rises*, 27–31. Hemingway took note of Chiappe's *épuration* as well, writing about it mockingly to F. Scott Fitzgerald: letter, Dec. 15, 1927, *Ernest Hemingway*, 267–9. Police action against homosexuals continued even after Chiappe's reign: see reports from the years 1934 and 1935 in APP B$^A$ 1690.

79. "Let 'Em Pet, Is Paris Prefect's Code for Lovers," *CT*, July 14, 1928, 2.

80. "Question de M. Fernand-Laurent"; Zimmer, *Septennat policier*, 168.

81. "L'épuration de Paris," Sept. 10, 1927, 2; "A travers Paris," Sept. 17, 1927, 5; and "L'épuration continue," Sept. 18, 1927, 4, all in *Le Mat*; "La police de Chiappe multiplie les rafles dans Paris," *L'Hum*, Sept. 10, 1927, 2; "Paris Cleans House for Visit of Legion," *NYT*, Sept. 10, 1927, 19; "Raids on Paris' Bright Spots Irk Legion Guests," *CT*, Sept. 15, 1927, 6; "Try to Clean Up Paris," *Lincoln State Journal*, Sept. 15, 1927, 3.

82. "Le service de la répression des ouvrages licencieux," March 19, 1931 in APP B^A 1689, dossier Pièces et Rapports Divers; "A.S. d'un incident au bar 'Jockey,'" June 29, 1923 in APP B^A 2010; photograph of policeman outside the Coupole in Lanzmann, *Paris des années 30*, 117; "Montparnasse Jazz Is Stilled by Police," *NYT*, Nov. 20, 1927, 2; J. A. Roger, "The Paris Pepper-Pot," *Pittsburgh Courier*, July 27, 1929, 7; McKay to William Aspenwell Bradley, July 5, 1929 quoted in Fabre, *From Harlem to Paris*, 105–6.

83. "Question de M. Fernand-Laurent."

84. Le Gallienne, *From a Paris Garret*, 56; "Extraits du discours de M. Jean Chiappe," in Merlet, *Vénus et Mercure*, 230–3; "Question de M. Fernand-Laurrent."

85. "Les 'Légionnaires' dans Paris-la-Nuit," Sept. 19, 1927, 2 and Marie Bréant, "Les bandes fascistes de l'American Legion et nous," Sept. 8, 1927, 4, in *L'Hum*; "Une saleté," *L'Œ*, Aug. 24, 1927, 1; "Expulsion d'un artiste américain," *LT*, Aug. 31, 1927, 3; "Question de M. Fernand-Laurent."

86. "Service de la brigade mondaine au parquet" in APP B^A 2242, dossier Obscénités: Statistique sur l'Activité du Service de Répression; report, Cmsr. Priolet, Jan. 28, 1933 in APP B^A 1689, Dossier: Pièces et Rapports Divers.

87. APP B^A 2242: "Trafiquants d'obscénités," Oct. 3, 1930 and "Interventions faites auprès des tenanciers de kiosques à journaux, bouquinistes et concessionnaires," Oct. 7, 1930 in dossier Obscénités: Statistique sur l'Activité du Service de Répression; report, Nov. 1930 and heaps of other documents in dossier Obscénités: Annonces Immorales; "Détail des condamnations . . . contre divers journaux illustrés," Nov. 1933 in APP B^A 1714, dossier Détail des Condamnations; report, Cmsr. Priolet, Jan. 28, 1933 in APP B^A 1689, dossier Pièces et Rapports Divers.

88. "Question de M. Fernand-Laurrent." Tellingly, police filed many reports on racy tabloids in their box for "Presse Etrangère."

89. Report, Cmsr. Priolet, Dec. 28, 1929, clipping, *La Vie Parisienne*, July 1933, and letter by L. Martin in APP B^A 2242, dossier Obscénités: Annonces Immorales; Boisson, *Coins et recoins de Paris*, 36–8.

90. "Affaire des journaux humoristiques" and "Jugement de la 12ème Chambre Correctionnelle du 19 novembre 1932" in APP B^A 1714, dossier Détail des Condamnations . . . contre divers journaux illustrés; "Cour d'appel de Paris, Présidence de M. Boucard, Audience du 27 octobre 1926," *Recueil de la Gazette des Tribunaux* (Paris: Rédaction & Administration, 1927), 347–9. On *Inversions*, Barbedette and Carassou, *Paris gay 1925*.

91. On Shanghai, Wakeman, *Policing Shanghai*.

92. "Defends Life in Harlem," *NYT*, Sept. 8, 1934, 3; Committee of Fourteen, *Annual Report* (New York: 1925–1927). Thanks to Chad Heap for pointing out the latter. On La Guardia's reforms, see Daniel Bluestone, "The Pushcart Evil," in David Ward and Olivier Zunz, eds., *The Landscape of*

*Modernity: Essays on New York City, 1900–1940* (New York: Russel Sage, 1992), 287–312 and his mayoral papers on microfilm at the New York City Municipal Archives, esp. Burlesque (Roll 14), Gambling (Roll 70), and Organ grinders (Roll 149). On Rome, Paris, and London as models for antinoise reform, see Noise (Rolls 146 and 148). Quote "purely sentimental" from La Guardia's form response to complaints about his ban on organ-grinders (roll 149) and quote "not a prude" from address to indecent magazine distributors, Aug. 19, 1940 (roll 97). On coverage of Chiappe's campaign in the regional American press, see "Try to Clean Up Paris," *Lincoln State Journal*, Sept. 15, 1927, 3 and "Reform Wave Shocks Paris Dens of Vice," *Ogden Standard Examiner*, Oct. 30, 1927, 1. On policing American nightlife more generally, Heap, *Slumming*, ch. 2.

93. "107—Question de M. Lionel Nastorg." See also "Paris Wins Praise of Police Prefect," *NYT*, Dec. 31, 1933, E2; Zimmer, *Septennat policier*, 93, 112–17.

*Chapter Five*

1. Marcel Cachin, André Marty, and Jacques Doriot quoted in "La fête nationale du 19 septembre," *L'Œ*, Aug. 24, 1927, 1 and "Les fascistes yankees complices du crime oseront-ils défiler?" *L'Hum*, Aug. 24, 1927, 1; Corday and Zévaès quoted in "Des encouragements à protester contre la honteuse fête," *Le Lib*, Sept. 10, 1927, 1.

2. Baker, *American Legion and American Foreign Policy*, esp. 12–29; American Legion, *Post Handbook*; Preston, *Aliens and Dissenters*; and Capozzola, *Uncle Sam Wants You*.

3. Pencak, *For God & Country*; Minott, *Peerless Patriots*, 29–41, 55–67, 70–96; Murray, *Red Scare*, 87–90, 182–9, 264–5, 270.

4. Levenstein, *Seductive Journey*, 271–5; Kennedy, *Over Here*, 363–7; Pencak, *For God & Country*, 97–9.

5. Shafer, *Second A.E.F*, xv; "Paris Wants Legion to Decide to Come," *NYT*, Oct. 9, 1926, 20; "How France Will Receive the Legionnaires," *Outlook*, Aug. 17, 1927, 495; "Les P.T.T. créent à Paris un bureau et des installations spéciales," Aug. 27, 1927, 2, and "Le 19 septembre sera jour férié," Sept. 6, 1927, 1, both in *Le Mat*.

6. FCTC, "The Second A.E.F.," *American Legion Weekly* supplement, Feb. 5, 1926.

7. Frederick Painton, "Proceedings of the Ninth National Convention of the American Legion," *70th Congress, First Session, House Document No. 66* (Washington, D.C.: U.S. Gov. Printing Office, 1928), 69–75; "On to Paris," *ALM*, Sept. 1927, 53–6.

8. Bowman Elder, "Proceedings of the Eighth National Convention of the American Legion," *69th Congress, Second Session, House Document No. 553*

(Washington, D.C.: U.S. Gov. Printing Office, 1927), 88–107; Charles Lindbergh, "They'll Be Glad to See You," Sept. 1927, 6; "On to Paris," May 1927, 49, 73, June 1927, 58–9, 84, July 1927, 59–62, and Aug. 1927, 57–9, 86–7; and ads for 1926–1927, all in *ALM*. On savings clubs, see pamphlet, "On to Paris Club," 1925 in WHSL.

9. Frederick Painton, "Why They Want to Go to France," *ALM*, April 1927, 40–2, 95; FCTC, "Second A.E.F."

10. Elder, "Proceedings of the Eighth National Convention"; FCTC, "Proceedings of the Ninth National Convention," *70th Congress*, 229–33; FCTC, "Second A.E.F."; "The Lines of Advance for the 1927 Paris Convention Pilgrimage," March 26, 1926, 10–11; "A Furlough in Paris," April 1927, 82; and "Over the Top of the World to Paris," June 1927, 87, all in *ALM*.

11. "Strict Measures Against Reds," Aug. 27, 1927, 2 and P. J. Philip, "Legion Visit Finds the French Uneasy," Sept. 11, 1927, E6, both in *NYT*; "Une protestation de la Ligue des Droits de l'Homme," Aug. 26, 1927, 2 and "Une démission au Comité de réception de l'American Legion," Aug. 24, 1927, 3, both in *L'Œ*; "Paris Assures Fete for Legion," *NYT*, Sept. 6, 1927, 19; "Les socialistes de France ne participeront pas à la fête de l'American Legion," *L'Œ*, Sept. 5, 1927, 2; "Le Comité Sacco-Vanzetti refuse de répondre à une convocation du Préfet de police," *Le Pop*, Sept. 10, 1927; Barbusse in "Des encouragements à protester contre la honteuse fête," *Le Lib*, Sept. 10, 1927, 1.

12. "Radicals Won't Join Legion Celebration," *NYT*, Aug. 31, 1927, 8; CGTU poster in APP B^A 1637; "Un manifeste du C.I.P. de l'Alimentation," Aug. 27, 1927, 5, "Boycottage de toute production américaine!" Sept. 4, 1927, 5, "Les organisations préparent le boycott des produits américains," Sept. 6, 1927, 5, "Les travailleurs boycotteront les produits américains," Sept. 10, 1927, 5, all in *L'Hum*.

13. "Déclaration des maires communistes de banlieue," *L'Hum*, Sept. 15, 1927, 1; "Un manifeste des municipalités de la banlieue parisienne," *L'Œ*, Sept. 17, 1927, 2; undercover reports, Aug. 23 and Sept. 2, 1927 in APP B^A 1643.

14. "L'état major de l'American Legion arrive à point!," Aug. 6, 1927, 2, "L'American Legion débarque à 15 heures gare Saint-Lazare," Aug. 18, 1927, 2, V. Gayman, "Lundi, à minuit" and "Debout contre le crime!" Aug. 20, 1927, 1, and "Contre le crime au Pré Saint-Gervais!" Aug. 21, 1927, 1, all in *L'Hum*.

15. Vaillant-Couturier, "Le drapeau étoilé à la hampe des matraques," *L'Hum*, Aug. 6, 1927, 1.

16. Dos Passos, "Boston (Massachusetts), le 7 août," Aug. 8, 1927, 1; Vaillant-Couturier, "Avec les martyrs face du dollar!" Aug. 23, 1927, 1, "'L'American Legion' ose démentir avoir exigé l'assassinat de Sacco et Vanzetti," Aug. 29, 1927, 1, "Legionnaires," Sept. 11, 1927, 1, "L'American Legion quatrième

pouvoir des États-Unis," Sept. 1, 1927, 1–2, and "Le général Pershing et l'état major de l'American Legion à Cherbourg," Sept. 17, 1927, 1, all in *L'Hum*.

17. Anonymous telegram in AFP, Series 8; "Quelques exploits de l'American Legion," Aug. 31, 1927, 1–2 and "L'American Legion sous son vrai jour," Sept. 19, 1927, 1, both in *L'Hum*. Correspondence from New York appeared on the front pages for Sept. 1, 3, 5, and 13, 1927.

18. Warner, "The Truth about the American Legion," *TN*, July 6, 1921, 7–10; July 13, 1921, 35–6; July 20, 1921, 65–6; July 27, 1921, 89–91. See also files on "Patrioteering Organizations" in American Civil Liberties Union Archives, Seeley G. Mudd Library, Princeton University, vols. 132, 189, 204, 252, 318–26, 331–4.

19. Hapgood, *Professional Patriots*, 2, 42, 56–63; ACLU pamphlet, 1927, quoted in Pencak, *For God & Country*, 6.

20. Boyer, *Urban Masses and Moral Order*, 191–219; John Cell, *The Highest Stage of White Supremacy: The Origins of Segregation in South Africa and the American South* (Cambridge: Cambridge University Press, 1982); Gary Gerstle, "Liberty, Coercion, and the Making of Americans," *Journal of American History*, Sept. 1997, 524–58; and Capozzola, *Uncle Sam Wants You*.

21. Between the wars, the American press carried an impressive amount of international news. Patriotic groups, too, worked to educate their members about communist threats around the world, albeit often with information riddled with errors. For example, in a characteristic blend of worldly engagement and virulent nationalism, the Better America Federation of California extensively detailed foreign developments in its bulletin, ranting against the "deprecatory Utopiate internationalist," who thought that America was not the best country in the world, while at the same time praising "world patriots," such as Marshal Foch and Myron T. Herrick—men of pronounced international sensibilities, but also men of the right with unwavering love of their own nations. See their *Bulletin: Survey of Americanism*, April 12, 1929 and Oct. 4, 1929, and copy of *The Patriot*, June 20, 1929 in MHP, folders 132 and 146.

22. Mussolini quoted in Payne, *History of Fascism*, 106; Mazower, *Dark Continent*, esp. 4–6.

23. "Program of the Communist International, 1928: Definition of Fascism," reprinted in Weber, *Varieties of Fascism*, 146–7; "The Terrorist Dictatorship of Finance Capital," ECCI Plenum, 1933 in Griffin, *International Fascism*, 59–62; Weber, *Hollow Years*, 113–14; Diggins, *Mussolini and Fascism*, 213–39.

24. Owsley in Hapgood, *Professional Patriots*, 61–2; Walter Wilson, "American Legion and Civil Liberty" [pamphlet] (New York: American League Against War and Fascism, [1936]), 19–20; Roszel, *Commanders' Tour*, 28–31.

25. MacLean, *Behind the Mask of Chivalry*, 177–88; Jenkins, *Hoods and Shirts*, ch. 3.

26. Pencak, *For God & Country*, 80–2, 138; Payne, *History of Fascism*, 10, 14; Gellermann, *American Legion as Educator*, 52–67, 158–66. Klan and Legion membership overlapped in the Midwest, but they remained competing organizations in the South. Interestingly, as Klan membership fell in the South in the late twenties, Legion membership grew in that region faster than in other parts of the country, suggesting that it benefited from the Klan's downfall. Also interesting are the parallels that can be drawn between the Legion and the French veterans' organization, the Croix de Feu, created only months after the Legion's parade. It, too, skirted the edges of fascism, while including elites among its members and moderating its use of violence: Irvine, "Fascism in France and the Strange Case of the Croix de Feu." Thanks to Jonathan Zatlin for the point about the Arditi and Stahlhelm.

27. For historiographical debates and working definitions of fascism, see Payne, *History of Fascism* and Griffin, *International Fascism*. On grounding in local traditions, Paxton, *Anatomy of Fascism*. For American fascisms, Jenkins, *Hoods and Shirts*, and for parallels stretching beyond the usual Bund and Blackshirt suspects, see Brinkley, *Voices of Protest*, 273–83.

28. American Legion, "Manual of Ceremonies," 1921 in WHSL. On the "promotion of small arms practice" for youths, see American Legion, *Post Handbook*, 28.

29. L.A. Legionnaires quoted in Pencak, *For God & Country*, 10; American Legion, *Americanism Manual*, 22–8; Duffield, *King Legion*, 129–43, 160, 169, 250–66; Hapgood, *Professional Patriots*, 96, 124, 147, 182–8.

30. For this framework, see Mosse, *Fascist Revolution*.

31. Americanism Commission quoted in Baker, *American Legion and American Foreign Policy*, 33; American Legion, "Manual of Ceremonies"; and "Official Catalogue of The American Legion Emblems and Supplies," 1922 in WHSL.

32. *Americanism Manual*, 8; Frank Belgrano, "The Command is Still Forward," 1934 and "The Legion Way Is the American Way," 1935 quoted in Gellermann, *American Legion as Educator*, 72, 99; American Legion, "Manual of Ceremonies."

33. *Americanism Manual*, 10–21; Gellermann, *American Legion as Educator*, 238; Hapgood, *Professional Patriots*, 58–9; Duffield, *King Legion*, 167–8, 315; Wilson, "American Legion and Civil Liberty," 4.

34. Savage quoted in "'High Power' Savage Leading the Doughboys Back to France," *LD*, Dec. 11, 1926, 50–5.

35. Sheldon Whitehouse to Sec. of State, Paris, Aug. 31, 1927, RDS, 851.00/927; "Le Boycott appliqué à Port-de-Bouc," *L'Hum*, Aug. 28, 1927, 1; "Strict Measures Against Reds," *NYT*, Aug. 27, 1927, 2; "La bombe sur le dancing de Juan-les-Pins," *L'Œ*, Aug. 28, 1927, 2; Préfet du Rhone to the Minister of the Interior, Sept. 8, 1927 and clipping, "Tous Dehors!"

*Le Lib*, Sept. 10, 1927 in APP B$^A$ 1637; report, Gardien de la Paix Vallet, Aug. 1927 in APP B$^A$ 1643.

36. Sarraut trans. in "Strict Measures Against Reds," *NYT*, Aug. 27, 1927, 2; "Pour renforcer l'action de la police," Aug. 27, 1927, 2 and Sept. 1, 1927, 2, in *Le Fig*; note to the press, Aug. 24, 1927 and "Note au sujet des services d'ordre," Aug. 25, 1927 in APP B$^A$ 1643; clipping, "Encore des agents," *Le Pop*, Sept. 2, 1927 and articles on "étrangers indésirables" the month following Aug. 23 in APP B$^A$ 1637. On Sarraut's measures, see Sheldon Whitehouse to Sec. of State, Paris, Aug. 24, Sept. 7, and Sept. 14, 1927, RDS, 851.00/926, 928–9.

37. "Pour recevoir dignement l'American Legion," *Le Mat*, Sept. 15, 1927, 1; UNC quoted in "Le voyage de l'American Legion," *LT*, Aug. 26, 1927, 3; "A la Tombe du Soldat Inconnu," *LT*, Aug. 28, 1927, 2. On France's veterans' associations more generally, see Prost, *In the Wake of War*. On the July 1926 protest against the debt accords, see APP B$^A$ 1851, dossier: Listes des Différents Manifestations, c. 1936; and correspondence, July 1926 in MHP, folder 64.

38. Jeunesses Patriotes quoted in "Le voyage de l'American Legion," *LT*, Aug. 26, 1927, 3. See also right-wing newspaper excerpts in "L'Opinion des autres," *Le Fig*, Aug. 26, 1927, 3 and "Revue de la Presse," *LT*, Aug. 26, 1927, 3. Even the reactionary Léon Daudet, no fan of Americans or the liberalism they were associated with, moved seamlessly from harangues against Sacco-Vanzetti supporters to effusive greetings for the Legionnaires on the front pages of *L'Action Française:* see Aug. 31, Sept. 2 and 19, 1927.

39. Letters to PP, Aug. 24 and 25, 1927 in APP B$^A$ 1637.

40. *Ibid.*

41. Laney, *Paris Herald*, 244; O'Brien, *P.S.*, 239–40, 248; Williams, *Autobiography of William Carlos Williams*, 252–3; Moody, *"Meet the King,"* 42–3.

42. "Paris in Gala Dress for Legionnaires," *NYT*, Sept. 2, 1927, 6; Moody, *"Meet the King,"* 15–16; Shafer, *Second A.E.F.*, 73; "Paris Decks Itself for Legion Parley," Sept. 8, 1927, 6 and "Paris Fast Taking On Gala Aspect," Sept. 13, 1927, 7, both in *PH*; "Hier des services religieux ont été célébrés en leur honneur à Notre-Dame," Sept. 19, 1927, 1 and "Avant les fêtes," Sept. 18, 1927, 2, both in *Le Mat*.

43. Moody, *"Meet the King,"* 44; James Barton, quoted in Roszel, *Commanders' Tour*, 11; *PH*, Sept. 19, 1927, 11.

44. Vaillant-Couturier, "A la 'GRANDE PARADE,'" *L'Hum*, Sept. 19, 1927, 1; Shafer, *Second A.E.F.*, 13–14; Treat, "Is This America?" *TN*, Oct. 19, 1927, 420–2; "Red Cross Attends to 60 Cases," *PH*, Sept. 20, 1927, 9.

45. John Gunther quoted in "The Legion's 'Second A.E.F.,'" *LD*, Oct. 1, 1927, 5–7.

46. Welles, "The Nature of the Enemy," 1945 speech quoted in Denning, *Cultural Front*, 380. The aesthetic pretensions and entertainment qualities

of fascism preoccupied many of Welles's contemporaries, from Walter Benjamin and Antonio Gramsci to William Shirer, and they have since received substantial attention from scholars. See, for example, Spotts, *Hitler and the Power of Aesthetics* and Falasca-Zamponi, *Fascist Spectacle*.

47. For detailed parade descriptions, see Shafer, *Second A.E.F.*, 13–22; "State Delegations Advertise Crops, Native Sons and Weather," *PH*, Sept. 20, 1927, 10–11; Philip Von Blon and Marquis James, "The A.E.F. Comes Home," *ALM*, Dec. 1927, 28–40, 66–81.

48. Edwin James, "Throngs Hail Marchers," *NYT*, Sept. 20, 1927, 2; Elmer Davis, "The State of the Nation," in Stokes, *Mirrors of the Year*, 35–52; "Les grandes journées des Légionnaires," *L'Ill*, Sept. 24, 1927, 277; "Avec ses costumes pittoresques," *L'Œ*, Sept. 20, 1927, 1–2.

49. "American Youth and French Battle-Scars," *LD*, Oct. 15, 1927, 38–44; *English Review* quoted in Moody, *"Meet the King,"* 45; Treat, "Is This America?"; Jean Guignebert, *Le Petit Journal* quoted in Shafer, *Second A.E.F.*, 82; "Avec ses costumes pittoresques," *L'Œ*, Sept. 20, 1927, 1–2. On the 1919 victory parade, Delamare, *Vingt années sans guerre*, 7–9 and Cohen, *Paris dans l'imaginaire national*, 26–32.

50. Moody, *"Meet the King,"* 12–13; A. J. Colman, "Legion Man Lauds Fine Spirit of Crowd" and Louis Smith, "Ladders, Boxes, Mirrors, Are Aid to Spectators," *PH*, Sept. 20, 1927, 1; Vaillant-Couturier, "Les deux cortèges," Sept. 20, 1927, 1 and "'Grande parade' de foire des légionnaires américains," Sept. 20, 1927, 1–2, both in *L'Hum*; "Paris, ému, joyeux et enthousiaste," *Le Mat*, Sept. 20, 1927, 1; Henri Vonoven, "La réception de Paris," *Le Fig*, Sept. 20, 1927, 1.

51. Sheldon Whitehouse to Sec. of State, Paris, Sept. 21, 1927, RDS, 851.00/930; "De l'Étoile à Notre-Dame Paris acclame la légion américaine," *Le Fig*, Sept. 20, 1927, 1–2; "Le défilé triomphal de la Légion américaine," *L'AF*, Sept. 20, 1927, 1–2; Othon Guerlac, "The American Legion Conquers Paris," *Current History*, Nov. 1927, 283–5.

52. Dir. Police Judiciaire to PP, Oct. 3, 1927 and "État des condamnations," Oct. 3, 1927 in APP B[A] 1637; "Les communistes ont manifesté à Clichy," *L'Œ*, Sept. 20, 1927, 4; "Deux légers incidents," *Le Mat*, Sept. 20, 1927, 2; "Quelques incidents," *L'Hum*, Sept. 20, 1927, 2; Rice, *Minority Report*, 233; O'Brien, *P.S.*, 264–5.

53. Capozzola, *Uncle Sam Wants You*, 124–5; Dubofsky, *We Shall Be All*, 175, 259–60; Mary Ryan, "The American Parade: Representations of the Nineteenth-Century Social Order," in Lynn Hunt, ed., *The New Cultural History* (Berkeley: University of California Press, 1989), 131–53.

54. "State Delegations Advertise Crops, Native Sons and Weather"; Von Blon and James, "A.E.F. Comes Home." Despite their claims to represent a cross-section of the United States, only 15 to 25 percent of former servicemen belonged to the organization. The Legion was strongest in small

towns, particularly in the Midwest, and among clerical workers, small-business owners, and skilled laborers. A small percentage of African American veterans joined segregated posts in the North, but they were excluded entirely from participation in most parts of the South and from the Legion's secret, elite club, "Societé des 40 Hommes et 8 Chevaux." In the Paris parade, only two African Americans marched. They found their own way to the capital, since the Legion's travel bureau refused to accept reservations from black members. Some three to four thousand female wartime volunteers and members of the Legion's Ladies Auxiliary also marched, appearing as subordinates or embodiments of abstract ideals rather than as men's equal partners: Pencak, *For God & Country*, 16, 68–9, 82, 99, 297.

55. "On to Paris," Sept. 1927, 53–6 and "The Second A.E.F.," Dec. 1927, 26–7, both in *ALM*; James, "Throngs Hail Marchers." The sympathetic French press also supported this idea. It was not "a Legion" that had marched, chimed in *Le Matin*, but "a people": "Paris, ému, joyeux et enthousiaste," Sept. 20, 1927, 1.

56. Julian Thomas, "Proceedings of the Ninth National Convention," *70th Congress*, 4–6, 41–9.

57. Lecoin, *Cours d'une vie*, 142–8; "Keeping Step," *ALM*, Dec. 1927, 46–7; Von Blon and James, "A.E.F. Comes Home"; "Ouverture de la convention nationale de la légion," *Le Fig*, Sept. 20, 1927, 2; "La séance d'ouverture de la 'convention,'" *L'Œ*, Sept. 20, 1927, 2; "Le congrès," *Le Mat*, Sept. 20, 1927, 2.

58. See, for example, "Vets of A.E.F. March Once More, in Paris," *Helena Daily Independent*, Sept. 20, 1927, 3 and "Legion Meeting Opens in Paris," *Bismarck Tribune*, Sept. 19, 1927, 1.

59. "Describes Welcome to Legion Men," *Syracuse-Herald*, Oct. 2, 1927, sec. 2, p. 4; George de la Fouchardière quoted in Treat, "Is this America?"; "What Legion Got in Paris," *NYT*, Oct. 3, 1927, 5; "Piercing Honks Will Advertise Legion's Return," *PH*, Sept. 21, 1927, 10; Shirer, *20th Century Journey: The Start*, 318; "Blame Attempts To Wreck Legion Trains on Sacco Case," *Decatur Daily Review*, Sept. 26, 1927, 1.

60. "You Buddies of '17-'18-'19" [advertisement], Lima, Ohio, in possession of the author; "American Colony Unanimous in Praise of Legion Visitors," *PH*, Sept. 29, 1927, 9. For all kinds of travelers during this era, trips abroad—to world fairs, battlefields, colonies—strengthened feelings of nationalism, a fact that would be recognized by the state-sanctioned tours popular during the 1930s. Like the Legionnaires, rowdy Nazis who participated in Strength Through Joy holidays abroad would revel in their own antics but would not always be welcomed by others: Holguín, "'National Spain Invites You'"; Jackson, *Popular Front*, ch. 4; Baranowski, *Strength Through Joy*, chs. 4–5.

61. Laney, *Paris Herald*, 243; "Paris Legion Convention Closes," *News-Palladium* (Benton Harbor, Mich.), Sept. 23, 1927, 1; "Legionnaires Start On Visit to Battlefields," *Charlestown Gazette* (W.V.), Sept. 21, 1927, 1; "Describes Welcome to Legion Men."

62. Paul, *Last Time I Saw Paris*, 159–60; Shirer, *20th Century Journey*, 318; Treat, "Is This America?"

63. "Cours-la-Reine Centre Will Provide Paris Home for Legionnaires," Sept. 1, 1927, 7, "Doughnut Demand Proves Too Great," Sept. 13, 1927, 8, "Cigarettes, Post-Cards and Soap Are Free at K. of C. Legion Hut," Sept. 13, 1927, 8, and "Legion Quarters are Now Deserted Save for Library," Sept. 25, 1927, all in *PH*; "Paris in Gala Dress for Legionnaires," *NYT*, Sept. 2, 1927, 6; Janet Flanner, "Paris Letter," *NY*, Oct. 1, 1927, 78–80.

64. Rice, *Minority Report*, 233.

65. "American Youth and French Battle Scars," *LD*, Oct. 15, 1927, 38–44; Moody, *'Meet the King,'* 12.

66. "Barbarus Americanus," *TN*, June 10, 1931, 623; Georges de la Fouchardière, "Le livre d'or du Mississipi [*sic*]," *L'Œ*, Sept. 27, 1927, 2.

67. "Les Légionnaires s'amusent et les Parisiens avec eux," *Le Mat*, Sept. 21, 1927, 3; "La soirée sur les boulevards et dans les rues de Paris," Sept. 18, 1927, 2 and "La légion américaine à Paris," Sept. 19, 1927, 1–2, both in *Le Fig*; "French Papers Praise Parade of Legionnaires," *PH*, Sept. 21, 1927, 11. Americans proudly detailed French leaders' participation in regional news accounts. See, for example, "High Officials of France Greet Legion Advance," *Charlestown Gazette* (W.V.), Sept. 19, 1927, 1, 12; "Foch Welcomes Legion to Paris," *San Antonio Express* (Tex.), Sept. 19, 1927, 2; and "Vets of A.E.F. March Once More in Paris," *Helena Daily Independent* (Mont.), Sept. 20, 1927, 1. On right-wing networking in general, see Morgan, *Fascism in Europe*, ch. 5.

68. Général Hellot, "La légion américaine en France," *Le Fig*, Sept. 21, 1927, 1 and Vonoven, "Réception de Paris." See also excerpts from right-wing press in "Voix de Paris," *Le Fig*, Sept. 21, 1927, 3 arguing for the parade's importance to showing Paris as a place of nationalism. On the fragile wartime *union sacrée*, see Becker, *Great War and the French People*.

69. "Paris, ému, joyeux et enthousiaste," *Le Mat*, Sept. 20, 1927, 1; "The Second A.E.F." and Frederick Palmer, "A Personal View," *ALM*, Dec. 1927, 26–7, 41.

70. Treat, "Is This America?" See also "Que prépare le gouvernement?" Sept. 14, 1927, 1 and "La légion lâchée dans Paris," Sept. 19, 1927, 1–2, both in *L'Hum*; clipping, "Tous dehors!" *Le Lib*, Sept. 10, 1927, 1 in APP B^A 1637. On the working-class sections of the city as the backdrop for Popular Front culture, see Rifkin, *Street Noises* and Rearick, *French in Love and War*, ch. 4.

71. Paul Bouthonnier, "Les travailleurs s'apprêtent à manifester," Sept. 17, 1927, 1, Vaillant-Couturier, "Sous le signe de Sacco & Vanzetti demain à

Clichy," Sept. 18, 1927, 1, "Grande manifestation aujourd'hui," Sept. 19, 1927, 1, and "Cent mille manifestants à Clichy," Sept. 20, 1927, 1–2, all in *L'Hum*; "The Other Paris Parade," *LA*, Nov. 1, 1927, 769–71. On *débaptisations*, Sylvie Rab, "Culture et loisirs, l'encadrement des prolétaires," in Fourcaut, *Banlieue rouge*, 80–98.

72. By enormous coincidence, the funeral procession of the dancer Isadora Duncan wound its way towards Père Lachaise cemetery the same afternoon the Legionnaires paraded. Like the rally in Clichy, it would be overshadowed by the veterans' display. A few hundred admirers followed Duncan's hearse across the city, but they were forced to detour south of the Champs-Elysées in order to make way for the celebration of her fellow countrymen. Details of her death rites were buried in the press beneath a barrage of Legion news. The cortege was called a "sad, motley, little procession" by an indifferent *Herald* reporter who veered off halfway to the cemetery in order to cover the parade. Shirer, *20th Century Journey*, 308–20; Desti, *Untold Story*, 278–9; Laney, *Paris Herald*, 240–5; "Few Attend Isadora Duncan's Rites as Compatriots Parade," *PH*, Sept. 20, 1927; Janet Flanner, "Paris Letter," *NY*, Oct. 15, 1927, 88–90.

## Chapter Six

1. Eugene Bagger, "Uprooted Americans," *HM*, Sept. 1929, 474–84.
2. "Pan America!—The Cry of the Expatriates," *LD*, Sept. 7, 1929, 46–51; Gilbert Seldes, "Uneasy Chameleons," Jan. 1, 1927, 78, 81–2, Jesse Sprague, "They Live in Europe!," March 29, 1930, 56–62, and Eleanor McDonnell, "The American Expatriate Intones a Dirge," Oct. 21, 1933, 16–17, 34–6, all in *SEP*; Thomas Craven, "The Bohemians of Paris," Feb. 1933, 335–49 and Eugene Bagger, "Expatriates in Time," Aug. 1933, 363–74, both in *HM*.
3. Harold Stearns, "Apologia of an Expatriate," March 1929, 338–41 and "Prodigal American Returns," May 1932, 293–5, both in *SM*. Similar apologies are offered in Waldo Frank, "I Discover the New World," Jan. 1926, 204–10 and Irwin Edman, "Look Homeward, America!" Dec. 1940, 53–60, both in *HM*. See also Susman, "Pilgrimage to Paris," 51–62.
4. Fitzgerald, *Babylon Revisited*, 210–30; Cowley, *Exile's Return*. See also Fitzgerald, "Echoes of the Jazz Age" and Farrell, "After the Sun Has Risen."
5. Dos Passos, *Fourteenth Chronicle*, 372.
6. Dos Passos, *Best Times*, 141; Ludington, *John Dos Passos*, 231–2, 240–1.
7. *Toronto Star* dispatches, April 13, 1922; Oct. 20, 1922; Oct. 28, 1922; and Nov. 14, 1922 in *By-Line*, 26–9, 51–60 and June 24, 1922 and Oct. 19, 1922 in *Hemingway on War*, 245–7, 264–6; Baker, *Ernest Hemingway*, ch. 3. These experiences figure in pieces for *In Our Time* (1925) and no doubt helped Hemingway to write the Caporetto retreat and childbirth scenes for

A *Farewell to Arms* (1929). On the relationship between journalism and fiction for Hemingway and Dos Passos, see Shelley Fisher Fishkin, *From Fact to Fiction: Journalism and Imaginative Writing in America* (Baltimore: Johns Hopkins University Press, 1985).

8. Dos Passos, *Best Times*, 91, 94, 99, 104, 123, 132, 141; Dos Passos, *Orient Express* (1927) reprinted in *Travel Books*, "building up" p. 255.

9. Herbst, *Starched Blue Sky of Spain*, 21–2.

10. Hughes, *Big Sea*, 13–34.

11. Herbst, *Starched Blue Sky of Spain*, 72–3; Ann Keene, "Elliot Paul," *American National Biography Online* [hereafter *ANB*] (Oxford University Press, February 2000), available at http://www.anb.org.

12. Kennedy, *Dreams in the Mirror*, ch. 6, notebook on 73–4; "double life" in Sawyer-Lauçanno, *E. E. Cummings*, 56; Herbst in Bevilacqua, *Josephine Herbst*, 2–3; Dos Passos, *Best Times*, 132.

13. Fitch, *Sylvia Beach*, ch. 2; quotations 24, 37–8.

14. Cowley, *Exile's Return*, 82; Cummings to his father in Sawyer-Lauçanno, *E. E. Cummings*, 105 and to his mother, Aug. 9, 1917 in *Selected Letters*, 28–36.

15. "Hotel childhood" from *Chosen Country* (1951) in Diggins, *Up From Communism*, 76; diary, Aug. 24–6, 1917 and letter to Rumsey Marvin, Aug. 23, 1917 in *Travel Books*, 671–6; *Best Times*, ch. 2, quotations 54–5; Hemingway, *Farewell to Arms*, 185; Dos Passos, *Three Soldiers*, 202, 214–15.

16. Shirer, *20th Century Journey: The Start*, 29–31, 94–109; Stansell, *American Moderns*, ch. 2; Sanford Smoller, "Robert Menzies McAlmon," *ANB*.

17. Cowley quoted in Gilbert Seldes, "Finding the Lost Generation," *SEP*, Aug. 30, 1930, 21, 69–70; Dos Passos, *Best Times*, 135; McAlmon, *Being Geniuses Together*, 3. See also Stansell, *American Moderns*, ch. 9.

18. Hughes, *Big Sea*, 3; Rampersad, *Life of Langston Hughes*, 75–7; Campbell, *Middle Passages*, ch. 5.

19. Hemingway to Dr. C. E. Hemingway, April 15, 1921, and Grace Quinlan, July 21, 1921, in *Ernest Hemingway*, 45–6, 51–2; Kennedy, *Dreams in the Mirror*, 211–12; Dos Passos, *Best Times*, 84; Fitch, *Sylvia Beach*, 38–9.

20. Whereas thousands of American students, artists, and writers settled in Paris, in Berlin there were only dozens. The thriving German capital of arts and culture sported only one American newspaper and a handful of other American establishments. Consequently, it offered far fewer opportunities for employment and social interaction for expatriates. Cummings called Berlin "big and imposturous." Matthew Josephson found it overly "sprawling": Cummings to Edmund Wilson, Dec. 26, 1930, in *Selected Letters*, 118; Josephson, *Life among the Surrealists*, 192; Costigliola, *Awkward Dominion*, 78, 173.

21. Cowley, *Exile's Return*, 133; Herbst, *Starched Blue Sky*, 73. Trains in particular—with their rhythmic lull and quickening pace—captured the excitement and urgency expatriates felt about travel, as though it were a

catalyst, stitching art and politics, timeless truths, and intruding current events all together. It was fitting that Claude McKay and Langston Hughes both wrote their most famous poems on trains. McKay composed "If We Must Die" (1919) while working on the railroads between New York and Pittsburgh; Hughes wrote "The Negro Speaks of Rivers" (1922) en route to Mexico.

22. Sheean, *Personal History*, 9, 37, 48–9, 187–8, 306; Sheean, *Between the Thunder and the Sun*, 77, 115.

23. Shirer, *20th Century Journey: The Start*, 17, 34–5, 128, 171.

24. Cummings, May 1917, in *Selected Letters*, 22–3; William Bolitho, "A Portrait of the American Tourist," *VF*, March 1928, 42, 110; Hemingway, *Sun Also Rises*, 60. Among the wittiest expatriate spoofs of American tourists are Donald Ogden Stewart's novels *Mr. and Mrs. Haddock Abroad* (1924) and *Mr. and Mrs. Haddock in Paris, France* (1926).

25. Kennedy and Bryer, eds., *French Connections*. Often evoked as an archetypal expatriate, Fitzgerald stands more as an outlier in terms of the themes of this chapter. Enamored of American high life, he was not interested in immersing himself in foreign customs or tramping through war-torn regions of the world. He hated Europe the first time he lived there and often behaved abroad not so differently from the insensitive tourists he looked down on as "fantastic neanderthals": "Echoes of the Jazz Age," 20–1; Meyers, *Scott Fitzgerald*, 110–35.

26. Cummings, *Enormous Room*, 69; Cummings to mother, c. Nov. 1917, in *Selected Letters*, 39–41; Hughes, *Big Sea*.

27. Lévy, *Transatlantic Avant-Garde*; Kaspi, *Paris des étrangers*; Edwards, *Practice of Diaspora*.

28. Herbst, *Starched Blue Sky*, 78.

29. Shirer, *20th Century Journey: The Start*, esp. pt. 3.

30. Shirer, *20th Century Journey: The Start*, 249–50, 279, 282.

31. Cummings, *Enormous Room*, 105.

32. Cummings to father, May 6, 1919 and Sept. 18, 1923 in *Selected Letters*, 46, 103–4; letters from Italy and Austria quoted in Sawyer-Lauçanno, *E. E. Cummings*, 216–19.

33. McAlmon quoted in Earnest, *Expatriates and Patriots*, 274; Rose, *Jazz Cleopatra*, 127–41.

34. "Paris 1922," reprinted in Baker, *Ernest Hemingway*, 90–1; "16 heures," *Is 5* (1926) in Cummings, *Complete Poems*, 273–4; Cummings to sister, Sept. 15, 1923 in *Selected Letters*, 101–3. Expatriates were among the many Americans detained (and even beaten) by the Paris police. Cowley was arrested for assaulting the proprietor of the Rotonde and the poet Hart Crane for starting a brawl at the Select. The clarinetist Sidney Bechet was jailed and then deported for engaging in a Montmartre gunfight in which a bystander was wounded. Cummings, no stranger to detention in France, was snapped up

again in 1923 (this time as a *pisseur*) and threatened with expulsion for not updating his *carte d'identité*.

35. McAlmon, *Being Geniuses*, 134–5; McKay quoted in Fabre, *From Harlem to Paris*, 108; Dos Passos, *Three Soldiers*, 352.

36. Hughes, *Big Sea*, 144–201; Hughes to Cullen and "world of color" in Fabre, *From Harlem to Paris*, 64–5; "Lament For Dark Peoples" and "I, Too, Sing America," in *Weary Blues*; Rampersad, *Life of Langston Hughes*, ch. 4. On the Harlem Renaissance in international perspective, see Edwards, *Practice of Diaspora*.

37. McKay, *Long Way from Home*, 52–3.

38. Greenfeld, *Ben Shahn*, 39–47; Pohl, *Ben Shahn*, 10–14.

39. Sheean, *Between the Thunder and the Sun*, 77–8.

40. Wineapple, *Genêt*, chs. 2–4.

41. Wineapple, chs. 4–6, 8–10, quote p. 139; Lesinska, *Perspectives of Four Women Writers*, 60–1. On Chiappe, see, for example, "Paris Letter," *NY*, Nov. 24, 1928, 104–5.

42. Hemingway to Fitzgerald, Apr. 12, 1931; to Dos Passos, March 26, May 30, and Oct. 14, 1932; to Ivan Kashkin, Aug. 19, 1935 in *Ernest Hemingway*, 339–40, 354–5, 359–61, 373–5, 417–21.

43. Denning, *Cultural Front*; Gerstle, *American Crucible*, ch. 4.

44. Pollack, *Aaron Copland*; Bevilacqua, *Josephine Herbst*.

45. Hughes, "The Negro Artist and the Racial Mountain," *TN*, June 23, 1926 and "Madrid's Flowers Hoist Blooms to Meet Raining Fascist Bombs," *Afro-American*, Nov. 27, 1937 in *Collected Works*, 31–6, 173–6; Hughes, *I Wonder as I Wander*, 28, 47; Hughes, *Chicago Defender*, Oct. 8, 1949 in *Good Morning Revolution*, 117–18; Rampersad, *Life of Langston Hughes*, chs. 8–11. On Zhabei, see Wakeman, *Policing Shanghai*, 189–94. On Haiti's importance in American political culture, see Renda, *Taking Haiti*, ch. 7.

46. Herbst quoted in Diane Johnson, introduction to *Starched Blue Sky*, xxiii. On leftist internationalism in Europe, see Horn, *European Socialists Respond to Fascism*, ch.7; Pennybacker, *From Scottsboro to Munich*.

47. Moorehead, *Martha Gellhorn*, 33, 67; Gellhorn to Stanley Pennell, May 1931 in *Selected Letters*, 10–12; Gellhorn to Harry Hopkins, Nov. 26, 1934 in *View from the Ground*, 23.

48. Hemingway, "An Old Newsman Writes: A Letter from Cuba," *Esquire*, Dec. 1934 in *By-Line*, 179–85.

49. Engerman, *Modernization from the Other Shore*; Dos Passos, *Best Times*, 194–5; Dos Passos to Cummings and to Hemingway, Sept. 1928 in *Fourteenth Chronicle*, 386–7; Ludington, *John Dos Passos*, 267–75.

50. Claude McKay, "Soviet Russia and the Negro," *Crisis*, Dec. 1923, in *Passion of Claude McKay*, 95–106; Hughes, "Moscow and Me," *International Literature*, July 1933, "Going South in Russia," *Crisis*, June 1934, and "The Soviet Union" series of articles in *Chicago Defender*, June–August 1946 in

*Good Morning Revolution*, 67–94; *I Wonder as I Wander*, chs. 3–5. On interwar American intellectuals and communism more generally, see Aaron, *Writers on the Left*; Diggins, *Up From Communism*; and Kelley, *Race Rebels*, ch. 5.

51. Cummings to father, June 22, 1920 and sister, May 3, 1922 in *Selected Letters*, 71–2, 83–7; Cummings, *Eimi*, xv, 20, 25, 50; Kennedy, *Dreams in the Mirror*, 307–14, 330–5. Kennedy speculates that "i sing of Olaf," which appeared in *ViVa* (1931), may have been inspired by the literary protests surrounding the Sacco-Vanzetti case: 320–1.

52. Sheean, *Personal History*, 185, 191. See also Herbst, "Yesterday's Road," in *Starched Blue Sky*, 101–27; Bevilacqua, *Josephine Herbst*, 5.

53. Dos Passos, *Best Times*, 205; Furet, *Passing of an Illusion*.

54. Hughes, "The Alliance of Antifascist Intellectuals," radio speech, Madrid, Sept. 1937 in *Collected Works*, 149–52; Gellhorn, *Face of War*, 13–14; Moorehead, *Martha Gellhorn*, 61–6. On American antifascism more generally, Kelley, *Race Rebels*, ch. 6; Denning, *Cultural Front*, and Wald, *Trinity of Passions*.

55. "Führer," *New Yorker*, Feb. 29, March 7 and 14, 1936 in *Janet Flanner's World*, 6–28; Wineapple, *Genêt*, 128–9, 142–6. Hemingway called Mussolini a "great organizer" who had a "genius for clothing small ideas in big words," but he also pointed out his shallow pretensions. Hemingway insisted, "There is something wrong, even histrionically, with a man who wears white spats with a black shirt." "Mussolini, Europe's Prize Bluffer," *Toronto Daily Star*, Jan. 27, 1923, in *Hemingway on War*, 256–7.

56. Gellhorn to Charles Colebaugh, July 17, 1941, in *Selected Letters*, 112–14; Moorehead, *Martha Gellhorn*, 71. On shifts toward more interpretive foreign correspondence between the wars, see Heald, *Transatlantic Vistas*.

57. Shirer, *Berlin Diary*, 16–19, 65. See also Shirer, *"This is Berlin"*; *20th Century Journey: The Start* and *The Nightmare Years*. Thompson got her start in journalism in Paris, too, writing exposés about Zionists, Sinn Fein radicals, and Russian refugees and churning out cheap publicity for the Red Cross while agonizing over her poor attempts at fiction in her rented room on the boulevard Raspail: Kurth, *American Cassandra*.

58. Hughes, "Alliance of Antifascist Intellectuals," and "Soldiers from Many Lands United in Spanish Fight," *Afro-American*, Dec. 18, 1937 in *Collected Works*, 149–52, 178–81; Hughes, *I Wonder as I Wander*, 27; "Too Much of Race," Second International Writers' Congress, Paris, July 1937, in *Good Morning Revolution*, 97–9.

59. Sheean, *Not Peace but a Sword*, 88, 121, 138; Gellhorn, *Face of War*, 68; "Dying, Well or Badly," *Ken*, April 21, 1938 in *Hemingway on War*, 292–4.

60. Gellhorn, *Face of War*, 14; Shirer, *20th Century Journey*, 347; Dos Passos, *Best Times*, 32–3; "tea-table" in Diggins, *Up From Communism*, 3; "old time" in letter to Edmund Wilson, March 23, 1934, *Fourteenth Chronicle*, 435–6;

Gellhorn to Allen Grover, Oct. 4, 1936 and to Hemingway, Nov. 30, and Dec. 4, 1939 in *Ernest Hemingway*, 40–1, 76–80.

61. Shirer, *20th Century Journey: The Nightmare Years*, xiv, 3, 11; Sheean, *Personal History*, 49, 139–42, 150, 160; Good, *Journalist as Autobiographer*, 114–15. Hemingway made similar points about the Italian invasion of Abyssinia in *Esquire*. Speculating about the self-interested calculations that led the French and British to tolerate Mussolini's expedition, he urged Ethiopians to learn from the Riffians. He expressed sympathy for the common Italian soldiers trapped in the horrors of African warfare but loathing for the political ploys that brought them there: "Notes on the Next War," Sept. 1935, and "Wings Always over Africa," Jan. 1936 in *By-Line*, 205–12, 229–32.

62. Haney, *Naked at the Feast*, 196–7; Rose, *Jazz Cleopatra*, 149, 184. On stage and on screen, Baker delighted in roles as colonial heroines, not only portraying an African temptress but also "La Petite Tonkinoise," an Annamese mistress, as well as a Tunisian goat girl in *Princess Tam Tam*. At the same time, she publicized herself as a latter-day Eliza Doolittle, overcoming her humble black beginnings to embrace French culture. This helps to explain why officials proposed to make her "Queen of the Colonies" for the 1931 Exhibition. On publicity for France in African American newspapers, see "Color Line Gets Acid Test in France," Aug. 18, 1923, pt. II, 13 and "French Democracy Versus American Race Prejudice," Sept. 1, 1923, both in *Chicago Defender*.

63. McKay, *Negroes in America*, 50–1; McKay to James Ivy, Paris, Sept. 20, 1929 and "Race and Color in East Asia," *Opportunity*, August 1939 in *Passion of Claude McKay*, 147–8, 294–9; Fabre, *From Harlem to Paris*, ch. 7; Hughes, "Johannesburg Mines" (1928), "The English" (1930), "The Same" (1932), "Merry Christmas" (1930), and "Cubes," (1934) in *Good Morning Revolution*, 9–12, 26–7. See also Janken, "African American and Francophone Black Intellectuals" and Stephens, *Black Empire*.

64. Dos Passos, *Rosinante to the Road Again* (1922) in *Travel Books*, 24; Paul, *Life and Death of a Spanish Town*; Hemingway to James Gamble, Dec. 12, 1923 and to Howell Jenkins, Nov. 9, 1924 in *Ernest Hemingway*, 106–8, 130–2.

65. Hemingway, "Dying, Well or Badly," *Ken*, April 21, 1938 in *Hemingway on War*, 292–4; Hughes, "Negroes in Spain," *Volunteer for Liberty*, Sept. 1937 in *Collected Works*, 156–7; Gellhorn to Eleanor Roosevelt, July 1937 and April 1938 in *Selected Letters*, 54–5, 59–60. On volunteers, see Wald, *Trinity of Passions* and Kelley, *Race Rebels*, ch. 6.

66. Hughes, *I Wonder as I Wander*, ch. 8; Hughes, "Madrid Getting Used to Bombs," *Afro-American*, Nov. 20, 1937 and "Laughter in Madrid," *TN*, Jan. 29, 1938 in *Collected Works*, 169–73, 191–4; Herbst, *Starched Blue Sky*; Hemingway, NANA dispatches, April 14, 1937 and May 22, 1937 in *Hemingway at War*, 281–91; Dos Passos, "Madrid Under Siege," *Journeys*

between *Wars* (1938) in *Travel Books*, 463–71; Sheean, *Not Peace but a Sword*, 239.

67. Herbst, *Starched Blue Sky*, 146; Gellhorn to Betty Barnes, Jan. 30, 1937 in *Selected Letters*, 48–9. Like Gellhorn and other women in this cohort, Herbst regarded herself as "a girl with the ambitions and aspirations of a boy." Fighting for a greater role in professions like foreign journalism, such pioneers smarted at the masculine bravado that infused the period's leftist political culture but also tried to adopt it for their own tough and savvy new models of femininity: Herbst quoted in Diane Johnson, introduction to *Starched Blue Sky*, xii.

68. Paul, *Life and Death of a Spanish Town*, 23–4, 206, 295; "Innocents Abroad." *SEP*, May 14, 1927, 32; Sheean, *Personal History*; Seldes, *Lords of the Press*. Paul would offer an equally rich and enduring portrait of the downfall of the Third Republic from the point of view of his Left Bank neighborhood in *The Last Time I Saw Paris* (1942).

69. Orwell, *Homage to Catalonia*; Preston, *Spanish Civil War*. Hughes was deeply disturbed by the use of Moorish troops on Franco's side, depicting them as duped and hapless conscripts. Focusing on the problems of race and empire, he sidestepped the religious convictions that motivated many on the rebel side, including some North Africans, who saw the conflict as a war against godlessness. Religion, for Hughes and likeminded expatriates, served foremost as a tool of oppressors, used to coat imperialist plunder in Christian veneer or to pull enraptured crowds into reactionary mass movements.

70. Dos Passos, *In All Countries* (1934) in *Travel Books*; "breathlessly" in *Best Times*, 174; "war zone" and Harlan County, in Ludington, *John Dos Passos*, 297–9, 324–5; Diggins, *Up From Communism*, 85–90.

71. Dos Passos, *Villages are the Heart of Spain*, 14–15; Dos Passos, "Farewell to Europe!," *Common Sense*, July 1937 and "The Death of José Robles," *NR*, July 19, 1939 in *Travel Books*, 618–25. On Dos Passos's growing impatience for "rubber stamp" labels and ugly partisanship leading up to the Spanish Civil War, see his correspondence from the mid-thirties in *Fourteenth Chronicle*.

72. Sheean, *Not Peace but a Sword*; Flanner, "Salzburg," Aug. 29, 1938 and "Vienna" Sept. 5, 1938 in *Janet Flanner's World*, 40–5; Gellhorn, "Obituary for a Democracy," *Collier's*, Dec. 1938 in *View from the Ground*, 49–64; Wineapple, *Genêt*, 153–4, "we must be ready" p. 167; Shirer, *20th Century Journey: The Nightmare Years*; and *Berlin Diary*.

73. Gellhorn, *Travels with Myself and Another*, 9–57, quote p. 24; Gellhorn to Allen Grover, July 1941 in *Selected Letters*, 111–12; Gellhorn, *Faces of War*, 67–70; Moreira, *Hemingway on the China Front*; Hemingway to Henry Morgenthau, July 30, 1941 reprinted in Moreira, 201–8; Hemingway, articles for *PM*, 1941 in *By-Line*, pt. 4.

74. For a contrary view of Americans' new international commitments in the 1940s as an extension of the domestic New Deal, see Borgwardt, *New Deal for the World*.

## Epilogue

1. Quotation from Carrot, *Maintien de l'ordre en France*, 77.
2. Weber, *Hollow Years*, 131–6; Carrot, *Maintien de l'ordre*, 81–6; quotations p. 80; and Pellissier, *6 février 1934*. Jean Chiappe went on to serve as president of the Municipal Council and then deputy for the Department of the Seine in 1936. Chiappe died toward the end of 1940, his plane shot down over the Mediterranean as he flew to assume the post of Vichy's high commissioner in Syria.
3. Shirer, *20th Century Journey: 1930–1940*, 82–4, 96–7; Bove, *Paris Surgeon's Story*, 99–105.
4. Mowrer, *Journalist's Wife*, 319–20; Gibbs, *European Journey*, 14–15. On the army kitchen in the Crillon's basement, see Thurber, "First Time I Saw Paris," 6–17.
5. Mannin, *Forever Wandering*, 76–9; Bove, *Paris Surgeon's Story*, 107; "German problem" in Morgan, *Fascism in Europe*, 9.
6. Paul, *Last Time I Saw Paris*, 299.
7. Gibbs, *European Journey*, 18–19, 30; Levenstein, *We'll Always Have Paris*, 6, 25–6; Shack, *Harlem in Montmartre*, 77–81.
8. J. C. Furnas, "The Vanished American," *SEP*, Dec. 8, 1934, 23, 88–93.
9. Flanner, "Paris, Germany," Dec. 7, 1940 in *Janet Flanner's World*, 50–61; Sheean, *Between the Thunder and the Sun*, 148; Jones, *Paris*, 413–25.
10. Sheean, *Between the Thunder and the Sun*, 151.
11. Sylvia Beach Papers, Box 35, Dept. of Rare Books and Special Collections, Princeton University Library.
12. Wineapple, *Genêt*, ch. 11; Flanner, "Letter from Paris," *NY*, Dec. 23, 1944 cited in Wineapple, 186–7.
13. Schwartz, *It's So French!*, ch. 1.
14. Jean d'Yvoire, *Radio-ciné*, Aug. 10, 1952 trans. in Schwartz, *It's So French!*, 49.
15. Cowley, *Exile's Return*, 289, 309; Hemingway, *Moveable Feast*, 210–11. "Good and evil are embodied in men who struggle," Cowley had originally written in his final paragraph; "Tragedy lives in the stories of the men now dying in Chinese streets or in German prisons for a cause by which their lives are given dignity and meaning." It was not the inner psychological worlds of the artist but the "outer world that is strong and colorful and demands to be imaginatively portrayed": 332.
16. See the 1994 Penguin publication of Cowley's *Exile's Return*, which includes excised portions of the 1934 version and Donald Faulkner's discussion of

the text's reception in the 1950s. On postwar intellectual trends, see Daniel Bell, *The End of Ideology: On the Exhaustion of Political Ideas in the Fifties* (Cambridge: Harvard University Press, [1960], 2000), esp. ch. 13.

17. Kuisel, *Seducing the French*; "Historical Perspectives on Anti-Americanism," *American Historical Review* 111.4 (Oct. 2006): 1041–129.

*Primary Sources*

Acheson, Edward. *Password to Paris: Advice for the Thrifty*. New York: William Morrow, 1932.

Adams, Eustace. *The Family Sees France*. New York: Brewer and Warren, 1931.

*Almanach franco-américain; French American Directory*. New York: Moniteur Franco-Américain, 1928.

American Legion. *Americanism Manual: "To foster and perpetuate a one hundred percent Americanism."* Indianapolis: National Americanism Commission, c. 1932.

———. *Post Handbook of the American Legion*. 8th ed. Indianapolis: American Legion National Headquarters, c. 1929.

Andrews, C. E. *The Innocents of Paris*. New York: D. Appleton, 1928.

Baker, Josephine, and Jo Bouillon. *Josephine*. New York: Marlowe, 1988.

Barrère, Albert. *Argot and Slang: A New French and English Dictionary of the Cant Words, Quaint Expressions, Slang Terms and Flash Phrases Used in the High and Low Life of Old and New Paris*. London: Hugo's Language Institute, [1889], 1911.

Beach, Joseph. *Meek Americans & Other European Trifles*. Chicago: University of Chicago Press, 1925.

Beach, Sylvia. *Shakespeare and Company*. New York: Harcourt, Brace, 1959.

Bechet, Sidney. *Treat It Gentle*. New York: Hill and Wang, 1960.

Bercovici, Konrad. *Nights Abroad*. New York: Century, 1928.

Bertaut, Jules. *Les belles nuits de Paris*. Paris: Flammarion, 1927.

———. *Le boulevard*. Paris: Flammarion, 1924.

———. *Paris, 1870–1935*. Translated by R. Millar. New York: D. Appleton Century, 1936.

Bidou, Henry. *Paris*. Paris: Gallimard, 1937.

Bizard, Léon. *La vie des filles*. Paris: Grasset, 1934.

Blanc, Édouard. *La ceinture rouge: Enquête sur la situation politique, morale et sociale de la banlieue de Paris*. Paris: Spes, 1927.

Boisson, Marius. *coins et recoins de Paris*. Paris: Bossard, 1927.

Bonney, Thérèse and Louise. *A Shopping Guide to Paris*. New York: Robert McBride, 1929.

Bost, Pierre. *Le cirque et le music-hall*. Paris: Au Sans Pareil, 1931.

Boucher, François, and Frances Wilson Huard. *American Footprints in Paris*. New York: George H. Doran, 1921.

Bove, Charles, with Dana Lee Thomas, *A Paris Surgeon's Story*. Boston: Little, Brown, 1956.

Brace, A. M., ed. *Americans in France: A Directory*. Vol. 3. Paris: American Chamber of Commerce in France, 1927–1928.

Branguyn, John [Charlotte Hirsch]. *Everybody's Paris*. New York: National Travel Club, 1935.

Brassaï [Gyula Halász], *Henry Miller: The Paris Years*. Translated by Timothy Bent. New York: Arcade Publishing, [1975], 1995.

———. *The Secret Paris of the 30's*. Translated by Richard Miller. New York: Thames & Hudson, 1976.

Brewster, Paul, ed. *The American Directory & Who's Who in Europe*. New York: Alfred Knopf, c. 1922.

Bricktop [Ada Smith], with James Haskins. *Bricktop*. New York: Atheneum, 1983.

Brooks, Van Wyck. *America's Coming-of-Age*. New York: Octagon Books, [1915], 1975.

Bucovich, Mario. *Paris*. New York: Random House, 1930.

Carco, Francis. *Images cachées*. Paris: Albin Michel, 1929.

Chancellor, John. *How to Be Happy in Paris without Being Ruined!* London: Arrowsmith, 1926.

Charters, Jimmie. *This Must Be the Place: Memoirs of Montparnasse by Jimmie "The Barman" Charters as Told to Morrill Cody*. New York: Collier, [1934], 1989.

Chiappe, Jean. *Paroles d'ordre*. Paris: Eugène Figuiere, 1930.

Clarke, William. *My Travelogue: Sketches and Observations Made on a Tour of the Principal Cities of Europe Shortly after the World War*. Toledo, Ohio: Kraus & Schreiber, n.d., [1922].

Cobb, Irvin. *Both Sides of the Street*. New York: Cosmopolitan Book Corporation, [1927], 1930.

Cohen-Portheim, Paul. *The Spirit of Paris*. Philadelphia: J. B. Lippincott, 1937.

Commission Municipale du Vieux Paris. *Procès-verbaux*. Paris: Imprimerie Municipale, 1909–1931.

Communist Party of Great Britain. *The Communist International: Between the Fifth & the Sixth World Congresses, 1924–8.* London: Dorrit, 1928.

Conseil Municipal de Paris. *Rapports et documents: Première partie de 1 à 70: Année 1933.* Paris: Imprimerie Municipale, 1934.

Cook, Joel. *A Holiday Tour in Europe Described in a Series of Letters Written for the Public Ledger During the Summer and Autumn of 1878.* Philadelphia: J. B. Lippincott, 1879.

Cowley, Malcolm. *Exile's Return.* New York: Penguin, [1934], 1994.

Croy, Homer. *They Had to See Paris.* New York: Harper, 1926.

Cummings, E. E. *Complete Poems, 1910–1962.* Edited by George Firmage. London: Granada, [1968], 1981.

———. "Conflicting Aspects of Paris." In *A Miscellany*, edited by George J. Firmage, 58–61. New York: Argophile, 1958.

———. *Eimi: A Journey through Soviet Russia.* New York: Liveright, [1933], 2007.

———. *The Enormous Room.* New York: Penguin, [1922], 1999.

———. *Him.* New York: Boni & Liveright, 1927.

———. *Selected Letters of E. E. Cummings.* Edited by F. W. Dupee and George Stade. New York: Harcourt, Brace, 1969.

———. "selfdiscovery; nonlecture three." In *i: Six Non-Lectures.* Cambridge: Harvard University Press, [1953], 1959.

Davis, Richard Harding. *About Paris.* New York: Harper, 1895.

de Catalogne, Gérard. *Dialogue entre deux mondes: Reportage.* Paris: Librairie de la Revue Française, 1931.

de Gramont, Elisabeth. *Souvenirs du monde de 1890 à 1940.* Paris: Bernard Grasset, 1966.

Degras, Jane, ed. *The Communist International: 1919–1943 Documents.* Vol. II (1923–1928). London: Frank Cass, [1960], 1971.

Delamare, George. *Vingt années sans guerre (1919–1939): Souvenirs de Paris.* Paris: France Littérature, 1956.

de Miomandre, Francis. *Dancings.* Paris: Flammarion, 1932.

Derval, Paul. *Folies-Bergère.* Translated by Lucienne Hill. New York: E. P. Dutton, 1955.

Desti, Mary. *The Untold Story: The Life of Isadora Duncan, 1921–1927.* New York: Horace Liveright, 1929.

Dos Passos, John. *The Best Times: An Informal Memoir.* New York: New American Library, 1966.

———. *The Fourteenth Chronicle: Letters and Diaries of John Dos Passos.* Edited by Townsend Ludington. Boston: Gambit, 1973.

———. *John Dos Passos: Travel Books and Other Writings, 1916–1941.* New York: Library of America, 2003.

———. *Three Soldiers.* New York: Bantam, [1921], 1997.

———. *The Villages Are the Heart of Spain.* Chicago: Esquire-Coronet, 1937.

Dougherty, George. *Exploits of a Detective in Europe*. New York: Pusey Press, n. d.

Duffield, Marcus. *King Legion*. New York: Jonathan Cape & Harrison Smith, 1931.

Duhamel, Georges. *America the Menace: Scenes from the Life of the Future*. Translated by Charles Miner Thompson. Boston: Houghton Mifflin, 1931.

Edwards, George Wharton. *Paris with Drawings in Color and Monotone*. Philadelphia: Penn Publishing, 1924.

Émile-Bayard, Jean. *Montmartre: Hier et aujourd'hui*. Paris: Jouve, 1925.

Ewan, Ruth Osborne. *Mr. and Mrs. Europe*. Atlantic City: Amusement Publishing, 1922.

Fanning, Michael. *France and Sherwood Anderson: Paris Notebook, 1921*. Baton Rouge: Louisiana State University Press, 1976.

Farrell, James T. "After the Sun Has Risen" and "Scrambled Eggs and Toast." In *An Omnibus of Short Stories*. New York: Vanguard, [1942], 1956.

———. "Paris Scene: 1931." In *When Boyhood Dreams Come True*. New York: Vanguard, 1946.

Fegdal, Charles. *Choses et gens des Halles*. Paris: Athéna, 1922.

———. *Coins curieux de Paris*. Paris: Delamain, Boutelleau, 1924.

———. *Dans notre vieux Paris*. Paris: Stock, 1934.

———. *La fleur des curiositez de Paris*. Paris: Revue Contemporaine, 1922.

Fitzgerald, F. Scott. "Babylon Revisited." In *Babylon Revisited and Other Stories*. New York: Simon and Schuster, 1996.

———. "Echoes of the Jazz Age." In *The Crack-Up*. City: New Directions, 1931, 1945.

———. *The Letters of F. Scott Fitzgerald*. Edited by Andrew Turnbull. New York: Scribner, 1963.

Flambeau, Viktor. *Red Letter Days in Europe with a Glimpse of Northern Africa*. New York: George Sully, 1925.

Flanner, Janet. *Janet Flanner's World: Uncollected Writings*. Edited by Irving Drutman. New York: Harcourt, Brace, Jovanovich, 1979.

———. *Paris Was Yesterday, 1925–1939*. New York: Viking, 1972.

Fréjaville, Gustave. *Au music-hall*. Paris: Monde Nouveau, 1923.

Garey, E. B. *American Guide Book to France and its Battlefields*. New York: MacMillan, 1920.

Gautherot, Gustave. *Le monde communiste*. Paris: Spes, 1925.

Gellermann, William. *The American Legion as Educator*. New York: Bureau of Publications Teachers College, Columbia University, 1938.

Gellhorn, Martha. *The Face of War*. New York: Atlantic Monthly, [1959], 1986.

———. *Selected Letters of Martha Gellhorn*. Edited by Caroline Moorehead. New York: Henry Holt, 2006.

———. *Travels with Myself and Another: A Memoir*. New York: Jeremy P. Tarcher/Putnam, [1978], 2001.

———. *The View from the Ground*. New York: Atlantic Monthly, 1988.

Gibbs, Philip. *European Journey*. Garden City, New York: Doubleday, Doran, 1935.

Goddard, Chris. *Jazz Away from Home*. New York: Paddington, 1979.

Gopnik, Adam, ed. *Americans in Paris: A Literary Anthology*. New York: Library of America, 2004.

Gravigny, Jean. *Montmartre en 1925*. Paris: Montaigne, 1924.

Greer, Carl Richard. *What a Buckeye Cover Man Saw in Europe and at Home*. Hamilton, Ohio: Beckett Paper Company, 1923.

Gress, Edmund. *A Dash through Europe with Snapshots by the Way*. New York: Oswald Publishing, 1923.

Griggs, Arthur. *My Paris: An Anthology of Modern Paris from the Works of Contemporary French Writers*. New York: Dial Press, 1932.

*Guide de l'étranger à Montmartre et à Paris/Guide of the Stranger to Montmartre and to Paris: French and English Edition: Montmartre by Day and by Night: Music-Halls-Amusements-Night's Establishments*. Pamphlet, c. 1909.

*Guide des plaisirs à Paris: Paris le jour, Paris la nuit*. Paris: Quai des Grands-Augustins, n.d. [c.1930s].

Hamel, Maurice, and Charles Tournier. *La prostitution: Enquête*. Nice: Imprimerie Nouvelle de la Madeleine, 1927.

Hapgood, Norman. *Professional Patriots*. New York: Albert & Charles Boni, 1927.

Hawkins, Eric, with Robert Sturdevant. *Hawkins of the Paris Herald*. New York: Simon and Schuster, 1963.

Hayes, Carlton. *France: A Nation of Patriots*. New York: Columbia University Press, 1930.

Hemingway, Ernest. *By-Line: Ernest Hemingway*. Edited by William White. New York: Simon and Schuster, 1967.

———. *Dateline: Toronto: The Complete Toronto Star Dispatches, 1920–1924*. Edited by William White. New York: Charles Scribner's Sons, 1985.

———. *Ernest Hemingway: Selected Letters, 1917–1961*. Edited by Carlos Baker. New York: Charles Scribner's Sons, 1981.

———. *A Farewell to Arms*. New York: Scribner's, [1929], 1969.

———. *Hemingway on War*. Edited by Séan Hemingway. New York: Scribner, 2003.

———. *A Moveable Feast*. New York: Collier, [1964], 1987.

———. *The Sun Also Rises*. New York: Simon & Schuster, [1926], 1954.

Henri-Jacques. *Moulin Rouge*. Paris: Seheur, 1925.

Henriot, Gabriel. *Nouvelles devantures et agencements de magasins*. Paris: C. Moreau, n.d. [late 1920s].

Herald, Don. *Doing Europe—and Vice Versa*. Boston: Little, Brown, 1932.

Herbst, Josephine. *The Starched Blue Sky of Spain and Other Memoirs*. New York: Harper Collins, 1991.

Herbst, René. *Nouvelles devantures et agencements de magasins parisiens*. Paris: C. Moreau, 1927.

Holland, Clive. *Things Seen in Paris*. New York: E. P. Dutton, 1926.

*How to Enjoy Paris and the Smart Resorts: A Guide-book of a New Kind for the Discriminating*. Paris: International Publications, 1927–1928.

Huddleston, Sisley. *Articles de Paris: A Book of Essays*. New York: MacMillan, 1928.

———. *Back to Montparnasse: Glimpses of Broadway in Bohemia*. Philadelphia: J. B. Lippincott, 1931.

———. *Paris Salons, Cafés, Studios*. Philadelphia: J. B. Lippincott, 1928.

Hughes, Langston. *The Big Sea*. New York: Hill and Wang, [1940], 1993.

———. *The Collected Works of Langston Hughes: Essays on Art, Race, Politics, and World Affairs*. Vol. 9. Edited by Christopher De Santis. Columbia: University of Missouri Press, 2002.

———. *Good Morning Revolution: Uncollected Social Protest Writings*. Edited by Faith Berry. New York: Lawrence Hill, 1973.

———. *I Wonder as I Wander*. New York: Hill and Wang, [1956], 1993.

Josephson, Matthew. *Life among the Surrealists*. New York: Holt, Rinehart and Wilson, 1962.

Josephy, Helen, and Mary Margaret McBride. *Paris Is a Woman's Town*. New York: Coward McCann, 1929.

Keely, Robert. *Paris and All the World Besides*. Philadelphia: Howard Myers, 1930.

Laney, Al. *Paris Herald: The Incredible Newspaper*. New York: D. Appleton-Century, 1947.

Laughlin, Clara. *So You're Going to Paris!* Boston: Houghton Mifflin, [1924], 1934.

Leake, Chauncey and Elizabeth. *1938 Travelog: Being an Account of a European Trip Written for the Amusement of the Friends of Chauncey and Elizabeth Leake*. San Francisco: privately printed, 1938.

Lecoin, Louis. *Le cours d'une vie*. Paris: 1965.

Le Gallienne, Richard. *From a Paris Garret*. London: Richards Press, 1943.

———. *From a Paris Scrapbook*. New York: Ives Washburn, 1938.

Léon-Martin, Louis. *Le music-hall et ses figures*. Paris: Editions de France, 1928.

Levinson, André. *Figures américaines: 18 Etudes sur des écrivains de ce temps*. Paris: Victor Attinger, 1929.

Lewis, Sinclair. *Dodsworth*. New York: Penguin, [1929], 1967.

Lewisohn, Ludwig. *Mid-Channel: An American Chronicle*. New York: Harper, 1929.

Lhande, Pierre. *Le Christ dans la banlieue: Enquête sur la vie religieuse dans les milieux ouvriers de la banlieue de Paris*. Paris: Plon, 1927.

Lineberger, Walter. "The Diplomatic and Consular Service of the United States: The Activities and Need for Reorganization and Improvement of the Nation's Foreign Service." Pamphlet, 1924.

Logan, Rayford. "Confessions of an Unwilling Nordic." In *The Negro Caravan: Writings by American Negroes*, edited by Sterling Brown, 1043–150. New York: Dryden, 1941.

Longstreet, Stephen. *We All Went to Paris: Americans in the City of Light, 1776–1971*. New York: MacMillan, 1972.

Loos, Anita. *Gentlemen Prefer Blondes*. New York: Liveright, [1925], 1998.

Loud, Marguerite. *An Elegant Time: Letters from an American Student in Paris, 1923–1924*. Princeton: Princeton University Press, 1990.

Louvrier, Henri. *Le guide du chauffeur de taxi, 1926–1927*. Paris: Etienne Chiron.

Lucas, E. V. *A Wanderer in Paris*. London: Methuen, [1909], 1925.

Lyons, Eugene. *The Life and Death of Sacco and Vanzetti*. New York: International Publishers, 1927.

Mac Orlan, Pierre. *Aux lumières de Paris*. Paris: G. Crès, 1925.

Mannin, Ethel. *Forever Wandering*. New York: E. P. Dutton, 1935.

McAlmon, Robert, with Kay Boyle. *Being Geniuses Together, 1920–1930*. San Francisco: North Point Press, [1968], 1984.

McKay, Claude. *A Long Way from Home*. New Brunswick: Rutgers University Press, [1937], 2007.

———. *The Negroes in America*. Port Washington, N.Y.: Kennikaat, 1979.

———. *The Passion of Claude McKay: Selected Poetry and Prose, 1912–1948*. Edited by Wayne Cooper. New York: Schocken, 1973.

Merlet, Janine. *Vénus et Mercure*. Paris: Vie Moderne, 1931.

Miller, Francis, and Helen Hill. *The Giant of the Western World: America and Europe in a North Atlantic Civilisation*. New York: William Morrow, 1930.

Miller, Henry. *Tropic of Cancer*. New York: Grove, [1934], 1961.

———. *Quiet Days in Clichy*. New York: Grove, [1956], 1965.

Miller, Webb. *I Found No Peace: The Journal of a Foreign Correspondent*. New York: Simon and Schuster, 1936.

Milton, Arthur. *Paris in Seven Days: A Guide for People in a Hurry*. New York: Robert McBride, 1923.

Montorgueil, Georges. *Le vieux Montmartre*. Paris: Hachette, 1925.

Moody, H. G. *"Meet the King": Story of Second A.E.F.'s Pilgrimage after Hitting the Paris Trail*. New York: Winwick, 1931.

Morain, Alfred. *The Underworld of Paris: Secrets of the Sûreté*. London: Jarrolds, 1930.

Morand, Paul. *Paris to the Life*. Translated by Gerard Hopkins. London: Oxford University Press, 1933.

Mott, T. Bentley. *Myron T. Herrick: An Autobiographical Biography*. Golden Day, N.Y.: Doubleday, Doran, 1929.

Mowrer, Lilian. *Journalist's Wife*. New York: William Morrow, 1937.

Mowrer, Paul Scott. *The House of Europe*. Boston: Houghton Mifflin, 1988.

Muller, J. W. *"Ever Thine": A Title not Inappropriately Chosen for a Fairly Coherent Selection of Excerpts from the Travel Letters of J. W. Muller; Made into Book Form Wholly without his Knowledge or Consent for the Diversion of Friends of the Bartlett Orr Press*. New York: Bartlett Orr, 1928.

Neagoe, Peter, ed. *Americans Abroad: An Anthology*. The Hague: Servire, 1932.

Nevill, Ralph. *Days and Nights in Montmartre and the Latin Quarter*. New York: George H. Doran, 1927.

Newman, E. M. *Seeing Paris*. New York: Funk & Wagnalls, 1931.

Newton, Edward. *A Tourist in Spite of Himself*. Boston: Little, Brown, [1926], 1930.

*Night Guide for Gentlemen: Paris After Dark: Containing a description of the fast women, their haunts, habits, etc. to which is added a faithful description of the Night Amusements and other resorts also all particulars relative to the working of the Social Evil in the French Metropolis*. Pamphlet, n.d. [c. 1877].

O'Brien, Howard Vincent. *P.S. by the Author of Wine, Women and War*. New York: J. H. Sears, 1928.

Ogilvie, F. W. *The Tourist Movement: An Economic Study*. London: P. S. King & Son, 1933.

Orwell, George. *Homage to Catalonia*. Orlando, Fla.: Harcourt, [1938], 1980.

Overton, Grant, ed., *Mirrors of the Year: A National Review of the Outstanding Figures, Trends and Events of 1926–27*. New York: Frederick Stokes, 1927.

Paul, Elliot. *The Last Time I Saw Paris*. New York: Random House, 1942.

———. *The Life and Death of a Spanish Town*. New York: Random House, 1937.

Phelps, Clyde. *The Foreign Expansion of American Banks: American Branch Banking Abroad*. New York: Ronald Press, 1927.

Pollock, John. *Paris and Parisians*. London: Geoffrey Bles, 1929.

Préfecture de la Seine. *Annuaire statistique de la ville de Paris: Années 1925 et 1926*. Paris: Société Anonyme de Publications Périodiques, 1930.

———. *Annuaire statistique de la ville de Paris: Années 1927 et 1928*. Paris: F. Deshayes, 1932.

Putnam, Samuel. *Paris Was Our Mistress: Memoirs of a Lost and Found Generation*. New York: Viking, 1947.

Rascoe, Burton. *We Were Interrupted*. Garden City, N.Y.: Doubleday, 1947.

*Revue des Folies-Bergère*. Albums 1–6. Paris: Art Editions, 1923–1928.

Reynolds, Bruce. *A Cocktail Continental Concocted in 24 Countries Served in 38 Sips and A Kick Guaranteed*. New York: George Sully, 1926.

———. *Paris with the Lid Lifted*. New York: George Sully, 1927.

Rice, Elmer. *Minority Report: An Autobiography*. New York: Simon and
Schuster, 1963.

Richard, Élie. *Le guide des grands ducs*. Paris: Monde Moderne, 1925.

Roszel, B. M., and the American Legion. *The Commanders' Tour, September
24th–October 11th, 1927*. Richmond, Va.: Garrett & Massie, 1928.

Roth, Joseph. *Report from a Parisian Paradise: Essays from France, 1925–1939*.
Translated by Michael Hofmann. New York: Norton, 2004.

Roubaud, Louis. *Music-hall*. Paris: Louis Querelle, 1929.

Sachs, Maurice. *The Decade of Illusion: Paris, 1918–1928*. Translated by
Gwladys Matthews Sachs. New York: Alfred Knopf, 1933.

Seldes, George. *Lords of the Press*. New York: Julian Messner, 1938.

———. *World Panorama, 1918–1933*. Boston: Little, Brown, 1933.

Sézille, L. P. *Devantures de boutiques*. Paris: A. Lévy, 1927.

Shachtman, Max. "Sacco and Vanzetti: Labor's Martyrs." New York:
International Labor Defense, 1927.

Shafer, Chet. *The Second A.E.F.: The Pilgrimage of the Army of Remembrance*.
New York: Doty, 1927.

Shaw, Elizabeth. *Painted Maps*. New York: Dial, 1931.

Sheean, Vincent. *Between the Thunder and the Sun*. New York: Random
House, 1943.

———. *Not Peace but a Sword*. New York: Doubleday, Doran, 1939.

———. *Personal History*. New York: Garden City: Doubleday, Doran, 1935.

Sheridan, Clare. *West and East*. New York: Boni and Liveright, 1923.

Shinkman, Elizabeth Benn, ed., *So Little Disillusion: An American
Correspondent in Paris and London, 1924–1931*. McLean, Virginia: EPM
Publications, 1983.

Shirer, William. *20th Century Journey: A Memoir of a Life and the Times, The
Start: 1904–1930*. New York: Simon and Schuster, 1976.

———. *20th Century Journey: The Nightmare Years, 1930–1940: Volume II of
a Memoir of a Life and the Times*. Boston: Little, Brown, 1984.

———. *Berlin Diary; the Journal of a Foreign Correspondent, 1934–1941*.
New York: Knopf, 1941.

———. *"This is Berlin": Radio Broadcasts from Nazi Germany*. Woodstock,
N.Y.: Overlook, 1999.

Sieburg, Friedrich. *Dieu est-il-français?* Paris: Bernard Grasset, 1930.

Siegfried, André. *America Comes of Age*. Translated by H. H. and Doris
Hemming. New York: Harcourt, Brace, 1927.

Slocombe, George. *Paris in Profile*. Boston: Houghton Mifflin, 1928.

———. *The Tumult and the Shouting*. London: William Heinemann, 1936.

Smith, F. Berkeley. *How Paris Amuses Itself*. New York: Funk & Wagnalls,
1903.

Soupault, Philippe. *The American Influence in France*. Translated by Babette
and Glenn Hughes. Seattle: University of Washington Chapbooks, 1930.

Southard, Frank. *American Industry in Europe*. Boston: Houghton Mifflin, 1931.

Spivak, John. *A Man in His Time*. New York: Horizon Press, 1967.

Spoerri, William. *The Old World and the New: A Synopsis of Current European Views on American Civilization*. Zurich: Niehan, 1937.

*Statistique générale de la france: Annuaire statistique*. Vol. 47, 2$^e$ Partie, Tableau VI. Paris: Imprimerie Nationale, 1931.

*Statistique générale de la france: Résultats statistiques du recensement général de la population effectué le 7 mars 1926*. Tome III. Paris: Imprimerie Nationale, 1930.

Stead, W. T. *The Americanization of the World: Or, The Trend of the Twentieth Century*. New York: Horace Markley, [1901], 1902.

Stearns, Harold. *The Street I Know*. New York: Lee Furman, 1935.

Stein, Gertrude. *Paris France*. New York: Norton, [1940], 1996.

Stewart, Donald Ogden. *Mr. and Mrs. Haddock Abroad*. Carbondale: Southern Illinois University Press, [1924], 1975.

———. *Mr. and Mrs. Haddock in Paris, France*. New York: Harper & Brothers, 1926.

Stokes, Horace Winston, ed. *Mirrors of the Year: A National Review of the Outstanding Figures, Trends and Events of 1927–28*. New York: Frederick Stokes, 1928.

Story, Sommerville. *Dining in Paris: A Guide to Paris à la Carte and Table d'Hôte*. New York: Robert McBride, 1927.

Street, Julian. *Where Paris Dines*. Garden City, N.Y.: Doubleday, Doran, 1929.

Stuart, Graham. *American Diplomatic and Consular Practice*. New York: D. Appleton-Century, 1936.

Thurber, James. "The First Time I Saw Paris." In *Alarms and Diversions*. New York: Harper & Brothers, 1957.

Union Temporaire contre la Prostitution réglementée et la Traite des Femmes. "Discours prononcés le 6 février 1931 à la Salle des Sociétés Savantes." Pamphlet, 1931.

Vaillant-Couturier, Paul. *The French Boy*. Translated by Ida Treat. Philadelphia: J. B. Lippincott, 1931.

Valentino, Henri. *Les Américains à Paris au temps joyeux de la prospérité*. Paris: Perrin, 1936.

Valti, Luc. *Femmes de cinq heures: Enquête sur les maisons de rendez-vous de Paris*. Paris: Editions de France, 1930.

van Paassen, Pierre. *Days of Our Years*. New York: Hillman-Curl, 1939.

Verne, Maurice. *Aux usines du plaisir: La vie secrete du music-hall*. Paris: Editions des Portiques, 1929.

Vernier, M. V. *How to Enjoy and Get the Very Best of Paris*, Translated by Fitz Gerald. Paris: M-V. Vernier, [1921], c. 1923.

Vorse, Mary Heaton. *A Footnote to Folly: Reminiscences of Mary Heaton Vorse*. New York: Farrar & Rinehart, 1935.

Warnod, André. *Les bals de Paris*. Paris: Georges Crès, 1922.

———. *Les plaisirs de la rue*. Paris: L'Edition Française Illustré, 1920.

———. *Visages de Paris*. Paris: Firmin-Didot, 1930.

Wells, H. G. *The Way the World Is Going*. New York: Doubleday, Doran, 1929.

Wharton, Edith. *A Backward Glance*. New York: Simon & Schuster, [1933], 1998.

Williams, William Carlos. *The Autobiography of William Carlos Williams*. New York: Random House, 1948.

———. *A Voyage to Pagany*. New York: New Directions, [1928], 1970.

Wilson, Mary Lena. *Ladies Third: Six Weeks in Europe for Six Hundred Dollars*. New York: Duffield, 1927.

Wilson, Robert Forrest. *Paris on Parade*. New York: Robert McBride, 1924.

Wilson, Walter. *American Legion and Civil Liberty*. New York: American League Against War and Fascism, [1936].

Windstaff, W. W. *Lower than Angels: A Memoir of War & Peace*. Silver Spring, Md.: Enigma, 1993.

Woon, Basil. *The Paris That's Not in the Guide Books*. New York: Brentano's, 1926.

Zimmer, Lucien. *Un septennat policier: Dessous et secrets de la police républicaine*. Paris: Arthème Fayard, 1967.

*Secondary Sources*

Aaron, Daniel. *Writers on the Left*. New York: Columbia University Press, [1961], 1992.

Abel, Richard. *The Red Rooster Scare: Making Cinema American, 1900–1910*. Berkeley: University of California Press, 1999.

Allen, Robert Clyde. *Horrible Prettiness: Burlesque and American Culture*. Chapel Hill: University of North Carolina Press, 1991.

Allen, Tony. *Americans in Paris*. Chicago: Contemporary Books, 1977.

"Americans in Paris: Catalogue of an Exhibition: Princeton University Library, May 4–June 30, 1956." Princeton: Department of Rare Books and Special Collections.

Augé, Marc. *Paris années 30: Roger-Voillet*. Paris: Hazan, 1996.

Avrich, Paul. *Sacco and Vanzetti: The Anarchist Background*. Princeton: Princeton University Press, 1991.

Bailey, William. *Americans in Paris, 1900–1930: A Selected, Annotated Bibliography*. New York: Greenwood Press, 1989.

Baker, Carlos. *Ernest Hemingway: A Life Story*. New York: Charles Scribner's Sons, 1969.

Baker, Roscoe. *The American Legion and American Foreign Policy*. New York: Bookman Associates, 1954.

Baranowski, Shelley. *Strength through Joy: Consumerism and Mass Tourism in the Third Reich*. Cambridge: Cambridge University Press, 2004.

Barbedette, Gilles, and Michel Carassou, *Paris gay 1925*. Paris: Presses de la Renaissance, 1981.

Bayly, C. A. *The Birth of the Modern World, 1780–1914: Global Connections and Comparisons*. Malden, Mass.: Blackwell, 2004.

Beale, Marjorie. *The Modernist Enterprise: French Elites and the Threat of Modernity, 1900–1940*. Stanford: Stanford University Press, 1999.

Beaumont-Maillet, Laure. *Atget Paris*. Paris: Hazan, 1992.

Becker, Jean-Jacques. *The Great War and the French People*. New York: St. Martin's Press, 1986.

Becker, Jean-Jacques, and Serge Berstein. *Histoire de l'anti-communisme en France: Tome 1: 1917–1940*. Paris: Olivier Orban, 1987.

Beckert, Sven. *The Monied Metropolis: New York City and the Consolidation of the American Bourgeoisie, 1850–1896*. New York: Cambridge University Press, 2001.

Bell, David, Douglas Johnson, and Peter Morris, eds. *Biographical Dictionary of French Political Leaders since 1870*. New York: Simon & Schuster, 1990.

Bender, Thomas. *A Nation among Nations: America's Place in World History*. New York: Hill and Wang, 2006.

Benstock, Shari. *Women of the Left Bank: Paris, 1900–1940*. Austin: University of Texas Press, 1986.

Berlière, Jean-Marc. *Le Préfet Lépine: Vers la naissance de la police moderne*. Paris: Denoël, 1993.

Berry, David. *A History of the French Anarchist Movement, 1917–1945*. Westport, Conn.: Greenwood Press, 2002.

Bevilacqua, Winifred. *Josephine Herbst*. Boston: Twayne, 1985.

Blake, Jody. *Le Tumulte Noir: Modernist Art and Popular Entertainment in Jazz-Age Paris, 1900–1930*. University Park: Pennsylvania State University Press, 1999.

Blumenthal, Henry. *Illusion and Reality in Franco-American Diplomacy, 1914–1945*. Baton Rouge: Louisiana State University Press, 1986.

Borgwardt, Elizabeth. *A New Deal for the World: America's Vision for Human Rights*. Cambridge: Belknap Press of Harvard University Press, 2005.

Boudard, Alphonse, and Romi [Robert Miquel]. *L'âge d'or des maisons closes*. Paris: Albin Michel, 1990.

Boyer, Paul. *Urban Masses and Moral Order in America, 1820–1920*. Cambridge: Harvard University Press, 1978.

Brinkley, Alan. *Voices of Protest: Huey Long, Father Coughlin, and the Great Depression*. New York: Random House Vintage Books, 1983.

Butler, Leslie. *Critical Americans: Victorian Intellectuals and Transatlantic Liberal Reform*. Chapel Hill: University of North Carolina Press, 2007.

Campbell, James. *Middle Passages: African American Journeys to Africa, 1787–2005*. New York: Penguin, 2006.

Cannistraro, Philip. "Mussolini, Sacco-Vanzetti, and the Anarchists: The Transatlantic Context." *Journal of Modern History* 68:1 (March 1996): 31–62.

Capozzola, Christopher. *Uncle Sam Wants You: World War I and the Making of the Modern American Citizen*. New York: Oxford University Press, 2008.

Carisella, J. P., and James W. Ryan. *The Black Swallow of Death: The Incredible Story of Eugene Jacques Bullard, the World's First Black Combat Aviator*. Boston: Marlborough House, 1972.

Carrot, Geroges. *Le maintien de l'ordre en France au XX$^e$ siècle*. Paris: Henri Veyrier, 1990.

Célati, Jean-Louis, and Rodolphe Trouilleux. *Chronique de la rue parisienne: Photos et articles de presse*. Paris: Parigramme, 1995.

Chadwick, Whitney, and Tirza True Latimer, eds. *The Modern Woman Revisited: Paris between the Wars*. New Brunswick: Rutgers University Press, 2003.

Chadych, Danielle, and Dominique Leborgne. *Atlas de Paris: Evolution d'un paysage urbain*. Paris: Parigramme, 1999.

Chauncey, George. *Gay New York: Gender, Urban Culture, and the Making of the Gay Male World, 1890–1940*. New York: Basic Books, 1994.

Chevalier, Louis. *Laboring Classes and Dangerous Classes in Paris during the First Half of the Nineteenth Century*. Translated by Frank Jellinek. Princeton: Princeton University Press, 1973.

———. *Montmartre du plaisir et du crime*. Paris: Robert Laffont, 1980.

Cocks, Catherine. *Doing the Town: The Rise of Urban Tourism in the United States, 1850–1915*. Berkeley: University of California Press, 2001.

Cohen, Évelyne. *Paris dans l'imaginaire national de l'entre-deux-guerres*. Paris: Sorbonne, 1999.

Cohen, Lizabeth. *Making a New Deal: Industrial Workers in Chicago, 1919–1939*. Cambridge: Cambridge University Press, 1990.

Collomb, Michel. *Les années folles*. Paris: Belfond, 1986.

Copley, Anthony. *Sexual Moralities in France, 1780–1980: New Ideas on the Family, Divorce, and Homosexuality*. London: Routledge, 1989.

Corbin, Alain. *Women for Hire: Prostitution and Sexuality in France after 1850*. Translated by Alan Sheridan. Cambridge: Harvard University Press, 1990.

Corn, Wanda. *The Great American Thing: Modern Art and National Identity, 1915–1935*. Berkeley: University of California Press, 1999.

Costigliola, Frank. *Awkward Dominion: American Political, Economic, and Cultural Relations with Europe, 1919–1933*. Ithaca: Cornell University Press, 1984.

Creagh, Ronald. *Sacco et Vanzetti*. Paris: Découverte, 1984.

de Grazia, Victoria. *Irresistible Empire: America's Advance through Twentieth-Century Europe*. Cambridge: Belknap Press of Harvard University Press, 2005.

———. "Mass Culture and Sovereignty: The American Challenge to European Cinemas, 1920–1960." *Journal of Modern History* 61:1 (March 1989): 53–87.

Demangeon, Albert. *Paris: La ville et sa banlieue*. Paris: Bourrelier, [1946].

Denning, Michael. *The Cultural Front: The Laboring of American Culture in the Twentieth Century*. London: Verso, 1997.

Desmond, Robert. *Crisis and Conflict: World News Reporting between Two Wars, 1920–1940*. Iowa City: University of Iowa Press, 1982.

Dewitte, Philippe. *Les mouvements nègres en France, 1919–1939*. Paris: Harmattan, 1985.

di Borgo, Ronald Pozzo. *Les Champs-Élysées: Trois siècles d'histoire*. Paris: Martinière, 1997.

Diggins, John. *Mussolini and Fascism: The View from America*. Princeton: Princeton University Press, 1972.

———. *Up from Communism: Conservative Odysseys in American Intellectual Development*. New York: Columbia University Press, 1994.

Dubofsky, Melvyn. *We Shall Be All: A History of the Industrial Workers of the World*. Urbana: University of Illinois Press, 2000, abridgement of Quadrangle Books, 1969.

Earnest, Ernest. *Expatriates and Patriots: American Artists, Scholars and Writers in Europe*. Durham: Duke University Press, 1968.

Edwards, Brent. *The Practice of Diaspora: Literature, Translation, and the Rise of Black Internationalism*. Cambridge: Harvard University Press, 2003.

Eksteins, Modrus. *Rites of Spring: The Great War and the Birth of the Modern Age*. Boston: Houghton Mifflin, 1989.

Eley, Geoff. *Forging Democracy: A History of the Left in Europe, 1850–2000*. New York: Oxford University Press, 2002.

Endy, Christopher. *Cold War Holidays: American Tourism in France*. Chapel Hill: University of North Carolina Press, 2004.

Engerman, David. *Modernization from the Other Shore: American Intellectuals and the Romance of Russian Development*. Cambridge: Harvard University Press, 2003.

Erenberg, Lewis. *Steppin' Out: New York Night Life and the Transformation of American Culture, 1890–1925*. Westport, Conn.: Greenwood Press, 1981.

Esnault, Gaston. *Dictionnaire historique des argots français*. Paris: Larousse, 1965.

Evenson, Norma. *Paris: A Century of Change, 1878–1978*. New Haven: Yale University Press, 1979.

Ezra, Elizabeth. *The Colonial Unconscious: Race and Culture in Interwar France.* Ithaca: Cornell University Press, 2000.

Fabre, Michel. *From Harlem to Paris: Black American Writers in France, 1840–1930.* Urbana: University of Illinois Press, 1991.

Falasca-Zamponi, Simonetta. *Fascist Spectacle: The Aesthetics of Power in Mussolini's Italy.* Berkeley: University of California Press, 2000.

Ferguson, Priscilla Parkhurst. *Paris as Revolution: Writing in the Nineteenth-Century City.* Berkeley: University of California Press, 1994.

Fierro, Alfred. *Histoire et dictionnaire de Paris.* Paris: Robert Laffont, 1996.

Fitch, Noel Riley. *Sylvia Beach and the Lost Generation: A History of Literary Paris in the Twenties and Thirties.* New York: Norton, 1985.

Flonneau, Mathieu. *Paris et l'automobile: Un siècle de passions.* Paris: Hachette, 2005.

Ford, Hugh. *Four Lives in Paris.* San Francisco: North Point, 1987.

———. *Published in Paris: A Literary Chronicle of Paris in the 1920s and 1930s.* New York: Collier, 1975.

Fourcaut, Annie, ed. *Banlieue rouge, 1920–1960: Années Thorez, années Gabin.* Paris: Autrement, 1992.

Furet, François. *The Passing of an Illusion: The Idea of Communism in the Twentieth Century.* Translated by Deborah Furet. Chicago: University of Chicago Press, 1999.

Garel, Sylvain. *Louis Lecoin: An Anarchist Life.* Translated by Paul Sharkey. London: Kate Sharpley, 2000.

Garrigues, Jean. *Images de la révolution: L'imagerie républicaine de 1789 à nos jours.* Paris: May, 1988.

Gilbert, David, and Claire Hancock. "New York City and the Transatlantic Imagination: French and English Tourism and the Spectacle of the Modern Metropolis, 1893–1939." *Journal of Urban History* 33:1 (November 2006): 77–107.

Gilfoyle, Timothy. "The Moral Origins of Political Surveillance: The Preventive Society in New York City." *American Quarterly* 38:4 (Autumn 1986): 637–52.

Golan, Romy. *Modernity and Nostalgia: Art and Politics in France between the Wars.* New Haven: Yale University Press, 1995.

Good, Howard. *The Journalist as Autobiographer.* Metuchen, N.J.: Scarecrow, 1993.

Greenfeld, Howard. *Ben Shahn: An Artist's Life.* New York: Random House, 1998.

Griffin, Roger, ed. *International Fascism: Theories, Causes and the New Consensus.* London: Arnold, 1998.

Gronberg, Tag. *Designs on Modernity: Exhibiting the City in 1920s Paris.* Manchester, U.K.: Manchester University Press, 1998.

Haney, Lynn. *Naked at the Feast: A Biography of Josephine Baker.* New York: Dodd, Mead, 1981.

Hanna, Martha. "French Women and American Men: 'Foreign' Students at the University of Paris, 1915–1925." *French Historical Studies* 22 (Winter 1999): 87–112.

Hansen, Arlen. *Expatriate Paris: A Cultural and Literary Guide to Paris of the 1920s.* New York: Arcade, 1990.

Heald, Morrell. *Transatlantic Vistas: American Journalists in Europe, 1900–1940.* Kent, Ohio: Kent State University Press, 1988.

Heap, Chad. *Slumming: Sexual and Racial Encounters in American Nightlife, 1885–1940.* Chicago: University of Chicago Press, 2009.

Herring, George C. *From Colony to Superpower: U. S. Foreign Relations since 1776.* New York: Oxford University Press, 2008.

Higham, John. *Strangers in the Land: Patterns of American Nativism, 1860–1925.* New Brunswick: Rutgers University Press, [1955], 1994.

Higonnet, Patrice. *Paris: Capital of the World.* Translated by Arthur Goldhammer. Cambridge: Belknap Press of Harvard University Press, 2002.

Hobsbawm, Eric. *The Age of Extremes: A History of the World, 1914–1991.* New York: Vintage, [1994], 1996.

Hoganson, Kristin. *Consumers' Imperium: The Global Production of American Domesticity, 1865–1920.* Chapel Hill: University of North Carolina Press, 2007.

Holguín, Sandie. "'National Spain Invites You': Battlefield Tourism during the Spanish Civil War." *American Historical Review* 110:5 (Dec. 2005): 1399–426.

Horn, Gerd-Rainer. *European Socialists Respond to Fascism: Ideology, Activism, and Contingency in the 1930s.* New York: Oxford University Press, 1996.

Igo, Sarah. *The Averaged American: Surveys, Citizens, and the Making of a Mass Public.* Cambridge: Harvard University Press, 2007.

Irvine, William. "Fascism in France and the Strange Case of the Croix de Feu." *Journal of Modern History* 63:2 (Jan. 1991): 271–95.

Jackson, Jeffrey. "Artistic Community and Urban Development in 1920s Montmartre." *French Politics, Culture and Society* 24:2 (Summer 2006): 1–25.

———. *Making Jazz French: Music and Modern Life in Interwar Paris.* Durham, N.C.: Duke University Press, 2003.

Jackson, Julian. *The Popular Front in France: Defending Democracy, 1934–1938.* Cambridge: Cambridge University Press, 1987.

Janken, Kenneth. "African American and Francophone Black Intellectuals during the Harlem Renaissance." *Historian* (Spring 1998): 487–505.

Jeanne, René, and Charles Ford. *Paris vu par le cinéma.* Paris: Hachette, 1969.

Jenkins, Philip. *Hoods and Shirts: The Extreme Right in Pennsylvania, 1925–1950*. Chapel Hill: University of North Carolina Press, 1997.

Jones, Colin. *Paris: The Biography of a City*. New York: Penguin, 2004.

Jones, Richard Seelye. *A History of the American Legion*. Indianapolis: Bobbs-Merrill, 1946.

Judt, Tony. *La reconstruction du parti socialiste, 1921–1926*. Paris: Fondation Nationale des Sciences Politiques, 1976.

Jules-Rosette, Bennetta. *Josephine Baker in Art and Life: The Icon and the Image*. Urbana: University of Illinois Press, 2007.

Kaspi, André, and Antoine Marès, eds. *Le Paris des étrangers depuis un siècle*. Paris: Imprimerie Nationale, 1989.

Katz, Philip. *From Appomattox to Montmartre: Americans and the Paris Commune*. Cambridge, Mass.: Harvard University Press, 1998.

Kear, Jon. "Vénus noire: Josephine Baker and the Parisian Music-hall." In *Parisian Fields*, edited by Michael Sheringham, 46–70. London: Reaktion, 1996.

Kelley, Robin D. G. *Race Rebels: Culture, Politics, and the Black Working Class*. New York: Free Press, 1994.

Kennedy, David. *Freedom from Fear: The American People in Depression and War, 1929–1945*. New York: Oxford University Press, 1999.

———. *Over Here: The First World War and American Society*. Oxford: Oxford University Press, 1980.

Kennedy, Gerald, and Jackson Bryer, eds. *French Connections: Hemingway and Fitzgerald Abroad*. Basingstoke and London: Macmillan, 1998.

Kennedy, Richard. *Dreams in the Mirror: A Biography of E. E. Cummings*. New York: Norton, 1994.

Kuisel, Richard. *Seducing the French: The Dilemma of Americanization*. Berkeley: University of California Press, 1993.

Kurth, Peter. *American Cassandra: The Life of Dorothy Thompson*. Boston: Little, Brown, 1990.

Lacorne, Dennis, Jacques Rupnik, and Marie-France Toinet, eds. *The Rise and Fall of Anti-Americanism: A Century of French Perception*. Translated by Gerald Turner. London: Palgrave Macmillan, 1990.

Lanzmann, Jacques. *Paris des années 30*. Paris: Fernand Nathan et Keystone, 1987.

Lebovics, Herman. *True France: The Wars over Cultural Identity, 1900–1945*. Ithaca: Cornell University Press, 1992.

Lees, Andrew. *Cities Perceived: Urban Society in European and American Thought, 1820–1940*. Manchester, U.K.: Manchester University Press, 1985.

Leininger-Miller, Theresa. *New Negro Artists in Paris: African American Painters and Sculptors in the City of Light, 1922–1934*. New Brunswick: Rutgers University Press, 2001.

Lesinska, Zofia. *Perspectives of Four Women Writers on the Second World War: Gertrude Stein, Janet Flanner, Kay Boyle, and Rebecca West*. New York: Peter Lang, 2002.

Levenstein, Harvey. *Seductive Journey: American Tourists in France from Jefferson to the Jazz Age*. Chicago: University of Chicago Press, 1998.

———. *We'll Always Have Paris: American Tourists in France since 1930*. Chicago: University of Chicago Press, 2004.

Levine, Lawrence. *Highbrow/Lowbrow: The Emergence of Cultural Hierarchy in America*. Cambridge, Mass.: Harvard University Press, 1988.

Lévy, Sophie, ed. *A Transatlantic Avant-Garde: American Artists in Paris, 1918–1939*. Berkeley: University of California Press, 2003.

Lucan, Jacques. *Eau et gaz à tous les étages: 100 ans de logement*. Paris: Pavillon de l'Arsenal, 1992.

Ludington, Townsend. *John Dos Passos: A Twentieth Century Odyssey*. New York: E. P. Dutton, 1980.

MacLean, Nancy. *Behind the Mask of Chivalry: The Making of the Second Ku Klux Klan*. New York: Oxford University Press, 1994.

Maitron, Jean, and Claude Pennetier, eds. *Dictionnaire biographique du mouvement ouvrier français: Quatrième partie, 1914–1939*. Vol. XLII. Paris: Éditions Ouvrières, 1992.

Manela, Erez. *The Wilsonian Moment: Self-Determination and the International Origins of Anticolonial Nationalism*. New York: Oxford University Press, 2007.

Marchand, Bernard. *Paris, histoire d'une ville: XIX$^e$–XX$^e$ siècle*. Paris: Seuil, 1993.

Martin, Benjamin. *Crime and Criminal Justice under the Third Republic*. Baton Rouge: Louisiana State University Press, 1990.

———. *France in the Après Guerre, 1918–1924: Illusions and Disillusionment*. Baton Rouge: Louisiana State University Press, 1999.

May, Henry. *The End of American Innocence: A Study of the First Years of Our Own Time, 1912–1917*. New York: Columbia University Press, [1959], 1992.

Mazower, Mark. *Dark Continent: Europe's Twentieth Century*. New York: Vintage Books, [1998], 2000.

McDermott, Kevin, and Jeremy Agnew. *The Comintern: A History of International Communism from Lenin to Stalin*. Basingstoke and London: MacMillan, 1996.

McGirr, Lisa. "The Passion of Sacco and Vanzetti: A Global History." *Journal of American History* 93:4 (March 2007): 1085–115.

McMeekin, Sean. *The Red Millionaire: A Political Biography of Willi Münzenberg, Moscow's Secret Propaganda Tsar in the West*. New Haven: Yale University Press, 2003.

McMillan, James. *Housewife or Harlot: The Place of Women in French Society, 1870–1940*. New York: St. Martin's Press, 1981.

Mead, Robert. *Atlantic Legacy: Essays in American-European Cultural History*. New York: New York University Press, 1969.

Mellow, James. *Walker Evans*. New York: Basic, 2001.

Méral, Jean. *Paris in American Literature*. Translated by Laurette Long. Chapel Hill: University of North Carolina Press, 1989.

Merrick, Jeffrey, and Bryant Ragan, eds. *Homosexuality in Modern France*. New York: Oxford University Press, 1996.

Merrick, Jeffrey, and Michael Sibalis, eds. *Homosexuality in French History and Culture*. New York: Haworth Press, 2001.

Meyers, Jeffrey. *Scott Fitzgerald: A Biography*. New York: Harper Collins, 1994.

Miller, James, Susan Pennybacker, and Eve Rosenhaft. "Mother Ada Wright and the International Campaign to Free the Scottsboro Boys, 1931–1934." *American Historical Review* (April 2001): 387–430.

Milza, Pierre, ed. *Les Italiens en france de 1914 à 1940*. Rome: École française de Rome, 1986.

Minott, Rodney. *Peerless Patriots: Organized Veterans and the Spirit of Americanism*. Washington: Public Affairs Press, 1962.

Miquel, Pierre. *La main courante: Les archives indiscrètes de la police parisienne, 1900–1945*. Paris: Albin Michel, 1997.

Moorehead, Caroline. *Martha Gellhorn: A Life*. London: Chatto & Windus, 2003.

Moreira, Peter. *Hemingway on the China Front: His WWII Spy Mission with Martha Gellhorn*. Washington, D.C.: Potomac, 2006.

Morgan, Philip. *Fascism in Europe, 1919–1945*. London: Routledge, 2003.

Mosse, George. *The Fascist Revolution: Toward a General Theory of Fascism*. New York: Howard Fertig, 1999.

Moura, Clóvis. *Sacco e Vanzetti: O protesto brasileiro*. São Paulo: Brasil Debates, 1979.

Munholland, John. "Republican Order and Republican Tolerance in Fin-de-Siècle France: Montmartre as a Delinquent Community." In *Montmartre and the Making of Mass Culture*, edited by Gabriel Weisberg, 15–36. New Brunswick: Rutgers University Press, 2001.

Murray, Robert. *Red Scare: A Study of National Hysteria, 1919–1920*. New York: University of Minnesota Press, 1955.

Noiriel, Gérard. *The French Melting Pot: Immigration, Citizenship, and National Identity*. Translated by Geoffroy de Laforcade. Minneapolis: University of Minnesota Press, 1996.

Nolan, Mary. *Visions of Modernity: American Business and the Modernization of Germany*. New York: Oxford University Press, 1994.

Nora, Pierre, ed. *Realms of Memory: The Construction of the French Past*. Translated by Arthur Goldhammer. Vol. 3. New York: Columbia University Press, 1998.

Nord, Philip. *Paris Shopkeepers and the Politics of Resentment*. Princeton: Princeton University Press, 1986.

O'Leary, Cecilia Elizabeth. *To Die For: The Paradox of American Patriotism*. Princeton: Princeton University Press, 1999.

Orvell, Miles. *The Real Thing: Imitation and Authenticity in American Culture, 1880–1940*. Chapel Hill: University of North Carolina Press, 1989.

Pascal, Pia. *Les livres de l'enfer: Bibliographie critique des ouvrages érotiques dans leurs différents éditions du XVIᵉ siècle à nos jours*. Paris: C. Coulet et A. Faure, 1978.

Paxton, Robert. *The Anatomy of Fascism*. New York: Knopf, 2004.

Payne, Stanley. *A History of Fascism, 1914–1945*. Madison: University of Wisconsin Press, 1995.

Pellissier, Pierre. *6 février 1934: La république en flammes*. Paris: Perrin, 2000.

Pells, Richard. *Not Like Us: How Europeans Have Loved, Hated, and Transformed American Culture since World War II*. New York: Basic Books, 1997.

Pencak, William. *For God & Country: The American Legion, 1919–1941*. Boston: Northeastern University Press, 1989

Peniston, William. *Pederasts and Others: Urban Culture and Sexual Identity in Nineteenth-Century Paris*. New York: Harrington Park, 2004.

Pennybacker, Susan. *From Scottsboro to Munich: Race and Political Culture in 1930s Britain*. Princeton: Princeton University Press, 2009.

Pérez, Louis A. Jr. *On Becoming Cuban: Identity, Nationality, and Culture*. Chapel Hill: University of North Carolina Press, 1999.

Phillips, Ann Yaffe. *Crosscurrents: Americans in Paris, 1900–1940*. New York: Hirshl & Adler Galleries, 1993.

Plazy, Gilles, ed. *Paris, History, Architecture, Art, Lifestyle, in Detail*. Translated by Deke Dusinberre. Paris: Flammarion, 2003.

Pohl, Frances Kathryn. *Ben Shahn*. San Francisco: Pomegranate Art Books, 1993.

Pollack, Howard. *Aaron Copland: The Life and Work of an Uncommon Man*. New York: Henry Holt, 1999.

Preston, Paul. *The Spanish Civil War: Reaction, Revolution, and Revenge*. New York: Norton, 2006.

Preston, William. *Aliens and Dissenters: Federal Suppression of Radicals, 1903–1933*. Urbana: University of Illinois Press, [1963], 1994.

Prost, Antoine. *In the Wake of War: 'Les Anciens Combattants' and French Society 1914–1939*. Translated by Helen McPhail. Providence, R.I.: Berg, 1992.

Rabinbach, Anson. *The Human Motor: Energy, Fatigue, and the Origins of Modernity*. New York: Basic, 1990.

Rahv, Philip. *Discovery of Europe: The Story of American Experience in the Old World*. Boston: Houghton Mifflin, 1947.

Rampersad, Arnold. *The Life of Langston Hughes*. Vol. 1. New York: Oxford University Press, 1986.

Rearick, Charles. *The French in Love and War: Popular Culture in the Era of World Wars*. New Haven: Yale University Press, 1997.

Reed, Ralph. *"American Express": Its Origin and Growth*. New York: Newcomen Society in North America, 1952.

Renda, Mary. *Taking Haiti: Military Occupation and the Culture of U. S. Imperialism, 1915–1940*. Chapel Hill: University of North Carolina Press, 2001.

Rifkin, Adrian. *Street Noises: Parisian Pleasure, 1900–1940*. Manchester, U.K.: Manchester University Press, 1993.

Roberts, Mary Louise. *Civilization without Sexes: Reconstructing Gender in Postwar France, 1917–1927*. Chicago: University of Chicago Press, 1994.
———. *Disruptive Acts: The New Woman in Fin-de-Siècle France*. Chicago: University of Chicago Press, 2002.

Rodgers, Daniel T. *Atlantic Crossings: Social Politics in a Progressive Age*. Cambridge, Mass.: Belknap Press of Harvard University Press, 1998.

Roger, Philippe. *The American Enemy: A Story of French Anti-Americanism*. Translated by Sharon Bowman. Chicago: University of Chicago, 2005.

Rogger, Hans, and Eugen Weber, eds. *The European Right: A Historical Profile*. Berkeley: University of California Press, 1965.

Rose, Phyllis. *Jazz Cleopatra: Josephine Baker in Her Time*. New York: Doubleday, 1989.

Rosenberg, Clifford. *Policing Paris: The Origins of Modern Immigration Control between the Wars*. Ithaca: Cornell University Press, 2006.

Rosenberg, Emily. *Spreading the American Dream: American Economic and Cultural Expansion, 1890–1945*. New York: Hill and Wang, 1981.

Russell, Francis. *Tragedy in Dedham: The Story of the Sacco-Vanzetti Case*. New York: McGraw-Hill, 1962.

Rydell, Robert, and Rob Kroes. *Buffalo Bill in Bologna: The Americanization of the World, 1869–1922*. Chicago: University of Chicago Press, 2005.

Sabatès, Fabien. *Les Champs-Elysées*. Paris: Olivier Orban, 1983.

Sabrié, Marie-Lise. *Le Nouveau Montparnasse: De la Porte Océane à la Seine*. Paris: Albin Michel, 1990.

Sallée, André, and Philippe Chauveau. *Music-hall et café-concert*. Paris: Bordas, 1985.

Saunier, Pierre-Yves. "La toile municipale aux XIX$^e$–XX$^e$ siècles: Un panorama transnational vu d'Europe." *Urban History Review* 34:2 (Spring 2006): 43–56.

Sawyer-Lauçanno, Christopher. *E. E. Cummings: A Biography*. Naperville, Ill.: Sourcebooks, 2004.

Schor, Ralph. *L'Opinion française et les étrangers, 1919–1939*. Paris: Sorbonne, 1985.

Schwartz, Vanessa. *It's So French!: Hollywood, Paris, and the Making of Cosmopolitan Film Culture.* Chicago: University of Chicago Press, 2007.

———. *Spectacular Realities: Early Mass Culture in Fin-de-Siècle Paris.* Berkeley: University of California Press, 1998.

Seigel, Jerrold. *Bohemian Paris: Culture, Politics, and the Boundaries of Bourgeois Life, 1830–1930.* New York: Viking, 1986.

Shack, William. *Harlem in Montmartre: A Paris Jazz Story between the Great Wars.* Berkeley: University of California Press, 2001.

Sirinelli, Jean-François, ed. *Dictionnaire historique de la vie politique française au XX$^e$ siècle.* Paris: Presses Universitaires de France, 1995.

Sonn, Richard. *Anarchism and Cultural Politics in Fin-de-Siècle France.* Lincoln: University of Nebraska Press, 1989.

Soucy, Robert. *French Fascism: The First Wave, 1924–1933.* New Haven: Yale University Press, 1986.

Spotts, Frederic. *Hitler and the Power of Aesthetics.* London: Hutchinson, 2002.

Stansell, Christine. *American Moderns: Bohemian New York and the Creation of a New Century.* New York: Metropolitan Books, 2000.

Stead, Philip John. *The Police of France.* New York: MacMillan, 1983.

———. *The Police of Paris.* London: Staples Press, 1957.

Stephens, Michelle. *Black Empire: The Masculine Global Imaginary of Caribbean Intellectuals in the United States, 1914–1962.* Durham: Duke University Press, 2005.

Stora-Lamarre, Annie. *L'enfer de la III$^e$ République: Censeurs et pornographes (1881–1914).* Paris: Imago, 1990.

Stovall, Tyler. *Paris Noir: African Americans in the City of Light.* Boston: Houghton Mifflin, 1996.

———. *The Rise of the Paris Red Belt.* Berkeley: University of California Press, 1990.

Stowe, William. *Going Abroad: European Travel in Nineteenth-Century American Culture.* Princeton: Princeton University Press, 1994.

Strauss, David. *Menace in the West: The Rise of French Anti-Americanism in Modern Times.* Westport, Conn.: Greenwood Press, 1978.

Surkis, Judith. *Sexing the Citizen: Morality and Masculinity in France, 1870–1920.* Ithaca: Cornell University Press, 2006.

Susman, Warren. *Culture as History: The Transformation of American Society in the Twentieth Century.* New York: Pantheon, 1984.

———. "Pilgrimage to Paris: The Backgrounds of American Expatriation, 1920–1934." PhD diss., University of Wisconsin-Madison, 1958.

Sutcliffe, Anthony. *The Autumn of Central Paris: The Defeat of Town Planning, 1850–1970.* London: Edward Arnold, 1970.

Sutcliffe, Anthony, ed. *Metropolis, 1890–1940.* London: Mansell, 1984.

Studeny, Christophe. *L'Invention de la vitesse: France, XVIII$^e$–XX$^e$ siècle.* Paris: Gallimard, 1995.

Tamagne, Florence. *Histoire de l'homosexualité en Europe: Berlin, Londres, Paris, 1919–1939*. Paris: Seuil, 2000.

Tartakowsky, Danielle. *Les manifestations de rue en France, 1918–1968*. Paris: Sorbonne, 1997.

Temkin, Moshik. *The Sacco-Vanzetti Affair: America on Trial*. New Haven: Yale University Press, 2009.

Thompson, Emily. *The Soundscape of Modernity: Architectural Acoustics and the Culture of Listening in America, 1900–1933*. Cambridge: MIT Press, 2002.

Topp, Michael. *The Sacco and Vanzetti Case: A Brief History with Documents*. Boston: Bedford/St. Martin's, 2005.

Trachtenberg, Alan. *The Incorporation of America: Culture & Society in the Gilded Age*. New York: Hill and Wang, 1982.

Verhagen, Marcus. "The Poster in *Fin-de-Siècle* Paris: 'That Mobile and Degenerate Art.'" In *Cinema and the Invention of Modern Life*, eds. Leo Charney and Vanessa Schwartz, 103–29. Berkeley: University of California Press, 1995.

Van Holthoon, Frits, and Marcel Van der Linden, eds. *Internationalism in the Labour Movement, 1830–1940*. 2 vols. Leiden: E. J. Brill, 1988.

Wald, Alan. *Trinity of Passions: The Literary Left and the Antifascist Crusade*. Chapel Hill: University of North Carolina Press, 2007.

Wall, Wendy. *Inventing the "American Way": The Politics of Consensus from the New Deal to the Civil Rights Movement*. New York: Oxford University Press, 2008.

Walz, Robin. *Pulp Surrealism: Insolent Popular Culture in Early Twentieth-Century Paris*. Berkeley: University of California Press, 2000.

Wakeman, Frederic. *Policing Shanghai, 1927–1937*. Berkeley: University of California Press, 1995.

Ward, John. "The Meaning of Lindbergh's Flight." *American Quarterly* 10:1 (Spring 1958), 3–16.

Weber, Eugen. *The Hollow Years: France in the 1930s*. New York: Norton, 1994.

———. *Peasants into Frenchmen: The Modernization of Rural France, 1870–1914*. Palo Alto: Stanford University Press, 1976.

———. *Varieties of Fascism: Doctrines of Revolution in the Twentieth Century*. Princeton: D. Van Nostrand, 1964.

Weber, Ronald. *News of Paris: American Journalists in the City of Light between the Wars*. Chicago: Ivan R. Dee, 2006.

Weinberg, Barbara. "The Lure of Paris for American Painters, 1850–1910." In *Americans in Paris, 1850–1910: The Academy, the Salon, the Studio, and the Artists' Colony*, edited by Hardy George, 8–33. Oklahoma City: Oklahoma City Museum of Art, 2003.

Wiebe, Robert. *The Search for Order, 1877–1920*. New York: Hill and Wang, 1967.

Wineapple, Brenda. *Genêt: A Biography of Janet Flanner*. New York: Ticknor & Fields, 1989.

Wohl, Robert. *French Communism in the Making, 1914–1924*. Stanford: Stanford University Press, 1966.

Worley, Matthew, ed. *In Search of Revolution: International Communist Parties in the Third Period*. London: I. B. Tauris, 2004.

Wyman, Mark. *Round-Trip to America: The Immigrants Return to Europe, 1880–1930*. Ithaca: Cornell University Press, 1993.

Sphinx (brothel), 136, 139
St. Louis, 32, 50, 55, 231, 277n66
Stalin, Joseph, 243, 253, 259
Stavisky, Alexandre, 257
*Stays and Gloves*, 143
Stead, William T., 269n3
    *Americanization of the World*, 2
steamship passengers, 21–22
Stearns, Harold, 36, 116, 214
    *Civilization in the United States*, 36
Steffens, Lincoln, 216, 241
Stein, Gertrude, 1, 7, 31, 39, 138, 225, 244
Stock Market crash, 259
Stoddard, Lothrop, 62
street trades, 43, 48, 100, 145, 150
strikes, 8, 35, 61, 95, 175, 184, 203, 237, 253
students, study abroad, American, 6–7, 20, 22, 24,
    26, 29–30, 31, 33, 41, 146, 204, 206
suburbs (*banlieue*), 4, 8, 9, 89, 97, 99, 112, 113, 115,
    210, 211. *See also* Red Belt
Sunday, Billy, 108, 130
Sûreté Générale, 157
surrealism, surrealists, 38, 62, 79, 214, 229, 236
Switzerland, 60, 100, 107, 121. *See also* Geneva;
    Zurich
syndicalists, 98, 99, 102
Syria, 217, 315n2

tabloids. *See journaux humoristiques*
Taittinger, Pierre, 130
tango (dance), 51, 63, 67, 138
Tardieu, André, 88
taxis, taxi drivers, 17–18, 21, 30, 42, 44, 46, 47f,
    48, 60, 66, 67, 80, 82, 88, 100, 150, 200,
    205, 276n52
    as underworld guides, 132, 136, 137, 164. *See
    also* automobiles
Taylor, Frederick Winslow, 20
    Taylorism, 51, 80, 184
Tehran, 217
*Temps, Le*, 121
Tertre, place du, 44
Thayer, Webster, 107
Théâtre Vaudeville, 79
Thiers, Louis-Adolphe, 132
Third Reich. *See* Germany
Third Republic, 8, 72, 97, 148, 185, 257, 281n40
    downfall of, 130, 212, 314n68
Thomas Cook, 21, 76
Thompson, Dorothy, 27, 245, 312n57
Thomson, Virgil, 31
Thurber, James, 273n20
Tiflis, 217
Tijuana, 142
Tin Pan Alley, 37
tipping, 42, 48, 70, 79, 138, 145
Tomb of the Unknown Soldier, 117, 118, 124, 147,
    193, 198, 205
*Toronto Star*, 48, 216, 224

Toulouse-Lautrec, Henri de, 262
tour buses (charabancs), 21, 48, 70, 71, 152, 154,
    154f, 193
tourism, 8, 21–22, 63, 155, 169, 272n14, 273n16
    in Paris, 8, 63, 65, 72, 82, 135, 143, 162, 165
"Tourist Third," 22, 41
tourists, American, 6, 21, 22, 31, 48, 49, 199, 216,
    249, 260, 262, 270n17, 290n69, 310n25
    attacks on, 42, 70, 129, 154f, 193
    fleecing, conning, blackmailing of, 48, 145
    making moral judgments, 134, 152–53, 155, 170
*Tournée des américains*, 154, 155
*Tout-Paris*, 77, 83
train stations, 4, 17, 18, 135, 145, 148. *See also*
    *individual entries*; trains
trains, 9, 17, 27, 35, 37, 42, 120, 176, 217, 225–26,
    227, 260, 309n21
*Transatlantic Review* (little magazine), 283n70
*transition* (little magazine), 229
travel bureaus, 23, 138, 273n16. *See also* American
    Express
Treat, Ida, 196, 206, 210, 230
Tresca, Carlo, 100
Trotsky, Leon, 120, 242
Tunisia, 62
Turkey, 222
    Turks, 217. *See also* Constantinople; Istanbul
Twain, Mark, 155
    *The Innocents Abroad*, 21

Union Nationale des Combattants (UNC), 193
United Artists, 79
United Press Service, 240
United States, 8, 13, 14, 62, 87, 101–2, 105,
    218–20, 245, 246, 249
    social, cultural fragmentation before World War
    I, 2, 34–35
    and debates about, defining the nation, 20,
    30–31, 37–39, 49, 57–58, 202
    and exports, 20, 25, 27, 57, 78
    and Great Depression, 236–37, 238, 240, 241
    and growing international power, 5, 18, 19, 20,
    25, 40, 45, 53, 179, 206, 266
    and perceived cultural inferiority to Europe, 2,
    19–20, 35–36
    and postwar problems, repressions, 1, 30,
    140–42, 174–75, 213, 230
    and concept of American civilization or way of
    life, 2–3, 11, 20, 34–37, 39, 40, 89, 265
    and vice, 139, 150, 166, 169
    and violence and vulgarity, 19–20, 56, 108,
    127, 209. *See also individual cities and regions*;
    Americanism; Americanness
United States Congress, 3, 108, 177
Universal Service, 245
University of Delaware, 29
urban chroniclers, French, 57, 65–66, 122
urban modernity, 58, 64, 81–82, 87, 135, 156, 167,
    264

urban preservationists, 57, 85, 89, 93, 122, 127, 159. *See also* Commission Municipal du Vieux Paris
urinals, 9, 138, 139

Vaillant-Couturier, Paul, 120, 127, 128, 158, 180, 211, 230, 291*n*74
Vanderbilt, Cornelius Jr., 45, 52
*Vanity Fair*, 154f
Vanzetti, Bartolomeo, 94, 106, 195, 211, 228, 233
*Variety Magazine*, 152
Vavin, rue and carrefour, 81, 82, 83
Vendôme, place, 18, 23, 28, 41, 45, 76, 116, 135, 147
Verdun, 117, 222
Verlaine, Paul, 229
Versailles Treaty. *See* Paris Peace Conference
veterans' groups, 99, 112, 118, 119, 192, 193. *See also* American Legion; parades
Vichy regime, 133, 148, 209, 315*n*2
Victor-Hugo, boulevard, 200
Vienna, 231, 235, 245, 253
Villette, La, 44
Visas. *See* passports
*voie publique, la*, 112, 114
Vorse, Mary Heaton, 111

Wagons-Lits tour company, 74f
waiters, 21, 45, 51, 150, 180, 208, 258, 262
Walker, Jimmy, 52, 164
war debts, 8, 42, 50, 56, 59, 107, 112, 173, 176, 179, 205, 207, 211, 278*n*4
Warner, Arthur, 182, 183
Warnod, André, 66, 85
Warsaw, 261
Washington Club, 24
Washington, George, 176, 192
Washington Naval Conference, 56
Weimar Republic. *See* Germany
Welles, Orson, 197, 200, 305*n*46
Wells, H. G., 104, 108

W. H. Smith (bookstore), 164
Wharton, Edith, 25, 228
Whitman, Walt, 232
Williams, William Carlos, 195
 *In the American Grain*, 39
Wilson, Edmund, 103
Wilson, Woodrow, 104, 184, 199, 220, 279*n*20
 Wilsonian ideals, 64, 86, 107
Wood, Grant, 31, 218, 219, 225, 229, 237
 *American Gothic*, 40
World Court, 206
World War I, 176, 217, 250
 humanitarian relief efforts, workers, 25–26, 28
 and Franco-American relations, 56, 59, 69–70
 and left-wing radicalism, 100–1
 and Paris, 6, 10, 26, 124–25, 135, 139, 141
 and travel and communication, 14, 22, 26, 101
 and the United States, 37, 174, 191, 200
 commemoration of, 177. *See also* Tomb of the Unknown Soldier
 nostalgia, glamorization of, 178, 181, 188, 190, 198–99, 209–10
 legacies in France, 8, 59, 97, 138, 207. *See also* expatriates: World War I service
World War II, 57, 256, 260–61, 263
writers, American. *See* expatriates

xenophobia. *See* immigration

*Yachting Magazine*, 144
Young Women's Christian Association (YWCA)
 Foyer International des Etudiantes, 30
Yugoslavia, 128

Zagreb, 231
Zelli's (nightclub), 32, 42, 48
Zévaès, Alexandre, 174
Zhou Enlai, 254
Ziegfeld's Follies, 152
Zionists, 312*n*57
Zurich, 22, 98

Made in the USA
Las Vegas, NV
16 August 2021